OPENING THE TREASURES

A Book of Daily Homily-Meditations

OPENING THE TREASURES

A Book of Daily Homily-Meditations

Charles E. Miller, C.M.

"The treasures of the Bible are to be opened up more lavishly so that richer fare may be provided for the faithful at the table of God's Word" (Constitution on the Sacred Liturgy, 51).

ALBA · HOUSE NEW · YORK

SOCIETY OF ST. PAUL, 2187 VICTORY BLVD., STATEN ISLAND, NEW YORK 10314

Library of Congress Cataloging in Publication Data

Miller, Charles Edward, 1929-
  Opening the treasures.

  1. Catholic Church—Sermons. 2. Sermons, American.
I. Catholic Church. Lectionary for Mass (U.S.).
Sundays and feasts. II. Title.
BX1756.M554063   252'.6   81-19095
ISBN 0-8189-0424-0   AACR2

Imprimi potest:
John A. Grindel, C.M.
Provincial, Province of the West

Nihil Obstat:
Newman C. Eberhardt, C.M.
Censor Deputatus

Imprimatur:
Cardinal Timothy Manning
Archbishop of Los Angeles
April 15, 1981

Designed, printed and bound in the United States of
America by the Fathers and Brothers of the
Society of St. Paul, 2187 Victory Boulevard,
Staten Island, New York 10314, as part of their
communications apostolate.

---

4 5 6 7 8 9 (Current Printing: first digit).

FOREWORD

This book is offered to priests as a help in preparing daily homilies and as a source of reflection for others who wish to meditate on the scriptural readings as found in the lectionary.

Every priest should make time to study, reflect, and pray as a preparation for his homilies, but it is my conviction that a busy priest deserves an aid, a "starter" for his own preparation. And this book intends to be nothing more than a starter, not a substitute for one's own preparation. I envision a daily homily which will be brief, between two and three minutes in length. I have generally concentrated on the first reading because the gospels usually receive rather full attention on Sundays, as they should. By emphasizing the first reading, a preacher fulfills the ideal of the *Constitution on the Sacred Liturgy* (51): "The treasures of the Bible are to be opened more lavishly so that richer fare may be provided for the faithful at the table of God's Word." I have unabashedly taken the homilies for the weekdays of Advent and Lent from my earlier books, *Until He Comes* and *Repentance and Renewal*, which are now out of print. The rest is new material, although I have been unable in some instances to avoid repetition because of the similarity of many readings.

For the final typing of the manuscript I am grateful to Mrs. Angela De Simone of the staff of St. John's Seminary. If this book is even a little help, especially to priests, I will judge that God has by his grace moved me to do something in accord with the heritage which is mine as a son of St. Vincent de Paul.

Charles E. Miller, C.M.

INTRODUCTION

The homily at Mass is an integral part of the Liturgy of the Word. We read in the eighth chapter of the Acts of the Apostles about an official from the court of the Queen of Ethiopia returning from Jerusalem. While reading Isaiah the Prophet, he was encountered by Philip the Deacon. Asked if he understood what he was reading, he replied, "How can I understand unless someone explains it to me?" He speaks for all of us.

To fill this need, many commentators have addressed themselves to various segments of the liturgical readings. We are enriched by all of them. It is particularly gratifying to have such a collection from the spiritual reservoir of Father Charles Miller, C.M. He is the Rector of our Theologate, a veteran of spiritual skills and already an approved author.

With a great measure of joy and gratitude we preface this present series. May it enjoy a wide circulation, be a source of spiritual enrichment for many, and assist the homilist in providing substantive comment to the readings of each day's liturgy.

Timothy Cardinal Manning
Archbishop of Los Angeles

April 14, 1981

TABLE OF CONTENTS

THE SEASON OF EASTER

THE SEASON OF THE YEAR (I & II)

OPENING THE TREASURES

THE SEASON OF ADVENT

Monday of the First Week

Human beings of all times have yearned for peace. Isaiah in the Old Testament prophesied that peace would come from Israel, provided the people learned to walk in the light of the Lord. He said that if Israel would turn to the Lord, the nations would stream to the house of the God of Jacob to seek instruction as to how to walk in the paths of the Lord. What a beautiful picture he painted: "They shall beat their swords into plowshares and their spears into pruning hooks; one nation shall not raise the sword against another nor shall they train for war again."

Isaiah did not understand that his words would be fulfilled only in the Church, the New Israel. With the coming of Christ the angels heralded the message of "peace on earth." But has the Church failed as did Israel? Where is the peace which Jesus came to bring?

In one sense the kingdom of peace and justice is still in the future. It will be realized only in the final coming of Christ. We, like the Israelites, are a people who must look to the future. On the other hand, we should not expect the final coming of Christ to effect a sudden reversal in the state of the world. We must work for the final coming of Christ by making the Church, that is, ourselves, as much like the final kingdom of justice and peace as possible. Transforming the world through Christ is a gradual process. To draw men to Christ in the Church is the first step. Living as Christ has taught us, with love for all men, can move people to say, "Come, let us climb the Lord's mountain, to the house of God, that he may instruct us in his ways and we may walk in his paths." If the nations are ever to beat their swords into plowshares, we must beat down our own personal feelings of hatred and contempt into love and concern. If the nations are ever to turn their spears into pruning hooks, we must turn our selfseeking into generosity and service. Should we look to the future for a kingdom of peace? Yes, but we must realize that the future comes to be only because of the present.

Alternate (A cycle only)

The prophet Isaiah foresaw a day when the Lord would come to purify Israel of her sins. It was not really a gloomy prophecy since Isaiah promised that the Lord would thereafter pour out his blessings upon the faithful remnant of his people.

Advent, besides preparing us for Christmas, looks toward the final day of the Lord when he will come again to purify the whole world. Sometimes we think of the end of the world as a time of terrible destruction, a pretty gloomy outlook. Actually we should long for that coming because God will not destroy the world; he will bring it to perfection. God does not destroy what is good, only what is evil. And the world is good, at least basically. The world does need a purification, and we can get a hint from Isaiah of what God's final action will be, for he says that God will wash away the filth of the daughters of Zion, that is, of the people. It is people who bring evil into the world. When all people are purified by God our world will emerge in a new beauty. God's glory will then be a shelter and protection from any further evil.

Despite all of the evil and hatred in our world now, we should never fall into a pessimistic or despairing spirit. Optimism and hope should characterize our outlook. No matter what others may do, our concern should be to work with God in his purifying action by cleansing ourselves of sin here and now. Our prayer should be: "In your mercy keep us free from sin and protect us from all anxiety as we wait in joyful hope for the coming of our Savior, Jesus Christ."

Alternate

The centurion in today's gospel was a man of faith and humility. He had the faith to recognize that Jesus possessed the power to cure his paralyzed servant, that he needed Jesus. At first glance this gospel may strike us as a strange reading for the first weekday of Advent. Actually, however, the faith and humility of this military man serve to remind us of what our attitude should be during this season as we prepare to celebrate Christmas.

Jesus came into our world to cure the human race paralyzed by sin. He wanted to free us of a spiritually crippling disease so that we could live a full, human life as children of God. But he does not force his cure on anyone. First, we must have faith that Jesus, and Jesus alone, has the power to help us. Secondly, we have to be humble enough to admit that we need Jesus, that of ourselves we can do nothing, that all human resources are insufficient to make us spiritually sound. Jesus offers us his healing power in the sacraments, especially in the Eucharist. The effect of the Eucharist upon us is not instantaneous, as was the power of Jesus upon the paralyzed boy, mainly because our faith and humility are not deep enough. To help us grow in faith and humility the Church has adapted the words of the centurion and put them on our lips before we receive the Eucharist: "Lord, I am not worthy to receive you, but only say the word and I shall be healed."

If we make those words an expression of real faith and humility, then our celebration of Christmas will take on more meaning, for Jesus was born to cure human beings paralyzed by sin.

Tuesday of the First Week

Today's lesson is preceded by a passage which describes Judah, destroyed by invading Assyrians, as a forest cut down and burned. A stump remains among the ruins; it is symbolic of Jesse, the father of David from whom Judean kings were descended. The image of the shoot coming from the stump indicates that the dynasty will not die out. It is a hopeful picture, for the prophet says that "from his roots a bud shall blossom."

Isaiah probably wrote of some ideal Davidic king who would meet the needs of the people through the spirit of God possessed by him in a special way. It is not at all likely that Isaiah had in mind the person of the Messiah as we know him. The Church, however, reading this passage in the light of further revelation understands that Isaiah's prophecy of the ideal king was eminently fulfilled in the person of Jesus Christ, himself of the Davidic line. Jesus was a unique king, one who could call both God and David his father. As the angel said to Mary of her son, "Great will be his dignity and he will be called Son of the Most High; and the Lord God will give him the throne of David his father (Lk 1:32). Jesus was the end of the Davidic line since he completed it. After him there was no need for another king to succeed him, for "his reign will be without end" (Lk 1:33).

The prophet Isaiah would have been thrilled into ecstasy had he known that the hope which he held out for his nation was to be realized in Jesus Christ, the God-man. And yet how easy it is for us to take the reality of Jesus Christ for granted. The story of his birth in Bethlehem, David's city, we have heard since we were children. Perhaps we still have only a child's appreciation of its meaning. We should pay heed to the words of today's preface: "When Jesus humbled himself to come among us as a man, he fulfilled the plan God formed long ago and opened for us the way to an eternal kingdom." During Advent we should meditate on this great truth so that we may see how much we need to give thanks and praise to God for sending his son to be our king.

Alternate

Scholars maintain that William Shakespeare was a great success not only because he possessed literary genius but also because he was born at the right time and in the right place. When he came upon the scene, the English language and the drama had developed to such an extent that they were excellent means for the expression of his talent. The time when a person is born can make all the difference.

Many magnificent persons were born before the time of Christ, prophets like Isaiah and Jeremiah, kings like David and Solomon. And yet ordinary people like us have an unimaginable advantage over them. We live in the age of Jesus Christ. The time of our birth has made all the difference. The revelation of God's love and goodness in the words and deeds of Jesus Christ is the perfection for which the people of the Old Testament unconsciously yearned. Indeed through faith they could see God's love for them, especially in their freedom from slavery in Egypt, but they had no inkling that God so loved the world that he would send his own son as a savior. They could sense God's goodness in his care and concern for them as a people in their homeland, but they did not fully realize that God's goodness was so great that he has prepared an eternal homeland in heaven.

We should be amazed that God has placed us in this age of fullness, this age of Christ, and that he has put us in circumstances in which we have responded to his gift of faith. How grateful we should be, for we are truly more blessed than many prophets and kings!

Wednesday of the First Week

Isaiah painted a picture of the great day of the Lord in images of a magnificent banquet: "a feast of rich food and choice wine." The splendid meal will be as joyful as it will be sumptuous, for "The Lord God will wipe away tears from all faces; he will destroy death forever."

In the Mass we have an image of the magnificent banquet of heaven. The image, however, is already the reality by anticipation. In the Mass the Lord provides for us, his people, not a feast of rich food and choice wines, but the spiritual nourishment of the body and blood of Jesus Christ. In the Mass the Lord wipes away the tears from our faces, for in the Eucharist, the sacrament of the death and resurrection of Jesus Christ, we have a guarantee of our own resurrection from the dead. Jesus said. "He who eats my flesh and drinks my blood has life eternal and I will raise him up on the last day" (Jn 6:54). How fitting is our proclamation of the mystery of faith, "Dying you destroyed our death; rising you restored our life; Lord Jesus, come in glory."

For the Mass to mean what it should, our faith must be more

than a proclamation on our lips. It must penetrate our whole beings and transform our entire outlook. Yes, real, deep faith is what we need—to see that whether the Mass is celebrated with the quiet simplicity of a weekday in our own church or amid the impressive splendor of a special feast in St. Peter's Basilica in Rome, it is the spiritual meal which anticipates the glory of eternal life. In every Mass we can say: "Behold our God, to whom we looked to save us! This is the Lord for whom we looked; let us rejoice and be glad that he has saved us!"

Alternate

The names of very few cities hold as much meaning for us as that of Bethlehem. That name calls to our minds images of Mary and Joseph bending in loving care over the newborn baby, of shepherds looking on in wonder and awe, and of angels singing their "Glory to God in the highest." And yet the greatest significance is found in the literal meaning of the word "Bethlehem" in Hebrew: "house of bread."

Among many ancient peoples bread was the fundamental source of nourishment and therefore a symbol of all the good things needed to sustain life. Even now we ourselves speak of a person who earns a living for his family as the "bread-winner." In today's gospel Jesus fed the people miraculously with bread. This miracle was a sign that he wanted to give all good things to us, that he wanted to give us a share of his own life of happiness. Jesus later made a promise. He said, "The bread that I will give is my flesh for the life of the world." He made good that promise at the Last Supper, and he continues to keep his promise in every Mass we celebrate.

Jesus was made flesh in the womb of Mary and born in Bethlehem, the "house of bread," so that he could give us his flesh as our spiritual bread. His birth was the turning point in history. How privileged was Mary to give birth to the Child. How blessed was Joseph to share Mary's joy. How fortunate were the shepherds and the angels to witness the event. And yet we need not feel deprived.

Though Bethlehem took place many centuries ago, its purpose is fulfilled whenever we receive the body of Jesus in communion as our church becomes a new Bethlehem, a house of spiritual bread.

Thursday of the First Week

In today's lesson God warned through the prophet, Isaiah, that he would humble those in high places and tumble their city to the ground. The proud who thought they could get along without God were doomed to failure. On the other hand, God wanted his faithful to realize that they had to stand before him and profess that without his help they could not possibly make a true success of life. This spirit is summarized in today's responsorial psalm: "It is better to take refuge in the Lord than to trust in princes." Mary, the mother of Jesus, had this spirit of humility. When her cousin, Elizabeth, praised her for having been chosen to become the mother of Jesus, Mary took no credit for herself and gave none to any other human person. She responded to Elizabeth's praise by directing the praise to God: "My being proclaims the greatness of the Lord, and my spirit finds joy in God my savior, for he has looked upon his servant in her lowliness."

It is a foolish person who wants to be self-reliant or who thinks he can depend only on other human beings to make life worthwhile. It is not that we are bad or that other human beings are bad. It's just that without God no one can make us happy. Turning to God and depending on him is the only realistic approach to life.

One of the great marvels of Christmas is that the eternal Son of God did not deem divinity something to cling to, but humbled himself to come among us as a man. He chose to be as dependent on his Father in his humanity as we are in ours. That act of humility is the model for all of us.

Alternate

Christmas is favored with some of the most beautiful music ever composed. The marvelous carols we hear during this season help to put us in the right mood, to stir up within us the Christmas spirit whereby we really want to have good will toward all men. But a funny thing happens on December 26th. Abruptly all the carols come to an end. And usually, so does the Christmas spirit.

Jesus says, "None of those who cry out, 'Lord, Lord,' will enter the kingdom of God but only the one who does the will of my Father in heaven." Perhaps our singing of Christmas songs is all too like crying out "Lord, Lord," without any persevering effort to carry out God's will in our lives. God's will is that we learn to live together as his children, as brothers and sisters, with love and concern for each other, with patience and acceptance. The feelings we have on Christmas day are good, but not enough. We must not build our religion upon a foundation of emotions alone. Emotions change, like shifting sand. God wants us to live together as his children all the time, not just when we are feeling good or when others are pleasant with us. We need the firm foundation of unrelenting, determined effort to be unselfish, to be generous with others—in a word, to be more like Christ himself.

During this time of Advent we need to think about how we treat others. We have to get serious about putting our religion of love into practice. We must devote more time to praying that God will help us to follow his will in our dealing with each other. Maybe then we can have Christmas every day this coming year.

Friday of the First Week

If we had to be deprived of one of our human faculties, I suspect that most of us would be least willing to give up our power of sight. The prospect of never again seeing the faces of those we love, the beauty of a Spring day, even a movie or television, is indeed frightening. We can close our eyes and try to imagine what it would be like to be totally blind—but of course all the while we know that we can simply open our eyes to see again.

The scriptures frequently present sinfulness in terms of blindness, and redemption in terms of seeing. In this context Isaiah wrote, "Out of gloom and darkness the eyes of the blind will see." Because of the coming of Jesus Christ we live in the age of redemption. In baptism our eyes were opened to see the Lord in faith. But do we keep our eyes open?

God is present for us to see everywhere, especially in people. His joy is in the smile of an infant. His acceptance of us is in the affection of a child. His vibrance is in the energy of an adolescent. His power is in the strength of an athlete. His beauty is in the loveliness of a young girl. His concern is in the devotion of a parent. His wisdom is in the prudence of the elderly. Every human person has something of the goodness of God within him. What a shame it is to close our eyes to God's presence, to live in darkness and gloom, when all we have to do is open our eyes in faith to see him.

Alternate

These are days for dropping little hints about what we would like to get for Christmas. Even though it was not Christmas for the two blind men in the gospel, they left no doubt as to what they wanted. They were not satisfied with hints. They went crying after Jesus and begging him to have pity on them by giving them sight. Jesus granted their request in response to their faith.

We can consider ourselves fortunate if we do not have a need as great as that of the blind men. But we do have needs, and we like to think that we have faith as well. Imagine yourself, then, as being given the opportunity of asking God for anything you wanted. What would you ask for? What is the one great favor you would like to receive?

Frankly I find this question very difficult to answer. I can think of a thousand things to ask for, but one and only one . . . well, I am just not sure. Heaven? Yes, of course, I want to get to heaven. But that is probably still far away and there is a lot of living to do before I can get there. Should I pray for wisdom as did Solomon? Should I ask for the patience of Job or the charity of St. Vincent de Paul? Wait a minute! Wasn't Jesus himself the night before he died in a position of asking his Father for one thing? As Jesus knelt in the garden of Gethsemane his prayer was simple: "Not my will but yours be done." I could not have a better prayer, for that simple prayer includes everything. It expresses supreme faith in the power of God and complete hope and trust in his goodness. Above all it manifests real love. It is no wonder that Mary's prayer at the annunciation was so similar: "Be it done to me according to your word."

"Not my will but yours be done." How I must make that prayer my own.

Saturday of the First Week

Isaiah paints a picture of the goodness of God toward his people: "He will be gracious to you when you cry out. He will give you bread you need. A voice shall sound in your ears: 'This is the way; walk in it.' " It is a beautiful picture of God's goodness, and it is a picture which comes to life in the Mass.

We approach God in the Mass by crying out to him, "Lord, have mercy." That cry is more than a plea that God forgive our sins, for "mercy" includes all that we understand by the words "love" and "kindness." Our first prayer of the Mass is a request that God show us his concern and his guidance. God is then indeed gracious to us. He does not hide himself nor is he deaf to our prayer. Rather, he speaks to us in the words of sacred scripture. As we listen to the lesson and the gospel, we should realize that it is God's voice sounding in our ears and saying, "This is the way; walk in it."

God does not point out to us how we should live without giving us the strength needed to walk in his way. He feeds us with a bread more marvelous than the manna which came from heaven, more beneficial than any human nourishment, more joy-giving than the most sumptuous banquet. He gives us the Eucharist.

The Mass, however simply celebrated, is something we must

never fail to appreciate. We should praise the Lord, for he is good to us. We should sing praise to our God, for he is gracious to us.

Alternate

The scene in today's gospel is a touching one. The heart of Jesus was moved with pity for the crowds who were like sheep without a shepherd. God had sent Jesus into the world as his own special Gift to just such people, among whom we are numbered. We are so used to this picture of Jesus that we may fail to notice his final words in today's gospel: "The gift you have received, give as a gift."

God has favored us by giving us faith in Jesus. This gift, however, is not to be hoarded as if it were too precious to be shared with others. Faith is different from material things. If you give someone money, you necessarily have less yourself. If you give someone faith, you not only do not have less, you actually have more. In fact, to grow in our Christian life we must share with others this most precious gift from God. We associate with people every day who do not enjoy our gift of faith. While we must respect their own personal convictions, we should never be reluctant to try to draw them to full faith in Jesus Christ by our words, our good example, our interest, our own obvious sense of conviction and dedication.

A five-year-old girl, an only child received a whole carload of presents from her parents for Christmas. Her mother noticed, however, that she seemed strangely reserved and subdued as she played with some of her new toys. She asked her daughter, "Aren't you happy with what Santa Claus brought you?" "Yes," the little girl answered, "but I didn't give Santa Claus anything for Christmas." In her simplicity that child had caught a real meaning of Christmas and of Christianity itself. We should be grateful for our gifts from God, but we must learn to be givers as well as receivers.

Monday of the Second Week

Charles Dickens in his famous novel, *David Copperfield*, created a delightful character by the name of Wilkins Micawber who was forever in financial difficulty. He was alternately buoyed by the hope that at last fortune was to be his and reduced almost to despair by sudden, unaccountable reverses. And yet it is his optimism which readers remember, since Mr. Micawber was constantly "looking for something to turn up."

Caricature though he is, Mr. Micawber is a reflection of the great prophets of the Old Testament. The prophets were at times reduced almost to despair because of the people's repeated infidelities to God and the consequences of those infidelities in war and destruction. And yet it is always their optimism which we should remember, since the prophets were constantly "looking for something to turn up." That something was the Day of the Lord when all wrongs would be righted. Today's lesson is typical. It was written during a bleak period in the history of God's people, a time of punishment in exile far from their homeland and their precious temple in Jerusalem. The prophets proclaimed a message of hope and encouragement to the people, the promise that the Lord would come.

The Day of the Lord arrived in the coming of Jesus Christ. But this "day" of the Lord was not a day of twenty-four hours nor was it a period of thirty-three years, for Jesus is still coming into our world. He is working even now to right the wrongs of the world through people who allow him to enter their lives. How long this day will last, we do not know. Whether we are still only at the dawn or have moved toward noon is uncertain. One thing is definite: despair is no part of the Christian outlook. "Something will turn up," and that something is the final coming of Christ when the Day of the Lord will reach its eternal zenith.

Alternate

We tend to take words for granted since we speak and hear so many of them every day. In this gospel Jesus spoke human words which sounded no different from any other human words. And yet what a difference there was, for behind his human words was his divine power. Jesus proved the power of his words to forgive sins by showing that his words could cure physical paralysis. In the day of creation God said, "Let there be light," and there was light. In the day of salvation Jesus said, "Your sins are forgiven," and they were forgiven.

The words of Jesus are with us still. We hear them through the voice of a fellow human being, the priest, and yet behind those words is the divine power of Jesus himself. They are sacramental words—words such as "I absolve you from your sins" and "This is my body; this is my blood." No proof is given now along with the words as was the case for the paralytic. Ours is the gift of faith rather than the gift of physical healing.

During Advent we are preparing for our celebration of the coming of Jesus Christ into the world as a human being. The incarnation was a marvelous manifestation of God's love for us, and that incarnation is continued and extended through the sacraments, especially Penance and the Eucharist. We must never take sacramental words for granted. Instead we should be filled with awe and give praise to God by saying "We have seen and heard incredible things."

Tuesday of the Second Week

A man driving from work was in a near-fatal accident. When his wife received the word she rushed to the hospital where he had been taken. A young intern informed her that her husband had received emergency treatment upon arrival and was now undergoing surgery. Though his condition was critical, he was still alive. The intern tried to comfort the wife by reminding her that where there is life, there is hope. The words struck the distressed woman as banal, as perhaps they would us in a similar situation. And yet the simple words, "Where there is life, there is hope," contain a profound truth.

Our world is in critical condition. It is near death because of war, social injustice, and pollution. Everything we try to do seems little better than emergency treatment, and there is small comfort in that. But the world is not dead, and where there is life, there is hope. Most important of all, a surgeon, a divine physician, is even now working to repair the serious injuries done to the world through sin, the real cause of all our ills. From time to time, as in today's first lesson, he sends a message to us, "Comfort, give comfort to my people." All will yet be well. Unlike the woman in the hospital we can do more than just wait. Hope does not mean passivity. But at least just for this moment, let us realize that the hope we have is derived not from human activity, however important, but from God. To all the prophets of doom we should not fear to counter with the words of the prophet of hope and consolation: "Here is your God. Here comes with power the Lord God."

Alternate

Sometimes we say of a person whom we esteem that he is worth his weight in gold. That means a newly born baby would be valued at about four thousand dollars and a fully grown man at about one hundred thousand. According to this measure the president of the United States in a year's time is worth twice his weight in gold.

God, however, does not measure the worth of people according to monetary values; he is not on the gold standard. Rather his standard is the life of his son, for people have been redeemed not with perishable things, with silver or gold, but with the blood of Christ which is beyond all price (cf. 1 P 1:18f). Jesus suggested that God is like a shepherd who values even one sheep so much that he leaves the ninety-nine to search for the one that is lost, for with God every human person is precious, even "little" people whom the "big" people of this world may despise. Grown men and babies, presidents and ordinary citizens are all valuable in the eyes of God.

In Advent we are thinking about God's sending his Son as the redeemer of the human race. We should draw from our devotions a real respect and esteem for every human person without exception, big people and little people, black and white people, rich people and poor people. Don't measure anyone by your own standard. Use God's standard, the blood of his Son which is beyond all price.

Wednesday of the Second Week

In the earlier days of movies a cartoon was a regular part of the program in every theater. I remember seeing a cartoon in which a bear, before settling down for his hibernation, wound and set an alarm clock. The winter went by and the selected time. When the alarm sounded, the clock went haywire, with hands and screws and springs flying wildly about. Through it all the bear continued to sleep soundly.

Some people seem to picture God to be like the bear in the cartoon, as if he created the world, wound it up and let it run all by itself. Now the world is indeed beginning to go haywire and they think that, despite the alarms sounded all around us, God is still asleep and completely unconcerned. Their only hope is that God will at last awaken and finally "intervene in human history" to set things right through a brilliant second coming of his Son.

Today's lesson gives us a completely different picture of God. The Jewish exiles in Babylon to whom the lesson was addressed felt as if they had been abandoned by God. The prophet assured them that God by his great might and the strength of his power is always active in the world, that he never grows faint or weary and is aware of everything that is going on. The truth is that God's act of creation is continuous, and without his constant almighty power the entire universe would lapse into nothingness.

No, God is not asleep nor will the final coming of his Son be a sudden "intervention," for God is without interruption actively in control of his creation, gently and wisely directing it to the goal of perfection in the second coming of his Son, a plan he has had in mind all along.

Alternate

You've had it happen to you. Something very serious has gone wrong and you are depressed. When a friend tries to cheer you up, your retort is: "It's fine for you to be so cheerful; you don't have any problem." And you turn away from your friend.

Jesus wants to be a friend to us. He invites us to come to him to find refreshment from the weariness brought on by all the burdens of life. We should never reject his invitation on the grounds that he does not understand our human situation. He has been through it all. In the mystery of the incarnation Jesus became as human as we are in everything except sin. His humanity was no fiction, no make-believe. The Vatican Council reminds us of this truth: "By his incarnation the Son of God has united himself in some fashion with every man. He worked with human hands, he thought with a human mind, acted by human choice, and loved with human heart" (*Church in the Modern World,* 22).

Have you suffered the loss of a loved one? In his youth Jesus had to bury his foster father, Joseph, and later wept real tears before the tomb of his friend Lazarus. Are you plagued by bills and financial losses? Jesus assumed the obligation of caring for twelve apostles even though he had no place to lay his own head and frequently did not know where his next meal was coming from. Do you find that you lack peace and quiet, that people are always making demands on you and your time? Jesus had crowds of people following him and asking for all kinds of favors.

Has someone you loved and trusted turned his back on you and hurt your feelings? Jesus in his passion was betrayed by Judas, denied by Peter, and abandoned by the other apostles.

When Jesus says, "Come to me and I will refresh you," have no doubt that he understands your problems. He has been through it all.

Thursday of the Second Week

The period of the Babylonian captivity was a difficult time for the Jews. Living conditions apparently were not as bad as in the previous Egyptian captivity, but the devout Jew missed the worship of the temple in Jerusalem and in a strange land he eventually felt abandoned by God. He was somewhat like a child who while playing with friends has wandered a little too far from home. As it begins to get dark the child suddenly realizes that he is lost, and his only thought through all his fears and anxieties is to get back home. Then he looks up and sees his father coming toward him. He rushes gratefully into his open arms, and hand in hand the two make their way home.

God, the Father of his people, said to them in exile: "I am the Lord, your God, who grasp your right hand; it is I who say to you, 'Fear not, I will help you.' " And God says the very same thing to us today. We have here no lasting city but we look for the city that is to come (Heb 13:14). In this life we are exiled from the Lord (2 Cor 5:6). We should not be surprised if at times our world appears dark and we experience a sense of being lost, of being all alone. The world is good and people are good, but God is our Father and heaven is our home. All human groping for happiness is ultimately a search for God and as St. Augustine said, our hearts will be restless until they rest in God.

God wants to lead us home. Through all the dark, lonely days of life we need to pray for faith—a faith that will open our ears to hear the consoling words of a Father: "I am the Lord, your God, who grasp your right hand; it is I who say to you, 'Fear not, I will help you.' "

Alternate

Evil cannot tolerate good because it sees good as a threat. John the Baptist preached repentance in an attempt to turn people back to God, but Herod saw him as a personal denunciation of his depraved life and beheaded him. Jesus proclaimed a kingdom of love and peace, but the Pharisees viewed him as an exposer of their corrupt religious leadership and conspired to put him to death. And so through the long history of the Church, men and women have paid with their lives for their commitment to the goodness of Jesus Christ. Evil correctly views good as a threat, for the two are quite incompatible.

Jesus warned that the kingdom of God suffers violence, for it is good confronting evil. But then Jesus added an enigma: "the violent take it by force." The meaning of these obscure words seems to be that evil must be met with resistance, and that only those who are brave enough to engage evil in a life and death struggle can become part of his kingdom. Passivity on the part of good leads only to victory for evil.

We are mistaken, however, if we think that the struggle between good and evil is going on only outside us. The real battle is within. Each one of us contains something of good and something of evil. We must come to grips with the fact that it is difficult to be a follower of Jesus Christ. Do we really listen to the teaching of Jesus Christ or do we dismiss it as impractical or irrelevant or as directed to others but not to us? His teaching, remember, is a threat to our complacency, our selfishness, and our laziness. To follow his teaching we must be willing to do violence to ourselves. Otherwise we will find to our regret that passivity has led to a victory for evil.

Friday of the Second Week

An important duty of parents is to teach their children to talk. In the long, laborious process, there is one word which every child seems to learn all by himself, a word which no one has to teach him. And that one word is "no." There are many things most children say "no" to, such as eating the right kind of food and going to bed at the proper time. It would be the easiest thing in the world for parents simply to allow a child to do whatever he wants—no more tears and no more pouting. Such peace! But complete permissiveness is in no way a sign of love. Parents who do not take the time and effort to guide their children have abandoned their role and are not worthy to have children under their care. Children cannot be expected to know what is good for them. Parents have the right and the duty to discipline their children because they are wiser and more experienced.

God is infinitely wise and his experience is eternal. His love is without measure. That is why he can and does say, "I, the Lord, your God, teach you what is for your good, and lead you on the way you should go." No matter how old we may be, in relation to God we are like children. Without his guidance we would be worse off than a little child trying to grow up without parents. Ignoring God's commandments can only make a shamble of our lives. This was the bitter lesson the Jews had to learn, for their period of exile was the result of their disobedience.

We should be grateful to God that he loves us enough to take the time and effort to guide us through life by means of his commandments. The biggest mistake we can make is to say "no" to God.

Alternate

Abraham Lincoln said that you cannot fool all of the people all of the time. He could just as correctly have said that you cannot please all of the people any of the time. John the Baptist led an austere life and preached repentance, so some people dismissed him as a fanatic. Jesus lived in a normal fashion and proclaimed God's merciful love for everyone, and they accused him of being a laxist.

Much the same sort of thing is going on today. Some say that the Church since Vatican II has moved too fast, others that it has moved too slowly. Some maintain that the Church has abandoned her role as a moral guide, others that the Church is still bogged down in legalism. Some want to return to the past, and others feel that we haven't yet moved into the present. How true it is that you cannot please all of the people any of the time!

There is no simple solution to this problem. The Church is our concern, and every Catholic has a right to work for what he thinks should be changed or restored in the Church. But concern is not enough. The Bible says that God made man in his own image and likeness, and he did the same with his Church. We are in grave error if we attempt to reverse the process. It is God's will we must seek, not our own; his plan we must strive to follow, not our own.

We need humility and docility. For every word of criticism we have uttered, how many prayers have we addressed to God for guidance? For every moment of discontent, how often have we placed ourselves in the hands of God and said, "Your will be done"? Our real concern should be to please God all of the time.

Saturday of the Second Week

Elijah was a great prophet extraordinarily favored by the Lord. It was believed that he did not die but was taken up to God at the end of his earthly life in some marvelous fashion. This belief led to a tradition that Elijah would appear again on the earth before the coming of the Messiah. According to the New Testament Elijah did appear again in the person of John the Baptist. This teaching does not reflect a belief in reincarnation; rather, it makes clear that the purpose of Elijah's prophetic office was fulfilled by the mission of the Baptist as he prepared the people to receive Jesus Christ.

In this sense we could correctly maintain that all the prophets of the Old Testament made a new appearance on this earth when John began his preaching, for the entire Old Testament era was intended to get the world ready for Christ. The future coming of the

Savior was proclaimed by all the prophets. We spend a few weeks preparing for the celebration of Christmas, but God dedicated centuries to his preparations. Throughout the long history of salvation in the Old Testament God was at work, patiently and wisely directing events toward the marvelous moment when his Son would be one of us. When Jesus humbled himself to come among us as a man, he fulfilled the plan God formed long ago and opened for us the way to salvation (*Advent Preface I*).

Our preparation for Christmas is short in comparison with God's. That is why we must try to be as intense about it as possible. Daily Mass is an excellent means if we listen attentively to the readings and use them as a motive for giving thanks and praise to God in the Eucharist. When Christ comes at Christmas he should find us watching in prayer, our hearts filled with wonder and praise (*Advent Preface II*).

Alternate

Some high school students were decorating their school auditorium in preparation for a Christmas celebration. Since the crucifix did not seem appropriate for the season, they were thinking of removing it from the wall when one of their teachers, a priest walked in. The priest urged them to allow the crucifix to remain. "After all," he said, "that is why Jesus was born—to die on the cross."

It was a point Jesus himself had to make. The episode in today's gospel occurred just after the transfiguration wherein Jesus gave three of his apostles a preview of the glory that would come to him in his resurrection. The transfiguration was intended to prepare them for the ordeal of the passion which would be a supreme test of faith for all the followers of Jesus. Jesus appreciated how difficult it would be for them to accept the fact of his death, and so he took the occasion of their question about Elijah to emphasize once again the necessity of his death. The second coming of Elijah was realized in the person of John the Baptist, a man who went unrecognized by the Jewish leaders and who was put to death. And Jesus added,

"The Son of Man will suffer at their hands in the same way." In God's plan the evil action of men would be the means of achieving the glorification of his Son and the salvation of the world.

For those who fail to recognize the true meaning of Christmas, the crucifix may seem out of place, but it is not. Jesus was born to die. Let the crucifix remain. It is a sign, not of ignominy, but of glory.

Monday of the Third Week

When the Israelites were about to pass through Moab on their way from Egypt to the promised land, Balak, the Moabite king, feared that they would take over his country. He commissioned Balaam, a pagan diviner or seer, to curse the Israelites and render them powerless, but God would not permit Balaam even to utter the words of the curse. Four times he made the attempt, but on each occasion his words turned into a blessing. A person does not usually like to have someone put words in his mouth, but that is what happened to Balaam. Today's lesson summarizes two of his oracles.

The Balaam incident symbolizes God's providential care of his people and the fact that salvation comes from his power alone and not from any human resources. By all odds the Israelites should have vanished from the earth long before the coming of the Messiah. Apart from the golden era of David and Solomon, their history was generally marked by religious infidelities and military defeats culminating in the destruction of Jerusalem by the Babylonians in 587 B.C. Living in a tiny land, bereft of many natural resources and surrounded by powerful and hostile neighbors, the Jews were the last people that human wisdom would have chosen as the source of the Messiah-King. Only God had power to lead Israel to its fulfillment in the coming of Jesus Christ.

God's ways are not our ways. The Church, the New Israel, has survived for twenty centuries. It began in Jerusalem with a small band, for the most part simple, unassuming people. From there it has spread over all the world. At times the Church has been rich and influential, at times poor and persecuted. Through it all the power of God has been at work, despite human weakness and corruption, and his power alone will bring the Church to its true golden age in the second coming of Jesus Christ.

Alternate

At first glance the objection voiced by the Jewish leaders in today's gospel seems reasonable enough. Jesus had just driven from the temple those engaged there in buying and selling, and was now teaching in the temple precincts. In the eyes of the Jewish leaders Jesus was no more than an itinerant preacher, and they demanded to know by what authority he was interfering in the activities of the temple. What is a little surprising is that Jesus, rather than offering an explanation, chose to embarrass them with his question about the Baptist and then refused to answer their demand.

The Jewish leaders were the only people with whom Jesus was abrupt and even harsh at times. Since they had closed their eyes to what he had done, Jesus knew that they would close their ears to anything he would say. They of all people should have been able to read the meaning of the signs since they professed to be experts. They just could not bring themselves to believe that God was at work in this ordinary, untutored carpenter from Nazareth. They had blinded themselves by their smugness.

The marvel of Christmas is that God comes to us in the flesh of a baby. He continues to come to us in the unpretentiousness—one is tempted to say the plainness—of the Eucharist. Only faith can see through the veils of the humanity of Jesus, and only faith can see beyond the appearances of bread and wine. But faith is not for the smug, the sophisticated, the self-reliant. It is for those who are willing to respond to the wonderful simplicity of God's almighty power at work among us.

Tuesday of the Third Week

Zephaniah's prophecy sounds as if it were addressed to modern America with its problems of riots and ecology: "Woe to the city, rebellious and polluted. . . ." The prophet, however, had in mind something even more serious than the rebellion expressed in riots, for the people in turning to the worship of false deities were guilty of rebellion against the one true God. He protested against a situation more devastating than pollution of the environment, for the people had polluted their own minds and hearts, and the smog of selfishness had obscured their vision of God's commandments concerning love for others. With their abandonment of God came grave social injustices.

Is Zephaniah's prophecy addressed to us? We profess the true religion and we worship the one God as our regular participation in Mass gives witness. So the answer seems to be no. Religion, however, is not confined to church. St. Augustine wrote: "The perfection of religion is to imitate the One you worship."* God is made present to us in Jesus Christ, and our religion means imitating him. Did Jesus show love and care for all without exception? Did he not resist the social evils of his day?

The means employed by some demonstrators these days is more than questionable, but maybe we condemn their means as a way of justifying our own complacency and inaction. Political and social questions are admittedly complex, but perhaps we use complexity as an excuse for turning off a priest who from the pulpit is disturbing our conscience.

If we think religion means no more than coming to church, we are living in a polluting smog which is obscuring our vision of what God intends. "The perfection of religion is to imitate the One you worship." A question we all must ask ourselves is: "What would Jesus do in my situation?"

*De Civitate Dei, VIII, 17.

Alternate

When Jesus taught the people, he liked to take something of their experience as his starting point. He talked about sheep and coins and farmers. In today's gospel, in speaking about two sons, he drew from his own experience. Jesus, we must remember, is God's son. Each of the two young men he spoke about was like Jesus and unlike him. The elder was like Jesus in that he readily agreed to do what his father asked of him, and he was unlike him in that he failed to carry out his father's will. The younger was unlike Jesus in his initial refusal, and he was like him in his subsequent obedience.

It is obvious that Jesus approved of the younger son, the one who at first refused but later obeyed. Actions count, not words. Jesus also sympathized with the younger son. He knew how the boy felt. Though Jesus himself agreed to do his Father's will, it was a human struggle for him to accept his passion and cross. In the Garden of Gethsemane, when it was perfectly clear what his Father would ask of him on the next day, Jesus prayed, "My Father, if it is possible, let this cup pass me by." The prospect of having to die on the cross for the salvation of the world was not easy to accept. As a human being Jesus, like us, would have preferred a way out. But Jesus quickly added, "Still, let it be as you would have it, not as I" (Mt 26:39). And the next day, opening his arms on the cross, he freely accepted death.

I personally feel that we should not be discouraged if at times of crisis we find a wave of rebellion surging within ourselves. Our first response cannot always be the best. Our actions, however, show what we are. That is why Jesus did not stop at teaching us to say, "Thy will be done." He also gave us a perfect example of accepting God's will. We should hope and pray that we will never say to God: "No, I will not," and yet the more important thing is not what we say but what we do.

Wednesday of the Third Week

The Israelites were surrounded by pagans who worshipped

creatures, such as the moon and the stars or even rocks and trees. The chosen people stood out as unique in their belief in one Supreme Being, the Lord and Master of all creation. Their belief was not born of human instincts or superstitions, but was a gift of God's personal revelation of himself to his beloved people. Despite this revelation, the people frequently drifted into the idolatry of their neighbors, and the prophets had constantly to call them back to the worship of the one true God.

Belief in one Supreme Being is so much a part both of our Catholic faith and our Western Civilization that we generally look upon worshippers of idols as being primitive and unsophisticated people. How unnecessary it seems for the creator of the heavens, the maker and designer of the earth, to protest to intelligent people: "I am the Lord and there is no other." The fact is, however, that we ourselves are surrounded by pagans who worship idols, pagans who exercise a considerable influence on us. Their idols are money, prestige, power, success, glamor . . . The list could go on and on, but I suppose it could be summed up in one word: selfishness. "What's in it for me?" is more than an often repeated question. It is the expression of a form of religion.

Christmas reveals to us the goodness and love of God. Its message, like the proclamation of a modern prophet amid the allurements of idolatry, calls us from selfishness to a renewal of the worship of the one true God, who alone is worthy of a complete and total dedication.

Alternate

They say that you can know a man by the company he keeps. In that case Jesus gave rather surprising credentials for himself. Really you would expect a king, for such was Jesus, to hobnob with the wealthy, influential people of his day, and yet Jesus claimed as his intimates the poor, the blind, the crippled, and the lepers: people whom few would esteem as friends and whom many would not even want to be bothered with.

When Jesus came into our world as the long awaited Messiah-

King, he did not look for his own comfort and pleasure either in the way in which he lived or in choosing to associate only with people who were pleasant and could return favors. He was born poor, he lived poor, and he died poor. The kind of people he most frequently associated with were those who needed him and who put something of a burden on him, people without any means for returning favors.

If Christmas is going to mean something to us this year, we must try through its celebration to become more like Jesus. It is true that we need friends who are agreeable and helpful to us; even Jesus had special friends. And in this sense charity begins at home, but it only *begins* there. Our love and concern must spread beyond a small circle of companions. We cannot treat eveyone in the same way, but we must not deliberately exclude anyone from our love and respect, whether it be because of his color, his religion, his nationality, or just plain old orneriness. In fact, if we want to be more like Jesus, the "undesirables" of this world have a special claim on us.

When Jesus comes again I wonder if he will know us as his disciples by the company we keep.

Thursday of the Third Week

God is love, and in his revelation God has been at pains to make it clear that he wishes to share his love, himself, with his people. One of the most beautiful images used for this purpose in the Old Testament is that which presents God and his people as husband and wife. As with human marriages, however, the relationship was not always ideal. Today's reading, addressed to the people in exile, takes on a particularly human quality wherein God admits, "For a brief moment I abandoned you (the period of exile) but with great tenderness I will take you back." God's love is so deep that despite the repeated "adulteries" of his spouse he cannot bring himself to divorce her.

The greatest expression of divine love was reached in the coming of Jesus Christ. Jesus entered into a new covenant, a new marital relationship, not with the chosen people alone but with the entire human race. Usually for a wedding the groom is dressed elegantly and his bride is attired in a beautiful gown. The marriage is sealed through the exchange of consent in a nervous but joyful atmosphere. The wedding of Jesus Christ and his people was unique. The groom hung naked upon a cross, his body battered and bloody. His bride was robed in the ugliness of sin. The marriage was sealed in the blood of Jesus. This ceremony, despite its outward appearances, was a profoundly glorious event, for the blood of Jesus was the sign of faithful, total love. "Christ gave himself up for his bride to make her holy and immaculate without stain or wrinkle" (Ep 5:25f).

Even with all our imperfections Jesus Christ loves us more than any husband has ever loved his wife, and he himself will make us beautiful and attractive. He could not have taken greater pains to show his love for us.

Alternate

John the Baptist was a person of austere virtue, an outstanding prophet, even a martyr. I find it difficult to think of myself as greater than this man, and yet Jesus assures us that the least born into the kingdom of God is greater than he. The point of comparison is the kind of birth one has, and therein lies the explanation of Jesus' remarkable statement.

John's birth was extraordinary in that his father was very elderly and his mother long past her childbearing years, but John as born of a woman is no match for one born of water and the Holy Spirit (Jn 3:3ff). Through the birth of baptism we are born into the kingdom of God. That birth is a marvelous, mysterious introduction into the family of God, a sharing in his own divine life, the source of a new people.

The words of Jesus in today's gospel have the ring of finality. They proclaim the end of an epoch and the beginning of the last era of the world. All that has transpired in the Old Testament period, a period summed up in the person of John the Baptist, is fulfilled in the kingdom of Jesus Christ. John, great though he was, belonged to the old age. We, simple though we may be, have been born into the new kingdom. And that has made all the difference.

Friday of the Third Week

Some Old Testament people developed a spirit of exclusiveness whereby they believed that only Jews could be saved. Isaiah in today's lesson made it clear that no one is excluded from God's favor, not even non-Jews living outside Palestine. In this spirit of Isaiah theologians are giving renewed emphasis to the mercy of God who wills the salvation of all men, an emphasis which gained approval in the Second Vatican Council. As a result, some Catholics are wondering what is the use of trying to win converts, or of trying to be a good Catholic, since God does indeed will the salvation of everyone.

The point is that religion is concerned with salvation in the future, of giving some guarantee of getting into heaven. Religion is also concerned with salvation here and now, which means leading people to achieve the real purpose of human existence in this life. The teachings of Jesus and the grace he won are intended to give us direction and help to live life to the full on this earth, as well as in heaven.

God wants all human beings to be now what they should be: people who worship him as their Father and who love one another as brothers and sisters. We still need a zeal that will move us to draw all men to Jesus Christ in his Church. The Second Vatican Council pointed out that good example is very important but that even more is required, for a true Christian "looks for opportunities to announce Christ by words addressed either to nonbelievers with a view of leading them to faith, or to believers with a view to instructing and strengthening them and motivating them toward a more fervent life" (*Decree on the Laity*, 6).

We should want to make the Church a house of prayer for *all* peoples.

Alternate

Jesus had spoken of God as his own Father, thereby making himself God's equal (Jn 5:18). His claim had not gone unchallenged by his enemies. In response Jesus asserted that he could bring forth witnesses, John the Baptist for one, but more importantly he had recourse to a truth which we ourselves accept: actions speak louder than words. And so Jesus stated: "I have testimony greater than John's, namely, the works the Father has given me to accomplish." His works, especially his miracles, could have come from God alone."

At Christmas we profess our faith that the baby born of Mary in Bethlehem had only God as his Father. That belief is fundamental to Christianity, and without it Christmas would be little different from our celebration of Washington's birthday. Some say that Jesus was only a social reformer, a religious philosopher, a great humanist. Jesus is actually none of these things. A social reformer struggles to find a way to right the wrongs of the day, but Jesus is himself the Way that we all must follow. A religious philosopher seeks to discover and contemplate the truth about God, but Jesus is himself the Truth that we must discover and contemplate. A humanist values and celebrates life and all its goodness, but Jesus is himself the Life that can bring goodness to us. Jesus, being God, is the Way, the Truth, and the Life (Jn 14:6).

Without Jesus any path a person follows simply goes around in circles. Without Jesus any search for truth becomes engulfed in darkness and confusion. Without Jesus even the longest and best life must come to an end. With Jesus we have a sure way to happiness, we find the truth that can set us free, and we enjoy the life that will last forever.

No readings are listed in the lectionary for a Saturday of the Third Week of Advent *since this day is always replaced by one of the days beginning on December 17.*

PART TWO

December 17th-24th

December 17

When Jesus Christ was born, the Jews inhabited a tiny, insignificant province within the mighty empire of Rome. From a human standpoint it would have made more sense for God to have chosen another people as the source of the Messiah-King—the Assyrians when their armies were all powerful, the Greeks when their philosophical wisdom was at its height, or the Romans of the day with their genius for law and government. But God knew what he wanted. He chose the tribe of Judah, the Jews, and from within that tribe he selected the house of David. He insisted that through David and his descendants the scepter, the ruling power, would never depart from Judah. In an eminent degree the prophecy of today's lesson was fulfilled in the person of Jesus Christ, born of the house of David as the Messiah-King.

God not only knew what he wanted; he also knew what he was doing. He was making it clear that he alone was God. He did not have to rely on mighty armies to conquer evil in the world. He did not have to appeal to philosophical wisdom for the spread of his truth. He did not have to rely on any human government to bring about justice and peace. God made his saving power present in a Jewish infant, Jesus Christ—an act which appears to be folly in the eyes of the wise of this world. He chose to pour out that salvation upon mankind through the blood of Christ poured out on the cross—an act which seems to be weakness in the eyes of the powerful of this world. God did what he did as a sign that we attain salvation, not by our own human efforts, but by his free gift in Jesus Christ.

No human wisdom, no human force can be given credit in place of God. It is right and just that we should give all the praise to God alone for the work of our salvation.

Alternate

Family trees are not very interesting until you know something about the people who are the branches, especially the unsavory characters. Three of the four women named by Matthew in the family tree of Jesus are not exactly the kind of people most of us would be proud to claim as our ancestors.

Tamar deceived her father-in-law, Judah, into an incestuous union. Rahab was a prostitute. And Solomon's mother, Bathsheba, was David's partner in an act of adultery which was followed by the murder of her husband, Uriah. These skeletons could easily have been kept hidden in the family closet, but Matthew chose to open the door for us to peek in. Precisely why he did so is not at all clear. The purpose of the entire genealogy is to show that Jesus Christ is the summit of the salvation history which began with the promise made to Abraham. Perhaps Matthew had in mind the fact that the Savior would be known as a friend of publicans and sinners (Mt 11:19), that he himself would declare that he had been sent to the lost sheep of the house of Israel (Mt 15:24), and that even in his death on the cross he would be flanked by two robbers (Mt 27:38).

Jesus was born to save sinners, not just those named in his genealogy, but all of us. Through the disobedience of "Adam" we were all constituted sinners, but through the loving obedience of Jesus on the cross we were freed from sin. The family tree of the human race, which began with the sinner, Adam, was transformed by the tree on Calvary. How fortunate we are that we can now trace our spiritual genealogy back to Christ, the new head of our human race.

December 18

On the night before he died, with his apostles gathered around him at the supper table, Jesus prayed to his Father for the unity of his followers: "That they all may be one as we are one" (Jn 17:21). Jesus wanted us to live together in harmony and peace. That he prayed for this intention on the very night before his death shows how close it was to his heart.

In the Mass, as we gather around the eucharistic supper table to commemorate the death of Jesus, we pray for the same intention: "May all of us who share in the body and blood of Christ be brought together in unity by the Holy Spirit." We offer a sign of peace to those present as an expression of our desire to make this prayer bear fruit in the way in which we live with one another. If we are not living together harmoniously, whom do we have to blame?

Before the time of Christ, the prophet Jeremiah accused the kings of Judah of not guiding the people properly and of therefore being responsible for their dispersion from the promised land. If Jeremiah were alive today he would not blame earthly rulers for any lack of harmony among us. Instead he would stand before us and say, "Don't you realize that you now have a king, a righteous shoot to David, who reigns and governs wisely, who does what is just and right in the land?" He would remind us that we have Jesus Christ, the Messiah-King, present among us not only to guide us in our lives, but also to give us the means of achieving real unity through the Eucharist. He would preach the same doctrine as did St. Paul: "Because the bread is one, we though many, are one body, all of us who partake of the one bread" (1 Cor 10:17). If we are not living together harmoniously, we really have no one to blame but ourselves, for we have the means of doing so in the Eucharist.

Alternate

Today's gospel shows how Joseph, a descendant of David, took Mary as his wife and adopted her child as his own. The result of his action was that Jesus was incorporated into the house of David in fulfillment of Old Testament prophecies. But the gospel contains a puzzling element. The angel assured Joseph that he should not fear to take Mary as his wife. What was Joseph afraid of? Knowing Mary, could he possibly have thought that she had been unfaithful to him? If so his reaction would not have been fear, but revulsion and indignation. Moreover, the evangelist clearly states that Mary "was found with child through the power of the Holy Spirit." The person who found her with child through the power of the Holy Spirit could have been only Joseph himself. It was the most natural thing in the world for Mary to confide in him.

Joseph's fear, then, was not about Mary. It was about himself. Humble as he was, he could not see how he of all people should presume to become the husband of someone who had been touched by God. He felt unworthy to take part in so holy a situation. The word of the angel did not give Joseph information but direction—to go ahead with his marriage.

Christmas is appealing to us because it makes God so close to us. Jesus is indeed "Immanuel," God with us in a simple, human way. But we should never allow the simplicity and humanness of Christmas to dull our sense of wonder and awe. We would do well to imitate Joseph in his humility because we are really much less worthy than he, a great saint, to take part in so holy a reality. Humility does not mean backing off in fear from the mystery of Christmas; rather it should move us to praise God for his goodness in calling us to be so close to him in the person of his Son made flesh. As we prepare to celebrate the birth of Jesus Christ our hearts should be filled with wonder and praise.

December 19

We look upon jealousy, the intolerance of any rival, as being a vice, a flaw of character. And so to speak of God as being jealous strikes us as unthinkable. Yet God is jealous, and in him jealousy is a virtue. It would be both unjust and untruthful for God to allow some rival to receive credit for what he alone accomplishes. And God must be both just and truthful.

In today's lesson we have an example of God's jealousy—perhaps we should say his justice and truthfulness. The people needed a leader like Samson to deliver them from the Philistines. They needed a Savior. Samson's being born of a woman who was naturally barren was a sign that God was at work. He was the real Savior of his people. We see much the same sign in the gospel narrative of the conception of John the Baptist in the womb of Elizabeth who had been sterile and was advanced in years. This sign of God at work reaches its finest expression in Mary who, though young, conceived Jesus without the cooperation of any human male.

Pelagius, a British monk who lived at the turn of the fifth century, ignored the jealousy of God. He taught that human beings can accomplish good without God's grace. Among us today we have a smattering of Pelagianism in those who see the Eucharist only as an experession of a good life. They insist that it is hypocritical to celebrate the Mass until one has proven his goodness. The Eucharist, it is true, should be an expression of goodness, but it is also a means to goodness. To think that we should not celebrate the Mass until we have arrived at perfection or even near-perfection is to fall into a modern form of Pelagianism. A more subtle form of Pelagianism is found in those who say that it is more important to love your neighbor than it is to bother with the liturgy. That is putting the cart before the horse, the effect before the cause.

The Vatican Council clearly taught that the Eucharist is not only the summit toward which all the activity of the Church is directed but also the font from which all her power flows (*Constitution on the Liturgy*, 10). Jesus rightly said at the last supper, when he instituted the Eucharist, "Apart from me you can do nothing" (Jn 15:5).

Alternate

Poor Zechariah! In the moment when two lifelong desires were fulfilled, he faltered. His first desire had been to have a child. Then when he and his wife were both advanced in years, God told him through the angel that Elizabeth would bear a son. But Zachary doubted. As a devout Jew and a priest he believed without qualification in God's power. He did not doubt that God *could* give him a son in his advanced age; he doubted only that God *would* give him a son. In other words, though he believed in God's power, he did not trust that God loved him enough to use that power in his behalf.

And what a time he chose to falter! For Zechariah's second

lifelong desire had been to have the privilege of offering incense in the sanctuary of the Lord. Only once in his lifetime did each priest offer incense; having once done so, he was never again given the privilege. It was a privilege determined by the drawing of lots, and through his many years the lot had not fallen on Zechariah. Now in this supreme moment, when God had granted him this priestly favor, at a time above all times when he should have trusted in God's love for him, Zechariah doubted.

We should not judge Zechariah harshly, for God did not reject him in his moment of hesitation. Instead, we should see whether we are not somewhat like Zechariah. We believe in God and everything about him which our faith teaches. But do we really trust that God loves us enough to use his almighty power in our behalf? We do not doubt that God can do something for us, but maybe we are not sufficiently convinced that he *will* do it, especially if we have waited a long time. In the supreme moment of the Mass, when God shows us both his power and love, at this time above all times we should trust completely in God, even if we have to wait a lifetime, as did Zechariah, to see God use his almighty power out of love for us.

December 20

Ahaz, king of Judah, was playing a dangerous game with Isaiah the prophet. Ahaz wanted to enter into an alliance with Assyria to protect himself from his neighboring kings. When Isaiah heard of the plan, he insisted that Ahaz should put his trust in God, not in some foreign military power, and even promised him a sign of God's fidelity. Ahaz refused the offer, saying in effect, "I wouldn't be so bold as to ask God for a sign." Actually Ahaz was afraid that if he were to receive a sign he would have to abandon his alliance with Assyria, and the truth was that he had more confidence in the power of Assyria than he did in the power of God.

Isaiah, refusing to play games, gave Ahaz the sign anyway: "The virgin shall be with child and bear a son." This child, a pledge that the kingdom of Judah would survive through a descendant of David, was a sign of God's continued presence and protection. The prophecy of Isaiah, as read in the Church and understood in the light of further revelation, is seen as being eminently fulfilled in the Virgin Mary's son who is truly Immanuel, "God with us" (*Constitution on the Church*, 55).

Through all the difficulty, frustration, and dangers of life, we must learn to depend on God as Ahaz did not. The birth of Jesus Christ from the Virgin Mary stands as a perpetual sign to us of God's continued presence and protection. Soon we will celebrate Christmas, a feast rich in meaning. Today, however, let us reflect on one aspect of that feast: the sign that in Jesus Christ, our Immanuel, God is indeed still with us.

Alternate

Two statements of Mary at the time of the annunciation are important for understanding our relationship to God as our Savior: "Let it be done to me" and "I am the maidservant of the Lord."

First, "Let it be done to me." Sin came into the world through human free will, and God wanted salvation to come into the world equally through human free will. And so the angel was sent to Mary to seek her consent to the Incarnation. St. Thomas Aquinas taught that Mary, like a new Eve, the mother of all the living, gave her consent in the name of the whole human race (III, q. 30, a. 1), an opinion supported by Pope Pius XII in his encyclical on the Mystical Body (127). When Mary said, "Let it be done to me," the salvation of the world through Jesus Christ began (cf. also the *Constitution on the Church*, 55-56). Though Mary consented to salvation in our name, we must confirm that consent, each one for himself. God wills the salvation of all men, but he respects human freedom so much that he forces his salvation on no one. God will not give us salvation without our cooperation.

But it is not quite that simple. We must remember the second statement of Mary, "I am the maidservant of the Lord." A maidservant is one who is totally dependent on her master, and

Mary in her humility, her honesty, recognized that she was totally dependent on God. As such, not even Mary could have given her consent without God's grace. And we are so totally dependent on God that we cannot freely consent to our salvation unless he moves us to do so. Though it is beyond our comprehension, God has the power to move us to accept salvation without destroying our freedom.

Complicated? Yes, but it is vital to recognize that while we must work for our salvation, salvation is still a gift since the work itself cannot be done without God. Salvation is so gratuitous that without God we cannot even say "yes" to the salvation he freely offers us. Like Mary we should say "Let it be done to me," but all the while we must realize that, like Mary, we are totally dependent on God.

December 21

The love song in the first lesson today is one of many in the Bible which have traditionally been understood as symbolic of the love between God and his people. These songs celebrate young love; a thrilling, absorbing, ardent affection, an attachment which is tender, yet strong, unselfish, yet fulfilling.

Young love is a wonderful symbol of God's love for us, but there is one big difference. Young love in time tends to weaken with familiarity; its luster grows dim with routine; its ardor lessens in the harshness of daily living. Not so with God's love. His love is constant, unchanging, and always faithful.

Young love is also a symbol of our love for God. Perhaps we have never quite felt the intensity of young love in our relationship with God, but it is very likely that our feeling of love has weakened with familiarity, its luster has grown dim with routine, its ardor has lessened in the harshness of life.

It is often said that love is blind, but that is not true. Real love sees attributes in another which no one else has the vision to perceive. And yet familiarity, like a cataract, obscures the vision of love. Our familiarity with even the signs of God's love can dull our vision. One of these familiar signs is the mystery of Christmas: God so loved the world that in the fullness of time he sent his only Son to be our Savior. But the feast of Christmas contains a light bright enough to get through our dimmed vision if we look intently enough with faith at this great mystery. We should pray that this year we may see the birth of Jesus Christ in such a light that our love for God may become more like his love for us.

Alternate

Christmas carols help to heighten our feelings at this time of the year. A very popular carol begins, "Joy to the world, the Savior reigns; let earth receive her king." If there is one emotion which should be ours at Christmas it is joy.

The prophet Zephaniah proclaimed joy to the faithful of Judah even during a time of religious degradation when in the city of Jerusalem itself some had fallen into idolatrous worship of the sun, the moon, and the stars. His proclamation looked to the future, to a great day of the Lord when once again it would be said to Jerusalem, "The Lord, your God, is in your midst, a mighty Savior." We too live in an era of idolatry when some worship materialism and pleasure. God proclaims joy to us in our celebration of Christmas as we look to the past to see the coming of the Lord, a mighty Savior, into our world. Our Christmas joy, however, is not derived only from the past. It is also a present reality and a future hope. The birth of Jesus is more than history. In a real sense by the power of God Jesus is born in each of us through our Christian liturgy. His coming is as fresh and new for us as it was for Mary his mother. The liturgy proclaims "The Lord, your God, is in your midst, a mighty Savior." And like Zephaniah we also look to the future, for though Christ is present he is also yet to come on the great day of the Lord. And what a festival of joy that day will be when the whole world receives her king!

As Christians, as the faithful of the Lord, we should sing in our hearts: "Joy to the world, the Savior reigns; let earth receive her king."

Alternate

For a very long time Elizabeth and her husband, Zachariah, had prayed and yearned for a child as a fruit of their marriage. When Elizabeth finally conceived in her old age, when all natural hope for a child had been exhausted, she recognized that she had been especially blessed by God. She was awed by the miracle which had taken place in her womb. But when Elizabeth saw her cousin, and the child stirred in her womb, she realized that an even greater work of God was present in Mary. Enlightened by the Holy Spirit she cried out to Mary: "Blessed are you among women and blessed is the fruit of your womb." She was so awed by the miracle which had taken place in Mary's womb that she felt unworthy even to be in her presence: "Who am I that the mother of my Lord should come to me?"

We have received many blessings from God, none perhaps as dramatic as that granted to Elizabeth and Zachariah, but striking nonetheless. We should praise and thank God for all these favors, but at this time of the year we must think especially about the meaning of Christmas: God himself comes to us in the person of his Son made flesh in the womb of Mary. We need to reflect on this great mystery of God's love for us. Each one of us, in awe and wonder, should ask, "Who am I that the Lord himself should come to me?" Before receiving Jesus in holy communion we are invited to confess, "Lord, I am not worthy to receive you." We are not worthy indeed, and if we had only a natural hope of receiving God's favor we would have to turn away from the table of the Lord in despair. But the Holy Spirit enlightens us to see that, though we are not worthy, God loves us so much that he wishes to give us the great gift of his own Son. And that is really something to praise and thank God for.

December 22

Hannah had prayed long and earnestly for a son and promised that if her prayer were answered she would consecrate her child to the Lord. Today's lesson recounts how after Samuel was born to her, she and her husband presented the Child to the Lord together with the sacrifice of a young bull. Samuel became their gift to God, and they left him in the temple.

One of the most difficult things for devoted parents to do is to let go of their children. Even if parents do not desire a child as earnestly as did Hannah, when he does come along they usually become very attached to him. Every child, whether eagerly or reluctantly accepted, is given to parents only for a while. Ties must eventually be broken so that a child may have the freedom to fulfill his own purpose in life. Children do not belong completely to their parents.

Perhaps parental ties could be severed with less pain if each one of us were to realize that we do not belong completely even to ourselves. We belong to God. He is the one parent with whom ties should never be broken. True freedom means giving ourselves totally to him, for that is the purpose of life. We must do for ourselves what Hannah did for Samuel as she offered him to the Lord.

In the third Eucharistic Prayer, wherein we offer to God the sacrifice of his own Son, we say these words: "May he make us an everlasting gift to you." An everlasting gift—that means an offering which is never taken back and a giving which has no reservations. The only way to real happiness in this life and in the next is to put ourselves with trust and love in the hands of God so that he may do with us as he wills.

Alternate

Christmas in our society is supremely a day for children. What a joyful, happy time it is for them as they open their presents and begin to play with their toys! Adults too want to share their simple pleasures. We have developed almost a caricature of that attitude in the picture of a father who spends more time in playing with an electric train than does his son to whom the present was given.

Actually Christmas is not meant for children any more than it is for adults. It is meant for anyone, whatever his age, who has faith and humility as Mary did. When Elizabeth praised her for being given the gift of Jesus Christ as her son, Mary manifested how profound was her faith and how great was her humility: "My spirit finds joy in God my Savior, for he has looked upon his servant in her lowliness."

To feel the joy of Christmas we must have the faith to believe that the almighty God himself came into our world in the flesh of an infant. To experience the thrill of Christmas, we must accept the awesome paradox, that, as G.K. Chesterton expressed it, in the cave of Bethlehem "the hands that had made the sun and the stars were too small to reach the huge heads of the cattle." To derive benefit from Christmas, we have to receive Jesus Christ as God's special gift to us, to open our arms to embrace him, to let him become a part of our lives, as Mary did. And even if we are mature adults, with serious responsibilities, we must be humble enough to admit that we need Jesus, that without him we cannot make any sense of our lives or accomplish any worthwhile purpose.

All the happiness which should be a part of Christmas can be ours if we join Mary in saying, "My spirit finds joy in God my Savior, for he has looked upon his servant in her lowliness."

December 23

Today's lesson does not seem to be in accord with the joyful spirit of Christmas. Malachi told the people that the Lord would come, which sounds cheerful enough, but he warned them that the Lord would purify them as silver and gold are refined in fire, which sounds somewhat ominous.

An old proverb is applicable here: one man's meat is another man's poison. The point of Malachi's prophecy was that the coming of the Lord would be painful only for those who were not ready, and he said that Elijah, the prophet, would come first to prepare the people. Jesus himself stated that this Elijah, this special prophet, was actually John the Baptist (cf. Mt 11:10ff).

John came preaching repentance as a preparation for the Messiah. Repentance means a turning away from sin and a turning toward God. Part of our Christmas preparation has traditionally been the making of a good confession and that is a practice in accord with the message of the Baptist, as we make use of this sacrament in order to turn away from sin. From this sacrament we should also seek to derive the grace to turn our thoughts to God, to center upon Christmas as a spiritual celebration of God's love for us in the coming of his Son. Many good people lament the commercialism which has obscured this spiritual meaning of Christmas, but it seems better to make a positive use of today's Christmas practices. The giving of gifts should make us think of God's Christmas gift to us. Christmas carols, even nonsensical ones like *Jingle Bells*, help to create an atmosphere of joy, an emotion which should be ours at this time. A big Christmas dinner can remind us that God calls us to share in the spiritual banquet of the Mass, which is a foreshadowing of our eternal blessedness in heaven.

The so-called material aspects of Christmas don't have to be our poison. They can be a refreshing nourishment which helps us open our eyes with renewed vigor to the true beauties of our Christmas celebration.

Alternate

William Shakespeare in *Romeo and Juliet* wrote, "What's in a name? That which we call a rose by any other name would smell as sweet." People's names don't have much significance these days, and yet, though we don't often reflect on it, some surnames, such as Farmer or Baker, apparently evolved from a person's occupation. Biblical names are often rich in meaning. God himself insisted that the son of Zachariah and Elizabeth be named John for a very good reason. That name in Hebrew literally means "The Lord has shown favor." The Baptist was the last of the Old Testament prophets, and in a sense he summed up in his person all the favors

3

God had shown to the chosen people through his spokesmen, the prophets. Everything that God did in the Old Testament pointed to the person for whom John was to be the herald, Jesus Christ.

John's extraordinary conception and birth as the herald of Christ were the last steps in God's preparation for the saving mission of the Messiah. Nor were his parents' names a matter of chance. "Elizabeth" means "The Lord has sworn," and recalls the solemn promise God made to send the Messiah. "Zachariah" means "The Lord has remembered," and indicates the faithfulness of God in keeping those promises.

What's in a name? In the names of the three principal characters of today's gospel we have a symbol of what our celebration of Christmas ought to be. Our hearts should be filled with praise and thanks to God for having remembered his great favor through the person of his Son, born into our world to be our Savior.

December 24

David told Nathan the prophet that he wanted to build a house for the Lord, meaning a beautiful temple. God in his turn, through a play on words, told David that he would establish a house for him, meaning a royal dynasty, which we have come to refer to as the "house of David." This promise of God, spoken through Nathan, became the basis of Jewish expectation of a kingly messiah, son of David—an expectation which Jesus Christ, born of the house of David in David's city of Bethlehem, fulfilled in an eminent way.

God's promise contained the idea that people were more important than a temple, that God would work out his plan of salvation through human beings who would prepare for the coming of Christ. When Jesus Christ did come, God's preference for people did not change. People are more important than the physical structure of a church, however appropriate and beautiful. As God chose people to lead up to the coming of Christ, so now he chooses people to continue the presence of his son in the world. We are those people, a chosen race, a royal priesthood.

Through faith and God's grace Jesus Christ is present within us, but his presence can grow. Or perhaps it is better to say that we can grow in our openness to accept him. The ocean is there. Only the container we bring limits how much of it we can take. In our liturgical celebration of Christmas Jesus wants to be born anew in us. He invites us to open our hearts to receive him. Are you willing to let Jesus take over your being, to flood your mind and body with his presence so that through you he may spread his kingdom on earth? His kingdom is one of justice, love, and peace. It is worth the effort to have a share in bringing that kingdom to all men.

Alternate

Zachariah thought that in his old body and that of his wife, Elizabeth, there was no hope for a child, for the gift of life. He hesitated to believe that God loved him enough to use his almighty power in his favor. As such Zachariah is a symbol of modern man with all his doubts and anxieties. It is not surprising that in the face of war and hatred, greed and injustice, people are pushed to the edge of despair. The young accuse the old of having made a mess of the world, and the old blame the young for only making it worse. Our world in the view of some is too decrepit to contain any hope for a new life.

Zachariah changed his view when he received a sign from God. That sign was the birth of his son, John. In response to this evident work of God, the old man sang the beautiful song found in today's gospel. In it he praised the faithful love of God.

If at times we are tempted to share in a pessimistic world view, we should remember that we too have received a sign from God. That sign is the birth of God's own son, Jesus Christ. And it is a sign which is not confined to the past, for it becomes a present reality in our liturgical celebration of Christmas. Every Christmas is a testimony from God that he has not given up on the world.

Zachariah's song should become our Christmas hymn: "Blessed be the Lord the God of Israel because he has visited and ransomed his people. He has raised a horn of saving strength for us in the house of David his servant."

PART THREE

Saints' Days During Advent

November 30
Feast of St. Andrew, Apostle

The feast of St. Andrew seems to be out of harmony with the season of Advent just when we are beginning to prepare to celebrate the birth of Jesus Christ. As a matter of fact, St. Andrew the Apostle helps to put the Christmas mystery into proper perspective. St. Andrew lived in the shadow of his more famous brother, St. Peter, so that we do not know a whole lot about him. Several very ancient traditions, however, assert that Andrew, like Jesus himself, met death by means of crucifixion. From the day that Andrew accepted, without any conditions, the invitation of Jesus, "Come after me," he was headed for the cross.

It is understandable that we would like to share in the resurrection of Christ without the cross, to gain life without death, to enjoy happiness without suffering. But today's feast reminds us that when Jesus took human flesh, he made himself vulnerable. When he was born into our world, he opened himself to the necessity of suffering physically, mentally, and emotionally. According to the plan of the Father as revealed in Jesus Christ, resurrection comes through the cross, life through death, and happiness through suffering.

When we accepted the invitation, "Come after me," as did Andrew, we made ourselves vulnerable. We opened ourselves to the necessity of suffering with Christ physically, mentally, and emotionally. Advent preparation for Christmas should indeed be joyful, but our joy should be put into proper perspective. According to the plan of the Father, if we wish to share in the lasting happiness of Jesus, we must also be willing to share in his cross as well.

December 3
Memorial of St. Francis Xavier

What an extraordinary man was St. Francis Xavier! As a missionary he preached the gospel of Jesus Christ in Japan and six other countries of the Far East. His name, "Xavier," in Spanish means "Savior," and true to his name he brought Jesus the Savior to a vast number of people. His converts numbered in the hundreds of thousands. Exhausted by his labors, he died in 1552 in Sancian, an island off the coast of China, far from his home in Spain.

This great saint was mindful of the fact that Jesus came to save all men, no matter who they were or where they happened to live. Quite appropriately Pope Pius X made him patron of the missions. Even though we are not missionaries to some distant country, we can and should follow the example of St. Francis in our own way. At Christmas time we recall that Jesus was born into our world as the savior. We should be grateful that through our faith as Catholics we have accepted the meaning of his coming. But there is more. The name, "Catholic," means "universal." To be a true Catholic we must have a universal interest in our fellow human beings. We are surrounded by a vast number of people for whom the faith of Jesus Christ has little or no meaning, people who are in as much need as were the people of the Orient in the sixteenth century. Why are we so timid and so reluctant to speak of Christ to others? Why are we so unwilling to make even a little effort when a man like St. Francis made a supreme sacrifice to spread the truth of our religion? Today we should pray that God may give us a share in the great zeal and courage of St. Francis Xavier.

By bringing the truth of Jesus Christ to others we can be true to our name, the name of "Catholic."

December 7
Memorial of St. Ambrose, Bishop

The memory of St. Ambrose is kept on December 7th because it was on this day in the year 374 that he became a bishop. This saint, in keeping with his office as teacher of the Church in the diocese of Milan, wrote extensively on the role and importance of Mary in our salvation (in his treatise on virginity). His emphasis should remind us that there is no Christmas without Mary, no crib without the Virgin, no Christ Child without his mother.

Celebrating Christmas without Mary is worse than celebrating the Fourth of July without the flag. The flag is only a symbol of our country, but Mary as mother is the true sign that God actually did become human like us in all things but sin. Mary is our link with divinity. Within her womb the divine Son of God took human flesh. In the temple of her body a unique wedding took place, the joining of divinity and humanity in the person of Jesus Christ. From her the God-Man was born into this world of ours in order to accomplish the work of our salvation.

Christmas is a day surrounded with tenderness and emotion, but it is not by mere sentiment that we include Mary in our celebration. She is an integral part of the mystery of Christ's coming.

I think St. Ambrose is pleased by our taking his memorial as an occasion to emphasize once again the place of Mary in the great truth of the birth of Jesus Christ.

December 8
Solemnity of the Immaculate Conception

A mother is a special person. No matter what our human relationships may be through the years, the relationship with our mother remains unique. We began life within the safe, protective confines of her womb. There we were nourished and grew until we were born. And though the cord uniting us to our mother was severed at birth, our union with her was not broken. We were fed at her breast and consoled in her warm embrace. Later we listened for the loving words of her gentle voice, and we told her of our needs and worries, our joy and happiness. Yes, a mother is a very special person. And yet as we grew older we realized that our mother, however wonderful, was not perfect, for she was as human as we.

It is no wonder that Jesus wanted his mother to be perfect. Because he was divine and preexisted his mother, he could fashion his mother exactly as he pleased. He brought to bear on her his almighty power as he preserved her free of original sin from the time of her conception. It was a unique privilege befitting the unique relationship between Jesus and Mary. The Immaculate Conception is an Advent feast, for Mary was preserved from sin so that she could be a worthy source from whom the Son of God would be born into the world. She was conceived immaculate in her mother's womb for the moment described in today's gospel when Jesus was conceived in her womb.

Even though we have not shared in the immaculate conception, this privilege of Mary has meaning for us. It is more than a family secret which has been told us as we peer in from the outside. It is more than a humanly appealing fact, that in God's plan a perfect woman is inseparably connected with the coming of the Savior. Perhaps above all, Mary's immaculate conception should stand as a sign of hope to us since it reveals the greatest masterpiece of the savior's power. In 1821 William Wordsworth wrote these beautiful words about Mary:

> Mother! whose virgin bosom was uncrost
> With the least shade of thought to sin allied;
> Woman above all women glorified,
> Our tainted nature's solitary boast. . . .*

We should boast about Mary. We should cry out to the whole world: "See what the power of Christ has done for a member of our race." And therein lies our hope. If the power of the Savior is great enough to preserve Mary, a human person like ourselves, from sin, then it is great enough to cure us of the effects of sin.

As we make our Advent preparations we should recognize with humility and honesty that we are not worthy of God. And yet God wants us. St. Paul reminds us of our calling (second reading): "God chose us in Christ before the world began, to be holy and blameless in his sight, to be full of love. . . ." As we look at ourselves we should be able to see that we are far from our calling. But that is no reason

*Ecclesiastical Sonnets, Part II, no. 25, "The Virgin."

for discouragement. Remember that the same Savior who pre-served Mary free from sin wishes to cleanse us from sin.

In the Mass before communion we proclaim: "Lord, I am not worthy to receive you, but only say the word and I shall be healed." What is this word of healing? Its finest expression is found in the sacrament of penance when Jesus says through the priest, "I absolve you from your sins." That word of Jesus both repairs injuries of the past and gives strength for the future. Confession is a traditional part of our preparation for Christmas, and that practice should continue. We are not immaculate as was Mary, but because of her immaculate conception we should have the confidence that through confession we can prepare ourselves to receive the grace of Christ at Christmas. His grace can lead us to our calling, to be holy and blameless and full of love.

December 13
Memorial of St. Lucy, Martyr

The feast of St. Lucy is a very ancient one, its celebration dating back to the sixth century in Rome. She has been honored in the Church ever since because she went to her death rather than abandon her faith. And yet it is an aspect of her life rather than her death which makes her celebration appropriate for the season of Advent. According to the traditional story told about her, when Lucy came of age she asked her mother for her dowry. Instead of using the money, according to the custom of the day, to secure a husband, she gave all her money to the poor. Her generosity to God's poor was greater than her natural desire for marriage and a family of her own.

During Advent we are thinking about the gifts we will give at Christmas. Isn't it true that for the most part we give gifts to persons who are very close to us, people who usually respond by giving us a gift in return. There is nothing wrong with that. We should give gifts to people as a sign of our love for them. But think about St. Lucy.

She gave her gifts to people who were really in need, people who could not return the favor. Perhaps we could do well on this feast of St. Lucy to reflect on the fact that we should develop a greater spirit of generosity in our Christmas celebration. A good resolution would be to make sure that we help someone who really has a serious need. And if we want to be as generous as possible, we can give the gift anonymously. That way we can be sure that we won't even be looking for a "thank you" in return.

St. Lucy is a good model for our Christmas giving.

December 14
Memorial of St. John of the Cross

St. John of the Cross died at the age of forty-nine after having lived a laborious and difficult life. He wrote several books on prayer and the spiritual life which are classics and which reflect his own inner struggle to grow in his love for God. Most of his prayer was a reliving of the prayer of Jesus in Gethsemane, "Not my will but yours be done." He expanded much effort in reforming the Carmelite Order, of which he was a member, but his good intentions often met with resistance and rebuffs. Like Jesus, "to his own he came, yet his own did not accept him."

It is related that when St. John was coming to the end of his life, Jesus appeared to him and asked what reward he desired. He replied, "Lord, to suffer and to be despised for you." And that, to a large extent, is what makes the difference between St. John of the Cross and ourselves. He had the courage *to ask* to suffer and be despised. I for one do not have that same courage, but I do recognize that like this saint all of us are required to suffer and to be despised.

Advent is a time for becoming more aware of the kind of life Jesus led when he took flesh and became one of us. It is also a time for becoming more like Jesus in our own lives. St. John of the Cross reminds us that becoming like Jesus involves the need to suffer and be despised. Our prayer becomes a form of suffering when we have a battle against distractions and boredom, and struggle to say and mean, "Not my will but yours be done." Our best intentions will at times meet wtih resistance and rebuffs, even from those whom we love the most. Perseverance will win a reward, not indeed the one St. John asked for, but the one he merited: a life of perfect happiness with Jesus when he comes again in glory.

The Season of Christmas

December 26
Feast of St. Stephen

We have scarcely concluded our celebration of the birth of Christ when today we are asked to look beyond the time of his own death and resurrection to the day of the death of St. Stephen, the first Christian martyr. St. Stephen gave witness to his faith by willingly accepting death.

This feast of the martyrdom of St. Stephen helps to put the meaning of Christmas into perspective for us. We need not lay aside all the beautiful images of Mary and Joseph bending over their God who chose to assume the helplessness of a human infant. And yet we must recognize that in becoming human like us in all things but sin, Jesus made himself vulnerable as was St. Stephen. He opened himself to the possibility of suffering and death. From the time of his conception and birth, Jesus was destined to win the salvation of the world by means of his death on the cross. In a real sense Jesus was born to die. From death he was born to the fullness of life in the resurrection.

The death and resurrection of Jesus are the great central event of his entire life. Everything about him led up to that momentous act of sacrifice. That is why yesterday when we celebrated his birth, we did so by means of the Mass, which makes present for us once again the mystery of his death and resurrection.

It is quite right for us to contemplate the sweetness of the scene at Bethlehem, but today's feast calls us to the realization that Jesus himself was born to be a martyr, that is, a witness to God the Father's immense love for us. The sign of that love is his sacrifice, a sacrifice which was a reality only because he had first become human like us in all things but sin.

December 27
Feast of St. John the Evangelist

When many people think of St. John, the first thought which

comes to their minds is that he is the apostle of love. He sensed God's love for himself through the person of Jesus Christ so intensely that he was consumed with the desire to make others aware of this great love.

From all the passages from his gospel the Church has chosen for his feast that moment when John himself came to faith in the resurrection of Jesus. He went into the empty tomb; he saw and believed. Yesterday the feast of St. Stephen helped us to realize that by becoming human, Jesus made himself vulnerable; his humanity made it possible for him to suffer and to die. Today's gospel helps us to see that death for Jesus led to the glory of the resurrection.

The resurrection of Jesus is not only the sign of the Father's great love for his beloved Son; it is also the sign of the Father's great love for us. Jesus is the plan, the blueprint for our lives. What happened to him will happen to us. We too are vulnerable, subject to death. But death for us will also lead to resurrection. The Father loves us so much that he wants us to share in his glory and the everlasting life of his Son.

The Christmas season is a time of great joy. St. John in the first reading stated that his purpose in writing was that our joy might be complete. Our joy at the birth of Christ is complete when we realize that our fellowship is with the Father and with his son, Jesus Christ. This fellowship, this oneness, will come to full fruit in our own resurrection from the dead.

December 28
Feast of the Holy Innocents

There are always bullies in this world, people who use their power to oppress the poor, the simple, the humble, and the defenseless. But God is always at work, often in mysterious ways, to defend his people who are poor in spirit.

No one is more defenseless than a child. When the Hebrews

were enslaved in Egypt, Pharoah decreed that all their male children were not to be allowed to live. And yet from their slaughter arose a great man, rescued by the providence of God. This man was Moses, the savior of his people. (Cf. today's Office of Readings.) King Herod decreed that all the boys, two years and younger, born in Bethlehem were to be murdered. And from that slaughter arose Jesus Christ, our Savior.

We are God's people, just ordinary people who are not the powerful of this world. We are called to be simple and humble, relying on God to protect us and to give us justice against evil. God worked for the good of his people through Moses and now he works for our good through Jesus Christ. But he wants us to be concerned about others as he is concerned about us, to allow Jesus to continue his good work within us.

The poor, the downtrodden, the underprivileged should be our favorites as they are God's favorites. In particular on this feast of the Holy Innocents, we ought to think of those unborn children, completely defenseless, who are victims of abortion. It is not right for us to identify pro-abortionists with Pharoah or Herod, for they may be acting out of ignorance. Nonetheless we must never compromise with the false theory which pretends that abortion is anything other than the killing of an innocent child. The Second Vatican Council has declared that "from the moment of its conception life must be guarded with the greatest care, while abortion and infanticide are unspeakable crimes" (*Church in the Modern World*, 51).

December 29
5th Day of Christmas

A little more than a week ago we experienced the shortest day of the year, that day when the least amount of sunshine is possible. From that time on the days grow longer and gradually there is more and more sunlight. The Church takes this natural phenomenon as a symbol of the coming of Christ into the world. That is why we celebrate Christmas when we do. Christ is the light of the world and of our lives. As St. John says, "The darkness is over and the real light begins to shine."

Simeon understood this meaning of the birth of Christ. Holding the infant in his arms he cried out: "My eyes have witnessed your saving deed displayed for all the people to see: A revealing light to the Gentiles, the glory of your people Israel." With this light to lead him Simeon was willing to make the passage through the dark, awesome doors of death. With absolute confidence he said to God, "Now, Master, you can dismiss your servant in peace."

Christmas has come and gone once more for us, but we must not forget its great meaning. Jesus is the light of our lives. He is the one who through his teaching which we read daily in the scriptures here at Mass gives meaning and purpose to our very ordinary lives. I can think of nothing worse than to have no purpose in life, no sense of direction, only confusion and frustration. With Jesus himself to guide, we should with confidence live each day of our lives until that great day when it will be time for us to say, "Now, Master, you can dismiss your servant in peace."

December 30
6th Day of Christmas

Some people think that Christmas is only for children. Of course that is seeing Christmas as a day of toys and games. The truth is that Christmas is for everyone because of God's gift, his own son.

Yesterday we saw the old man, Simeon, embrace Jesus and recognize that salvation had come to him and to the world. Today the elderly prophetess, Anna, sees the child, Jesus, and gives thanks to God. But she does more. In her role as prophetess she spoke about the Child to all who looked forward to the deliverance of Jerusalem.

What Anna did for the people in the temple, the writers of the

New Testament have done for us, all of us. St. John in the first reading today is at pains to omit no one as he has words of advice for little ones, children, young people, and adults. St. John encourages all those whom he addresses, but his final word is the most important of all: "The man who does God's will endures forever." That exhortation puts the coming of Christ into perspective for us. Sentiment and emotion are part of the Christmas celebration, but they are empty without a determination to be followers of God's will.

Jesus came, among other reasons, to show us and to teach us his Father's will. We see his example and we hear his teaching chiefly in the gospels. During the coming year this gospel will gradually be unfolded during our daily Masses. A good New Year's resolution is to try to be as faithful as we can to daily Mass. Through daily Mass the meaning of Christ's birth and life on this earth can more easily be fulfilled.

December 31
7th Day of Christmas

Usually an author of a book on any serious subject begins in a simple way so that the reader may get an easy start. St. John began his gospel in just the opposite way by thrusting us back into the day of eternity, that non-moment before time began when there was only God, nothing else. It is impossible for us to form a picture of what St. John presents. In fact it is very difficult even to talk about it.

What is clear is that before creation God was not alone. Without any reference to concepts such as past or future, God the Father begets his Son, equal to him in all things. This is an act which is an eternal "now." God is in fact begetting his Son in this very moment. Among other things this idea means that in God there is great dynamism. He is not static, like a great mountain. Rather he is suffused with life, power, and activity.

In the moment of creation God shared this life, this dynamism, by allowing his goodness to spread outside himself. It was like speaking the words, "Let there be creation." This creation is a sharing in the being of his Son, whom St. John calls the eternal "Word." Later in time this same eternal Word became flesh to show us the meaning and purpose of creation, of life itself.

We are now at the end of another year. This fact reminds us that one day time will end, but life will not. We ourselves will be caught up into the never ending life, which is God. Jesus Christ, the Word of God, has empowered us to become children of God. As children we share now in his life and we are his heirs, and we stand to inherit everlasting life. Earthly existence will end where St. John's gospel begins, in the eternal presence of God.

January 2
Memorial of Sts. Basil the Great
and Gregory Nazianzen

St. Basil and St. Gregory were both bishops and great teachers in the Church. Although they lived and died in the fourth century, they believed and taught the same faith which we hold today. The reason they share the same feast day is that they were the closest of friends. They were brought together by the intense desire each felt to know as much about God as possible. The knowledge they sought together was not a theoretical understanding of God, but a practical one which would affect their lives.

As St. Gregory wrote, "Our single object and ambition was virtue, and a life of hope in the blessings that are to come . . . Our great pursuit, the great name we wanted, was to be Christians."

As Bishops they were like St. John the Baptist whose whole mission was to direct people to the person of Jesus Christ. Their virtue was zeal and their knowledge led to instruction. All they did was not for themselves, but for God and his people.

These two saints, though far removed from us in time, illustrate for us today that being a follower of Christ means sharing in a community of believers. We do not walk alone in our journey to

God. Rather we progress with others, just as in coming to receive communion we do so in company with those who share our faith. We are called to help each other by good example, by mutual encouragement, and by being ready to help in any kind of need.

What we enjoy in faith with each other, we must try to share with others as did Basil and Gregory, and as did St. John the Baptist. That is the spirit to which Christ calls all of us. "Church" means people, united in faith and love, who are eager to draw others into the community of God's people.

January 3

People often failed to recognize the true identity of Jesus during his public ministry. John the Baptist desperately tried to call people to follow Jesus for who he was. He himself had seen the Spirit descend upon Jesus, marking Jesus out as God's chosen one, his beloved Son.

Another St. John, the author of the letter we heard today, was eager that we recognize not only who Jesus is but who we have become because of him. He says to us, "Dearly beloved, we are God's children." Scarcely could such a simple statement bear such a monumental truth. To be God's own children is the greatest privilege and dignity that could be alloted to us mere mortals.

Do you believe that God the Father loved Jesus, his Son? Do you think that he cherished him and cared for him? Can you imagine how proud he was of his Son and how he wished only the best for him? A great mystery of our faith is that in making us his children, God the Father looks upon us and sees within us the person of his beloved Son. He pours out upon us much the same Fatherly affection he has for Jesus.

Our real worth in God's eyes is not what we do or accomplish but simply who we are. Good parents do not demand that their little children earn their love and affection. They do not have to pay for food and lodging. Good parents give to their children not because their accomplishments are world shaking but simply because of who they are.

We should always want to follow God's will, but we should never think that we must earn anything from God. He gives to us freely because we are his children. Heaven is not something we will buy from God. It is something we will simply inherit. Nothing is greater than this simple truth: "We are God's children."

January 4
Memorial of St. Elizabeth Ann Seton

Elizabeth Ann Seton is the first American born saint and a truly extraordinary woman. She was the wife of William Seton and mother of their five children. She was reared as an Episcopalian, but was impressed by a Catholic family in Italy while visiting there with her husband. Her husband died there when he was only age 30 and she was left alone to support her five small children. She became a Catholic shortly after the death of her husband.

To support her children she opened a school in Baltimore, and soon a group of young women began to form around her. They eventually became the American Sisters of Charity and followed the rule of St. Vincent de Paul. By the time of her death on this day in 1821 she had seen her sisters expand their work from Baltimore to New York and as far west as St. Louis.

Many aspects of her ministry could be emphasized, but toward the end of her life she herself expressed the wish that she be known as a daughter of the Church. She understood well the truth which would later be expressed by the Vatican Council in these words: "It has pleased God to make men holy and save them not merely as individuals without any mutual bonds, but by making them into a single people" (*Const. on The Church*, 9). God wants us to come to know him and to serve him by means of the relationships we have with each other. We see this truth, which was so impressed on Mother Seton, reflected in today's gospel. Jesus wanted to draw disciples to himself as a beginning of the Church. When Andrew was called, he did not think only of himself. "The first thing he did was to seek out his brother Simon and tell him." That is the spirit of community, the spirit of the Church.

We never stand alone in our relationship with God. It is a relationship we enjoy in union with all the members of the Church.

January 5
Memorial of St. John Neumann

John Neumann was born in Bohemia in 1811. He came to the United States and was ordained a priest here with the desire to serve the poor immigrants who had very few priests to care for them. In his own life he had found Jesus as the Messiah, and he wanted to share that good news with others.

Much to his surprise as well as his dismay he was appointed Bishop of Philadelphia in 1852. He worked very hard to increase the number of parishes in the diocese and to establish parochial schools. All the while in his humility he felt unworthy of his position as Bishop of Philadelphia. In fact he sent a letter to the Holy See stating his preference for a smaller and poorer diocese. In his letter he wrote: "The care of temporal things weighs upon my mind and it seems to me that my character is little suited for the very cultured world of Philadelphia" (cf. Office of Readings for today). Though he was obliged to stay on in Philadelphia, he turned all temporal matters over to his auxiliary bishop.

John Neumann's sense of values was different from that of those people who are consumed by ambition and whose only thought is to rise to wealth and power. He understood well why Jesus himself was born in simplicity and poverty. He was consumed by humility and his only thought was to please God and to serve his people. Although he was a bishop, he is for all of us an excellent model of humility and zeal.

January 6

Throughout history there have been men who have wanted to conquer the world: Alexander the Great, Napoleon, Adolph Hitler, to name only some. They were consumed with a lust for power and they thought their goal could be achieved by bloodshed. Adolf Hitler and his regime were responsible for more deaths than anyone can count and more atrocities than anyone can comprehend.

Ironically St. John in today's reading tells us that one who is the conqueror of the world is the one who believes that Jesus is the Son of God. Of course he is speaking of a different kind of conquest, one which overcomes sin, evil, and everlasting death. We can become conquerors through faith in Jesus Christ because he has won the great victory for us. This would be a strange kind of victory in the twisted mind of someone like Hitler. Strangest of all, the victory has come about through blcodshed, not the blood of innocent millions but the blood of one truly innocent person, Jesus Christ.

Ambition is a drive which can become so strong that it blinds a person to true values. Faith in Jesus should be like a light which illumines reality so that we can see the real purpose of life and to perceive what we really should be working for. We have a promise that this goal is already ours in every Mass we celebrate. Jesus declares to us: "This is the cup of my blood, the blood of the new and everlasting covenant." This covenant is God's promise that eternal life is ours. This promise is sealed in the blood of Christ, the same blood of which we partake under the appearance of wine. Alexander was called the Great, but God has made us great through the blood of his Son.

January 7

We have many reasons for coming to daily Mass. One reason is so that we can pray not only for ourselves but for others, especially those who are in the greatest need. Our prayer of the Faithful is an important part of Mass.

St. John today declares that we have confidence in God, that he hears us whenever we ask for anything according to his will. That of course is the ideal we should all have. Mary is an excellent example for us. In the gospel she is so confident that Jesus will respond to her observation that the wine had run short that she simply instructed the waiters to do whatever Jesus told them.

Sometimes we can become very discouraged with prayer. It is only natural for us to want immediate results. When results do not appear to be forthcoming we may be tempted to give up. But God wants us to persevere. He is pleased with persistent prayer. This kind of prayer is actually a profound form of worship in which we acknowledge two things about God. The first is that he is powerful. If we did not believe that God is powerful, we would seek help elsewhere. The second is that God is all loving. If we did not believe that God loves us enough to answer our prayers, we would not bother asking him.

We are called to be like Mary at the marriage feast of Cana. We should be concerned about others and we should respond to that concern by means of confident prayer to God.

Monday after Epiphany

Yesterday we celebrated the Solemnity of the Epiphany. "Epiphany" is a Greek word which means "manifestation." Jesus in welcoming the Magi, who were Gentiles, manifested the truth that he is the Savior for all people without exception.

Actually the entire life of Jesus is a manifestation or revelation of God. Jesus is God in the flesh, and he reveals the Father in a way which we can perceive and understand. In today's gospel he shows us that our God is one who heals. The people carried to Jesus all those afflicted with various diseases and those racked with pain: the possessed, the lunatics, the paralyzed. Jesus cured them all.

Jesus will cure and heal us too. First he will heal the wounds of sin. But he cares about our total person. Some of us here may at this moment stand in need of some physical cure. Eventually all of us must see our bodies wither and be corrupted in death. We should not think that Jesus is unconcerned about these physical realities, as if only our souls counted and not our bodies. A complete cure for our physical weakness will not come in this life. It will come on the day of resurrection. Then we will be raised body as well as soul to the fullness of perfect life. We have a promise of that in our communion with the glorified body of the Risen Lord. Jesus has promised solemnly, "He who eats my flesh and drinks my blood has life everlasting and I will raise him up on the last day." That last day God will manifest what a great healer he truly is.

Tuesday after Epiphany

In a fancy restaurant, the tip which is left for the waiter or waitress is referred to as a gratuity. Such is a corrupt use of the word. A gratuity is something which is given to another freely without any consideration of merit. A waiter or waitress, especially one who has given good service, is entitled to some recompense. A tip is actually part of his wages, not really a gratuity.

God acts gratuitously toward us in the proper sense of that word. St. John makes the point quite clearly when he says that love consists in this: not that we have loved God, but that he has loved us and has sent his Son as an offering for our sins. It is not as if we did something to merit the sending of God's Son. God took the initiative. While we as a race were still sinners, God loved us nonetheless and manifested that love in a practical way.

Throughout his life Jesus continued to show this kind of gratuitous love. Jesus taught the vast crowd. He was not under contract, like a professor in a university, paid to teach students who in turn had paid their tuition. It was an act done out of love, free of charge.

Jesus then went a step further. He fed the crowd miraculously—that kind of an act cannot be purchased.

It is essential that we recognize that everything we have comes as a gift from God: our lives, our faith, our families, even the energy and talent with which we earn a living on this earth. And what Jesus did for the crowd he continues to do for us in every Mass. He teaches us through the scriptures and he feeds us with his own body and blood. Nothing can buy what God gives us. Everything is a gift.

Wednesday after Epiphany

We cannot buy God's love. It is a gift, something freely given to us. And yet God does ask some recompense, some return for his favor. St. John sums it up in one sentence: "Beloved, if God has loved us so, we must have the same love for one another." One idea which runs through the scriptures, especially in the writings of St. John, is that God wants his love for us to be the motive of our love for each other.

God has revealed that he is a Father. Like all good parents, he yearns to see his children living together in peace and harmony, eager to help each other. He is upset by bickering and selfishness. He wants us to have a generous spirit toward each other, not that spirit in which one child insists that it is not his turn to do the dishes, not that spirit in which one child refuses to help his brother or sister because it is not his turn to do the chores. When it comes to loving and helping another, we should not ask whether he deserves it or whether he has ever done anything for us. Real love does not set limits or conditions.

In every Mass we are asked to express our love for one another by offering the sign of peace. This gesture should be a prayer that others may receive the gift of God's peace, but it should also be the outward expression of an inner attitude of love. In return for his great love for us, God asks that we love each other.

Thursday after Epiphany

We have always heard that the church is the house of God. Since God is our Father and we are his children, his house is our home. We come here to worship God our Father, but we must not neglect his children. Being aware of other people, quietly and respectfully greeting them before and after Mass, and extending to them the sign of peace during Mass is what God wants from us. As St. John tells us today: "One who has no love for the brother he has seen cannot love the God he has not seen . . . Whoever loves God must also love his brother."

There is a time and a place to be alone with God. The place can be anywhere. The time we must set aside. But the Mass is always community worship, the prayer of God's family. It is never a private devotion of an individual. We come to Church for Mass not as to a place of convenience but as to a home where God's family gathers for worship.

In the past before Vatican II people often prayed privately in their own way during Mass, perhaps saying the rosary or reading from a devotional book. The rosary and private devotions are still important, but during the Mass we must pray together in the same words as a family. Most important of all we must seek a unity among ourselves which comes from our communion, our mutual sharing in the body and blood of Jesus Christ.

What we do during Mass must be reflected in our lives. Since we address each other as brother and sister here at Mass, we must treat each other as brother and sister outside of Mass. God wants our love for him to overflow into love for all his children.

Friday after Epiphany

In the time of Jesus leprosy was a hideous disease without any means of prevention or cure. The incidence of leprosy has been greatly reduced in our own time because of modern medicine and even serious cases have at least been arrested. In other words, leprosy does not pose the threat which it did in the time of Jesus. Nonetheless the cure of which we heard in today's gospel is important to us, not indeed because we may acquire leprosy but because the episode tells us something about Jesus.

Jesus did indeed work his cures out of a motive of compassion for the people. And yet he did not choose to end all sickness and disease during his life on this earth. What he did for people was intended to unfold gradually who he is. He is the almighty God who has come among us in our humanity. He has entered into the human condition whereby he shows his feelings for our weakness and our needs. In other words, we do not have a God who is aloof or unconcerned about our situation. But Jesus wants us to respond to him not merely as a miracle worker but as a God of love. He does not want us to see him as an extraordinary doctor or physician to whom we turn only when we need him. If you think about it, the only time you see your doctor is when you are sick. Jesus does not want that kind of relationship with us.

We have all received many blessings from God, blessings upon which we should frequently ponder. All of these blessings should help us to see how good God is and how much we should love him for Himself.

Saturday after Epiphany

St. John the Baptist had for his purpose, not to draw attention to himself, but to focus a light on the person of Jesus Christ. He sums up his mission by saying about Jesus, "He must increase," and about himself "I must decrease."

We have recently celebrated the feast of Christmas. That day has been placed after the shortest day of the year, the winter solstice. From the time that we celebrate Christmas the amount of daylight increases each day as a symbol of Christ the Light coming into the world. By contrast the birth of St. John the Baptist is celebrated after the longest day of the year, the summer solstice.

From the time we celebrate his birth on June 24th the amount of daylight each day decreases as a symbol of John's words, "I must decrease."

Most people consider ambition a natural incentive. To want to be the first or the best is viewed as normal and surely the only way to get ahead in this world. John the Baptist shows us a value which is just the opposite. His only ambition was to get out of the way so that Jesus could become first in the hearts of his own disciples. He wanted people to see that following Jesus and not himself was the best thing that could happen to them.

John the Baptist indicates to us one important aspect of our Christian vocation. We should help to focus a light on Jesus Christ. When we do good for others, we should do so with the intention that they will see the goodness of Christ within us. When people praise us, we should politely let them know that any talent we may have is a gift from God to whom the credit is due. John the Baptist, with his unusual kind of ambition, is a model for all of us.

The Season of Lent

Ash Wednesday

When Joel spoke the prophecy we heard in the first reading, the people were suffering from a great plague of locusts which were destroying their crops. The prophet saw the plague not only as a punishment for sin, but also as a warning that God would come one day in judgment. He therefore called the people to repentance—all the people without exceptions, the old, the young, the newly married, and even the priests.

Centuries later St. Paul, in writing to his converts at Corinth, proclaimed the same message of a need for repentance. In his message there was a sense of urgency: "Now is the acceptable time! Now is the day of salvation!"

On this Ash Wednesday the Church once again calls us to repentance by means of the ceremony of the ashes. This call is meant for all of us without exceptions, for the ashes remind us, first, of our human weakness. No matter who we may be, no matter how good we may think we are, because of our weakness we have been guilty of sin and need repentance. The ashes also remind us of the coming judgment of God, for the ashes are a symbol of the inevitability of death when we must face God to give an accounting of our lives. Finally there is a sense of urgency about this call to repentance because we have no idea of when death will claim us.

Repentance means a turning away from sin and turning toward God, a real change of heart necessary for all of us. Daily Mass during Lent is an excellent way to achieve true repentance. In the lessons you will hear what God's will is for you, that is, just what you are to do to practice repentance. In the Mass you look to God to receive the grace you need to follow out what you learn in the lessons. This Lent is the acceptable time, the time of salvation. We do not know whether we will have another.

Alternate

Lent, which begins today, is a time of preparation. It looks forward to our annual commemoration of the paschal mystery of Christ at Easter wherein we celebrate his victory over sin and death.

Today in the ceremony of the ashes the Church insists that we face the awesome reality of death: "Remember man that you are dust and unto dust you shall return." A fascinating aspect of death is that it is both certain and uncertain. It is certain in the sense that we know we will one day die. Our ancestors died before us. There were people sitting in church at this time last year who are not here today for one reason: they are dead. And yet this death which is so certain in itself is most uncertain as to time, place, and circumstances. We simply do not know when, where, or how we will die. Most important of all is the question of whether death will find us worthy to share in the victory which Jesus won over sin and death itself—will our death lead to resurrection with Jesus?

Death is also final. None of us can expect to be given a second chance. God has given us an allotted time in which to work out our salvation. It is up to us to use our time well. One moment wasted by infidelity to God can never be captured. We may work harder after a failure, but the one moment lost has passed into eternity, never to return. Nor can we depend on some kind of death bed conversion. On the other hand, if we have really tried to be faithful to God throughout life we need not fear that at the moment of death we will make a sudden reversal and abandon God. It is the present that counts; we cannot change the past nor can we predict the future.

The liturgy has given a sober and awesome reminder: "You are dust and unto dust you shall return." The way in which we live now will determine our future after death. As we live, so shall we die, and as we die, so shall we be for all eternity.

Thursday After Ash Wednesday

Today we are presented with the great issues of life and death—not only this temporal life, but also the eternal life of happiness in heaven; not only death as we know it, but also the unending death of damnation. In the gospel Jesus tells us that he himself must first suffer and endure physical death before entering into eternal life through his resurrection. It is a proclamation of his paschal mystery.

The paschal mystery, put as simply as possible, means that in God's plan Jesus passed through suffering to joy, through humiliation to glory, and through death to life. God's plan for us is that we should share in this same great mystery.

Our first contact with the paschal mystery was our baptism. We then went through a form of death with Christ, a death to sin. And through that death we rose with Christ to share in his life of grace. That was the beginning of our Christian vocation. But all through our lives we share in the paschal mystery in different ways. The Mass is that mystery, for in the Mass Jesus makes present once again the reality of his death and resurrection so that we may share in it. All of our Lenten penance is a sharing in this mystery, as is the suffering that comes to us, be it physical, mental, or emotional. Throughout Lent we look forward to a full liturgical participation in the paschal mystery during Holy Week and Easter.

Moses in the first lesson tells the people that if they are faithful and loyal to God, they will receive life and many blessings. Jesus is more explicit in the gospel. He warns that faithfulness and loyalty as his disciples means taking up the cross of suffering daily. But he promises us, not merely a temporal blessing, but a sharing in his own eternal life in heaven.

Alternate

In the days of the reformation in England a bishop refused to recognize the validity of the divorce of King Henry from Catherine of Aragon. There was a principle involved concerning not only the teaching of the Church on marriage and divorce but also the authority of the Pope. It was a principle, and a matter of conscience, for which the bishop was willing to die. As a matter of fact, for his refusal he was condemned to death. It is related that while he was in prison some of his friends came to his cell to plead with him to reconsider in order to save his life. He told his friends that he would give in to their request if they could answer satisfactorily but one question which he would put to them at the end of one week.

During the week the men tried to settle on answers to the questions they thought he would ask about marriage and divorce and papal authority. At the end of the week they approached him and indicated that they were ready for his question. The prisoner said that his question was this: "What profit does he show who gains the whole world and destroys himself in the process?" To this question, originally posed by Jesus himself, the men could offer no answer. Sadly they walked away as the bishop gladly went to his death. As a follower of Christ he had accepted the truth of his words, "Whoever loses his life for my sake will save it." Today he is known as St. John Fischer.

Whatever our temptations may be to abandon Christ, let us pray in the Mass that we will have the courage and the conviction of St. John Fischer, for it will indeed profit us nothing to gain even the whole world if we do not have Jesus to save us from eternal death.

Friday After Ash Wednesday

In recent times there has been a new emphasis about Lent. The fact, however, that we are obliged to fast only on Ash Wednesday and Good Friday does not mean less self-denial. What is asked of us now is greater self-denial in the form of unselfish love and service of others in the manner described in the first lesson today.

God tells us through this lesson that we are to share our bread with the hungry, to shelter the oppressed and the homeless, and not to turn our backs on anyone. To be concerned about others, to be aware of their needs—that takes real self-denial. If we are concerned only with our own convenience, our own comfort, our own rights, or even our own perfection, we will never follow the teaching of our Lord. His teaching requires that we go out of ourselves to love and care for others, and that is our Lord's point in today's gospel about fasting.

In the law of the Old Testament fasting was required only on the Day of Atonement, but it had become a pious practice among the Jews to fast more often. Jesus did not condemn fasting as such. He pointed out that the messianic era had arrived, that like a bridegroom he would draw his spouse, the people of God, into an intimate relationship of love. His great love for us required that we love one another, and our love must be like his own; unselfish and self-sacrificing. That is the kind of fasting he wishes.

Alternate

When some objected to Jesus that his disciples did not fast, he said that for them to fast while he was still with them would make as much sense as mourning at a wedding banquet in the presence of the groom. He said that the time for fasting would come when he would be taken away.

Where does that leave us? Is Jesus still with us so that we should not fast or has he been taken away so that we should fast? The most obvious answer is that Jesus is not with us; he has been taken away into heaven. In a sense that is correct, and so fasting is in order. But fasting has been de-emphasized in the modern Church partly because of the realization that Jesus is indeed still with us, not only in the Eucharist, but in ourselves as members of his Church through baptism. Jesus has entered into a union of deep love with us, not unlike the marriage union as scripture attests. Because of this union of love our lives should be characterized by a spirit, not for mourning, but of joyful and generous love which overflows to others.

Maybe you know a couple, obviously in love, whose home is always open to anyone. Their natural love is so great that they seem to have a lot of love left over to share with others. Not only do the parents and the children have many friends, but the whole family without fail is ready and eager to help other people.

We as members of the Church must try to realize that the love

Christ has given us must overflow, for we are indeed the family of God. That is why in the first lesson God tells us that what he wants of us is sharing our bread with the hungry, sheltering the oppressed and the homeless, and not turning our backs on anyone. Yes, Jesus is still with us, and he wants his love to spread from our hearts and through our hands.

Saturday After Ash Wednesday

Suppose you are not feeling very well. You go to your doctor and after a thorough examination he tells you that you have a severe case of diabetes. You must go on a very strict diet. You have to give up most of your favorite foods, and drinking is out of the question. The doctor warns you that it is a matter of life or death. I think you would go along with what the doctor says. You would indeed be very foolish to ignore his diagnosis and pretend that you are not sick at all. The best doctor in the world would be of absolutely no help to you unless you were first willing to admit that you were sick, that you needed his services.

The Pharisees and the scribes in today's gospel were very foolish people. They were self-righteous, that is, right in their own eyes but not in the eyes of God. When Jesus said, "The healthy do not need a physician," he was being ironic, meaning the opposite of what he said in the sense that the Pharisees and the scribes were not healthy at all. They were seriously sick with the spiritual disease of selfishness and pride. They needed to go on a spiritual diet like the one prescribed in the first lesson today: they needed to give up following their own ways and seeking their own interests. But even Jesus could not help them because they were unwilling to admit that they were sick.

Jesus is our spiritual physician. He has the skill and the means to cure us of sin if we only follow his advice and his directions. First we must be humble and honest enough to accept his diagnosis. Today before communion we will admit to Jesus that we are spiritually ill and that we need his help. We will say, "Lord, I am not worthy to receive you, but only say the word and I shall be healed." That humble admission is the first step on the road to a full recovery from the sickness of sin.

Alternate

When Levi, whose other name was Matthew, was called by Jesus to be an apostle, his occupation was that of a tax collector, usually a lucrative position in those days. In view of the great reception he was able to give in his own home for Jesus, he was apparently a wealthy man. St. Luke notes that when he was called, Levi left everything for Jesus. Considering his wealth, his decision to follow Jesus involved a greater sacrifice than that of the apostles called earlier, who were fishermen. It was a point missed by the Pharisees.

When the Pharisees objected to Jesus' association with men like Levi, an undesirable in their eyes, and others who did not keep the Law according to their interpretation, he answered that he had come to call sinners. When Jesus used the term, sinners, he did not intended that it should be understood according to the mind of the Pharisees. Actually it was his way of saying that he had come to call everyone, since all men in one way or another are sinners. Even the Pharisees would have been called, except that they precluded themselves by their self-righteousness, by their judgment that they were better than anybody else, and by their blind decision that they did not need Jesus.

Today the Church of Jesus Christ calls everyone; only those are excluded who have excluded themselves. It is indeed a sad, scandalous situation when the members of any parish refuse to welcome someone warmly into their number, whether it be because of his low economic or social status or because of his poor reputation. It is your business to make everyone feel welcome in church, no matter how he may be dressed, or how unappealing he may appear, or what others may say of him. The fact that he comes to church must be taken as a sign that he wishes to respond to

Jesus, and, who knows, his response may involve an even greater sacrifice than that of Levi. To wish to exclude anyone is to be guilty of the self-righteousness of the Pharisees, who alone deserved to be excluded.

Monday of the First Week

It must have been a wonderful thing to have lived with Jesus when he was on this earth. What a great privilege it was for Peter, James, and John to have known our Lord personally and intimately. We naturally wish that we could have lived with Jesus, and I think we feel that we would have been completely devoted to him.

As a matter of fact many people who lived with Jesus either did not recognize him or failed to respond to him. And today it may be that we ourselves sometimes do not recognize Jesus or fail to respond to him. We do not have to wish that we could have lived at the time of our Lord. The truth is that he is living among us right now. He is present in this world not only in the Eucharist but also in the people with whom we live. He is all around us.

In today's gospel Jesus tells us that what we do to one of his brothers we do to him. Notice that he does not say that it is *as if* we do it to him, or that he will *consider* what we do to others as done to himself. We must not water down the truth. Jesus lives in others. What we do to them, we do to Jesus.

In the first reading today we heard many practical directives for dealing with people, all of which are summed up in the one command, "you shall love your neighbor as yourself." Among the Old Testament people the word "neighbor" was understood as referring to a fellow Israelite. Jesus gave this commandment two new dimensions. First, neighbor includes everyone. Secondly, Jesus lives in our fellow human beings, our neighbors.

There is no sense in daydreaming about how much we love Jesus or in imagining all the great things we would like to do for him. We are right in seeking him here in the Eucharist, but still more is needed. He is all around us in the people we live with and meet every day. When our time for judgment comes, Jesus will want to know whether we have loved him, not only by our worship of him in the liturgy, but also by finding him and serving him in our fellow human beings.

Alternate

When St. Martin of Tours was but a catechumen and a soldier in the army, a poor man approached him and asked for an alms. Martin had no money, but seeing the man shivering in the cold he took his cloak from his shoulders, cut it in two with his sword, and gave half to the beggar. Later that night Martin was rewarded with a vision of Jesus wearing the half of the cloak he had given away.

Upon hearing this story, some people immediately think that Jesus had come down from heaven and disguised himself as the beggar. Such was not the case, as we learn in today's gospel. Jesus said quite plainly, and his words must be taken as they stand, "I assure you, as often as you did it for one of my least brothers, you did it for me." Jesus is present and living in others, those whom we are privileged to serve in love. This great truth has been understood by the saints, and has motivated their manner of acting.

St. Vincent de Paul, for example, made meditation and prayer a very important part of his life. Despite the great value he placed on them, whenever someone needed him he quickly and cheerfully left the chapel to be of service. When a priest of his congregation once aksed him if it were not more important to remain at prayer, Vincent replied, "I am leaving God for God." He understood the lesson taught by our Lord in today's gospel.

We do well in praying to God at Mass, and this is necessary. At the end of Mass you hear these words, "Go in peace to love and serve the Lord." Indeed, we will fulfill these words if we go forth to serve others for the love of God.

Tuesday of the First Week

The power of speech, or communication, is one of the most wonderful gifts that God has given us. Through words we can tell others our thoughts, our feelings, our hopes, and our joys. What we say to others in words can change completely their attitude toward us and establish a new relationship.

God's word is found in the sacred scriptures, a word that we hear every day in Mass. Through his word God tells us of himself, his thoughts, and his wishes for us. Through his word he wants to establish a special relationship with us, one of love. And this word of God has real power to accomplish a change in us. As we just heard in today's lesson, God says, "My word shall not return to me void, but shall do my will, achieving the end for which I sent it." The word of God, however, will not produce its effect without our cooperation. We must try to listen to God's word actively and attentively, especially at Mass. Here we can learn what God is like, how he feels toward us, and what he expects from us.

And God wants to hear our words too. Words spoken to God are prayer. Simple words are best, words like "I love you—I need you—I'd do anything for you." This simplicity in prayer is what Jesus had in mind when he said, "In your prayers do not rattle on like the pagans." The prayer he taught, the *Our Father*, was intended to be a model for prayer. Jesus did not mean that the words of the *Our Father* are the only ones we should use in prayer. It is the spirit behind those words which counts, a spirit of simplicity, directness and sincerity.

Words are wonderful, especially the word of God. We must listen to that word with great attention. Our words will be pretty wonderful too if we pray in the way our Savior taught us.

Alternate

Throughout his life Jesus referred to God as "*my* Father." And of course God, the first person of the Trinity, is the Father of Jesus in a unique sense. The striking thing about Jesus' lesson on how to pray is that he told his disciples and us that we should address his Father in heaven as "*our* Father." Obviously we can never be the child of God in the same way as Jesus, for we would then be God too as Jesus is, but in our own way we really do become God's child through baptism.

A person becomes the child of someone by receiving life from him. In baptism we really do receive a share in the life of God, which we call sanctifying grace. Jesus chose water as the sacred sign of baptism, and a fitting sign it is. Without water the growing things of the earth wither and die. You have experienced this fact if, during the heat of the summer, you have neglected to water your lawn. But with water the plants and the trees and the grass come alive with a vibrant growth. And with the water of baptism we came alive with the vitality of God himself. God from eternity has given his life to his Son, and through his Son in baptism he has given a share in his life to us so that we have become his children.

A good parent does more than pass on life. He enters into a relationship of love with his child. He cares for him and is concerned about him. And that is God's relationship with us through Christ.

To call God "our Father" is no fiction. Rather it reflects a profound truth upon which we should meditate, not only so that we may appreciate God's gift of divine life to us, but also so that our prayer may be in the right spirit. When we pray we speak not only to God who has made the universe and who is the Lord and Master of all creation, but also to God who truly is our Father, and who has love and concern for us as his children.

Wednesday of the First Week

One of the most impressive of all Catholic shrines is that of Lourdes in France. There miraculous cures have occurred, many of them authenticated through the most intense scrutiny by a team of experts. To see, and even more to experience personally, such a miracle would indeed be a tremendous bolstering of one's faith.

The people in today's gospel were looking for some such miracle from Jesus, some spectacular proof of his claims. But Jesus refused to give any extraordinary sign to them. His preaching of the word of God should have been sign enough. He pointed out that the people of Nineveh, pagans though they were, accepted Jonah, and he was much greater than Jonah.

Though we are people of faith, it is only natural that once in a while we wish for some extraordinary sign from God to confirm our faith. For the most part, however, we must live by and accept the ordinary signs of God's activity among us, the most important of which are found in the Mass. First is the sign of our coming together as God's people. We ourselves are a sign of the presence of Jesus, for as Jesus promised, "Where two or three are gathered in my name, there am I in their midst." Actually it is Jesus who continues to pray within us as members of his Body. The word of God is also a sign. The *Constitution on the Sacred Liturgy* reminds us that Jesus "is present in his word, since it is he himself who speaks when the holy scriptures are read in the Church" (7). It is Jesus who renews the offering of himself in the sacred sign of the consecration, and Jesus who comes to us under the sign of food and drink.

Summing up these ideas, the *Constitution on the Sacred Liturgy* declares, "In the liturgy the sanctification of man is signified by signs perceptible to the senses and is effected in a way which corresponds with each of these signs; in the liturgy the whole public worship is performed by the mystical body of Jesus Christ, that is, by the head and members" (7).

The signs of the Mass are simple, but their spiritual effects are extraordinary, for they are a sign of the presence and activity of one who is much greater than Jonah or anyone else. It is Jesus himself who lives and acts through the sacred signs of the Mass.

Alternate

Whenever we hear of Jonah, we think of the incident in which he was swallowed by the great fish. Actually that story was but a prelude to today's first lesson about Jonah. God wanted Jonah to preach to the pagan city of Nineveh, but Jonah felt that only Jews should hear the word of God, and so he tried to run away. In a storm at sea, brought on by God's anger, he was cast into the water only to be swallowed by the fish and then vomited on the shore. He received a second command from God to preach to the pagans of Nineveh. This time he obeyed, and much to his surprise the people heeded the word of God and repented. The point of the story is that God cares about *all* men and wills their salvation.

There are times in life when we are tempted to wonder whether God really cares about us or even has time for little people like us. Is he too busy running the universe, too concerned about the big important people who are responsible for the major events which shape history itself? God does care and has a great concern, because he has sent someone to us who is even greater than Jonah. In the Mass we hear the words of Jesus. In the Mass we pray to God through, with, and in Jesus. In the Mass God gives us the gift of his Son in holy communion.

God showed his care and love for the people of Nineveh by sending Jonah to them. His love and concern for us are greater in the degree in which Jesus is greater than Jonah.

Thursday of the First Week

Imagine this scene which takes place somewhere every day. A person surrounded by his family lies dying in a hospital bed. The doctors have admitted that the case is medically hopeless. A member of the family quietly says, "I guess all we can do now is pray." All we can do now is pray. . . . Such a statement betrays an attitude that prayer is but a last resort in dire circumstances.

How different was the attitude and teaching of Jesus about prayer. His words to us today indicate that prayer must be an habitual part of our life in all of its circumstances. A little child does not turn to his parents only when he is in serious trouble. He is completely dependent on them and somehow knows that all good things come from them. He looks to his parents for food when he is hungry, he runs to them for comfort when he has skinned his knee or had his feelings hurt, he seeks solace from them when he is lonely and blue. Above all he wants to feel that he belongs, that he has their love and interest all the time.

No matter how young or old we may be, in relation to God we are like little children, and God is a Father more loving and interested than even the best of human parents. He wants us to look to him in all the circumstances of our lives, not merely when we are in serious trouble. It is true that the prayer of Esther in today's first reading was a plea when her life was in danger. She was about to intervene with King Xerxes to thwart a plot to destroy her fellow Jews, even though the law of Persia stated that anyone who approached the King in his inner court without being summoned would suffer the penalty of automatic death. Esther's prayer in her moment of supreme danger was prompted by her habitual practice of turning to God for help. She was not praying because there was nothing else she could think of. Her words show that she understood not only God's concern and power, but also her complete dependence on him: "You alone are God. Help me, who am alone and have no help but you." It was the prayer of a little child before God her Father.

Prayer, then, is not some last ditch effort to ward off impending disaster as suggested in the words heard so often, "All we can do now is pray." It should instead be a child's confident turning to God as a loving Father in all the circumstances of our lives.

Alternate

The words of our Lord, "Ask and you will receive," indicate that God does answer our prayers. Our Lord's insistence on this fact puts one in mind of the well-known story of the little girl who was taunted by her friends that God had not answered her prayer because she did not receive something she had prayed for. The little girl responded, "God answered my prayer; it's just that his answer was 'No.'"

The truth of the matter is that God does not have to be informed as to what our needs are. He knows them better than we, and actually grants what we really need, though not always what we think we need. St. Augustine put it succinctly when he said, "If our prayers seem not answered, it is because either we do not ask rightly or we do not ask for the right thing."

God, more than the best of parents, is concerned with giving us the right thing, but he does will that his gifts come to us in answer to our prayers. Every parent should be able to understand why God wants us to ask for things. Good parents will take care of their children, but they are pleased when their children turn to them with confidence, as well as politeness, for they thereby show that they recognize both the ability of their parents to help as well as their love which will move them to help.

All prayer should be worship of God, that is, recognition of God's power and love, even the prayer of petition. When we pray to God with humility, realizing his almighty power, and with confidence, recognizing his love, he will give us the good things we need.

Friday of the First Week

A high school boy was very eager to play with his school's football team. His father was delighted with the idea, but he warned his son that he had to keep up his studies. He told him that if his marks went down after the first year of football, he would not be allowed to play the following year. All the while the father was hoping that the boy would continue to do well in his classes because he did not want to punish his son by not letting him play football.

Almost all parents have had the feeling that discipline of children is harder on them than it is on the children, but they know that it is something they must do. God as our Father definitely takes no delight in punishing us for our sins, but it is something that he does in justice. The words of the first lesson reveal God's attitude, "Do I indeed derive any pleasure from the death of the wicked says the Lord. Do I not rather rejoice when he turns from his evil way that he may live?"

On the other hand, God does not lower the standards required of us; he demands that we keep our grades up. That is what Jesus is talking about in today's gospel. He points out that mere external observance of the letter of the Law (getting by with D's) is not good enough. It is the observance of the spirit of the Law found in the supreme law of love (getting straight A's) that really counts, and it is this holiness, which surpasses that of the scribes and the Pharisees, which will win entrance for us into the kingdom of God.

Though God demands much of us, he is in a sense pulling for us all the time. We must remember that God is a loving Father who wants to punish us even less than we want to be punished.

Alternate

Sometime or other you have heard someone say something like "Any friend of Fred is a friend of mine." The expression of course means that the person has a high regard and esteem for Fred. And out of consideration for Fred, he would want to favor, and never offend, any friend of his.

Jesus had the same principle in mind when he said that we should first be reconciled with anyone we have offended before offering our gifts at the altar. Any friend of God should be a friend of ours, or to put it more correctly, we should love and respect any child of God. To fail to do so is to fail to love and respect God. God says, as would any good parent, "Love me, love my children."

We go to Mass to worship God by giving him a Gift in sacrifice. If we have enmity in our heart for anyone, God prefers that we leave the Gift and first become reconciled with the one we have offended. Otherwise our Gift giving is meaningless; it is the mere external observance of religion practiced by the Pharisees and resoundingly condemned by Jesus.

I suppose that it would be pretty dramatic if we all were to stop

Mass, leave Church, and seek out anyone we have willfully hurt. The very least we can do, however, is pray to God now for forgiveness, and, before we return to Mass, go to anyone we have offended and offer our apologies. Our next Mass then will have much more meaning and be much more pleasing to God.

Saturday of the First Week

The covenant of Sinai was mediated by Moses and sealed in the blood of animal sacrifice. It was an agreement whereby God would be the God of the Israelites and they would be his people, provided they kept his commandments. The new covenant was mediated by Jesus Christ and sealed in his own blood on the cross. We by our baptism are the new people of God, the people of this new covenant, and we too are called upon to keep his commandments.

The blood of Christ is not only the seal of the new covenant, but also a special sign of the love of God for us, his people, as well as a sign of how great our love must be. In today's gospel Jesus emphasizes our love for our fellow human beings. It is to be a love like his own. When Jesus says that we must love even our enemies and pray for our persecutors, he is teaching a commandment he himself followed. From the cross he prayed for his persecutors and he died on the cross out of love for those who were his enemies by sin.

Christianity is a joyful, happy religion, but this does not mean that those whom we are commanded to love are limited to pleasant, agreeable people. True joy and real happiness come from being like Jesus, and Jesus excluded no one from his love, neither his big enemies nor his little ones—neither the people who put him to death nor those who merely nagged him and bothered him when he needed peace and quiet.

The people addressed in today's first lesson lived long after the actual sealing of the old covenant. These words were proclaimed to them in a liturgical rite so that they might personally renew for themselves the covenant with God. When we come to the end of Lent on Holy Saturday, we will be invited in a liturgical rite to renew our covenant with God through the renewal of our baptism. That renewal will mean little unless during Lent we have made even greater efforts to practice the great commandment of love, a love like that of Jesus which excluded no one.

Alternate

Today's first lesson was addressed to a generation of Israelites who lived long after the covenant of Sinai when God promised that the people would be peculiarly his own, provided they kept his commandments. The people to whom this passage was read in a liturgical rite were asked to renew the covenant with God by their own personal commitment to him.

The new covenant was sealed in the blood of Jesus, and we entered into that covenant through our baptism. It has been traditional in the Church that the season of Lent be dedicated in a special way to this sacrament. At the end of Lent we will be asked to renew our baptism in a formal manner during the Holy Saturday liturgy. That will be a very important liturgical rite, but we certainly do not have to wait until Holy Saturday to make a personal renewal of our baptism, our covenant with God, the pledge of our complete devotion to him. After all, married couples do not have to wait until the anniversary of their wedding to renew their marriage vows; it is something they should do every day as they express their love for each other. And so the renewal of our baptism is something we can do today within Mass.

During the Eucharistic Prayer the bread will become the body of Christ and the wine will become his blood, "the blood of the new and everlasting covenant." Thereby our Lord will re-present the sacrificial offering of himself to his Father, the expression of his completed dedication to the Father, his absolute fidelity, and his total love. He invites us today to join with him in this sacrifice. Let us say within ourselves, "Father, with Christ we make the complete gift of ourselves to you." And that will be a true renewal of our baptism, our covenant with God.

Monday of the Second Week

There are several lessons our Lord seemed never to tire of repeating. His favorite was the lesson of love, and one aspect of love that he insisted on was that of forgiveness. Perhaps he persevered in his teaching about forgiveness because he realized how difficult a virtue it is for us. How often have you heard someone say, "I forgive, but I just can't forget"? Maybe you have said it yourself. That attitude—forgiving but not forgetting—is in reality far from the ideal that our Lord had in mind. To nurse hurt feelings, while mouthing words of pardon, is not really Christian forgiveness at all. "I just don't want to get burned again," we say, and what we actually mean is that we now wish to alter our relationship with the person who has offended us.

Jesus wants us to practice his kind of forgiveness. After an injury, for which a person is sorry, nothing changes. Remember what Peter did to Jesus at the time of his passion. Not once, but three times he denied that he even knew Jesus. Before that denial Jesus had promised Peter that he would be the head of the Church, and despite Peter's denials Jesus stuck to his promise. Jesus didn't say, "Well Peter, I forgive you, but I just can't forget your disloyalty and so someone else will have to take your place." Even Judas could have been restored to his position as an apostle if he had not despaired.

We ourselves hope for forgiveness from God, real forgiveness. We pray that God will completely forget our sins and keep us in his loving care. Jesus warns, however, that we will enjoy such total forgiveness from God only if we have learned to practice it ourselves. True forgiveness involves a kind of spiritual amnesia, and it is a real part of the love that Jesus both taught and practiced.

Alternate

There are three words which most of us find very difficult to say and mean. Those three words are, "I was wrong." Simple words they are, but even in little matters they are hard to say. If we knock over a glass and break it, it is the fault of someone who left it where they should not have. If we are late for an appointment, it is the fault of the alarm clock which failed to go off. And even when we have sinned, it is hard to admit our fault; we look for excuses.

The prayer recorded in the first reading is refreshing in that it is an honest admission of guilt. In the prayer the people acknowledge that they have sinned, that they have been unfaithful to the covenant and disobeyed God and his messengers. In effect they say, "We were wrong," those words so difficult to say and mean.

There are three other words equally difficult to say and mean, and those words are, "I am sorry." They are words which should follow "I was wrong." Have we been wrong? If we have our ideals set as high as Jesus requires in today's gospel, maybe we can see how wrong we are. Are we as compassionate as God is? If not, then we are wrong. Are we as forgiving as God is? If not, then we are wrong. Are we as generous in giving as God is? If not, then we are wrong.

If we are wrong, we must bring ourselves to say, and to mean, "I am sorry." The sincerity of those three little words will be measured by our effort to match the ideal of goodness and love which Jesus has taught us by word and example.

Tuesday of the Second Week

A priest once remarked, "It is a shame that I do not practice what I preach, but it would be far worse if I were to preach what I practice." The statement was made in good humor, but as a matter of fact we are not inclined to like people who do not practice what they preach. More seriously, we are not inclined to listen to what they have to say. You can imagine how you would feel if your doctor were to insist that you give up smoking as he blows cigarette smoke in your face.

Sometimes we hear about people who have left the Church

because they maintain that bishops and priests do not practice what they preach. Even if their claims were true, such people should remember that our Lord in today's gospel told the people to follow the teaching of their leaders because they had succeeded Moses as teachers, even though they did not follow that teaching themselves. But wait a minute. Who really is the teacher of our faith? It is Jesus Christ. The pope, the bishops, the priests, only hand on to us the word of Christ.

The real question, then, is what about the example of Christ. He was one who indeed practiced what he preached. He told us to love our enemies, and he redeemed those who by sin were his enemies. He said that we should do good to our persecutors, and he forgave those who put him to death. He proclaimed that no one could have greater love than to lay down his life for a friend, and he died out of love for his Father and us.

The best sermon at any Mass is still the example of Christ, which in the Mass is made present on our altar: the sacrificial offering of himself to his Father.

Alternate

The background of today's first reading is that God was not pleased with the liturgical sacrifices of his people, for in God's eyes prayer and sacrifice without good living are worthless. This word of God to us today means that we must live our sacrifice of the Mass. Let's think about that a little.

In the Mass we offer ourselves with Jesus to God our Father to express our complete love for him; we make the gift of ourselves through, with, and in Christ. Then to show that he is pleased with our offering, God makes a return gift to us in holy communion. We receive the resurrected, glorified body of Christ and enter into intimate union with him.

When we leave this place of worship we should do so to continue a life of worship. The rest of the day must be a continuation of the offering of ourselves in the Mass. In the holy sacrifice we have said that we wish to give ourselves completely to God; now we must live in accord with that dedication. Throughout the day we must do nothing that we would have to be ashamed to give to God in the next Mass we offer. After all, when we come to Mass we can offer only what we are and what we have done. We must do nothing that would contradict the offering we have already made.

Our communion is a sharing in the resurrection of Christ, his victory over sin. We must then go forth to witness that resurrection by showing in our lives that Christ has conquered sin in us personally.

We must live the Mass.

Wednesday of the Second Week

The scene in today's gospel is a very natural one, a mother trying to gain a place of honor for her two sons. The context suggests that James and John were not at all hesitant about having their mother intercede for them. Our Lord's reply indicates that Christianity requires a generous service without the thought of reward as a motive. A reward there will be from the Father, and it is a strong incentive, but Jesus asks that we be as unselfish as he was in the service of his fellow men.

It is no easy thing to give of ourselves to others without some kind of recompense, but if we look for that kind of satisfaction I am afraid that we will not be very good disciples of Jesus Christ. If you are a parent, you know that children do not always appreciate what you are trying to do for them and take a lot for granted. Perhaps you have to take care of older parents, and the elderly without realizing it can be very demanding on your time with a considerable taxing of your nerves and your patience. It is especially difficult when the people you are helping manifest no gratitude at all, but the worst possible situation is to have them turn against you completely. Jeremiah the prophet was in just such a situation. Those who were plotting his death were the very ones for whom Jeremiah had prayed before the Lord.

Difficult though unselfish service is, it is what Jesus requires of us, and he teaches that true greatness comes from serving the needs of others without thought of compensation. Reward there will be, but that we must leave in the hands of God.

Alternate

Almost everyone enjoys a good meal, but if you are not a cook it may be difficult for you to appreciate all the time and hard work that go into preparing a really fine dinner. It seems that it is necessary to pay some kind of price for all good things, and apparently that is what James and John and their mother in today's gospel had forgotten. The two brothers wanted a share in the kingdom and the glory of Christ, the very place of honor, but our Lord had to remind them that there was a price to be paid. It was the price he himself had to pay for his glorification, namely his passion and death.

Jesus warned all the apostles that he had to go up to Jerusalem to suffer and die, and only then would he be raised to glory and come into the possession of his kingdom.

On several occasions our Lord likened his kingdom to a great banquet. In this Mass, the Eucharistic banquet, we have an anticipation of the heavenly banquet, but with this spiritual meal we are also reminded of the price to be paid. Christ is present as our food in the Mass only because he first makes himself present as a victim through the sacred sign of the consecration. We receive communion, a sharing in the resurrection of Christ, with the best dispositions only if we first identify ourselves with him as the victim of sacrifice. That identity means the total dedication of ourselves to God with Christ, even to death. Can we indeed drink of the cup of the Lord?

Thursday of the Second Week

The Pharisees, to whom today's parable was originally directed, are described in the gospel as being "fond of money." Our

Lord also referred to them as "blind guides," and it was their
fondness for money that made them spiritually blind to their neighbors, as well as deaf to the word of God.

Our Lord's object in the parable was not to condemn wealth as
such but to point up the evil consequences of its abuse. The rich
man dressed in finery and pampered his appetite for exquisite food
and drink. He was so taken up with his own pleasures that he failed
to pay any attention to poor Lazarus starving at his gate. In his
condition Lazarus would have considered the scraps from the rich
man's table a banquet but not even the scraps were offered to him.
The rich man had allowed his wealthy circumstances to blind him to
the need of others.

Secondly, abuse of wealth had induced spiritual deafness.
From the abode of the dead, the rich man pleaded with Abraham to
send Lazarus to warn his five brothers. Abraham answered, "They
have Moses and the prophets. Let them hear them." Abraham then
went on to say that if the brothers have been deaf to the word of God
found in Moses and the prophets, they would not be converted
even if one should rise from the dead.

Wealth is enticing because of the pleasures it can bring. But the
man who lives for pleasure alone will wither and dry up like the
barren bush described in today's first lesson. The person who
keeps his eyes open to the needs of others and listens attentively to
the word of God will be like the tree planted near running water. He
will yield good fruit, a fruit that will endure unto everlasting life.

Alternate

There is a paradox about poverty in the New Testament. On the
one hand Jesus tells us that a poor man is fortunate. On the other
hand he tells us that we should help to overcome the poverty of
others. How can this be?

The point is that Jesus wants us to be free. Freedom is the key
to the whole question of both poverty and wealth. If we are attached
to material things, we can lose our freedom. Look at the rich man in
today's gospel. He wore fine clothes and enjoyed a splendid ban-

quet every day, but apparently he was so wrapped up in his pleasures that he had no time for God or his fellow men. He had lost his freedom because of his attachment to wealth and the pleasures that wealth brought him. He would have been better off if he had been poor.

And yet being poor can be a problem for freedom too. We need God's material gifts in order to have the leisure of time and mind to worship God and be concerned about others. If a person has to spend all his time and effort in trying to acquire the very basic necessities of survival and has to actually wonder where his next meal is coming from, he can scarcely turn his attention to God or the needs of others. He has lost his freedom because of a poverty which is destitution.

It is unlikely that any of us here is either destitute or extremely wealthy. But how free are we? If we are neither destitute nor wealthy, are we satisfied with moderation, or deep in our hearts are we constantly yearning for more and more? A good test is to see what are the things we usually pray for. Another good test is to examine how generous is our charity in helping others. The rich man in today's gospel was condemned not because he was wealthy but because he was selfish. He was not willing to share even the scraps from his table with the poor man. How really free are we?

Friday of the Second Week

The brothers of Joseph in today's lesson were guilty of envy. They were saddened and even angered because of the favors received by Joseph, and they looked upon his good fortune as a threat to themselves. The evil men in the gospel parable were also guilty of envy. When they saw the property owner's son, they said, "Let us kill him and then we shall have his inheritance!"

Perhaps surprisingly, envy is a vice that even good people can sometimes be guilty of. If we are really trying to be good Christians, we may be led to wonder why it is that others seem to be more favored than we are by God and the circumstances of life. The problem is intensified if we see someone who does not seem to be a particularly good person prospering and enjoying comfort and security. It can even hurt us to hear someone else praised, especially if we think that maybe we deserve a little praise once in a while.

Of course envy is born of pride and selfishness. What we have to remember is that we are all children of God, that we are all brothers united in Christ and forming one body with him. As St. Paul teaches about the mystical body of Christ, the good qualities and achievements of one member help all the other members. What we are all working for ultimately is the glory of God, who gives us his gifts so that we may glorify him. In the final analysis, it is God's business to whom he gives his gifts.

At Mass today let us humble ourselves before God our Father. Let us thank him for his gifts to us, and ask him to give us the grace to be big enough to be happy that he also gives his gifts to others.

Alternate

There is an old saying that God can write straight with crooked lines. It is a comment which fits the story of Joseph in the Old Testament which we have just read. Joseph's brothers sold him into slavery. As he was led away to Egypt Joseph did not in any way realize how God would use that evil deed to save his brothers and their families from starvation. You know the touching story of how Joseph rescued his people during a time of famine after he had come to great authority in Egypt.

The same comment can be made about today's parable from the New Testament. The son, murdered by the tenant farmers, represents Jesus himself. The farmers through their evil deed hoped to have the son's inheritance. As a matter of fact the death of Jesus brought the grace of his heavenly inheritance to the whole world. God used the malice of some men to bring supreme good to all mankind.

We sometimes wonder where God's plan is to be found. We see natural disaster, riots, and war itself as part of our world. In our own personal lives we experience sickness, suffering and frustration. At the moment, like Joseph, we cannot see why God tolerates all these evils, let alone how he will use them to accomplish his good purposes. But we must never be fooled into suspecting that somehow God has lost control of human affairs or that evil has become so powerful that even God cannot draw good from it. Though it is true that God could prevent all evil, in his supreme wisdom and for his own good reasons he has chosen to write straight with crooked lines.

Saturday of the Second Week

Our Lord told the parable we have just heard because the scribes and the Pharisees had complained about his kind treatment of known sinners. By his parable he wanted to show that he was doing his Father's will in seeking out sinners to save them. The scribes and the Pharisees, had they been really good men, would have been glad to see sinners being led to repentance. In the parable they are represented by the older son who, by his own estimate anyway, had remained loyal to his father. This older son, however, was guilty of envy, and his father had to point out to him that he too should have rejoiced over the return of his brother. The younger brother had indeed been foolish in his sin, but the older brother was equally foolish in his self-righteousness and envy.

Where do we fit into the parable? Probably we do not completely match either son, but are a little bit like both of them. We certainly should realize that we are not perfect, that we are guilty of some sins, usually little ones but maybe serious ones at some time. During Lent we are expected in a special way to be honest about our sins. Whatever our sins may be, we know from this parable that God is a loving Father who welcomes back the repentant sinner with open arms.

In comparison with people whom some would be tempted to label as notorious sinners, we may look like saints. It may even be that a close friend or member of our family or a priest we have known has left the Church. In relation to such people we are in danger of acting like the older son of the parable, and so we must not fall into the sin of self-righteousness. If others have wandered away from their Father's home, they should be our concern. We should be praying for them. We should even attempt to search them out to lead them back to God. It certainly should be a source of great joy to know that a person has repented.

Whichever son we may resemble at the moment, at all times we must remember that God loves all his children and welcomes them with open arms.

Alternate

The story of the prodigal son is a parable; though it is not factual, it is in accord with the truth, and the truth it teaches has been manifested in the lives of many throughout the centuries. Here is a factual story which reflects that truth.

A child was born of devout parents. As a young man, however, he not only left home but also abandoned any attachment to the true faith. He lived what we would call a wild life and even fathered a son out of wedlock. One person stood by him, his mother. She never gave up praying for him. At her insistent urging he listened to the preaching of a very holy bishop. Struck by the preaching and influenced by his mother's prayers, he realized the mistakes he had made and changed his whole way of life. His conversion was so complete that he founded a religious order, was made a bishop, and became a famous preacher, writer, and theologian of the Church. At his mother's funeral he said in his sermon. "I weep for my mother, now dead before my sight, who wept for me for so many years that I might live in her sight." We now honor this man every year in the liturgy on August 28th as the great St. Augustine.

St. Monica, Augustine's mother, never gave up on him, just as God never gives up anyone, whether they be big sinners or little sinners. During Lent the Church calls us to repentance and like a good mother weeps for our sins and prays for our conversion. Though we have not abandoned our Father's home, we must do penance for all our sins, big or small, and we must try to cooperate with the grace of God who wishes to raise us even to the heights of sanctity.

Optional Mass for the Third Week

In their exodus from Egypt and their passage through the waters of the Red Sea, the Israelites were formed into the people of God. Despite their grumbling and recalcitrance during their journey to the promised land, God sustained them with the manna from heaven and the water from the rock.

We as Christians are formed into the people of God by our passage through the waters of baptism and on our journey to heaven God sustains us with the food and drink of the Eucharist.

The *Constitution on the Church* of Vatican II emphasizes that we are a pilgrim people, a people on a journey to our true home, which is heaven (cf. ch. 7). During our journey we are somewhat like the Israelites in their journey to the promised land. We can get discouraged, tired, hungry, and thirsty. The Israelites longed for food, and God strengthened them with the manna from heaven. They yearned for drink, and God refreshed them with water from the rock. We have our strength and refreshment in Jesus. In today's gospel he says, "The water I give will become a fountain, leaping up to provide eternal life." Through the symbol of water Jesus was referring to his grace. We receive this grace chiefly in the food and drink of the Eucharist, a nourishment that will lead us through this life to the eternal life of heaven.

At Mass you come in procession to the altar to receive the Eucharist. This procession is a sign that we are on a journey to heaven and we come to the altar to receive the food of pilgrims. The Eucharist will indeed strengthen us and bring us home to heaven, our promised land.

Monday of the Third Week

One of the most common failures of our human condition is to take things for granted, especially those which have become very familiar to us or which are very simple.

Jesus was rejected by the people of his home town of Nazareth because he was too familiar to them and his background too simple; they took him for granted. As we read in today's lesson, Elisha's directions to Naaman for the cure of his leprosy were at first spurned by Naaman because they seemed too simple and commonplace.

There is a real danger that we may take the Mass for granted because it seems so familiar and so simple to us. Actually the Mass is a wonderful experience. To help make it such, I have some suggestions.

As you drive or walk to church, or in the few moments you may have before Mass begins, make the effort to impress on yourself what is about to happen. Say to yourself: "God is about to speak to me in the scriptures, and I will speak to God in the prayers. Jesus will make the great sacrifice of the cross truly present on this altar and he will give me the opportunity, with my fellow Catholics here, to join with him in this offering to the Father. Then I will receive Jesus in holy communion as a pledge of my own resurrection as well as a means of strength to carry on until the day of resurrection." It will take you even less time to make this reflection than it takes me to say it now.

Then when Mass is over spend a moment or two in reflecting on what has happened, to try to realize that you must strive to live a life in accord with the offering of yourself to God. The Mass, simple and familiar though it be, is just too important to take for granted.

Alternate

There is one day in our lives which we usually consider pretty important, and that is our birthday. It would be a very rare person indeed who would not know the date of his own birth or who would not celebrate that day. As we grow older we may not be too eager to count how many birthdays we have had, but we still like to be greeted with a "happy birthday" from relatives and friends.

Actually we have two birthdays, one when we were born of our parents, and the one when we were born of God in baptism. The event related in the first lesson puts us in mind of the sacrament of baptism. Naaman suffered from leprosy. He was asked to do a simple thing by Elisha, to wash seven times in the water of the Jordan. After some reluctance he complied, and, as we saw, he was cured of his leprosy. It was a great day for Naaman, one he never forgot.

Our baptism was a very simple ceremony: a little water was poured over our heads, but it was a great day for us. Not only were we cured of the leprosy of sin, but more importantly God gave us a share in his divine life, and thereby made us his children. It was indeed our spiritual birthday.

It does not really matter too much, I suppose, if we do not know the actual day when we were baptized, but we certainly should celebrate the day with great joy and happiness. As you know, during Lent there is an emphasis on baptism, an emphasis which reaches its climax in the renewal of our baptism on Holy Saturday. Each time, however, that we come into church we should reflect on our baptism as we take holy water at the font, a symbol of baptism. Then as we see others in the church we should realize that we are all here in our Father's home, brothers and sisters of one another because of our spiritual birth from a common Father in baptism. Indeed, the day of our baptism was a great day for us, one we should never forget.

Tuesday of the Third Week

A man lay on his death bed. Having held public office, though never any major ones, he had experienced how a politician's motives and actions are open to the sometimes erroneous judgment of others. Despite his good intentions, he had made many enemies. After his confession, he said to the priest, "Father, I am grateful for one thing, that I will be judged by God and not by my fellow men."

The dying man had a point. Though we may fear to stand before God as our judge, we must remember that God is not only infinitely wise and powerful, but also infinitely merciful. His mercy exceeds any mercy a human being could possibly manifest. Notice in today's parable a detail you may have overlooked. The official, who owed the huge amount, pleaded with the master only for a delay: he said, "My lord, be patient with me and I will pay you back in full." The master not only heeded the plea but granted even more than the official dared ask: "Moved with pity, the master let the official go and *wrote off the debt.*"

The master of course represents God, who wishes to write off our debt of sin completely, but he will do so only if we learn to forgive those who have offended us. When our brother has wronged us, how often must we forgive him? Jesus says, "Seventy times seven times," that is, without any limit. When we are tempted to feel that enough is enough, maybe it will help to remember that any injury done us is trifling in comparison with the sins we have committed against God, as the gospel says, a mere fraction. Like the dying man, we too can be grateful that we will be judged by God, but only if we have learned to forgive our brothers without limit from our heart.

Alternate

Sin is a terrible evil because it offends God. We cannot even begin to imagine how bad sin is because we cannot appreciate how good God is. And yet we know that when we have sinned we can go to confession and have our sins forgiven, no matter how serious or frequent the sin may be. But God does warn us that his forgiveness depends on whether we forgive others from the heart.

Is it not true that we sometimes find it hard to forgive others? Someone says something behind your back. You find out about it.

Your indignation grows, and the more you think about it the less inclined you are to forgive this "enemy" of yours. Or someone insults you in front of others, or ignores you, or stands you up for an appointment. It may not seem important to anyone else, but it is important to you and you find the offense hard to forgive.

It is not surprising that we find it hard to forgive. That is the way human nature is. You see, it takes bigness to forgive. That is why it is easy for God to forgive, difficult for us. Jesus understood all this, and so he told the parable in today's gospel in order to motivate us to find the bigness needed for forgiveness. The official owed a huge amount; his master wrote off the whole debt, when merely asked for a delay, because he was a big man. But that same official could not forgive a small debt owed him by a fellow servant because he himself was a small man.

Any offense against us is a mere fraction of what we are guilty of by sin before God. The lesson of today's parable is strikingly clear: if we want forgiveness from God we must forgive those who have offended us.

Wednesday of the Third Week

We all realize that the purpose behind traffic laws is to provide for the safety of both motorists and pedestrians. Merely sticking to the letter of the law, however, can get you into trouble. For example, say someone runs through a stop sign when you have the right of way. The law is, strictly speaking, on your side, but insisting on your right of way at that moment may well be the way to an accident, perhaps even death itself. The spirit behind the law, not to mention common sense, would demand that you stop.

This illustration is close to the idea our Lord had in mind in today's gospel. He said that he had not come to abolish the law found in the Old Testament. That law was an expression of God's will for people, but because it was necessarily put in human words it was an imperfect expression of God's will. The spirit behind the law is what counts, and that spirit is found in the love of God and neighbor. Jesus fulfilled the law first by his own supreme example of love. It is his teaching and example that Jesus wants us to follow, and not merely the letter of the law.

For instance, no law requires that you be present at Mass on weekdays during Lent. But in the celebration of these Masses you are certainly fulfilling the spirit behind the command that we love God and pray to him. You won't find any explicit law which says that if your neighbor down the block has just come home from the hospital you must go and find out what help you can be, but taking the initiative in a case like that is in accord with the spirit of the law. If a friend of yours has abandoned the Church because of, say, an argument with his pastor there is no precise legislation requiring that you be the one to try to straighten him out. The spirit of the law, however, should motivate you to approach your friend with understanding and affection.

Perhaps a twist of John F. Kennedy's famous words from his inaugural address fits the idea: Ask not what the law demands that you do, but ask what you can do to fulfill the spirit of the law.

Alternate

Do you remember not long ago when there were as many ads on television against smoking as there were commercials pushing different brands of cigarettes? One episode showed a father walking down a country road with his young son. Everything the father did the little boy imitated: throwing a rock, admiring a bird, and stretching in the marvelous sunshine. Then the father sat by a tree and his son did the same. The punch of the ad came as the father took a cigarette, lay the pack on the ground, and the little boy slowly reached for the pack.

What we do, the way we live, the example we set, all influence others, adults as well as children. We would probably be amazed if we were to know how much we do affect others. Jesus says in today's gospel, "Whoever breaks the least significant of these commands and teaches others to do so, shall be called least in the kingdom of God." What a terrible thing it would be deliberately to teach evil to others. We hope and pray that we will never become so perverse. But we teach others not only by our words but also by our example. As a matter of fact, we recognize, at least in theory, that "actions speak louder than words." Someone put it another way when he said, "What you are speaks so loudly that I cannot hear what you say."

Some people maintain that they do not go to church because churchgoers are hypocrites. Such a position usually is an excuse to hide some deeper problem, but there is a good point here nonetheless. Our lives do have an influence on others, for good or ill. If our example "fulfills and teaches God's commands we shall be great in the kingdom of God."

Thursday of the Third Week

The history of our world is to a large extent the story of war, lust, greed and selfishness. What is behind it all? Today's gospel, as well as much of sacred scripture, implies that it is the devil. Many people say that believing that there is a devil is naive and childish, but the truth is that not accepting the reality of the devil is naive and childish. The Bible teaches that there are intelligent, highly powerful forces of evil in the world, known as devils. That teaching is in accord with reality.

Look at Nazism and all its horrors: millions of people exterminated. How could any human being ever wish such evil? Adolf Hitler was no doubt insane, but maybe part of the cause of his insanity was the power of Satan. Communism began with a certain sincerity and good intention on the part of Marx and Lenin, but how did it become such a monster today?

The devil puts ideas into people's heads under the guise that the ideas represent freedom and goodness. Look at the attack on human life in the movements for abortion, euthanasia, and compulsory sterilization. Or look at the blows dealt to human dignity in today's sexual revolution: premarital sex, wife swapping, the disintegration of marriage and the family.

Christianity does not mean no fun; it is not a religion for prudes, such as the scribes and the Pharisees in the gospel who were just waiting for Christ to do something wrong so that they could pounce on him. But we must make no mistake about the fact that there is a war going on, a war between good and evil, between Christ and the devil. Our Lord warns us today that we must take sides. We simply cannot fool around with the important issues of morality. If we are not for Christ and his teaching, then we are against him.

Alternate

Before our baptism we were, in a sense, like the mute in today's gospel. We were freed from the power of the devil by the grace of our baptism. Jesus warns however that the devil is strong, and that if we are not constantly on our guard he will overpower us. The devil we rejected in our baptism is insidious and persistent in trying to claim us for himself. Our only defense is to fill the void left by the devil with the love of God and neighbor.

The devil these days uses many different weapons in the hope of destroying Christian love in our hearts. One is rugged individualism, which in its false independence and pride refuses to see the necessity of depending on God for anything. Another is materialism which considers the accumulation of possessions and power as the goal of life, and not the love of God. Still a third weapon is indifference, which makes the Christian either unaware of the needs of others, or unconcerned with helping to meet those needs. Last to be mentioned here is the subtle yet extremely effective weapon of smug complacency, which makes the Christian feel, as did the people addressed in today's first lesson, that simply because he is baptized and has the faith his eternal salvation is assured, and that nothing more need be done except to fulfill the mere letter of the law. This last weapon is frequently the first to be used by the devil to get his foot in the door, for then he can utilize the destructive force of rugged individualism, materialism, and indifference to their fullest extent.

Jesus warns that if we are strong "our possessions will go undisturbed." Our greatest strength comes from an unselfish, generous love of God and neighbor.

Friday of the Third Week

The question asked by the scribe in today's gospel about the greatest commandment was not an idle one. The rabbis of the time had determined that there were 613 distinct commandments in the law, and they distinguished not only between great and small commandments, but even *very* great and *very* small ones. Moreover, some people lived according to what was an observance of merely the letter of the law without regard for its spirit, despite the warnings of the prophets throughout the history of Israel that external cult was insufficient.

The answer of Jesus, to love God and love the neighbor, not only indicated the greatest commandment, but also revealed the spirit and purpose behind all of the other commandments of the law. We are so familiar with this teaching of Jesus that we may fail to see its vital import in our lives.

Today in the Church we have gotten away from a lot of very small rules and obligations, which had their value at certain times and places. Some of you will remember when the fast before communion was so stringent that you dared not brush your teeth before Mass lest you accidentally swallow even a drop of water. There was a time too when you would not eat pork and beans on a Friday because of the almost minuscule amount of meat contained in them. And before you would reach almost any moral decision, you first consulted a priest. Today we enjoy a greater freedom, and we know that the Spirit is at work in all of us.

One lesson to be drawn from today's gospel is that our freedom must be exercised to allow for a greater love of God and our neighbor. The validity of any movement we think we feel from the Spirit is to be confirmed by how conducive that movement is to loving God and the neighbor more unselfishly.

As mature people we all want to enjoy freedom and do not wish to be restrained like children by a whole host of petty rules and regulations. Our freedom will be really mature and responsible if we learn to live according to the great command to love God and our neighbor. And then, like the scribe in today's gospel, we too will not be far from the reign of God.

Alternate

St. John the Apostle lived to a very old age. Toward the end of his life he was so feeble that he had to be carried to church. Though he could not preach at length because of his advanced age, he insisted on saying something at Mass. His message was brief and it was always the same: "My children, love one another." Everybody was bored with the sameness of his words, and finally someone got up enough courage to ask, "Master, why do you always say the same thing?" John patiently and calmly replied, "Because it is the command of the Lord; if only this is done, it is enough."

St. John was indeed imitating Jesus who never wearied of preaching the command of love, a command which we have heard once again, in today's gospel. To love God and love the neighbor is the greatest commandment of all. Our Lord never tired of repeating it; we must never tire of hearing it, because there is certainly a great need for love in our world.

John was right in saying, "If only this is done, it is enough."

If love were the controlling force on this earth, there would be no wars, no riots, no injustices. We know that we are far from this ideal. Where do we start? I think the answer is obvious. We must start within the framework of our personal lives. "Charity begins at home"—that is, with the persons we live with and work with every day. There is no point in complaining about the lack of love that produces wars and riots and injustice if love is not the motivating force in our personal lives. And the Lord knows that there is a lot more room for love in the lives of each one of us.

In coming to Church you will again and again hear about the

command of love. You must never tire of hearing it, and you must never give up trying to practice it. "It is the command of the Lord; if only this is done, it is enough."

Saturday of the Third Week

A young man was very conscious of the fact that he was rather short. He made a point of dating only girls who were much shorter than he, so that he could live under the delusion of thinking of himself as being tall. This self-deception, on a much more serious scale, was one of the problems of the Pharisee in today's gospel. His prayer, far from being a humble and honest admission of weakness, was a form of self-congratulations because he was making the wrong point of comparison. Rather than comparing himself with people who had the reputation of being grasping, crooked, and adulterous, he should have been comparing himself with God, who is perfection itself.

We here at Mass today could, I suppose, be thought of as being better than some people who have no regard for religion or morals. And yet, as we begin every Mass we are urged to call to mind our sins, and to say, in effect, "O God, be merciful to me, a sinner." Indeed we are sinners in comparison with the goodness of God. And it is God who should be the point of comparison since Jesus said, "Be perfect as your heavenly Father is perfect."

To stand before God with a humble, honest admission of our imperfection is the key to true, effective prayer. Notice that the Pharisee's "prayer" was a nauseous mixture of pride and self-complacency. He asked for nothing from God, and he gave nothing in return. The tax collector asked for mercy and he received justification from God. If our prayer is to be effective, it must begin with a plea for mercy.

Alternate

These days there are some people who seem to want to excuse

all sins. They say that heredity is to blame, or environment, or psychological factors, or something else. Still others maintain that a feeling of sinfulness is a guilt complex, a hang-up. They put one in mind of the man who felt he had a guilt complex and told his psychiatrist so. After spending a long time in many visits with the man, the honest psychiatrist said to him, "You don't have a guilt complex; you are guilty."

Certainly it is true that heredity and environment have influence on us, and a real psychological problem is no laughing matter. But we must remember that the mark of maturity is to accept responsibility for our free actions, not to seek excuses for our mistakes, and that a spiritually healthy person is honest with himself before God, while to deceive oneself habitually and to live in a make-believe world of self-righteousness is to border on mental as well as spiritual illness.

The Pharisee in the parable certainly had no guilt complex; in a sense you might say that he had an innocence complex. Rather than being straightforward and honest, he put forth a catalogue of shallow virtues to cover over the guilt of his deep pride. In contrast the tax collector acted grown-up; no excuses, no double talk, just the plain truth about himself as he prayed, "O God, be merciful to me, a sinner."

Of course we should not pretend to have sins of which we are not guilty, nor should we exaggerate our real sins. But with complete honesty we should admit our sins, and without fear we should turn to Jesus for mercy, who came to call sinners.

Optional Mass For the Fourth Week

For those of us who enjoy the gift of sight, it is impossible to appreciate what it means to be blind. We can close our eyes and pretend that we are blind, but of course we know that all we have to do is to open our eyes in order to see again.

The primary purpose of today's gospel story was to present a dramatic proof that Jesus is the light of the world who triumphs over the darkness of sin and gives eternal life to men. Unfortunately the Pharisees deliberately closed their eyes to Jesus and in doing so condemned themselves. To be saved, all they had to do was to open their eyes in order to see with the same faith that had come to the man born blind.

The early Church saw in the healing of the man born blind a symbol of baptism, wherein we are healed of the effects of sin and our eyes are opened in faith to Jesus. In the ceremony of baptism, a small candle is lit from the paschal candle, which represents Christ. The priest then says, "This child has been enlightened by Christic. . . . May he keep the flame of faith alive in his heart. When the Lord comes, may he go out to meet him with all the saints in the heavenly kingdom."

During the Holy Saturday service, the paschal candle is carried into the darkened church as a symbol of the light of Christ who came into a world darkened by sin. Later in the service we will all be invited to renew our baptism, to open our eyes to Christ with an even more intense faith in him. As Lent progresses we should look forward to that time of renewal with a prayer that our faith may become stronger day by day.

Monday of the Fourth Week

Modern medicine in recent times has made tremendous progress. And yet with all its wonders, all that the science of medicine can accomplish at most is to prolong life, to put off the inevitable day of death. It can do nothing once a person has died.

Through his miracles Jesus wanted to show that he had power not only over sickness but over death itself. The faith of the royal official in today's gospel was at first only a belief that Jesus had extraordinary healing powers, that he was some kind of super physician. Jesus rejected that type of faith. But the man struggled, with God's help, to deepen his faith and cried out: "Sir, come down before my child dies." When Jesus told him that his son would live, he put his whole trust in the words of Jesus and started for home. When he discovered upon returning home that his son was alive and well, he came to full faith in Jesus as the life-giver; he became a believer.

This final, complete faith of the official is the kind of faith we must have in Jesus. Jesus is not concerned merely with our temporal well-being. He wishes us to share one day in his own resurrection from the dead, so that we may enjoy his eternal happiness in heaven.

All during Lent we look forward to our celebration at Easter of the resurrection of Jesus from the dead. In faith we must see that Christ's victory over death as manifested in his resurrection is our victory as well. God will one day create new heavens and a new earth, as we heard in the first reading. Provided we keep our faith and trust in Jesus, we will enjoy that new creation through our resurrection with Jesus from the dead.

Alternate

The royal official of today's gospel was apparently in the service of Herod Antipas. As such he was a rather prominent person in the local community, a man of some dignity and stature in the eyes of the townspeople. Distraught though he was at the serious illness of his son, it must have taken quite a bit of humility for him to admit, first to himself, that things were out of his control, and then to go before the carpenter turned preacher and beg for his help. He had not been a follower of Jesus, one of those who had responded to his message and invitation. He saw in Jesus only a wonderworker, someone whose help he desperately needed at the moment. It was only later that he became a "believer," that is, a true follower of Jesus.

It is a very natural thing for us to forget all about God, for all practical purposes, when everything is going well for us. But just let something go wrong, and all of a sudden God becomes very important to us. When we need help, we humbly turn to him in prayer. Certainly we should ask God for help, but the prayer of petition does not exhaust our relationship with God. God is more than a super physician or a supreme righter of all wrongs. He is God, the center of our whole lives and one who deserves our prayer of praise and adoration. Our attitude toward God should be like that of the man—you ladies may think him extraordinary—who brings his wife flowers or a box of candy just to show his love. He is not trying to patch up an argument or coax a favor out of his wife. He only wants to let her know what he thinks of her.

A true believer does not think of God only in time of need. He wants to let God know what he thinks of him by means of the prayer of praise and adoration.

Tuesday of the Fourth Week

The first reading today paints a picture of how God will eventually restore this world to its original state of paradise. The water mentioned so prominently in the prophecy, is a symbol of the abundance of blessings, especially of life itself, that God will pour out upon his elect.

Perhaps it was this biblical use of water as a symbol of blessings that moved the people of our Lord's day to attribute curative powers to the pool of Bethesda. (As a matter of fact the gospel does not assert that the pool had curative power, but only that it was thought to have such.) Jesus took pity on the sick man, apparently a cripple, who clung to a faint hope that the water could restore him to health. Without recourse to any aid, not even that of the water, Jesus cured the man by his mere word, "Stand up! Pick up your mat and walk!"

When Jesus found the man later in the temple precincts, he said to him, "Give up your sins so that something worse may not overtake you." Jesus did not imply that the man's sickness had been a punishment for sin; rather, he wished to make it clear to the man that sin is worse than any physical ailment, for while his sickness had paralyzed him, sin would lead him to eternal death.

It is good for us to hear this lesson ourselves today. Physical debility and illness are very real and very close to us. If we ourselves are afflicted, or someone we love, the problem and the burden may seem almost overwhelming. But it is not a cliché to say that things could be worse. One serious sin is worse than all the physical suffering in the whole world. Whatever our problem, the words of Jesus are meant for us as well as for the sick man in today's gospel: "Give up your sins so that something worse may not overtake you."

Alternate

Jesus took pity on the man who had been sick, apparently as a cripple, for thirty-eight years. It was a long time to be sick, but in a moment by the power of his word alone, Jesus cured the man. In the confusion caused by the incredible objections of the Pharisees, the man disappeared in the crowd, and it was only later that Jesus found him and said, "Give up your sins." Jesus wanted to make clear to the man that he was interested in his whole well-being, both physical and spiritual. The order of events was different from Jesus' usual practice. Ordinarily he forgave sins before effecting a physical cure.

We can readily understand how Jesus would first be concerned about the sickness of sin. This particular miracle does help to make us realize, however, that indeed it is the whole person whom Jesus wishes to save. Maybe in the past we have put too much emphasis on "saving our souls," almost with the implication that what happens to our bodies does not really matter. As a matter of fact we are God's creature in body as well as soul, and our bodies, if we dare think of them as something separate from our persons, are precious in the eyes of God. Jesus came to save us as whole human beings, not as disembodied souls, and today's miracle is a sign that Jesus' saving grace will bring our whole being to a state of health and happiness.

The mother of Jesus was taken up body as well as soul into heaven, for she did not have to wait for her sharing in the resurrection of Christ. We yearn for the day of the final coming of Christ when he will take us body and soul to heaven to share in his glory.

Wednesday of the Fourth Week

One of the greatest problems facing the world today is a movement either to deny or ignore the divinity of Christ. There are some who would want to see Jesus as a great philosopher, or social reformer, or even as some kind of beloved beatnik. To be sure, Jesus has a human nature which creates great appeal for us: he graced the wedding banquet, blessed little children, ate and drank with sinners. But Jesus is much more than a man, even a very extraordinary one. He is truly God, and the Jews in today's gospel saw clearly that Jesus spoke of God as his own Father, thereby making himself God's equal.

Jesus forcefully manifested his claim of divinity by attributing to himself two works in particular which are distinctively God's works: these are the greater works which Jesus will show, greater, for instance than the cure of the man at the pool which we heard about in yesterday's gospel. First, Jesus gives life; he raises the dead to life. Second, he judges all men, and thereby grants them eternal life or sentences them to eternal condemnation, depending on whether they accept or reject him.

We accept Christ, we believe in his divinity. We should take this occasion to remind ourselves of what this belief entails. It is only by our faith in Christ that we can pass from death to eternal life. It is in Christ that we find God and in him alone. The divine life which God the Father has in himself he has given to us through the Son, by sending him into this world as life-giver and judge. To seek happiness in anyone or anything apart from Jesus is the worst of folly. In Jesus alone is our eternal salvation and our happiness.

Alternate

There are people who feel that God is very far away from us and completely unconcerned about what is going on in our world. They seem to think that God, after sending us into this world, has lost all interest in us, like some unscrupulous used car salesman whose only hope is that his client will not return with a complaint.

During the time of their exile in Babylon, the Israelites felt abandoned by God. They had been deprived of their homeland and led off into slavery. It was a difficult, discouraging period for them, and with one voice the people cried out, "The Lord has forsaken me; my Lord has forgotten me." God sent his prophet to protest that it was not so. In a beautiful image God replied to the people through his prophet, "Can a mother forget her infant, be without tenderness for the child of her womb? Even should she forget, I will never forget you."

There are times, perhaps even many times, when we are tempted to wonder whether God really cares about us. When someone we love very much dies, especially when least expected, we may question why it had to be. We are often in the dark as to reasons why other misfortunes come upon us. Sometimes nothing seems to make sense any more. But we must never think that God is unconcerned or that he has abandoned us, even if everybody else has abandoned us. The test of real faith comes not in good times, but in bad ones. It is then that we must cling to the belief that our God cares.

Thursday of the Fourth Week

In today's lesson we have witnessed an extraordinary scene: Moses standing before the irate God to intercede for the rebellious and ungrateful Israelites. God was angry with them because they had made a molten calf and worshipped it as God. He was so angry in fact, that in speaking to Moses he referred to them not as "my people," but as "your people." He had divorced himself from the Israelites and was determined to destroy them and make a new people for himself. How fortunate they were to have Moses as their mediator before God because at his intercession God "relented in the punishment he had intended to inflict on his people."

Someone even greater than Moses is here as our mediator before God, the one about whom Moses wrote, Jesus Christ himself. As we saw earlier in Lent, Jesus taught us *how* to pray, but more than that, he prayed *for* us and continues to pray for us and *with* us, especially in the Mass. It is true that we must humble ourselves before God and admit our weakness and our unworthiness as we do in the penitential rite of the Mass; however, we do not have to fear that God will reject our prayers or spurn our worship. We do not pray or worship alone or by our own power. We do so in union with Jesus.

Jesus, as it were, like a new Moses stands before his Father and says, "Why, O Lord, should your wrath blaze up against these people whom I have saved in my own blood. These are my people, for I have redeemed them, and therefore they are your people too." What we do today has value in the eyes of God because as he looks down upon us gathered for Mass he sees in us the person of his Son, our mediator, and he says: "This is my beloved Son in whom I am well pleased."

We should try to be especially conscious of our union with Jesus at the time of the consecration, when Jesus renews his sacrifice, and at the time when the solemn words of the great doxology are pronounced: "Through him, with him, in him, in the unity of the Holy Spirit, all glory and honor is yours, almighty Father, for ever and ever." To these words add your sincere and fervent "Amen" with the confidence that our worship is pleasing to the Father because Jesus is with us.

Alternate

Have you ever wondered why you have the faith? It is a good question to think about. Maybe you were born of parents who passed the faith on to you, but you could have been born of parents who had no religion. Maybe you are a convert, but you could have lived in a country in which people do not even hear the mention of

Jesus Christ. Still another question is why have you kept the faith and not changed your mind about it.

The Israelites were a people especially favored by God. They received the gift of faith through God's revelation to them, and experienced his salvation in the exodus. And yet "they forgot the God who had saved them." Incredibly they abandoned the true God; they "made a calf in Horeb and adored a molten image." Why should we be more faithful than they?

When Jesus came, his credentials were overwhelming: his good works done in the Father's name, his miracles, and the very testimony of scripture itself. And yet the leaders of the people failed to respond to Jesus. Why is it that we accept Jesus whereas those men did not?

I think we have all met people who are obviously very good people. We feel that they are much more worthy than we to enjoy the gift of faith, and yet it is we who have the gift and not they. Why is it so?

The gift of faith is indeed a deep mystery, one which theologians have struggled to understand for centuries, but without much agreement among themselves. One thing is certain: we should be grateful for our faith, not with a smug complacency that we are better than others, but with a sincere humility which recognizes that faith is God's gift of which we are unworthy.

Friday of the Fourth Week

In the science fiction stories which appear occasionally on television, the theme generally runs about the same. Some unusual creature appears from outer space. The earthlings, without any investigation, react with fear and their first thought is to kill the creature. Almost instinctively, though irrationally, they feel that his death is necessary for their safety.

The reaction of many to Jesus was even more irrational. Though it is true that Jesus, in a certain sense, came from outer space, he should have been recognized by the people as the Messiah because of his many signs and miracles. Far from being a threat to their safety, he came to be their salvation and to give them eternal life. And yet the leaders of the people plotted to kill Jesus. They felt that his death was necessary for their safety.

Perhaps the real reason for their plot can be found in the words of the wicked quoted in today's first lesson: "His life is not like other men's, and different are his ways. He judges us debased; he holds aloof from our paths as from things impure." Jesus was a living reproach to the leaders in their wickedness. And so they judged that the best thing to do was to kill him; that would get him out of the way for good. But "they knew not the hidden counsels of God nor did they count on a recompense of holiness." Death was not the end of Jesus, but only his gateway to eternal life and exaltation by his heavenly Father.

With Jesus we too must be bold enough to be different from the wicked; we must hold aloof from things that are impure. And we must face the consequences. There is enough evil in this world to make us suffer for trying to be good. Some may ridicule us as being odd, like some creature from outer space. But, as with Jesus, not even death will be our defeat, but only a gateway to eternal life and exaltation by our heavenly Father.

Alternate

Perhaps on first hearing you missed the full impact of one sentence in today's gospel: "They were looking for a chance to kill him." How chilling are those words; thinking about their meaning can make our blood run cold. They were looking for a chance to kill the very person who had come to save them from eternal death. And they had their foolish wish fulfilled when they saw Jesus dead on the cross.

Equally chilling are the words of the Epistle to the Hebrews in referring to those who have abandoned their faith: "They crucify again for themselves the Son of God and make him a mockery" (Heb 6:6). Though these words were written as a vivid picture of the malice of apostasy, they can be applied without exaggeration to the evil of any deliberate mortal sin.

A lot of people these days do not like to hear this kind of talk about mortal sin from the pulpit. Many of us priests are slow to speak about serious sin lest we seem negative or old-fashioned. It is true that sometimes in the past there was too much emphasis on sin, fear, judgment, and hell and not enough on virtue, love, mercy, and heaven. But sin is not imaginary. It is real and a distinct possibility in our lives. Many of the readings during this season of Lent warn about the danger of complacency in religion. It is like the person who has been feeling fine only to discover that all along he has had a lurking tumor which has exploded into cancer. Perhaps if he had not been complacent about his health, if he had taken the trouble to get a thorough examination, the tumor could have been discovered in time.

We hope that at this moment we are spiritually healthy. Now is the time to search out even the smallest tumor of venial sin to destroy it. Now is the time to build up our spiritual health against a sudden attack. Now is the time to do everything we can, without complacency, to make sure that one day we are not so foolish as "to crucify again for ourselves the Son of God and make him a mockery."

Saturday of the Fourth Week

Nicodemus was a Pharisee, a rabbi, and a member of the Sanhēdrin, the high court which formed the supreme governing body of the Jews. His first meeting with Jesus (Jn 3:1 ff), some time before the event of today's gospel, was a secret one at night because he was afraid of having his reputation tainted with his associates, all of whom vehemently opposed Jesus. On this occasion, however, he mustered enough courage to bring up a point of law in Jesus' favor. After the crucifixion, with still more courage, he assisted in the burial of Jesus (Jn 19:39).

Our Lord looked for men who would have at least the courage of their convictions as did Nicodemus, but he found few. How disappointed he must have been to hear some out of cowardice bring up specious arguments against him from scripture itself. How saddened he must have been to see others intimidated by the Pharisees. Jeremiah, in the first reading, was a man of tremendous courage, and though he knew he was like a lamb being led to slaughter, he stuck to his convictions.

Like Nicodemus and even more like Jeremiah, we must have the courage of our convictions. We must be witnesses for Christ before others. Our religion is not fulfilled only by prayer and worship, for the Church is, as the Vatican Council expressed it, "the Church in the Modern World." It is especially your office as lay people to bring Christ to modern men. The *Decree on the Laity* says that you do this by "the very testimony of your Christian life and good works done in a supernatural spirit," but it points out also that "a true apostle looks for opportunities to announce Christ by words addressed either to nonbelievers with a view of leading them to faith, or to believers with a view to instructing and strengthening them and motivating them toward a more fervent life" (6).

Neither fear for our reputation nor for our security is an excuse for failing to defend and proclaim Christ. Jesus wants, and needs, Catholics who have the courage of their convictions.

Alternate

You have noticed that when a man is arrested, reporters are careful to state that it is *alleged* that the man did so and so. The word, "alleged," or something similar is always used to avoid a statement indicating guilt before the case is tried in court. Moreover, when people are being selected for a jury, every effort is made to choose people who have no prejudice in the case. The reason for all this is that in our system of justice a man is presumed innocent until he has been proven guilty before a jury of his peers.

Nicodemus tried to make the same point with the Pharisees who had already condemned Jesus. "Since when," he protested, "does our law condemn any man without first hearing him and knowing the facts?" The Pharisees had rejected Jesus without even an attempt to investigate the facts. They protested that the Messiah-Prophet would not come from Galilee but from Bethlehem. With but little trouble on their part they could have discovered that, though Jesus grew up in Nazareth in Galilee, he was indeed born in Bethlehem. The Pharisees were guilty of rash judgment.

Rash judgment is coming to a conclusion before all the facts are known. Unfortunately it is a fault that even good people can fall into. We hear a rumor about someone and we accept it as truth. Maybe we notice that someone is not going to communion and we judge that he or she must be guilty of mortal sin. Perhaps we see a man having lunch with a woman who is not his wife, and we conclude that they are having an affair. If we think that the rash judgment of the Pharisees against Jesus was a terrible crime, we had better think twice before passing judgment on anyone. In all these matters and ones like them, a person should be innocent in our eyes until he has been judged guilty, not by a jury, but by the all knowing and just judge, God himself.

Optional Mass For the Fifth Week

The two awesome realities with which all humans must be concerned are life and death. We fear death and cling to life. We do everything we can to put off the moment of death, and we yearn for a good life that will never end.

In times past men searched for the fountain of youth so that they might always be young and might never have to die. Today scientists are probing into the aging process in the hope of finding a way to prolong life and eventually prevent death. Such searching and probing miss the point. The life for which we are made is not found in this world, but in heaven, and to find it we must, like Christ, pass through death to a sharing in his resurrection.

Jesus is the key to eternal life. He tells us today: "I am the resurrection and the life: whoever believes in me, though he should die, will come to life." The tremendous miracle related in today's gospel was not only an act of compassion, but also a sign of Christ's power over life and death. Jesus has the power to overcome death and to grant eternal life to those who are faithful to him.

We do not have to fear a physical aging process that will lead to death; we need only fear the disruptive power of sin which alone can destroy us. There is no fountain of youth except Jesus himself, who said, "The water I give shall become a fountain, leaping up to provide eternal life." Whoever believes in Jesus though he should die, will come to life.

Monday of the Fifth Week
(A and B Cycle)

It is true that the law of Moses stated that the penalty for adultery was death. The scribes and the Pharisees in today's gospel, however, seemed to enjoy the misery of the poor woman as they dragged her before Jesus. They were perverse in that they hoped to use her sad condition in order to trap Jesus. But our Lord would neither be trapped nor be partner to their gloating self-righteousness.

It is not that our Lord condoned the sin of adultery or pretended that it was not evil. Rather Jesus revealed that he is a judge who extends mercy to the sinner in order to turn him away from sin. Our Lord knew what was in the woman's heart, and it must have been that he saw there a spark of repentance, which won his forgiveness. He told her to avoid the sin in the future as a sign of her repentance.

Susanna, in contrast to this woman, was falsely accused of adultery. Until Daniel appeared on the scene, all the people believed her guilty and condemned her to death. In her innocence she had trusted in God, and her trust was rewarded by acquittal.

Sometimes we are rightly accused by others because we do make mistakes; we do commit sins. Some people may even seem to enjoy our misery at the time. We must remember, however, that Jesus is the judge who wishes to extend mercy to us, no matter what others may think about us, provided we show the spark of repentance. On the other hand, we are sometimes falsely accused, and in one way that can be an even more painful situation. It is then that we must turn to God, like Susanna, and put our trust in his power to vindicate us. In either case, it is how we stand in the sight of God that really counts.

Monday of the Fifth Week
(C Cycle)

Susanna, the wife of Joakim, was falsely accused of adultery by the two elders. How distressful it must have been for Susanna in her innocence to see herself being condemned, while the two elders in their guilt were going free. Indeed it looked as if the elders would have their day until Daniel appeared on the scene. Face to face with Daniel, and caught by his shrewdness, they condemned themselves. In much the same way, the Pharisees, who wished to accuse Jesus of blasphemy and deceit, face to face with Jesus manifested their own sinfulness by their rejection of him. Jesus had just said that he was the light of the world, and it was his penetrating light which revealed their wickedness.

Sometimes we may be tempted to be distressed about people who seem to be "getting away with murder." Maybe we feel spiteful toward them, or perhaps a little envious. We work hard, try to be good and to do the right thing all the time, while others who seem to have little care for God or anyone but themselves prosper and have everything their own way. We may think that we are better off than they morally, and yet they are better off than we financially, socially, and in every other material way. What happens to such people is God's concern. We should not wish evil for them, but as a matter of fact if they are guilty of sin they will be judged by God and receive his condemnation as did the two elders.

Actually we should be concerned with how we stand before God, without making any comparison of ourselves with others. Such comparison not only can lead to self deception, but misses the point. We are what we are before God, and we will be judged, not in contrast with our fellow human beings, but in the light of the holiness of Christ.

Tuesday of the Fifth Week

We have all heard about parents who have disowned their child. It may have been because of a marriage the parents did not approve, or because the son or daughter had gone off to live a hippie-type existence. Whatever the reason, it is a terrible thing to hear a father or mother say, "Out of my sight! You are no child of mine!"

So-called fire and brimstone sermons are no longer popular. Nor would such a sermon be appropriate for you. However, it is healthy sometimes to remember that it would be a very terrible thing for any of us to hear from God, "Out of my sight! You are no child of mine!" After all, the Church in this Mass had us listen to the words of Jesus, "You will surely die in your sins unless you come to believe that I am." If we do not wish to die in our sins, we must turn to Christ as our savior. When the Israelites in the desert were punished for their sins by means of deadly serpents, they were saved by turning in faith toward the bronze serpent lifted up by Moses. St. John the evangelist saw in the lifting up of the serpent a type or sign of Jesus' being lifted up on the cross, and he wrote, "Just as Moses lifted up the serpent in the desert, so must the Son of Man be lifted up, that all who believe may have eternal life in him" (Jn 3:14).

And so we turn to Christ in faith because we want to have eternal life. We want no part of mortal sin, but as God's children we should be concerned about even small offenses against God. Small sins count too. It is good for all of us to remember that we should take venial sins seriously, in the sense that we should really be trying to please God in all things. Jesus lifted up on the cross has the power to save us not only from the deadly bite of mortal sin but also from the minor prick of venial sin.

Alternate

Jesus told the Pharisees that where he was going they could not come. Somehow they foolishly interpreted his words to mean that Jesus was going to commit suicide, and consequently go to hell where they as "righteous" men could not follow. It was a case of supreme irony. As a matter of fact Jesus would lay down his life, not in suicide but in sacrifice, and he would thereby pass, not to hell, but to the glory of heaven where indeed the self-righteous Pharisees could not go because of their sins.

The gospels show that Jesus had come to call sinners out of love for them. He was considerate of the tax collectors, lenient toward the woman taken in adultery, and merciful toward those suffering because of their sins. Yet Jesus was stern with the Pharisees, and to no one else did he address such words as, "You will die in your sins; where I am going you cannot come."

The Pharisees had taken the heart and spirit out of religion. They thought their salvation was guaranteed because of their descent from Abraham, and they had reduced religion to nothing more than a hypocritical observance of a multiplicity of minute regulations. They were complacent; they thought they had it made. In their smugness they had placed themselves out of the reach of Jesus, and in their self-sufficiency they believed that they did not need the help of Jesus or anyone else.

Complacency is deadly, whatever be its cause. St. Paul (Ph 2:12) says that we must work out our salvation in fear—not the fear of God but the fear of ourselves for we are weak and without Jesus we can do nothing (Jn 15:5).

Wednesday of the Fifth Week

A growing problem in our society is that of drug abuse. Those drugs which are addictive, after giving temporary satisfaction, leave the user with a driving need for more and more. The addict loses his freedom; he becomes a slave of dope. If he finds no cure, he eventually becomes a dropout from his family, from society, from everything.

One can also become a slave of sin. Any sin gives only a temporary satisfaction. Unless one turns immediately back to God, sin leaves a person with a driving need for more and more in a blind, desperate search for happiness. Jesus said in the gospel today: "Everyone who lives in sin is the slave of sin." Jesus came to set us free from the slavery of sin. The Jews who heard the words of Jesus were insulted by his implying that they were slaves. They protested that they were free because they were sons of Abraham, and they thereby betrayed their mistaken belief that being a descendant of Abraham was an automatic guarantee of salvation. Jesus indicated that such physical descent was not enough, and that because of their evil works they were really slaves after all, and as slaves they had in effect become dropouts from the household of God.

The lesson for us is obvious. We are sons of God by our baptism, but just being a Catholic is no automatic guarantee of salvation. We too, amid all the confusing enticements and mixed up values of our society, run the risk of becoming slaves of sin. It is never a sudden process, just as the slavery of dope addiction is never a sudden process. Little by little small sins can get a hold on us until a serious sin becomes easy. Then one sin leads to another until we are enslaved. We cannot afford the luxury of complacency. With the grace of God we must constantly guard and nourish the filial love of God in our hearts lest, as slaves to sin, we become dropouts from the family of God.

Alternate

On July 10, 1970 Communist China released Bishop James

Walsh from prison, reportedly because of advanced age and ill health. The bishop had been arrested in 1958 and held incommunicado for almost two years before he was sentenced to twenty years in prison on charges of spying for the United States and the Vatican. When his brother was allowed to visit him in 1960, the bishop told him, "While no one likes to be confined, I am not unhappy here and I leave the future entirely in the hands of God." He had found that "four walls do not a prison make, nor iron bars a cage."

During those long years in a small cell of a prison on the outskirts of Shanghai, Bishop Walsh did not enjoy freedom in the ordinary sense, but he did learn the meaning of the words of Jesus, "If you live according to my teaching, you are truly my disciples; then you will know the truth and the truth will set you free."

Jesus taught that cells and prisons do not destroy freedom; sin does that. Sin makes us slaves. It chains the human spirit and restricts us from living in such a way as to achieve the real happiness for which we all yearn. Freedom is the liberty not to do whatever we want, but to do whatever we must in order to fulfill our spiritual destiny. Living a life of sin is like choosing to confine oneself within a run-down, one room hovel and pretending that is pleasure, when one could live in a magnificent mansion forever.

If we live according to the teaching of Jesus as his disciples, his truth will set us free—free from sin with the liberty to pursue the true purpose of life.

Thursday of the Fifth Week

A small time, virtually unknown politician in a campaign speech boasts that he is a better man than George Washington. What is the reaction of the crowd? Some are indignant at his presumption. Others simply reject him as a fool. Still others are so enraged that they want to run him out of town.

Jesus in today's gospel was not giving a campaign speech, for he was not running for election. He had been chosen and sent by God. But his claim to be greater than Abraham was, in the estimation of the Jews, even wilder than the politician's boast of being greater than George Washington, the father of our country. Abraham was indeed the father of the Jews, as well as of all the Semitic peoples, a man of faith, devotion, and courage. And yet the claim of Jesus to being greater than Abraham was no vain boast. The Jews may have thought of him as small town stuff, but he emphatically states that he is divine by declaring, "Before Abraham came to be, I AM." They may have looked upon him as virtually unknown, but Jesus was known and chosen by his Father to fulfill all of the covenant promises made to Abraham, who from heaven rejoiced to see Jesus coming into the world.

God promised Abraham, "I will maintain my covenant with you and your descendants after you throughout the ages as an everlasting pact, to be your God and the God of your descendants after you." Jesus came in fulfillment of this covenant, a greater fulfillment than even Abraham could ever have dreamed possible. We as Christians are the beneficiaries of that covenant and its fulfillment. How right and just it is for us to give thanks and praise to God in this Mass in which we renew our covenant with God in the blood of Jesus.

Alternate

Abraham, the father of the Israelites, was indeed a marvelous man. He had many virtues, such as courage, determination, and fortitude, but in today's lesson his greatest virtue is subtly manifested: his docile faith. God made astounding promises to this simple nomad, but Abraham did not say, "How can you do all these things?" or "What proof do you offer of your truth and your power?" He simply listened in reverent silence and accepted God's word on its face value, without confirming miracles or signs on God's part.

In contrast the Jews of today's gospel did nothing but oppose the teaching of Jesus. Scarcely had Jesus gotten the words out of his mouth when they were protesting and objecting to everything he had said. And they had plenty of reason at least to listen patiently to Jesus because of all the signs and wonders he had done to support his claims. For whatever reason, they did not have docile faith.

Some people say that faith is blind, but faith is no more blind than love is. Love sees through appearances to the true worth and beauty of a person which others, with but a superficial glance, easily miss. True love sharpens visions, and docile faith does the same. Our faith should make us see through the maze of confusion and conflict through which our lives are passing to the final goal of happiness toward which the living hand of God is directing us. Our faith should make us see through the frustration and turmoil of our present existence to the life of fulfillment which God had promised us.

God is patient. He took centuries to prepare the world for the coming of the Messiah in accord with the promises made to the docile Abraham. The saving work of Jesus continues in our world and will not be completed until the final coming of Jesus, a coming toward which we must look with docile faith.

Friday of the Fifth Week

One of the most amazing things in the life of Jesus is the fact that so many people rejected him. Jesus is the personification of all that is good and holy and desirable, and he wishes to draw all men to himself to make them perfectly and eternally happy. Not only did he preach the goodness and love of his Father for men, but he himself revealed that goodness and love by his actions. When some wanted to stone him, he protested, "Many good deeds have I shown you from the Father. For which of these do you stone me?" They then accused him of blasphemy because he made himself God, and yet he was but speaking the truth, and his claim to be divine was confirmed by signs and miracles.

The rejection that Jesus suffered was nothing new. Jeremiah, who did nothing but speak the truth in God's name, was likewise rejected (first reading). When he warned the people about the destruction of Jerusalem unless they repented, he was arrested, beaten, and put in stocks.

Yes, it is amazing that Jesus, as well as Jeremiah and other prophets in Israel, were rejected by so many people when they spoke the truth. Why were they rejected? There are many complicated reasons, but one reason is that sometimes the truth can hurt. When the truth makes us face our own failures and inadequacies, the easiest way to escape our responsibilities and the need to change is to ignore or deny the truth. When a teacher informs irresponsible parents that their child is both a scholastic and a disciplinary problem in school, that evaluation is a judgment of the parents as well as the child. Rather than face their own failure and the need to do something about the child, the parents take the easy way out and refuse to accept the teacher's report.

The truth can hurt, even the truth preached by Jesus. The truth of Jesus demands that we be different from others; it requires that we accept suffering and self-denial, and that we abandon our selfishness to be generous in our love and service of others. Let us pray in the Mass that we will never take the easy way out by rejecting Jesus and his truth.

Alternate

When Jesus was on this earth, his humanity was a stumbling block for his enemies. It was shocking to them that this former carpenter, who hailed from the inconspicuous town of Nazareth, laid claim to divinity. The leaders of the people, infuriated by his claim, accused him of blasphemy. "You who are only a man are making yourself God," they complained.

We look back upon Jesus through the eyes of faith. Because of our faith we are amazed that the people of the day were so blind to the divinity of Christ. It may even be that our faith in his divinity is so strong that we fail to appreciate the reality of his humanity. The leaders of the people were wrong in thinking of Jesus only as a man, falsely claiming to be God, but we are equally wrong if we think of him only as God, masquerading, as it were, in the costume of a human body. Jesus, though truly God, was just as human as we are in all things but sin.

During this coming week, Holy Week, we will meditate once more on the passion and death of Jesus. His pain and anguish during that ordeal were no fiction. When Jesus struggled with himself in the garden of Gethsemane to accept the chalice of suffering offered him by his Father, he experienced that same confusion that we ourselves have felt when face to face with a serious temptation. When Peter denied him and Judas betrayed him, he knew the same sadness we have known when a relative or friend has hurt us deeply. When the soldiers mocked him and spat on him, he was just as humiliated as we when we have been insulted or made little of. His pain in the crucifixion was true torture, and his agony was true torment.

Indeed it was God who suffered and died to save us from our sins, but he did so as a real human being.

Saturday of the Fifth Week

God has given us the precious gift of freedom, and he respects that freedom. Some people abuse their freedom by doing evil, but God, rather than take freedom away, uses his wisdom to draw good from evil. This is an important lesson that we see in today's gospel.

The chief priests and the Pharisees were afraid that if the people were to follow Jesus, the Romans would come and take over their temple and their country. Caiaphas, the high priest, using his freedom of decision, told his companions that the simplest solution to the problem was to kill Jesus. He pointed out that it was better for this one man to die than for the whole nation to be destroyed. From that day on the leaders of the people plotted to kill Jesus.

What Caiaphas and the others did not realize was that God would draw good from their evil plan, and even from the words of

Caiaphas. It was indeed better that Jesus die in sacrifice than the whole human race perish in sin. God the Father's plan was that the death of his son would atone for our sins. He allowed the leaders of the people to set in motion all the events that led to the death of Jesus because he knew that his son would accept death eagerly and willingly for the salvation of the world.

We are in a position to see how God worked good through the evil plot to kill Jesus. In our own lives at the present moment it is often difficult or even sometimes impossible to know just what God has in mind when he allows evil. But we must have the faith to believe that God knows what he is doing. His respect for freedom allows evil, but in his wisdom he knows how to draw good from evil and in his love he does so. Perhaps we think that if we were running the world we would do things differently. God's ways are not our ways, but his ways are best.

Alternate

Tomorrow we begin Holy Week, which at one time was referred to as "the great week." It is truly a great week because within it we will commemorate the events of our salvation. The liturgy, however, does not present the passion of our Lord in merely sad or sorrowful terms as if we did not know the outcome. There is no tragic note about the suffering and death of our Lord as if he were a failure, dragged down to defeat by the machinations of such men as Caiaphas and the Pharisees. Rather throughout the week there runs a feeling of joyful victory generated by the realization that the death of Jesus led to the glory of his resurrection.

We will begin the week tomorrow with the praise and glorification of Jesus as the Messiah-King in the procession of the palms. The shouts and cheers of the people of Palm Sunday are but a foreshadowing of the true glory bestowed upon Jesus by his heavenly Father in his resurrection on Easter Sunday. On Palm Sunday, after the triumphal procession, Jesus instructed his apostles in a veiled way concerning the mysterious events that were to follow. He said, "Unless the grain of wheat falls to the earth and dies, it remains just a grain of wheat; but if it dies, it produces much fruit" (Jn 12:24f). Jesus was that grain of wheat which had to die and be planted in the earth for three days. Then he would, as it were, push upward on Easter Sunday through the earth like a growing stalk of wheat bearing much fruit. That fruit was his glorification and our salvation. His life has become our life and his glory, our glory.

During this coming week the liturgy will give us the opportunity to relive with Christ his paschal mystery. Let us pray that our union with him through this week may bear the fruit of eternal life.

Monday of Holy Week

In today's gospel St. John makes one of his few chronological references. He notes that the anointing took place "six days before Passover." That was the day on which the Jews were instructed to procure the lamb that would be used for the Passover meal and to keep it until the day before Passover when it was to be slaughtered during the evening twilight (Ex 12:3). The Passover meal was a commemoration of the saving events of the exodus. The Israelites at the time of the exodus were told to sprinkle the blood of the lamb on the lintel and the two doorposts of their houses. Then at midnight the angel of God struck down all the first born of the Egyptians, but seeing the blood on the lintel and the two doorposts, he passed over the houses of the Israelites. They were saved because of the blood of the lamb.

It would seem that somehow in the mind of St. John the anointing of Jesus was his being selected and prepared to be the Christian paschal lamb. Indeed it is the blood of Christ that saves us from sin. Before communion you hear these words, "This is the lamb of God who takes away the sins of the world." As the true paschal lamb, Jesus is the fulfillment of all of those years of promise and preparation found in the Old Testament. For century after century God patiently directed his people toward the great events which we relive this week in the liturgy. We do not look to the future as did the

Jews of old; rather we have the privilege of sharing directly and personally in the saving mysteries of Jesus, the lamb who takes away the sins of the world.

Alternate

Mary's anointing of Jesus was indeed an extravagance. Judas, a shrewd calculator of monetary worth, estimated that the perfume could have been sold for three hundred pieces of silver (perhaps ten months' wages, and incidentally ten times more than Jesus was worth in his eyes). Jesus saw in Mary's impetuous act a beautiful sign of love (cf. Mk 14:6). Love does not always correspond with cold logic, and there is room in religion for deeds which spring more from the heart than from the intellect. It is true that the perfume could have been sold for the benefit of the poor, but Jesus, who took second place to no one in his concern for the poor, graciously accepted Mary's extravagance.

The protest of Judas was hypocritical, made from no concern for the poor, since his hope was to have pocketed the price of the perfume for himself. Today in the Church there has been a healthy renewal of concern for the poor, and in many respects we all need such a renewal. And yet some, though with a sincerity never felt by Judas, seem to be making of religion nothing but the service of the poor. No excuse should be manufactured for hoarded or abused wealth on the part of anyone in the Church; however, there is much more to religion than the alleviation of poverty, important though it be. Mary had learned that Jesus is the resurrection and the life, and her act was one of loving recognition. The wish to spend the money on the poor involved a lack of recognition of the real nature of Jesus as the Son of God. There must always be a time and place for service of the poor, but there must also be a time and place for the due worship of the person of the Son of God.

Tuesday of Holy Week

Two men in the gospel are alike, and yet totally different. They are Simon Peter and Judas Iscariot. They are alike in that they both failed Jesus, Peter by denial and Judas by betrayal. They are totally different from each other in their reaction to Jesus after their failure; Peter repented and Judas despaired.

Peter's character was so human that I think all of us can feel very close to him. He was eager, yet weak; sincere, yet faltering; devoted, yet temporarily disloyal. Above all he knew Jesus so well that he was quick to repentance and confident of forgiveness.

We hope and pray that we will not end up as Judas did but how like Peter most of us are. We are eager to form resolutions to do great things for Christ, but often we are remiss in carrying out those good resolutions. We are sincere in our zeal for Christ, but frequently we falter through human weakness. We are truly devoted to Christ, but sometimes we may live almost as if we did not know Christ and his teachings.

If we are like Peter in his faults, we should try to be like him also in his strong points. Peter came to know Jesus well. Because he knew Jesus well and had witnessed his love for sinners, Peter was confident of forgiveness. But what about Judas? We cannot afford to be like him in any way. Judas had the same opportunities to know Jesus that Peter had. He had heard his teaching and seen his example. He had been offered love by Jesus. But he squandered his opportunities to know Christ and he failed to respond to Jesus' offer of love.

During this Holy Week we have a valuable opportunity of knowing Jesus by meditating on the events of his passion and death. He suffered all that he had to endure out of love for us. Today let us pray for the grace to respond to love as Peter did.

Alternate

During the last hours of Jesus on this earth, St. Peter learned a bitter lesson: words are cheap. All you have to do is open your mouth and let them come out, but if they are not backed up by actions they are as worthless as counterfeit money or a bad check.

At the Last Supper poor Peter opened his mouth and let the

words come out. He said to Jesus, "I will lay down my life for you." At the moment he did not realize that his words were counterfeit. It was only later, when he was challenged concerning his association with Jesus, that he realized how worthless those words were. While Jesus was standing trial before the high priest, a servant girl noticed Peter in the courtyard and accused him of being a follower of Jesus. And this man, who a few hours before had said that he would die for Jesus, said to the girl, "I don't know what you are talking about." A little later when some bystanders accused him of the same thing, he replied, "I don't even know the man you are talking about!" Then he heard the second cock crow and broke down and began to cry. It was a bitter lesson for Peter to learn.

But learn the lesson he did. Peter determined to make good his words at the Last Supper, not with a bad check, but with a blank check on which he would allow Jesus to fill in the amount he wished. And so it was that many years after the crucifixion Peter followed his master to a martyr's death on a cross.

If we are good Christians we will tell Jesus that we will follow him to death rather than deny him or be disloyal to him in any way, even in little things. In fact, we should write Jesus a blank check and allow him to require any amount from us. We must remember, however, that our payment cannot be counterfeit; it must be backed up with the silver and gold of sincerity and truth.

Wednesday of Holy Week

When we look at a crucifix it is difficult for us to realize that Jesus is there because he wanted to be. It looks as if he were over-powered by his enemies and forced to die on the cross. Such was not the case. On one occasion the Pharisees tried to stone Jesus to death, but he easily escaped from them. On another occasion the people of his own town led him to the brink of a cliff with the intention of throwing him to death on the rocks below, but he simply turned and walked away with no one able to lay a hand on him. There are many incidents in which the enemies of Jesus tried to apprehend him to put him to death, but they were powerless to do so because, as our Lord explained, his "hour had not yet come." That hour was the time determined beforehand by his Father.

Jesus in today's gospel indicated that he knew that time set by his Father for his sacrificial death; he said, "My appointed time draws near." He also showed his foreknowledge of his death by his prediction that one of the twelve was about to betray him. But Jesus not only knew the time of his approaching death; more importantly he willingly accepted that death in loving obedience to his Father, in fulfillment of the scriptures.

In the conclusion of his presentation of himself as the Good Shepherd, our Lord said, "The Father loves me for this: that I lay down my life to take it up again. No one takes it from me; I lay it down freely" (Jn 10:17f). And at the Last Supper he said, "There is no greater love than this: to lay down one's life for one's friends" (Jn 15:13). These words express the motive according to which Jesus died.

On Good Friday, or whenever we look at a crucifix, let us realize that Jesus died because he wanted to. It was the perfect expression of his free, personal love for his Father and for us.

Alternate

Today's gospel tells how Judas finalized his plot to betray Jesus into the hands of the chief priests; in some places this day is referred to as "spy Wednesday." Though we realize that only God knows what was really in the heart of Judas, we do wonder just why he turned traitor. Was it mere avarice? The gospel does call him a thief and relates that he stole from the common purse which he held in trust for Jesus and the other apostles. But does it not seem that if he had had faith in Jesus, his faith should have conquered his greed?

The first mention of Judas as a traitor was on the occasion when Jesus promised that he would give his flesh to eat and his blood to drink. Jesus made that day of preaching on the Eucharist a supreme test of faith. When some of his own disciples walked away from him in protest that his words were hard to endure, he turned to the apostles to let them know that he demanded absolute faith as he asked, "Do you want to leave me too?" Though Peter manifested his faith in the name of the apostles, Jesus replied, "Have I not chosen you, the twelve? Yet one of you is a devil." And St. John comments, "He was speaking of Judas Iscariot . . . for he it was, though one of the twelve, who would betray him" (Jn 6:71-72).

It was from the supper table at which Jesus instituted the Eucharist that Judas left to carry out his betrayal. The impression, at least, is left that Judas turned traitor because he had failed to pass the supreme test of faith in the Eucharist.

Tomorrow, Holy Thursday, we celebrate the institution of the Eucharist. Let us take that occasion to profess our complete faith in Jesus, and let us pray that our faith will make us loyal and faithful to him.

Holy Thursday

At this time of the year devout Jews throughout the world continue to celebrate the Passover Supper in commemoration of God's deliverance of Israel from Egypt and his saving of the people in the Exodus. As presented in the New Testament, on Holy Thursday evening Jesus celebrated the Passover Supper with his apostles. Since this liturgical meal foreshadowed the Mass, our Lord instituted the Mass within its framework.

At the beginning of the supper certain incidents from the Bible were related, telling the story of the Exodus. It was the custom for the head of the house to give an explanation of this history and the symbolism of the meal; it was a kind of homily. Jesus himself performed this function at the Last Supper, and took the opportunity to elaborate on the Jewish ritual by giving a very long sermon. Prayers of praise and thanksgiving were said, and psalms were sung.

Unleavened bread and wine were served at the meal. At one point of the meal, Jesus set aside some of the bread and wine and changed them into his body and blood as a sacred sign of his sacrifice of the next day when he would pour forth all his blood from his body in death. As the sacrifice of the lamb in Egypt saved the Jews, so the sacrifice of the Lamb of God would save the new people of God. And as the Jews partook of the sacrificial lamb, so our Lord gave his body and blood in communion to the apostles as a sacred sign of their sharing in his resurrection. Psalms were sung and the first Mass was at an end.

After Pentecost the apostles fulfilled the command of Christ, "Do this in memory of me." At first, however, they did not omit the service of the synagogue (Acts 2:24). The synagogue service usually consisted of prayers, to which the people responded with "Amen." There were two lessons from the Old Testament, one from the Law of Moses and one from the prophets. Before and after the lessons certain interludes were sung, and then an explanation of the scripture text was given. In conclusion a sermon was preached by a rabbi.

After the break from the synagogue, this service was christianized and retained as a preparation for the Eucharist. Passages from the New Testament, then developing, were added. About the middle of the second century the basic plan of the Mass stood out clearly: lessons from the Old Testament or epistles, the gospel, homily, and prayers; all this was followed by the celebration of the Eucharist. Then over the centuries minor elements were introduced, some of which tended to obscure the basic simplicity of the Mass as instituted by Christ and handed down by the apostles.

The changes in the Mass which we have experienced since Vatican II have had for their purpose to make the Mass even more clearly a memorial of what our Lord did as carried out by the apostles and their earliest successors. For example, the prayers at the foot of the altar have been replaced by a brief penitential rite. This rite has the same purpose as the washing of the feet at the Last Supper, which, among other things, symbolized the fact that to share in the Lord's Supper the apostles had to be purified from sin. We then ask for God's mercy and praise him in the *Gloria*.

We next listen to God's word in sacred scripture and in the homily, and pray to God in the universal prayer or prayer of the faithful. This liturgy of the word obviously reflects elements of both the Last Supper and the synagogue service. In the offertory we set aside bread and wine from ordinary use, as our Lord set aside the bread and wine used in the Paschal Supper. This bread and wine become the body and blood of Christ just as at the Last Supper, as a sacred sign of his sacrifice on the cross. Then we receive Jesus in holy communion as did the apostles at the Last Supper.

Tonight on this Holy Thursday evening in a very special way we are keeping the command of Christ, "Do this in memory of me." But every Mass is the memorial of the Lord and of what he did to save us from the slavery of sin.

Alternate

On the night before he died our Lord thought of two things. He thought of heaven and he thought of earth. He thought of his Father in heaven and in his human mind he contemplated his wonderful relationship with the Father: all its glory and joy and even ecstasy. What a tremendous thing to be the son of such a Father and to be about to return home! Our Lord thought of earth as well, as he turned his attention to us who live here. Since he loved us, he wanted us to share in his own joy and happiness in being the son of God. "He had loved his own in this world, and would show his love for them to the end." His prayer for us to the Father was: "That all may be one as you, Father, are in me and I in you . . . All those you gave me I would have in my company where I am . . ." (Jn 17:21 ff).

It was in this frame of mind that our Lord instituted the Eucharist, the sign and cause of unity and love in the Church. It is true that we are united to Christ as sons of the Father by means of baptism, but that union is only a beginning, a rudimentary type of oneness. Our union with Christ grows and becomes perfect through our receiving him in holy communion. Little by little the Eucharist will transform us into Christ, enhancing and enriching and making more effective that relationship with the Father begun in baptism.

Our Lord instituted the Eucharist within the context of a family meal, the Last Supper, and we now receive the Eucharist within the context of a family meal, the Mass. A family eating together at the family table and partaking of the same food is a sign of unity. And so our unity with Christ is by its very nature a corporate reality, not an individual one only. It is impossible to come into union with Christ and through him with the Father without coming into union with the other members of God's family. Such union must find its expression in charity, love. This is why at the Last Supper Jesus gave both an example and a command of charity. His example of practical charity was one of service to the apostles: he washed their feet. His command was this: "I give you a new commandment: love one another; such as my love has been for you, so must your love be for each other" (Jn 13:34f).

The mysteries of this day center around the theme of the unity of the Church: in itself, in its cause which is the Eucharist, and in its application which is love. Let us through this liturgical celebration seek the grace to recognize and appreciate our oneness with Christ through the Eucharist, and let us ask for the grace to live this oneness by means of our love for one another.

Good Friday

In the ancient world in which our Lord lived, there was no worse death than that by crucifixion, and no penalty was more feared and despised. Consequently, the soldiers who crucified men expected them to be filled with bitterness and hatred. In fact it is related that executioners often cut out the tongue of the man to be crucified so that he could not curse them and blaspheme God.

The soldiers who crucified Christ were probably old hands at that sort of thing; it was just another day's work for them. Possibly they had seen many men die in crucifixion and in each instance they had witnessed the horror as well as the hatred in the eyes of the condemned man. They had heard his curses and his blasphemies. How amazed they must have been at what seemed to them to be serene resignation on the part of Jesus. If they had penetrated the meaning of the inscription on the cross proclaiming Jesus as King, they would have realized that his death was indeed a victory and the way to his glorification as King of all men. If they had known that Jesus was dying as victim of his own priestly sacrifice, they would have understood that far from wishing to curse them, he was dying for the salvation of all men, and that far from blaspheming God he was offering himself in supreme worship to the Father.

Today we are here not to lament the death of Christ, even though we are in sorrow over our sins because of which Jesus died. Rather we are here to rejoice in the great victory that Jesus the King won by his death. We are here to praise and thank God that he sent his son to be the high priest who won our salvation through the worship of the cross.

Alternate

Each year in the United States we have a Memorial Day in honor of the soldiers who have died on the field of battle in the struggle against the enemies of this country so that we might be preserved in life and freedom. We have been so concerned that none of these heroes be forgotten that in Arlington National Cemetery we have erected the tomb and monument of the unknown soldier.

Today the Church throughout the whole world is having a memorial day in honor of its great hero, its soldier who died. His battle was against Satan and sin, the enemies of our salvation. His battlefield was the cross, and he died that we may have supernatural life and the freedom of the sons of God. Perhaps to many he is an unknown soldier. To others he is little known and less honored.

And yet the whole life of Christ was one of love for people, a love which reached its climax on Good Friday. On the evening before he died, Jesus said at the Last Supper, "There is no greater love than this: to lay down one's life for one's friends." On the cross Jesus freely laid down his life for our salvation. But the amazing thing is that when Jesus did die for us we were not actually his friends. We were his enemies by sin. It is truly wonderful and understandable that a man should die for his loved ones, but it is unheard of that one should die for people who have offended him and are his enemies. St. Paul wrote, "It is rare that anyone should lay down his life for a just man, though it is barely possible that for a good man someone may have the courage to die. It is precisely in this that God proves his love for us: that while we were still sinners, Christ died for us" (Rm 5:7-9).

No one of us need wonder whether Christ loves us. Today we celebrate the memory and the reality of that great love.

Easter Vigil

Tonight, in the words of St. Augustine, we celebrate "the mother of all vigils." It is a fulfillment of the Jewish vigil before Passover. The book of Exodus says, "This was a night of vigil for the Lord, as he led them out of the land of Egypt; so on this same night all the Israelites must keep a vigil for the Lord throughout their generations" (Ex 12:42). Among the Israelites the yearly vigil of passover was a commemoration of the most glorious event of their past, their liberation from the slavery of Egypt. But it also looked to the future in expectation of the coming of the Messiah.

The Christian vigil is, as with all liturgical functions, past, present, and future in its outlook. St. Augustine wrote, "Our annual celebration is not simply a commemoration of a past event; it implies a present action on our part, which we accomplish by our life of faith and of which this vigil is the symbol. The entire course of time is in fact one long night during which the Church keeps watch, waiting for the return of the Lord, waiting 'until he comes.' " There is a very ancient belief, and St. Jerome says that it is apostolic in origin, that Christ will come in glory at the *parousia* in the night of the Easter vigil.

Tonight, then, in faith we have kept vigil, recalling the saving death of our Lord and his glorious resurrection. We have renewed our baptism, which was our original sharing in the death and resurrection of Christ. That baptism gave us the power to participate in the Mass, which makes his sacrificial death and victorious resurrection a reality among us.

Tonight we should make a special effort to join with Christ enthusiastically in the living offering of himself to the Father during the Eucharistic Prayer, and let us receive the glorious body of the resurrected Christ in a spirit of faith and joy.

The deep spiritual happiness that should be ours tonight is not something we can explain or even express. There is, however, one word repeated many times in the liturgy, a word that is meant to give voice to our almost inexpressible happiness, a word that should be in our hearts as well as on our lips as we wait for Christ to come again in glory, and that one word is "Alleluia!"

THE SEASON OF EASTER

Monday of the Octave of Easter

During this entire week the Church continues to celebrate the great feast of Easter. We celebrate not a moment in history, but the meaning of all history. This week of resurrection should make us think back to the week of creation. God in creating us gave us the gift of freedom. Freedom involves the risk of abuse, but God preferred a free service of love to one that would be imposed. Sin is the result of an abuse of our freedom.

In the moment in which God created us free, he also decreed an antidote for sin, the sending of his own Son. This Son through his death would destroy that death which is the penalty for sin, and by rising he would restore the eternal life forfeited by sin. In other words, the death and the resurrection of Jesus are the central event of all history.

On the morning of the resurrection Jesus greeted the women: "Peace," he said. Then he went on: "Do not be afraid!" That is the great Easter message from the Risen Savior. We no longer need be afraid as we journey through life. We can have peace in our hearts because we believe that Jesus has overcome the great obstacle of death. In faith we cry out in the memorial acclamation: "Dying you destroyed our death. Rising you restored our life. Come, Lord Jesus."

Wherever we go, whatever we do, no matter how rich or how poor we may be, one day each of us must face that dark, awesome moment of death. But as people of faith we approach that moment with the realization that Jesus has gone before us in death only to rise triumphant in glory. As we follow him in death, so will we follow him in resurrection.

Tuesday of the Octave of Easter

Mary Magdalen on Easter morning was in the depth of sadness.

Jesus had become the center of her life and now he was dead. Mary could not know how mistaken she was in looking for Jesus among the dead. The great truth of the resurrection had not as yet become part of her faith to dispel her sadness. Her vision still darkened by gloom, she at first failed to recognize Jesus standing before her. She needed to hear only a word from Jesus, and her mind was flooded with the light of faith. She realized that she was in the presence of the Risen Lord.

What happened to Mary Magdalen happens to each of us. The meaning of life is to search for and to find the Risen Lord, for he is the source of all life and happiness. Perhaps at times we make the mistake of looking for happiness among sinful pleasures which can only bring death. Perhaps we make the mistake of thinking that life can come from temporary values, such as financial success or social status. Jesus, the Risen Lord, alone is the source of lasting life and eternal happiness.

In a special way we find Jesus in the eucharist. We hear his word, "This is my body . . . this is my blood." That word is intended to flood our minds with the light of faith so that we can believe that by means of the eucharist we are in the presence of the Risen Lord. The eucharist is the very heart of our faith. Jesus in the eucharist does much more than merely stand before us. He invites us to take him into our being so that he can give us the gift of lasting life and eternal happiness.

Wednesday of the Octave of Easter

The engaging story which we have just heard in the gospel was composed by St. Luke in such a way that we should think about the Mass. By the time the gospel came to be written the expression, "the breaking of the bread," had become a Christian term to signify the Eucharistic celebration. More importantly, at Mass much the same thing happens to us as happened to the two disciples.

Jesus proclaimed to the disciples on the road what the

scriptures had to say about himself. Then he explained their mean- ing. In breaking bread he not only shared a meal with them but also revealed himself. Here at Mass every day we hear the scriptures read. They are explained in the homily. In our "breaking of bread," our spiritual meal, Jesus presents himself to us as the one who has passed through death to glory and thereby attained our salvation. In the Mass we come to know Jesus in two ways: through the words of scripture he enters our minds and through the eucharist he enters our hearts. We come to know him.

"To know someone" according to the scriptural usage means to enter into an intimate union with him. In fact, this is the same term used to describe the intimate sexual union of husband and wife. Jesus wants us to grow in our intimacy with him through our daily celebration of the Mass.

In one sense Jesus says, like the apostles in the first reading, that he does not give us silver and gold. Rather he gives us something much more precious, himself. We must never grow tired of this gift or fail to appreciate it. Part of the human condition is to take something for granted, especially something which happens every day. Few of us ever reflect on what a marvel it is that a new day begins, that the sun continues to shine, that our hearts go on beating. We take all this for granted. With each new day Jesus offers us the word of the scriptures to shine in our hearts and he gives us his body and blood to enliven our hearts. That indeed is something we must never take for granted.

Thursday of the Octave of Easter

In almost all of his resurrection appearances Jesus greets his disciples by saying, "Peace be with you." He seems eager to dispel any fear in their hearts. When you think about it, without faith we have every reason to live in fear. There is fear of sickness and disease, fear of economic uncertainty, fear of loneliness and rejec- tion, and even fear of annihilation in an atomic war. Human existence could easily be overwhelmed by fear, but such need not be the case if we have faith in Jesus Christ and his resurrection from the dead.

God has shown that we need have no fear about the future. We find a person trustworthy when he has proven himself. If a doctor has been able to cure you in the past, you have confidence in him when he tells you that you are going to recover from a current illness. If you are lost on a strange road with a driver who has always been able to find his way, you are willing to put yourself in his hands.

Jesus in his resurrection demonstrated that he had overcome sin and death. In fact, through his entire ministry, as well as in his death and resurrection, he revealed that he fulfilled all the promises God had made throughout the Old Testament era. That is the main point St. Peter wanted to make in the sermon we heard in the first reading today. In other words, God has shown us that he is trustworthy. We all suffered the sickness of sin, and the human race was ill unto death. Jesus, the divine physician, cured us of the ultimate effect of that sickness, which is eternal death. In another sense, we were lost on the way which leads to God and our heavenly home. Jesus knows the way; in fact he is the way to the Father. We can confidently place ourselves in his hands.

The words of Jesus, "Peace be with you," are not an empty greeting. They express the great gift which should dissipate all fear from our lives. Because of our union with Jesus we can live our lives with peace in our hearts.

Friday of the Octave of Easter

The episode in today's gospel took place sometime between Easter Sunday and Pentecost. The apostles were in a state of confusion. They felt lost and alone without Jesus and wondered what the future held for them. When Jesus appeared to them, the first thing he did was to give them something to eat. He did so because feeding a person is a profound sign of love.

Notice how mothers are always eager to show their love to their adult children when they return home for a visit. They want to feed them. Over any protest about not being hungry or being on a diet, a mother usually insists that her child eat something. I suppose that feeling is such a natural urge for a mother because a mother has the privilege of nourishing her infant at her breast. She does so with milk which she has created within her own body. In giving her own milk a mother comes very close to nourishing her infant with her own body and blood. What a mother cannot do, Jesus can. He can and does feed us with his own body and blood.

As a sign of his great love, Jesus has left us a special food and drink. For this food and drink, we must always hunger. A diet from this nourishment is the worst kind of foolishness. From the table of the Lord we must not absent ourselves. We are in the same period of time, between Easter and Pentecost, as were the apostles during their time of confusion. Lest we ever think that Jesus has gone away and no longer loves us, he has left us the Holy Eucharist, the spiritual nourishment of his body and blood. The Eucharist is the great sign of the love which Jesus has for us.

Saturday of the Octave of Easter

Faith is a gift from God. It is not something we can earn or acquire by our own efforts. There is a mystery about how God grants this gift. A person can read the whole Bible, study the best of theologians, and listen to the most persuasive of preachers without coming to faith.

St. Peter and St. John, as we heard in the first reading, went about preaching the resurrection of Christ. They even cured a cripple as a sign that their words were from God. And still the officials of the people would not believe them. We should not be surprised. It is no easy thing to believe that a man has come back from the dead! Mary Magdalen announced to the followers of Jesus the good news that she had seen Jesus alive after his death. They refused to believe her. Again, we should not be surprised. It is indeed no easy thing to believe that a man has come back from the dead!

What ought to surprise us is our own faith. Some of us may think we have faith because we happened to have been born of Catholic parents who saw to it that we were baptized as infants. Others may have become converts later in life and think that faith came from the good example or the teaching of others. But some people, baptized as infants, have rejected the faith later in life. Some people have witnessed good example and heard sound teaching without converting.

In the final analysis we must all stand before God in wonder that for his own good reasons, and without any merit of our own, he has freely chosen to give us faith as a gift. And faith makes all the difference in our lives. In this eucharist, this worship of thanksgiving, we must offer to God the most profound gratitude for the great gift of faith.

Monday of the Second Week of Easter

Throughout this Easter season our first reading at Mass will be taken from the Acts of the Apostles. This book, composed by St. Luke, tells the story of the pristine Church after the resurrection of Christ. The Church was born from the side of Christ dying upon the cross. When the physical Christ died, the mystical Christ was born. Jesus, like a mother dying in childbirth, gave up his life so that we might be given a new life in the Spirit.

What happened for the Church as a whole on Good Friday happened for us on the day of our baptism. We were born of water and the Spirit, given a share in the life of Christ and thereby made children of the Father. We became brothers and sisters of one another, the family of God. What we read in the Acts of the Apostles forms a plan for our own lives as Christians. For example, in today's reading we see that the Christians were a community of believers who were eager to share their faith, even in the face of dire threats. We also see that they were a prayerful people. In their prayers and in their lives they were led by the Holy Spirit.

The life of the Church is summed up in an earlier chapter of the Acts of the Apostles. It states: "They devoted themselves to the apostles' instruction and the communal life, to the breaking of bread and the prayers" (Ac 2:42). The apostles' instruction is preserved in the writings of the New Testament and in the sacred tradition of the Church. We hear this instruction every day at Mass. The "breaking of the bread" is the New Testament term for the Mass, which we celebrate with prayers. The communal life refers to the life of caring for each other in love. In other words, the life of the Church as described in the Acts of the Apostles is indeed the blueprint for our lives.

Tuesday of the Second Week of Easter

In today's first reading we see a beautiful ideal of Christian living. The community of believers were of one heart and one mind, and everything was held in common. This group in Jerusalem was so small that a family atmosphere prevailed. Their arrangement was ideal since through baptism they had all become God's children and brothers and sisters of one another. They were indeed a family.

Circumstances are vastly different for us. The church is now truly catholic, worldwide. Even within a single parish it is impossible to know every Catholic. Our economic system is complex, based on a highly competitive spirit and entangled in a tax system so elaborate that it is virtually out of control. Making money is for some a way of life rather than a means of support and social status is very often determined by one's monetary worth. In short, ours is a materialistic society. Within this context, in such shocking contrast with gospel values, it seems unrealistic to attempt to model our lives on the Jerusalem community of unselfish Christians who were dedicated to God and each other.

Some members of the Church attempt to follow the ideals of the Jerusalem community by joining a religious order and by taking a solemn vow of poverty. Such is, of course, not the vocation of every Christian. Nonetheless, we are all called by God to live with each other in a family spirit of unselfish sharing and mutual concern. We must not lightly dismiss this ideal as an impossibility in our world.

In the Mass we have a model of ideal Christian living as well as a source of strength to put that ideal into practice. Here we come together as one poeple of faith. Without charge we receive the most precious spiritual food from God who feeds us as a loving parent. This spiritual nourishment, the body and blood of God's son, unites us as one body, one spirit in Christ. To be true to the Mass we must have an unselfish love and concern for each other.

Wednesday of the Second Week of Easter

"Love" is a word which is used so frequently that it has practically lost its force. The word is also used in so many different senses that it has practically lost its value. People say that they love their children, their dog, and Monday night football.

Actually "love" is a precious word which we ought to use precisely and with meaning, never carelessly or cheaply. We should be prepared to back up the use of this word with action. God uses this word wisely and well. He does not use it in a shallow sense as do those who are merely infatuated with each other. Nor does he use it lightly as we do when we say that we love a good steak. God tells us that he loves us, and he means what he says.

We know that God has a profound love for us because he has backed up his words with action. One characteristic of true love is generosity, a generosity which knows no limit. Love and giving, when understood properly, are synonymous. How much does God love us? The answer is in today's gospel: "God so loved the world that he gave his only Son." God simply had no gift to give more precious than his only begotten Son. Nor is his gift merely precious and actually useless, as is a diamond which a man gives to his wife. God's gift is both immeasurably precious and eminently practical. The gospel goes on to say that God gave his only Son that whoever believes in him may not die but may have eternal life.

If ever we are tempted to wonder whether God loves us, we need only reflect on the words of today's gospel: "God so loved the world that he gave his only Son that whoever believes in him may not die but may have eternal life."

Thursday of the Second Week of Easter

When the apostles after Pentecost went about fulfilling their duty of proclaiming the word, they met with opposition, especially from the Sanhedrin, the ruling body of their people. They were threatened with death if they did not stop their preaching. Peter and the apostles responded in words which contain an important principle for us today: "Better for us to obey God than men!"

The Christianity proclaimed by the apostles is more than a body of teachings. It is a way of life. In fact the purpose of the teachings is to lead us to live in accord with God's will. In attempting to follow God's will, we will meet with opposition. Think about the pressures from our society, pressures to accept birth control, abortion, and now even incest! There are actually those who propose that friendly incest, as opposed to violent incest, is normal and acceptable. Young people are being brainwashed to believe that there is nothing wrong with premarital sex or the use of drugs. Much of the spirit of our economic system, based on the competitive syndrome, lead many to ignore the need for social justice and induces a contempt for the poor who can survive only on welfare.

The apostles were a small group but because of courage in their convictions they helped to transform the world. We should never think that we can do nothing. With God's grace we can be faithful and loyal to his teachings and we can influence others. Often we may not even be aware of how much good we are doing by the witness of our lives. In any event we must live by the words of the apostles, "Better to obey God than men!"

Friday of the Second Week of Easter

Today we began reading from a very long chapter in St. John's gospel. It is the sixth chapter and it is St. John's profound presentation of the eucharist. To borrow an expression from the first reading, the eucharist does indeed come from God and nothing has been able to destroy Catholic faith in the eucharist for almost two thousand years.

The chapter begins with an episode quite familiar to us, the miraculous feeding of the five thousand. What Jesus did was an act of compassion for the crowd who had been with Jesus all day and had nothing to eat. And yet we will look in vain for any mention of compassion by the evangelist. The reason is that he wanted us to understand this miracle on a deeper level. What Jesus did was a sign of extraordinary power over physical reality, bread in particular. Jesus showed that he had power over bread, a power which he exercises in the eucharist. We should not get caught up in the question of just how the miracle took place. Such is not the point. As Jesus somehow multiplied bread to satisfy a natural hunger, so in the eucharist he multiplies his presence under the appearance of bread to satisfy a spiritual hunger.

Ultimately the action of Jesus is indeed one of compassion, but his concern goes beyond physical need. Understanding our spiritual need and overflowing with love, he uses his divine power to give us the gift of the eucharist.

In writing this passage St. John noted that the Jewish feast of Passover was near. It was in connection with the Passover, while celebrating the supper with his disciples, that Jesus instituted the

Holy Eucharist and left it as a memorial of himself for all time. We, then, are the people who gathered around Jesus on that spring day. We are the ones toward whom he has shown the greatest love and compassion.

Saturday of the Second Week of Easter

Yesterday in the gospel we saw Jesus miraculously feed five thousand people. It was a miracle of compassion, not unlike the concern of the apostles mentioned in the first reading, but it was more. It was a sign of the power which Jesus has over material elements, bread in particular, a power which he exercises in the Eucharist. Today we see Jesus perform another sign, the walking on the water.

In the Old Testament power over water was seen as a sign of divinity. We need think only of the mighty power of God which parted the waters of the Red Sea for the passage of the Israelites. Jesus "conquered" the waters not only by walking over the waves but also by quieting the storm. This miracle was another step in the gradual revelation of his true character as Son of God. It was a sign of the power which Jesus as divine has over his own body.

The multiplication of the loaves and the walking on the water fit together as one sign concerning the Eucharist. They show that Jesus has the power to multiply the presence of his body under the appearances of bread. Jesus is concerned about our physical welfare, but he is even more deeply concerned about our spiritual welfare. These two events in the gospel of John are an invitation to have faith in the Eucharist, to believe that Jesus is so powerful that he can nourish us with his body and that he loves us so much that he is eager to give us the gift of himself in a most extraordinary manner.

Monday of the Third Week of Easter

Being misunderstood is probably one of the most disheartening of human experiences. Jesus worked great signs among his people, such as the multiplication of the loaves to feed five thousand, and yet the people failed to understand him. Jesus wanted to draw people to himself as their Savior, but they were interested only in satisfying their human needs.

St. Stephen, a deacon, followed in the footsteps of Jesus. He too worked great wonders and signs among his own people. His only intention was to draw them in faith to the person of Jesus Christ as their Savior. Not only did some of his own people fail to understand, they actually turned against him, and went so far as to bring false witness against him before the Sanhedrin, the ruling body of the Jews. Tomorrow we will see how he suffered a martyr's death.

Both Jesus and his follower, Stephen, were strengthened by the realization that they were doing God's will. Their pain was not lessened, but their determination was left undaunted.

No matter how careful we are with others, no matter how loving our intention, we will face misunderstanding, sometimes even actual rejection. The natural reaction is simply to give up on another person. But God calls us to an attitude and way of acting which at times may even be heroic. It is not the Christian approach to meet misunderstanding with disdain or rejection with contempt. God calls us to use every avenue possible to communicate properly with others and to overcome misunderstandings. Such an approach is especially vital toward those with whom we live or work. And through all our efforts at reconciliation, we should have a certain serenity and peace of mind derived from the realization that we are following the example given us by Jesus and the saints.

Tuesday of the Third Week of Easter

St. Stephen was the first Christian martyr. In the earliest days of the Church only those who, like St. Stephen, suffered a martyr's death were recognized as saints. The reason was that sanctity is conformity to Christ, and one who died as Christ did, a witness to the truth, was seen to be truly holy. When the period of persecution ended and martyrdom became rare, the Church examined its understanding of sanctity. She recognized that being like Christ is the correct criterion of sanctity but she realized that physical martyrdom was not the only sign of such conformity.

Today we recognize a very large number of people as saints who underwent a natural death. Each one of these saints manifested some special characteristics of Christ since no one saint can completely reflect the sanctity of Jesus himself. In St. Vincent de Paul we see the love and care which Jesus had for the poor. We observe in St. Francis of Assisi the poverty of Jesus himself. St. Therese, the Little Flower, shows us his simplicity and devotion to his Father. St. Piux X, who lowered the age for first communion from twelve to about seven, manifests the love which Jesus had for little children.

Each one of us is called to be a saint. We may never be canonized by the Church, but our basic vocation in life is to live as Jesus did. We need not, in my opinion, try to determine the specific manner in which we will be like Jesus. Rather we must draw upon the most important source for becoming like Jesus, and that is the Holy Eucharist. Jesus in the gospel today proclaims, "I am the bread of life." He wishes to give us a share in his own life, and that is what sanctity is all about.

Wednesday of the Third Week of Easter

Tertullian, an early Church Father who died about the year 230, declared that the blood of martyrs is the seed of Christians. It was his poetic way of declaring that the Church grows through suffering, especially the suffering of persecution. The persecution of the primitive Church which started with the martyrdom of St. Stephen saw the first spread of the faith beyond Jerusalem. This was the beginning of the Church as truly catholic, for from this time the faith was preached and received in all Judea and Samaria, throughout Asia Minor and Greece, and finally to Rome and the ends of the earth, as Jesus had commanded just before his ascension.

The faith was spread by devout men and women who endured much suffering, often martyrdom so that Christ could be known and loved. There is a mystery in God's plan which we cannot pretend to comprehend, but for some reason suffering plays an important part both in preaching the gospel and in following it. Jesus himself had to undergo crucifixion and death for our salvation. In fact, the Eucharist itself is the fruit of his death on the cross. He gives us the gift of the Eucharist so that we may have everlasting life, but the price of life is death.

Every human life is coupled with suffering, whether it be physical, mental or emotional. As people of faith we are asked to see God's loving hand for his own purposes in all the forms of suffering we must endure. During this Easter season as we continue to celebrate the resurrection of Christ, we must remember that for him glory came from suffering, joy came from sorrow, and life came from death. We follow in the footsteps of Christ and what was true for him is true for us. Because in faith we embrace the cross of suffering, we will have a resurrection to glory.

Thursday of the Third Week of Easter

We will not be amiss if we look upon the first reading today in a broad, symbolic fashion. Notice that the Ethiopian was reading the scriptures when Philip caught up with him. Philip asked, "Do you really grasp what you are reading?" The man replied, "How can I unless someone explains it to me?" Philip then became his teacher. In a real sense Philip represents the Church and all its tradition. The Ethiopian represents any person of good will who wishes to know more about his faith.

It is important for us to understand that the scriptures belong to the Church and must be understood in light of its tradition. In fact, the Church as a body of believers who preached their faith in Jesus Christ existed before the New Testament was composed. The oldest book of the New Testament, the First Letter to the Thessalonians, was composed no earlier than about the year 50 A.D. The Church today, looking back upon its tradition of twenty centuries, is the only final interpreter of the scriptures.

A good case in point is the teaching of Jesus in the gospel whereby he declares, "The bread I will give is my flesh for the life of the world." The Church understands that the Eucharist is truly the body of Christ which we receive in communion. This understanding was not even questioned until the eleventh century and then the matter was confounded in the sixteenth century. Many people today, for a reason I cannot understand, refuse to take this teaching of Jesus literally. And yet the Church assures us, not by a twentieth century interpretation, but by an ancient and abiding tradition, that Jesus meant what he said.

We should rejoice that we have the Church as a sure and safe guide for interpreting the scriptures. With her guidance and tradition we will never go astray.

Friday of the Third Week of Easter

Today's readings couple an important truth concerning the presence of Christ in people and in the Eucharist. They help us to see how Jesus Christ is truly the center and the heart of Christianity.

Saul was persecuting the Christians. On the road to Damascus he was struck to the ground and he heard the voice saying, "Saul, Saul, why do you persecute me?" It was the voice of Jesus Christ. This episode took place after the death and resurrection of Jesus. Saul had never even seen Jesus before his death on the cross. And yet Jesus was accusing Paul of persecuting him. The reason is that

Jesus truly lives in his followers. Note that Jesus did not say that it was as if Paul were persecuting him or that he considered what was done to his followers as having been done to himself. He declared quite plainly, "I am Jesus, the one you are persecuting." We must not water down these words of Jesus. We must take them literally, for Jesus does live in his followers.

With an equal emphasis Jesus in the gospel proclaims, "My flesh is real food and my blood is real drink." We must not water down these words of Jesus either. We must take them literally too, for Jesus is truly present in the Holy Eucharist, a spiritual food and drink.

Our faith must be complete. As we believe that Jesus is present in the Eucharist, so we must believe that he is present in his people. As we believe that Jesus is present in his people, so we must believe that he is present in the Eucharist. The two truths must be coupled as one, for they are in a sense the two sides of one coin.

Saturday of the Third Week of Easter

In today's first reading we see St. Peter performing miracles by curing the sick and even raising the dead. These are the kinds of things we are used to seeing Jesus do in the gospel. In fact, in the first reading we could have easily substituted the name Jesus for Peter and the reading would have sounded much like a gospel narrative—except for one important element. Jesus performed miracles in his own name and by his own power. St. Peter performed miracles but only in the name of Jesus and by his power. Notice how clearly St. Peter made this point when he said to Aeneas, the paralytic, "Aeneas, Jesus Christ cures you!"

This power of Jesus Christ is still with us in the Church, especially in the Holy Eucharist. In fact, Jesus made faith in his Eucharistic presence an ultimate test of true discipleship. As we have been hearing the past few days in the gospel of John, Jesus was unequivocal in his declaration that the bread he would give is his flesh for the life of the world. In today's gospel we see the reaction of many of the disciples who protested that the words of Jesus were hard to endure. When Jesus insisted on his doctrine, many of them broke away and would not remain in his company any longer. Jesus did not call them back. He did not say, "Wait, you do not understand; I am not talking literally, only figuratively." No, he let them walk away because faith in the Eucharist was critical to being a true disciple. Jesus even challenged the twelve, "Do you want to leave me too?" The day on which he promised the Eucharist was the day of decision.

Thanks be to God that we have responded to the gift of faith whereby we believe in the Eucharist. Today we ought to recognize how central the Eucharist is to our faith and how necessary for us it is never to waver from our appreciation of this great gift of the body and the blood of Jesus Christ.

Monday of the Fourth Week of Easter

Real baseball fans remember when Jackie Robinson broke into the major leagues with the Brooklyn Dodgers. Robinson was an excellent baseball player, but the notable thing about him in that era was that he was black. Until the owner of the Dodgers was bold enough to hire him, it was simply taken for granted that major league baseball was a sport for white men only. Although it is impossible now to think of professional baseball without black players, opposition to Jackie Robinson was rather forceful from some of the players and even some of the fans.

In the early Church it was at first taken for granted that Christianity was for Jews only. When some of the Christians at Jerusalem heard that Gentiles too had become followers of Christ, they objected. Peter was challenged on the point and responded by explaining the vision he had which makes it clear that God was calling all people to salvation through Jesus Christ. Jesus is the gate, as he declares in the gospel. Through him all peoples are invited to enter into the kingdom of God.

These days it is difficult for us to imagine how anyone could have thought that Christianity was meant to be exclusive. Nonetheless, we must constantly make sure that our attitude is the same as God's about people. Even the slightest hint of excluding anyone from our love and concern is not in accord with his will. Actually we must make positive efforts to reach out in sharing his love with everyone we meet.

Tuesday of the Fourth Week of Easter

The first followers of Jesus did not immediately give a name to themselves and their religion. Possibly their thinking was like that which Shakespeare would later formulate by writing in *Romeo and Juliet*, "That which we call a rose by any other name would smell as sweet." Today's scripture informs us that it was in Antioch that the disciples were called Christians for the first time. Apparently the name was coined spontaneously, but it is indeed an appropriate name.

Some names indicate only the nationality or the citizenship of a person, such as American, German, Italian, and so on. There is no intrinsic significance to these names, as is evidenced by the fact that one may easily change his citizenship. The same is true of the names given members of clubs or fraternities and sororities. But the name of Christian makes all the difference in the world and even in the next world. "Christian" indicates much more than nationality or citizenship and infinitely more than membership in a club. To be a Christian is to be like Christ himself, a child of God and an heir of God the Father's eternal kingdom. Through baptism we take on a whole new identity. In earlier times the popular name for baptism was christening, and that name brings out the true character of this fundamental sacrament. By baptism we are "christened," made like Christ.

Because we are Christians, we are most precious in the eyes of God. Jesus says about us, "I give them eternal life, and they shall never perish." Our new identity should give us great confidence in God's love. We can and should go through life with a sense of peace and serenity for we bear the name, "Christian."

Wednesday of the Fourth Week of Easter

God can deal with us in anyway he chooses. God is all powerful and so in our thinking we must never limit his way of acting. Still God most often interacts with us through other human beings. This is especially true since the time of the incarnation.

Jesus is the son of the Father from all eternity and equal to his Father in all things. Yet at the moment of the incarnation in accord with the will of his Father he became human like us in all things but sin. Jesus was sent to us in the flesh by his Father. That is what Jesus had in mind when he said, "Whoever puts faith in me believes not so much in me as in him who sent me." And as Jesus was sent by the Father, so other human beings are sent by the Holy Spirit to continue the mission of Jesus on earth. We see an example of this commissioning in the first reading. The Holy Spirit declared: "Set apart Barnabas and Saul for me to do the work for which I have called them."

In Jesus God wanted to be close to us in a way which we could understand and appreciate. God continues to be close to us through the bishops and priests and other ministers of the Church. We ought to rejoice that God has chosen to deal with us in a human way. This is still another sign of his love and concern for us. Although human ministers are weak and make mistakes, God in his wisdom sees that his way is best for us.

Thursday of the Fourth Week of Easter

Serious athletes are people of great dedication. They train and work for years, day in and day out. They diet, get regular sleep, and take good care of themselves. Their preparation, perhaps without their realizing it, goes back to their conception in which heredity gave them the means needed for developing healthy and strong bodies. Their preparation was taking form even during their years of growing up. For a man like Bruce Jenner, winning the decathlon in the Olympics was the culmination of such intense preparation and training.

St. Paul's thinking about Jesus as expressed during his sermon in the synagogue at Antioch reflected this same idea of culmination. He reviewed for his hearers the history of salvation. All that had happened to the Chosen People was part of God's plan, a long, patient plan of preparation for that supreme moment of history, known as the fullness of time, when Jesus came into the world, died and rose from the dead. This great event of the life, death, and resurrection of Jesus is rightly viewed as the culmination of all history, the center point of all time, the most significant happening of all human experience.

We have been born into the world during the continuation of this fullness of time. We stand at a vantage point of history when we have the opportunity, by God's grace, to participate fully in the death and resurrection of Jesus. Jesus has preserved the central point of history in the Holy Eucharist. The Mass is not the mere presence of Jesus. It is a happening, an event. It is the reality of the death and resurrection of Jesus Christ.

Friday of the Fourth Week of Easter

Sometimes famous men and women are asked to name the most influential person in their lives. The idea behind the question is that usually people do not rise to prominence without the help of some significant person in their lives. We may not think of ourselves as prominent, but as a matter of fact we are very important in God's eyes.

The most influential and significant person in our lives is Jesus Christ. He is our way, our truth, and our life. Without the way there is no going, without the truth there is no knowing, and without the life there is no living. But in following Jesus we can be sure that we are on the right way, a path that leads to true happiness. In embracing the truth that is Jesus we are certain that we have the correct understanding of, and approach to, human existence. And by accepting Jesus as the life we are made like him, children of God, favored and beloved by God the Father.

Someone once said that life without Christ is like living at O'Hare airport in Chicago. That airport is a confusing, impersonal, madhouse of bustling humanity. Amid thousands of people you can feel completely lost and alone. It is so large and sprawling that you are lucky to find your way on time to the right place for the departure of your plane.

But with Christ we are not a lost soul amid a madding throng. Rather through him we are in union with an untold number of brothers and sisters in the family of God, the Church. We are all on the same journey with the sure, safe guidance of Christ. Filled with the life of Christ we are already well on our way to our eternal destiny. How blessed we are that Jesus Christ is for us the way, the truth and the life.

Saturday of the Fourth Week of Easter

Although all of the first Christians were Jews, Paul and other preachers did not succeed in winning a mass conversion from among their own people. The purpose of their preaching was to gain acceptance for what Jesus himself proclaims to us in today's gospel, that he and the Father are one. Jesus is God in the flesh, come among us as our savior and the light of our lives to guide us in our journey toward the Father's heavenly kingdom.

We should not be surprised at the lack of success experienced by Paul since even today our own society as a whole does not in reality accept Jesus Christ. By some Jesus is relegated to the role of a good man with high ideals who in their judgment is not possessed of any divine attributes. By others he is summarily dismissed as a charlatan or the product of the imagination of his followers. We are not immune from these hostile influences which surround us.

Within our society there are those who are more willing to put their confidence in television commentators and newspaper editors than they are in Jesus Christ. They give more credence to the counsel of psychologists than they do to the teaching of the gospel. And they wish to follow the life of self-indulgence rather than accept the demands of discipleship for personal sacrifice and generosity. They mistake sexual license for true love, and pleasure for happiness.

Christianity is not meant to be a dour or sullen approach to life. Rather it is the source of true, lasting happiness. Abbot Marmion, a Benedictine monk who lived earlier in this century, liked to stress that "joy is the echo of God's life within us." There should be a joy within us as we attempt to follow Christ toward eternal life.

Monday of the Fifth Week of Easter

It seems to me that Paul and Barnabas could easily have given in to the temptation to accept being treated as gods by the people of Lystra. Up to this point they had been undergoing rejection and persecution by the leaders of their own people. Now the exact opposite was true. In a moment, if they wished, they could go from rejection to absolute authority and from persecution to adulation and riches. These days there are not only some people who have given in to this kind of temptation; there are those who under the guise of a phony religion have actually fostered for themselves the reaction paid to Paul and Barnabas.

Why were Paul and Barnabas so different that they were horrified at the mere suggestion that they were gods? The reason is that they knew full well that any power they possessed or any good they accomplished was due to God alone. They understood the truth of what Jesus teaches today in the gospel: "Anyone who loves me will be true to my word, and my Father will love him; we will come to him and make our dwelling place with him." God working within Paul and Barnabas cured the man lame from birth, and he was responsible for any worthwhile thing they achieved.

We do not expect to do anything as astounding as to cure a man lame from birth, but like Paul and Barnabas we must realize that God lives and acts within us. Whatever good we do or evil we overcome, is the result of that presence and action of God and not of any power or talent we may think we have as our own. In this Mass we are called to give praise, not to ourselves, but to the one true God who makes his dwelling place within us.

Tuesday of the Fifth Week of Easter

Peace is a beautiful reality, impossible to define and yet experienced by all of us at some time. Peace can be thought of in a negative way, such as an absence of war between nations, or a lack of turmoil within a family, or freedom from anxiety in one's heart. But true peace is something positive. Underlying all kinds of peace is a sense of tranquility and harmony which come from unity. Nations are truly at peace with one another, not when there is no relation at all between them, but when they cooperate with each other. A family is at peace, not when everyone has moved out of the house, but when they have learned to live together in harmony. A person is at peace, not when he ignores his problems, but when he has come to rest confidently in the loving arms of Jesus Christ.

Peace, then, is something positive and something very precious. It is this positive peace which is the farewell gift of Jesus to his disciples and to us. His words are earnest: "Peace is my farewell to you, my peace is my gift to you; do not be distressed or fearful." Jesus did not, however, stop with words. He gave us a means to find peace. And that means is his body and blood in the

Eucharist. There is a connection between peace and the Eucharist. That is why the prayers before communion turn to the theme of peace.

Putting it somewhat technically, the Eucharist is the effective sign of unity in the Church. This statement means simply that we all become one in Christ. We all receive one and the same Christ in communion. By uniting each individual to himself, he unites all of us with each other. He is our bond of union. His wish is that tranquility and harmony will come about through this unity.

If we are true to the Eucharist, if we respond to the grace granted us in holy communion, we will find a true peace in our hearts and we will live in peace with each other.

Wednesday of the Fifth Week of Easter

There are many aspects of our religion which today pose no particular problem for us, even though in earlier times they may have been the subject of controversy. For example, I doubt that any Catholic today would maintain that our religion should be limited to only one nationality or group of people, least of all the Jews. And yet the disciples of Jesus were all Jewish and the vast majority of the first Christians were also Jewish. After the resurrection of Jesus, many people believed that to be his followers it was necessary to follow completely the Jewish religion with all its laws and regulations. Put simply, they saw no real distinction between Judaism and Christianity.

This misunderstanding is the background of today's first reading. Tomorrow in the first reading we will see how the Church moved to correct the situation. But today's gospel gives us an important insight. Jesus by means of the allegory of the vine and the branches wished to indicate that he was the source of life for his followers. Earlier in St. John's gospel (Wednesday of the 2nd Week of Easter), we heard Jesus proclaim, "God so loved the world that he gave his only Son that whoever believes in him may not die but may have eternal life." In this statement, "world" does not refer to the planet but to all its inhabitants of all times without exception. Jesus is the Savior of all men, whether they be Jews or Gentiles, white or black, oriental or occidental. Ours is a truly catholic, that is, universal religion.

Today we should have a great sense of solidarity with all people of our faith throughout the world. We all believe one doctrine, follow one moral law, and celebrate one Eucharist. That worldwide unity is the hallmark of our religion. To be Catholic is to be universal in faith, in devotion, and in love.

Thursday of the Fifth Week of Easter

Yesterday we saw evidence of the controversy in the primitive Church concerning whether converts had to be circumcised and to follow the Law of Moses in order to be a Christian. St. Paul was adamantly in favor of freedom from the Jewish law. It is noteworthy, however, that he did not make a decision on his own. He returned to the Jerusalem community, the center of the faith at that time, to consult with the other apostles. Peter, the acknowledged head of the apostles, was the first to speak up and was followed by James who was in charge of the Jerusalem community.

The controversy over Mosaic practice is no longer of concern to us. That problem has been settled, but the manner in which it was settled is of importance to us. Paul needed to know what the entire community thought of the matter. The point is that in the Catholic Church there is no private interpretation. To put it more positively, God has revealed his truth, not to individuals, but to a community, the Church. The Second Vatican Council has delcared that "It has pleased God to save men and to make them holy not merely as individuals without any mutual bonds, but by forming them into a single people" (*Constitution on the Church*, 9).

The celebration of the Mass is the best manifestation of the nature of the Church. We celebrate, not as individuals, but as one people united in faith with fellow Catholics throughout the world and back across the centuries to the time of the apostles themselves.

Friday of the Fifth Week of Easter

As we have seen for the past two days in the first reading, the Church had to come to grips with the question of whether Christians were required to follow the law of Moses. Accepting the right doctrine was traumatic for many people. Many of the Jewish converts felt that the Church was taking away the traditions of their ancestors and depriving them of practices with which they had grown up. It was difficult for them to see what was essential to faith and what was peripheral and unnecessary. The distinction was important because the Church cannot impose unnecessary ideas as a matter of faith.

The body of the apostles who decided the matter has often been referred to as the Council of Jerusalem, and the Second Vatican Council bears a similarity to it. Since the Vatican Council a number of Catholics think that the Church has taken away the foundation of their faith and deprived them of practices which they enjoyed from their childhood. The matter is not a simple one because some people have perpetrated abuses in the name of Vatican II. On the other hand, we ought to understand clearly that the Council was guided by the Holy Spirit as surely as were those leaders of the Church gathered for the Council of Jerusalem. Following the clear directives of any ecumenical council of the Church will never lead us astray from sound doctrine or practice.

The Council wished to emphasize the essential practices of the Church in order to put them in clear light. For this brief homily, suffice it to say that the Mass and the Sacraments are the core of our Catholic practice. Other devotions are good and helpful for certain people at certain times. These devotions need to change with the needs of people. But the Mass and the Sacraments stand as absolutely essential. That is one clear and unmistakable message of the Second Vatican Council.

Saturday of the Fifth Week of Easter

St. Paul was a traveling missionary. He went from town to town and even country to country in order to preach the good news. His journeys were not like those of a tourist. They meant hard work and sleepless nights, with no place to call home. Nor was the reaction of the people always favorable. Paul fulfilled the words of Jesus in the gospel, "They will harry you as they harried me. They will respect your words as much as they respected mine." And yet when Paul in a vision heard the touching plea of the man of Macedonia, "Come over to Macedonia and help us," he responded immediately. The reason was his conviction that God had summoned him.

We have the faith because of St. Paul and others like him. Throughout the centuries earnest Catholics, both priests and lay people, have generously responded to the call to be missionaries. They helped spread the faith as witnesses to Christ in Jerusalem and in all Judea and Samaria and even to the very ends of the earth (cf. Ac 1:8).

The Church is missionary by its very nature, as Vatican II has proclaimed. That is why it is so important that we respond to missionary appeals through prayer and financial contributions. Such is an act of gratitude for our own faith. But there is more. Every Catholic is called to be a witness to faith in Jesus Christ by word and example. Faith is not a possession to be hoarded; it is a gift to be shared. We are called to show forth the power of faith by the goodness of our lives, especially the love we readily show others. Strengthened by the nourishment of the Eucharist, we should never hesitate to invite others to accept the gift of faith. Each one of us is a missionary in his own way.

Monday of the Sixth Week of Easter

St. Paul and his companions made a journey to Macedonia, not on a whim, but because Paul in a vision saw a man of Macedonia who pleaded with him, "Come over to Macedonia and help us." St. Paul responded because he was committed to follow the direction of Jesus in today's gospel, "You must bear witness." The result of his journey was a great success, for he founded a community of faith in Philippi, a leading city in the district of Macedonia. The Church flourished there and the Philippians became favorites among Paul's converts.

We may wonder just what was the nature of the vision Paul had. Who was the man who asked for help? Was it perhaps Christ himself in the guise of a Macedonian? We have no way of answering these questions, but something does stand out clearly for us. God can call us in anyway he chooses, but usually he does so in a very human way. Actually there was no need for Jesus to take up the guise of Macedonian since he acts in and through other human beings.

What this means for us is that in responding to others in need, we are responding to Christ himself. The poor and hungry person is Christ seeking something to eat. The lonely person who needs someone to listen to him is Christ seeking companionship. The person who is ill and suffering is Jesus in his passion. The needs of our fellow human beings contain the call of Christ to us to reach out with a helping hand and loving heart.

St. Vincent de Paul, the great apostle of charity, used to say, "Let us love God, but let it be at the expense of our arms and in the sweat of our brows." That was his way of saying that we must respond to the needs of Christ as they are found in other people.

Tuesday of the Sixth Week of Easter

Jesus promised that the Holy Spirit, the Paraclete, would reveal the truth about himself to the Church. This guidance of the Holy Spirit has fulfilled the words of Jesus and has manifested a great irony in the divine plan. He has shown that the view of the world about Jesus is just the opposite of the truth.

Think back to some circumstances of the crucifixion. Those who plotted the death of Jesus did so out of a false piety by which they pretended to be doing God's will. But the fact is that Jesus was not guilty of sin; they were guilty of sin by not believing in him. Some people ridiculed Jesus for calling God his Father, and jeered that if God were his Father he would save him. They did not understand that it was precisely through his death that Jesus would return to his Father in glory. Evil men saw the death of Jesus as the triumph of Satan, the prince of this world, over good. But it was the death of Jesus which condemned evil to impotency, for it was in dying that he destroyed death.

This kind of divine irony is always at work. In the first reading it was not Paul and Silas who were deprived of freedom in prison. It was the jailer, forced as he was to treat shamefully these innocent men. The Holy Spirit moved him to see the truth through the extraordinary event of the earthquake.

Christianity is a different way of living, a sharing in the divine irony, in which the poor are blessed, the sorrowing receive joy, and the dead rise to everlasting life.

Wednesday of the Sixth Week of Easter

There is no point in attempting to get high school students to read Shakespeare when the teacher recognizes that they need remedial English. We all know the principle that you have to take people where they are. St. Paul followed this principle. When St. Paul preached to the Jews of his time, he presumed that they had an understanding of God from the revelation given to their fathers. But when he went to Athens in Greece, he started with the basics that there is but one God who made the heavens and the earth.

Jesus himself worked slowly and patiently with his disciples. Even at the end of his life, he declared to them, "I have much more to tell you, but you cannot bear it now." His statement implied that there was something beyond the "now," a time when the disciples would advance in their knowledge and understanding of the truth. That time was the day of Pentecost, the moment of the coming of the Holy Spirit to guide the Church to all truth.

Jesus returned to the Father in order to send the Holy Spirit upon the Church. Jesus through his life and death had proclaimed the good news. He had formed the nucleus of the Church. Having fulfilled his mission, he returned in glory to the Father so that from them both could come forth the Holy Spirit to develop and guide the Church.

This Holy Spirit directs the life of the Church and of each individual member. He takes the Church wherever it is in any particular era and supplies its needs for a better understanding of the faith. He is the one who moved the bishops of the Second Vatican Council in their marvelous work. He is also the one who will help us in our need for a better understanding of our religion. This Holy Spirit is indeed a precious gift to us from God the Father and his Son.

Thursday of the Sixth Week of Easter (where Ascension is observed on Sunday)

During the era of the great immigrations to the United States, many a destitute man left his family in Europe in order to seek a fortune in the new world. It was a long journey, filled with uncertainty and fear, and the arduousness was compounded for the man because he knew that his family would not only continue to live in utter poverty but that they would also be deeply saddened by his absence. Some of these stories had a happy ending in which the man, economically successful, was able to send for his family and give them a happy life in the United States.

Today's gospel is taken from a discourse of Jesus at the last supper. He was about to go on a journey and leave his disciples behind. But the journey was for their good, even though they could not understand that fully at the time. Jesus tried to assure them that they would grieve for a time but their grief would be turned into joy. His journey was to be a passage through the awesome doors of death. This journey would lead him to the riches of everlasting life. These riches he wished to share with us. He went ahead to prepare a place for us, as did the man who left his family in Europe.

Now we are following his lead in our journey through this life to everlasting life. We have a symbol of this journey in our communion procession as we walk to the altar to receive Christ. This meeting with Christ in the Eucharist is a sign of what is in store for us when we complete our journey at the moment of death and are welcomed by Christ into our heavenly home.

Friday of the Sixth Week of Easter

It has often been observed that there is no physical pain which can be compared to that which accompanies giving birth to a child. Men must, of course, take this statement on faith and most men are undoubtedly grateful for that fact. Nonetheless, all of us have had the experience that time often blurs the memory of intense pain in the past. But there is another element to consider. When pain has accomplished something significant, it is not merely forgotten in the future. Rather it is considered to have been worthwhile.

Jesus was looking for a way to make his disciples understand that the sorrow and suffering involved in being his follower will not only be forgotten later but will be judged very worthwhile. That is why he talked about a woman giving birth to a child. The allusion was particularly apt because the pain of childbirth leads to a new life and the suffering of the Christian leads to everlasting life.

Jesus himself took the lead. He accepted suffering and death in loving obedience to his heavenly Father. Because of this his Father highly exalted him (cf. Ph 2:9). To be a follower of Christ means to share in his suffering, but it also means to share in his glory. The first reading today relates some of the sufferings of St. Paul. These sufferings he accepted in union with Christ, and his loving obedience led to glory for him as it did for Christ.

During this life we are like a woman in labor. There are pain and sorrow in this life. When our time comes, however, we will not give birth. Rather we will be the ones born to everlasting life.

Saturday of the Sixth Week of Easter

Apollos who is mentioned in the first reading is truly worthy of admiration for his docility and openness. He was acknowledged to be an authority on Scripture (meaning, of course, the Old Testament or Hebrew Scriptures since the New Testament had not yet been written). He was also instructed "in the new way of the Lord." And yet his knowledge was incomplete, especially regarding baptism. When Priscilla and Aquila took him home to explain the new teachings to him more fully, he did not resist. A proud person would have probably protested, "Who do you think you are, presuming to instruct me?" Apollos was eager to learn as much as he could.

We should never presume that we know everything there is to know about our religion. Great saints and scholars have spent a lifetime in studying and meditating on the mysteries of faith. But penetration into the mysteries comes not only from study and meditation. It comes also from dialogue with other people of faith and through prayer.

Sometimes Catholics are reluctant to talk about their faith. They are afraid to appear as pious or fanatical. Of course one can go to the extremes, but we ought to recognize that in discussing our faith we can grow in understanding. Rather than always talking about sports and politics, we need to tell each other what the faith means to us.

We also need to pray for better enlightenment. Jesus assures us that whatever we ask the Father in his name, he will give us. This kind of prayer is not exhausted by requests for good health or other benefits. It should also include petitions for a better understanding and love of the faith.

In this life we will never comprehend the mysteries of faith. We are called to use every suitable means to grow in our religion.

Monday of the Seventh Week of Easter

The first reading today makes a sharp distinction between the baptism performed by John the Baptist and the baptism performed by the apostles (which included what we now call confirmation). The distinction is helpful for our understanding and appreciation of Christian baptism.

The baptism by John the Baptist was a simple ceremony whereby a person publicly testified that he wished to repent, to change his life for the better, to abandon sin for a life of dedication to God. Christian baptism includes this reality and much more.

To begin with, the effect of the baptism by John was entirely dependent on the good will of the person. He indeed needed the grace of God to respond, but the baptism in and by itself had no power to change his life. Christian baptism has within it the power of the Holy Spirit. This power transforms us into the person of Christ. It gives us a whole new identity whereby the name Christian is given us, a name which indicates our new identity as a member of the Church, by which we become part of Christ, part of his mystical body.

A change of life is not the prerequisite for Christian baptism. Rather it is the result. It is our new identity which both demands a new way of living and which contains the grace for this life of dedication to God our Father. In turn God the Father looks upon us with a special favor, that same favor with which he looks upon his beloved Son, Jesus Christ.

This new identity should also give us courage in life. Jesus says to us, "Take courage! I have overcome the world." Because of our oneness with Christ we too have overcome the world, the symbol of sin and death. Christian baptism is indeed the great fundamental event of our lives.

Tuesday of the Seventh Week of Easter

Jesus by his life and ministry set an example for all of his disciples to follow. This example is manifested throughout the pages of the gospel, and we see a particularly beautiful instance in today's reading from St. John. Jesus is in prayer to his Father. His love and devotion to his Father are evident. The Father occupies his mind and absorbs his heart. But there is more. Jesus is praying to his Father for us, his followers. His love for his Father overflows into tender affection for us.

St. Paul followed this example of Jesus. The first reading today contains a sermon which he preached to the leaders of the Church he founded at Ephesus. He proclaimed to them how he served the Lord in humility and never shrunk from telling them what was for their own good. He summed up his dedication by saying, "I put no value on my life if only I can finish my race and complete the service to which I have been assigned by the Lord Jesus." St. Paul said all these things so that those coming after him would also follow the example of Jesus as he had done.

In Jesus and St. Paul we see two things: dedication to God and service of his people. This ideal is intended not only for bishops and priests but for all the people of the Church. It is your ideal too, for it is the fulfilling of the command to love God and to love our neighbor.

No one can begin to count the millions of words which have been written about the meaning of Christianity, but in the final analysis the message comes down to a single word: love. Love God. Love your neighbor. This simple message takes on a great profundity when we realize what the measure of our love should be. That measure is the love which Jesus himself has both for his Father and for his people.

Wednesday of the Seventh Week of Easter

The foundation of our political lives as Americans is the Constitution with the Bill of Rights. The safeguarding of this document has been left to the interpretation of the Supreme Court. The main purpose of the Court in this regard is to see to it that the Document is rightly applied in our own times. Although all do not agree that the Court has been true to its task, there is a need for some such authority since there are always those who would twist the Constitution for their own purposes.

St. Paul was aware that after his death some people would distort the truth of the Christian message which is found in the scriptures and the tradition of the Church. He warned the leaders of the Church at Ephesus about this problem. Jesus was aware of the same problem on the night before he died. He prayed to his Father, "As long as I was with them, I guarded them with your name which you gave me." Jesus knew that he was about to pass from this world and that the time of danger would soon arrive. And so he continued in his prayer, "Consecrate them by means of truth."

This prayer of Jesus has been effective. The Church as a whole, and in particular the Pope and the college of bishops, have been consecrated in truth so that error does not enter into the official teaching of the Church. We know that the Pope has been granted the gift of infallibility when acting as the supreme teacher of the Church in matters of faith and morals. The same gift is present within the entire Church and is further personified by all the bishops in union with the Pope. We have witnessed the exercise of this divinely granted authority in the Second Vatican Council, which for us is the sure and safe guide to the truth of Jesus Christ.

As Catholics we must be grateful to God that in following the Church we know that we are following Christ.

Thursday of the Seventh Week of Easter

After St. Paul returned to Jerusalem following one of his missionary journeys, he caused a riot in the temple by his preaching. He was rescued by Roman guards and subsequently turned over to the Sanhedrin, the ruling body of the Jews which was made up of Sadducees who did not believe in the resurrection and Pharisees who did. In proclaiming that he was on trial because of his hope in the resurrection, Paul was not only stating the truth but also using a clever tactic to turn the Sadducees and Pharisees against each other.

I have to imagine that there was a slight smile on Paul's face as he resorted to this tactic. Nonetheless, the matter of the resurrection, that of Jesus and ours as well, is at the heart of our faith. That is why the Lord appeared to Paul and declared: "Keep up your courage! Just as you have given testimony to me here in Jerusalem, so must you do in Rome." This testimony has come down to us and has shaped our faith in the resurrection.

In the Responsorial Psalm we proclaimed our faith in the resurrection, "You will show me the path to life, fullness of joys in your presence, the delights at your hand forever." This faith of ours is confirmed by the words of Jesus in the gospel addressed to his Father: "To them I have revealed your name . . . so that your love for me may live in them, and I may live in them." The love which the Father has for his own Son reaches out to us. This love has granted us a share in the life of the Son, and this sharing will one day blossom into the fullness of resurrection from the dead.

Friday of the Seventh Week of Easter

Life cannot continue without food and drink. The more complex an organism, the greater is its need not only for nourishment but for the proper nourishment. When he was about to leave this world for heaven, having already won for us the gift of divine life, Jesus was eager to leave with us the means to nourish this gift. In giving the pastoral charge to St. Peter, Jesus expressed his mission in terms of nourishment: "Feed my sheep."

The ministry carried on by the successors of St. Peter within the Church is that of spiritual nourishment which essentially takes two forms: the Word of Scripture and the Holy Eucharist.

The Second Vatican Council in its *Constitution on the Sacred Liturgy* (51) decreed that at Mass "the treasures of the Bible are to be opened up more lavishly, so that richer fare may be provided for the faithful at the table of God's Word." As a result we now have a three year cycle of readings on Sundays and a two year cycle on most weekdays. Catholics are now hearing more of the Bible at Mass than ever before. This same Constitution (47) also reminds us that the Eucharist is the "paschal banquet in which Christ is consumed, the mind is filled with grace and a pledge of future glory is given to us." The Constitution also wants us to recognize that "the two parts which . . . go to make up the Mass, namely the liturgy of the word and Eucharistic liturgy, are so closely connected with each other that they form but one single act of worship" (56).

The background of today's first reading is that St. Paul had been in custody at Caesarea for two years. This was only one among many incidents of hardships which he endured for Christ. He was able to bear all things for Christ for the same reason that we should be able to do so. He was nourished by the Word of God and by the Holy Eucharist.

Saturday of the Seventh Week of Easter

This is a day of conclusions. Our first reading was the conclusion of the Book of the Acts of the Apostles by St. Luke. The gospel was the conclusion of the Gospel according to St. John. And tomorrow with the Solemnity of Pentecost we conclude the Easter Season. And yet the Church will go on until the Lord comes again in glory.

Any conclusions we experience are but the prelude to something more in the divine plan. St. Luke concluded his story about the apostles with St. Paul in Rome. And yet we know that from Rome the faith spread throughout the whole world. St. John concluded his gospel by saying that if everything Jesus did were to be written about in detail, there would not be room enough in the entire world to hold the books to record them. And so his gospel was not to be the last word about Jesus. Saints and scholars for twenty centuries have blessed us with books and sermons about Jesus.

The great Easter event of the resurrection, although twenty centuries old, is not a thing of the past. The Risen Lord is still with us. And even though we complete one form of our Easter celebration tomorrow, we continue the celebration of Easter on every Sunday of the year.

With God there is no conclusion, for he is eternal. With God there is no limit to his goodness, for he is infinite. The great truth and beauty of God as revealed to us in Jesus Christ can never be exhausted by us, even in heaven.

As people of faith we have a great gift here on earth. But what we have to look forward to is far beyond our poor powers even to imagine.

THE SEASON OF THE YEAR (I & II)

Monday of the First Week (I)

For any person who is serious about the purpose of life, there are two supreme questions: What is God like and what does he want from us?

Down through the centuries God himself has supplied the answers, and for the most part he has done so through human representatives whom he himself has chosen. We call these people the prophets. It is possible for a "private" individual to receive revelations from God, but such is not usual and the person who thinks he has been so favored is subject to self-deception. The prophets, almost universally humble people who were reluctant to take up their task, never spoke in their own name. Their constant refrain was, "Thus says the Lord God."

In the time of fulfillment, mentioned in today's gospel, God the Father sent, not a human prophet, but his own Son. Jesus, because of his divinity as the very image of the Father, could speak in his own name. Not once did he use the prophetic refrain, "Thus says the Lord God." Rather, he proclaimed, "I say to you. . . ." Moreover, Jesus revealed the nature of God not only by his words but by his actions. In seeing Jesus in the gospel we see God in the flesh. The marvel of the incarnation is that God lived among us, human like us in all things but sin.

The person who thinks he is the receiver of a personal revelation from God runs the danger of creating a God in his own image and likeness, the kind of a God he wants. In Jesus as he is found in the gospels and proclaimed by the Church, we make no mistake. By hearing his words and following his example, we are on the right path to knowing the answers to the great questions of life: What is God like and what does he want from us?

Monday of the First Week (II)

As people of faith we are called to believe that God guides and directs our personal lives as well as world events. At times in order to emphasize his providential care, God acts in extraordinary ways. One of his favorite ways of acting is to surround with unusual circumstances the birth of certain persons who will be particularly instrumental in carrying out his plan. One of these persons was Samuel.

Hannah, the wife of Elkanah, was to become the mother of Samuel, but for years she was barren. In fact she had just about come to the point of recognizing that she would never be a mother. Tomorrow in the first reading we will see how God acted on her behalf. Her son, Samuel, would be the last of the judges, those men and women who ruled Israel in God's name before the age of Israelite kings. In fact Samuel was to be the person mainly responsible for establishing the monarchy in Israel.

These events, and all those of the Old Testament, are important because they form part of God's overall plan leading to the coming of his Son, and even that moment in the gospel today when Jesus said, "This is the time of fulfillment. The reign of God is at hand!" The history of the Old Testament is our history, our roots.

Today we should recognize that each one of us is part of God's plan. Even if we do not discern any extraordinary intervention of God in our lives, we are the beneficiaries of all that he has done in the history of salvation. We live in the time of fulfillment, and the reign of God has come to us in the person of Jesus Christ.

Tuesday of the First Week (I)

If you were a Christian living around the year 80, you would probably be faced with a serious difficulty. How could Jesus, who was so human that he endured death, be superior to the angels? The difficulty may strike us as strange, but among many people of the early Church the angels held a very sublime position.

That Jesus was truly human and died a real death is clear from the scriptures and is a dogma of our faith. The paradox of God's plan is that it was precisely through his death that Jesus was exalted above all creation. His death in loving obedience to his Father led to the glory of the resurrection whereby he was proclaimed as Lord of the universe. For us this is all still a matter of faith. "At present we do not see all things thus subject" to Jesus.

I doubt that we have any problem about Jesus' being exalted above the angels. Their prominence has faded from the thinking of Christians over the centuries. We need to consider other kinds of prominence. Are we tempted to put more confidence in any form of human experts than we do in Jesus? Some people are guided more by popular columns in newspapers and magazines than they are by the principles of the gospels. Others would rather follow the stock market than to hear the words of Jesus, "Blessed are the poor." Some prefer to have the favor of friends at the expense of the commandments of Jesus.

This is not a time to point the finger at others. Each one of us must be sure that in our hearts and in our actions Jesus Christ is our Lord, exalted far above anything or anyone merely human.

Tuesday of the First Week (II)

Today's gospel is unusual, not in that Jesus drove out the unclean spirit, but in that he did so without being asked. More often than not Jesus helped needy people in response to a petition. It is not as if Jesus had to be told what should be done. Rather he willed that his help would come as a result of faith manifested in a request.

God does not need to be informed about our needs. Such is not the purpose of the prayer of petition. Rather God has, for the most part, willed to respond to our needs in answer to prayer. To put it another way, and perhaps more accurately, God moves us to pray for what is right and good as part of his overall plan to do what is right and good for us.

All along Samuel was part of God's plan. He willed to send this extraordinary man to govern and direct his people because they needed him. But he wanted Hannah, as a representative of all the people, to pray that a son would be granted her despite her apparent inability to bear a child. And pray Hannah did. In fact she

204 / Wednesday of the First Week of the Year

prayed so fervently that Eli, observing her in the temple, thought she was drunk! In answer to her prayer she conceived and bore a son whom she called Samuel.

Our prayer of petition, especially our prayer of the faithful here at Mass, should be fervent and persevering. We do not pray, however, to inform God or to change his mind about something. Rather we pray because God wants us to pray, and he wishes to respond to our need in answer to our prayers.

Wednesday of the First Week (I)

One of the most beautiful truths of our faith is that the eternal, divine Son of God became human like us in all things but sin. Since Jesus did not come to save angels but human beings, he did not appear in some ethereal fashion, nor was he born amid the trappings of a royal court. The Second Vatican Council put it this way: "By his incarnation the Son of God has united himself in some fashion with every man. He worked with human hands, he thought with a human mind, acted by a human choice, and loved with a human heart" (*Const. on the Church in the Modern World*, 22).

When most of us are depressed or have a problem, we look for someone who will understand us, someone who can appreciate how we feel. Sharing a tragedy with someone who has gone through a similar ordeal is much more comforting than talking to some professional counselor who may be aloof and without any experience like our own.

Throughout the pages of the gospel we indeed see Jesus reaching out to others with understanding and empathy. In today's gospel he cured the mother of Peter's wife because he knew in his heart how he felt about his own mother, Mary. In fact throughout his life Jesus either experienced or shared in almost every possible human emotion, both joyful and painful. He knew the joy of a nice meal with friends and he suffered the pain of watching some of his disciples turn away from him.

In Jesus Christ our God is not far removed from us and our human situation. He is close to us in every aspect of our lives, and he is ready to hear our prayers with understanding and to direct them to God the Father with earnestness and concern.

Wednesday of the First Week (II)

God usually chooses to deal with people through other people. Of course he can reveal himself directly to anyone he wishes, as he did with Samuel in the temple. It is helpful to note, however, that Eli, the priest, had to make clear to Samuel that the voice he was hearing was the voice of God. Incidentally, Eli was not the most saintly of men; in fact, God was displeased with him because he had not reproved his sons who were guilty of blasphemy. The point is that God often works through people, and sometimes they are not necessarily very holy.

The greatest manifestation of God is through the humanity of Jesus. But even Jesus himself works in cooperation with others. Notice that Simon and Andrew call to his attention the fact that Simon's mother-in-law was ill with a fever. Later people brought to Jesus those who were sick and those possessed by demons.

God wants to act through us now. Perhaps we do not think that we are especially holy or that we are suitable instruments for God. Such is a thought we must put from our minds. We must be as eager as Samuel was to know what God's will is for us and then to be as zealous as he was in following God's will. Actually we find God's will all around us in people who are in need. The sick, the lonely, the discouraged—all these are signs to us that God wants us to act. In passing by or in neglecting anyone in need we are failing to listen to God. In searching out those in need and in helping them in any way we can, we are responding to God's voice which is calling out to us as clearly as he called out to Samuel in the temple.

Thursday of the First Week (I)

Today's first reading, although from the New Testament, has a long reference to a psalm from the Old Testament, psalm 95. This psalm is basically an invitation to worship God. The reference we heard is from the second part of the psalm in which the people are warned that they must not be like their ancestors who were disgruntled with God because of their hunger and thirst in the desert following their freedom from Egypt.

The people in the desert had not allowed the word of God, which held out the promise of a fruitful land, to penetrate their hearts. They hardened their hearts, refusing to take faith and trust from God's word.

The psalm is a call to worship. The reason for the second part is to indicate that worship does not mean only praising God or telling him of our needs. Worship includes listening as well. The psalmist proclaims, "Today, if you should hear his voice, harden not your hearts." We hear the voice of God through his inspired word in our daily worship. And we need that word. Think about the leper in the gospel. He knew his need for a cure. Don't you think he listened attentively to the words of Jesus, "Be cured."

In every Mass we are nourished by the body and the blood of Jesus Christ. He wishes also to nourish us with the inspired word of the scriptural readings. That word will strengthen our faith.

Our worship, then, is complete when we couple praise of God with listening to him. We must not harden our hearts but open them wide to hear God's word.

Thursday of the First Week (II)

During their history the Chosen People alternated between two extremes: one was a lack of sufficient trust in God and the other was complacency. The terrible defeat of which we heard in the first reading was the result of the second extreme, complacency. This attitude led the people to believe that God would take care of them regardless of whether they were truly faithful to him or not. Often complacency manifested itself in reliance on external acts of religion with no real interior devotion.

In the battle against the Philistines the leaders thought that bringing the ark of the covenant, which represented the presence of God, to the front line of battle would in itself bring about the defeat of the Philistines. The irony of the situation is clear in the fact that the ark was carried by two priests, Eli's sons, "who had respect neither for the Lord nor for the priests' duties toward the people" (1 S 2:12). The result was disaster. Earlier God had warned Eli that his sons would be destroyed, and God promised, "I will choose a faithful priest who shall do what I have in heart and mind" (1 S 2:35). No one fulfills this prophecy more than does Jesus Christ.

We see him in the gospel cure the leper. We know, however, that Jesus is more interested in an interior cleansing, a change of heart. As he did what the Father had in heart and mind, so for us real devotion must be a dedication to the Father's will. "Thy will be done" must be more than a phrase on our lips. It must be a way of life.

Friday of the First Week (I)

After the Israelites were freed from slavery in Egypt, they wandered in the desert for forty years. That generation of people were precluded from entering the promised land because of their unfaithfulness. The promised land was pictured as a place of contentment and rest. The Letter to the Hebrews used this same imagery of contentment and rest in referring to our promised land, heaven, and urges us to strive for that fulfillment.

Of course we have no clear picture of what heaven will be like. It is beyond our powers of imagination, nor is any single image sufficient even to suggest its wonders. Today's scripture, however, suggests for our consideration one aspect of heaven: rest. Thinking about that aspect can help us form some notion of heaven.

You are familiar with the prayer, "May the souls of the faithful departed through the mercy of God rest in peace." This does not mean the rest which is found in the grave. And it means much more than the rest of sleep. Rather we should think of the poetic image of God resting on the seventh day after his work of creation. God, so to speak, sat back and looked upon all he had done and saw that it was very good. His rest was not a relief from exhaustion; rather it was a contentment in what he had accomplished. His rest was one of fulfillment and satisfaction.

When our time comes for death, God will gather us to himself. He will invite us to enter into *his* rest. He will see our holiness as one of his own great accomplishments. We do not save ourselves or make ourselves holy. That is the Father's work through Jesus, who brings us forgiveness for our sins and makes us holy in God's eyes. God will, in effect, say to us in heaven: "I am very pleased with what I have done for you. Come rest with me and share in my joy."

Friday of the First Week (II)

Part of the human condition is to be dissatisfied with present circumstances. We are always looking for something better to turn up, to be like those who seem to be well off in life. The Israelites were dissatisfied that they did not have a king. They wanted to be like the nations around them, and they thought a king could unify them in their struggles against their enemies, especially the Philistines.

Samuel disagreed. He warned the people that a king could usurp their rights, take over their possessions, and oblige them to be at his service. Deep within him Samuel had an even stronger objection. He saw a monarchy in Israel as a contradiction. God alone was king in Israel, and he should not be abandoned in favor of a human king with all his foibles and weaknesses. The people were nonetheless so persistent that God allowed them to have a human king, but with the understanding that he would be a viceroy, a representative of God.

We need to ask ourselves what kind of a king or leader we want in our own lives. The Israelites were looking for someone who would insure safety and security. Do we want someone who can give us safety against foreign oppression or domestic criminals, or do we want someone who can safeguard us against sin which alone can ultimately destroy us? Do we want someone who can give us everlasting security in eternal life?

Jesus fulfilled the yearnings for kingship in Israel in a way which the people of that time could not imagine. He is our king. We must make him the center of our lives and of our hearts.

Saturday of the First Week (I)

We hear the word of God every time we celebrate Mass, and many of us probably read it at home as well. This word is living, not a relic from the past. Through his word God constantly invites us to strengthen our faith and to persevere in our love. His word is also a challenge to grow more in holiness, to be uncompromising in slashing any attachment to sin.

Often the word of God is intended to make us uncomfortable, to stir us out of complacency. God does not wish us to hear his word in a passive fashion as we might the interminable flow which comes at us from radio and television. Rather we must listen to this word as something always new.

The challenge of the word is not meant to frighten us. Jesus understands our weakness as sinners. That is what the gospel shows us today. He says, "People who are healthy do not need a doctor; sick people do. I have come to call sinners, not the self-righteous." Jesus is the divine physician who heals us of sin, our weakness, and gives us the help we need to respond to his word.

Here at Mass we have the perfect combination. First we hear the word of God. That is our challenge. Then Jesus comes to us in the form of food and drink as our spiritual nourishment. That is our strength. Jesus, in other words, does not offer us a challenge without supplying the means we need to meet that challenge.

Saturday of the First Week (II)

The episode in today's first reading, whereby Saul was called in very ordinary circumstances to be king and was anointed by Samuel with utter simplicity, changed the course of Israelite history. It set God's people upon a turbulent course. There was indeed a golden age under King David, despite his human weakness, but it was relatively brief. With his son Solomon a decay began which eventuated in a separation of the kingdom into north and south and led finally to disgrace and exile for the people. Corruption, lust, and an abandonment of God marked most of the kings.

In stark contrast is the person who fulfilled kingship in Israel. That person is Jesus Christ. Born in poverty in David's city of Bethlehem, he lived and died as a poor man. Lust was no part of him. Rather he was consumed with a passion to serve his people in love. His whole life was marked by a complete trust in his Father. An unusual king was Jesus Christ. He made himself at home with a tax collector, one of the most despised elements of Jewish society, and he insisted that he had come to call sinners, not the self-righteous.

The ideal is that people should love their king and be eager to serve him. How easy it should be for us to love our king and to be dedicated to his service!

Monday of the Second Week (I)

In the early days of the Church the word "priest" was reserved to Jesus Christ in order to emphasize that he is ultimately the only priest. Those whom we now call priests were referred to by various titles. But gradually around the seventh century the term priest came into common usage. Nonetheless we should strive to recognize that "priest" means Jesus Christ foremost and that the priesthood of the ordained and that of the faithful is a sharing in the one priesthood of Jesus Christ.

A priest is a mediator between God and men, a bridge which spans the gap which separates us from God. To accomplish its purpose a bridge must be in contact with both shores, like the magnificent expanse which is the Golden Gate bridge. Jesus Christ is our priest, our bridge with God. First Jesus is divine, God himself, from all eternity. In his divinity he is in contact with God the Father. Secondly when Jesus became human, he came into contact with us. Eternally begotten of the Father in his divinity and taken from among us in his humanity, Jesus is the perfect priest.

Jesus is our mediator to the Father. He takes our worship to the Father. He not only taught us how to pray, but he continues to pray for us and within us. He fulfilled the office of priest perfectly by his sacrificial death on the cross when he made the gift of himself to the Father for our sakes. Standing before the Father he could say: "These are my people. I am one of them because from them I have been taken. It is for them that I offer myself to you."

Jesus is among us at this moment. What we do is pleasing to the Father because Jesus is our priest, renewing his sacrifice and bringing our worship to the Father. We are a fortunate people to have Jesus Christ as our priest.

Monday of the Second Week (II)

The background of today's first reading is that King Saul had been commanded by God to wage a holy war against the Amalekites. Nothing of their possessions was to be spared. But King Saul made the mistake of putting his judgment above that of God. With good intentions, but in disobedience, Saul did not destroy the best of the sheep and oxen in order to sacrifice them to God.

God's reaction through Samuel, his prophet, was swift and sure. He declared that "obedience is better than sacrifice." Absolute dedication to God's will is preferred to any merely external act of religion. It was a point which Jesus himself had to make repeatedly. In the gospel he spoke out against a form of fasting which had become nothing more than an external act devoid of any real devotion to God. He insisted that this old form of religion had to go, to be replaced with a worship of God which came from the heart.

Most of us celebrate Mass together every day or almost every day. Through the readings we have heard, God wants to remind us that this celebration must be a constant rededication of ourselves to his will. Our celebration is a beautiful response to our prayer, "Thy will be done on earth as it is in heaven," for in heaven the blessed are constantly praising God for his goodness. From this celebration we can and must draw the strength to live lives which are in accord with God's will. God's will is done in heaven perfectly by all those who are constantly in his presence. We are still striving for that perfection. Each day should bring us a little closer to what happens in heaven. Loving obedience to God's will as best we can know it must be the identical twin of the worship we offer daily in the Eucharist.

Tuesday of the Second Week (I)

Sometimes when people are fishing in a small boat, they throw down an anchor to keep the boat from drifting away from the good fishing area. The boat is free to move slightly within a certain area depending on the length of the anchor chain. The anchor gives the fishermen a sense of security provided the chain is strong.

Yesterday we saw that Jesus is our priest. Although still with us, he has in another sense gone before us by means of his ascension into heaven. There he is rooted like our anchor. Our union with him through faith is like the chain of the anchor. The degree of our faith determines how strong the chain is. From this comes hope. Hope is a confident assurance that all is well and that we will not drift away from heaven.

Christian hope is not foolishness. It is not a complacency that, no matter what, God will save us. It is not like a fisherman who fearlessly goes out into a raging storm and throws out an anchor with a chain which is rusted and weak. To think that he is secure under such circumstances is not only foolishness; it is insanity.

Christian hope, founded on faithfulness, is meant to dispel needless fear. We should not be like the person who, despite a good life, fears that on his death bed he will deny God. Nor should we think that God will abandon us simply because we are humanly weak and still have many imperfections.

Christian hope is meant to give us a certain serenity as we go about our lives, trying to do God's will, to avoid sin, and to grow in his grace. This kind of hope brings to us the peace for which we pray in every Mass, a peace of mind that Jesus has gone before us, a firm anchor in heaven.

Tuesday of the Second Week (II)

God's ways are not our ways and his values are not our values. One of the characteristics of God as manifested in the Bible is that he is different. Think about our process for presidential elections. There are long, drawn out and very expensive campaigns in which the candidates try to sell themselves to the American public. Unbashedly they proclaim their qualities and virtues. And that is only for the primaries. The primaries are followed by even more intensive and expensive campaigns, marked not only by self proclamation but by sometimes vicious attacks on the opponent. Theoretically the process is supposed to produce the best man for the job. Whether it does or not, we leave to political analysts.

In stark contrast is God's approach to his choice of a king to succeed Saul. God sent his prophet, Samuel, to the little, out of the way town of Bethlehem. He did not tell the prophet to search out a famous governor or mayor, someone with experience or even someone with wealth or education. He told him to choose the least likely son of Jesse, one whom Jesse himself did not even consider as a possibility. That son was David, who became the greatest king in the history of the Israelites.

We have been chosen by God to be a kingly and priestly people. This choice has been freely made by God. It is not as if God looked around to discover the most qualified people, the most intelligent or the most influential and wealthy. It was God who made David king and it is God who has made us his people, both out of his own goodness. We do well always and everywhere to give thanks and praise to God for his unmerited goodness to us.

Wednesday of the Second Week (I)

Among the Israelites a man became a priest by being born from the descendents of Levi who were of the family of Moses' brother Aaron, who was made a priest by God. A levitical priest ceased being a priest upon his death and the priesthood was passed on to his sons. In contrast was Melchizedek, a Gentile priest in the time of Abraham. The Bible is deliberately silent about his ancestry as a symbol that he did not inherit his priesthood.

Jesus is compared to Melchizedek to emphasize that his priest-hood is different from the levitical priesthood. He does not inherit his priesthood but is made a priest directly by his heavenly Father. Moreover, his priesthood does not end with his death but continues because he is a priest forever. Incidentally the episode in today's gospel is just one instance whereby Jesus was showing that he supersedes the old order.

Most significant for us is the fact that we do not worship alone here at Mass. Jesus the priest is with us. He is present and active in you by virtue of baptism, and in me by virtue of ordination. He is present and active in the inspired word of Scripture and in a pre-eminent way in the eucharist. Jesus as priest is our mediator. He brings the Father's truth and love to us, and he presents our prayers and sacrifice to the Father.

What we do at Mass has great meaning and value not because of ourselves but solely because of Jesus Christ. He is our priest among us at this moment because he is a priest forever according to the order of Melchizedek.

Wednesday of the Second Week (II)

If anybody was betting on the battle between Goliath and David, I am sure that by taking David he could have gotten very good odds, probably about a hundred to one. It was like the Super Bowl champions playing a high school football team. In everybody's opinion, except his own, David did not stand a chance against the giant. And when people saw David with only a sling shot approach the fully armed Goliath, they were certain that all bets were off, that the cause was hopeless.

Yesterday we saw how God is different, how his values and approaches are different from human values and approaches. In the battle he did not align himself with the mighty and the powerful Philistines, as represented by Goliath. Rather he put himself on the side of the lowly and the weak in the person of David. David was confident because he believed that God was on his side. We know the outcome.

The Bible shows that God has a predilection for the poor, the humble, the defenseless. His attitude is that those who are so foolish as to rely on power and riches, and have rejected him, can fend for themselves. But God will take care of his own, provided they turn to him for help.

In life one of the most important attitudes we should have is humility. Humility recognizes that everything we are and have comes from God, and this humility in turn leads to a great confidence and trust in God. With humility we can face the difficulties of life with confidence like that of David when he faced Goliath. We express this attitude every day at Mass before communion when we say, "Lord, I am not worthy to receive you, but only say the word and I shall be healed." God is on the side of the humble and the lowly.

Thursday of the Second Week (I)

Whenever we come to Mass, we hear a certain phrase repeated again and again. In fact we hear it so often that its impact may be lost upon us. That familiar phrase is: "Through Christ our Lord." The constant use of that phrase should make us mindful of two truths about the Mass.

The first is that the Mass is not primarily the worship of Jesus, as is, for example, a eucharistic devotion outside of Mass. Rather the Mass is the worship of the Father by his children "through Christ our Lord." We are not children of God the Son or of God the Holy Spirit. God the Father by the power of his Spirit has made us his children in the image of his divine Son, Jesus Christ. We have been made children of the Father by means of baptism, and baptism calls us to the Mass to praise and thank God our Father and to pray to him. The Mass is not so much looking at the person of Jesus as it is looking in the same direction with him to the Father.

The second truth brought out by the phrase "through Christ our Lord" is the truth that we never stand alone at Mass. We are one with Christ. At Mass we never have to rely on our own merits. We need not be concerned with whether what we do can possibly be pleasing to the Father. Because we pray and worship through Christ, God the Father looks upon us and sees within us the person of his own Son with whom he is well pleased. Jesus is our priest, our intercessor with the Father.

In faith we have assurance of the teaching of the letter to the Hebrews: "Jesus is always able to save those who approach God through him, since he forever lives to make intercession for them." Nowhere is this truth more operative than in our celebration of the Mass through Christ our Lord.

Thursday of the Second Week (II)

Saul became envious of David because the people gave greater praise to David after his defeat of Goliath than they did to Saul as king. Saul was convinced that David, making capital of his popularity, would seize the throne. Actually he had little or no basis for that fear. David respected Saul and his position. He recognized that the same divine power which had allowed him to defeat Goliath had also established Saul as the rightful king. Saul, blinded by fear, failed to see God's hand at work and gave in to the vice of envy.

Envy is chagrin or discontent at the excellence or good fortune of another. It produces resentment and bitterness. Envy is a terrible vice not only because it manifests selfishness but also because it makes its victim miserable. It can plague not only an insecure king like Saul but ordinary people like ourselves.

There is a temptation for us to resent the fact that some people who seem to have no regard for God or their fellow human beings are the ones who are wealthy and powerful in this world. In our own struggles to make ends meet we can also become bitter about our situation. But envy knows no boundaries. We can envy even the good fortune of our best friends or members of our families.

Although there is a pettiness in all envy, its main cause is a lack of personal security, not the kind of security which comes from money but from the conviction that God loves us. By recognizing the wealth of God's blessings to us we need envy no one else. God's hand is always at work in our lives, directing us to what is best for us personally no matter what may seem to happen for others. Placing ourselves completely in the hands of God overcomes any temptation to envy and produces, not bitterness, but contentment.

Friday of the Second Week (I)

"Covenant" is a word which is not in very common usage today. A covenant is a contract, a binding agreement, but what makes a covenant distinctive is that it is based, not solely on law, but on love. For example, a marriage is a contract which is more properly termed a covenant.

Through Moses as mediator God entered into a covenant with the chosen people. It was indeed much like a marriage covenant whereby God agreed to love and care for his people and they in return promised faithfulness. Unfortunately faithfulness was not manifested by the people. In effect they divorced God.

Jesus is the mediator of a new and better covenant, our covenant with God. This is an everlasting covenant. It allows of no divorce. A contract or covenant to be valid must be signed and sealed. To show how earnest he was about his new covenant God signed and sealed it in the blood of his Son. We became part of this covenant by means of our baptism. God called each of us by name just as surely as Jesus called the apostles by name to be his followers. In responding to this call we must never waver.

Married people do well to renew their marriage vows in order to deepen their love for each other. We have the opportunity to renew our baptismal covenant with God here at Mass. Jesus declares to us: "This is the cup of my blood, the blood of the new and everlasting covenant." As we partake of his cup we should wish to renew our covenant with God, to pledge that we will strive to be a more loving and dedicated people.

Friday of the Second Week (II)

Despite the pleadings of his son, Jonathan, Saul was so consumed by bitter envy toward David that he continued in his plot to kill him. In today's reading we saw that David had an opportunity to put Saul to death. He did not do so out of respect for Saul as king, the Lord's anointed. It was an extraordinary act on David's part and reflected not only an esteem for the king but for God from whom the dignity of the king came.

In baptism we were anointed as a kingly and priestly people, sharing in the royal priesthood of Christ. We are called by baptism to love each other as brothers and sisters. But before we can really love people, we must respect them. We must first see the source of Christian dignity, which is God's free choice. All the baptized are called by God just as surely as were the apostles mentioned in the gospel today. This is not to say that the unbaptized are excluded, for God wills that all men be saved and ultimately come to the dignity which has been granted to the baptized.

The truth is that the values of our society are not such as to foster proper respect. A well dressed person usually receives respect, but not the poor, especially one who is termed a "bum" or a "wino." A wealthy person usually receives respect, but not an alien, especially an illegal alien who cannot speak English. An influential person usually receives respect, but not the powerless or the defenseless, especially a child in the womb.

We are called to turn those values around. One might say that it was easy for David to respect Saul because Saul was a king. But all the people we meet are either part of the kingly people of God or called to be such. For them we must have respect before we can truly love them.

Saturday of the Second Week (I)

Jesus is unique, being at the same time both human and divine. In becoming man he made himself vulnerable, open to human suffering and death. As divine he had dominion over his own life, something no human person has.

The priests of the Old Testament, being only human and not divine, did not have dominion over their own lives. They could not offer their own lives in sacrifice for the people; such would have been suicide, which God forbids. Instead they offered the blood of animals in atonement to God as representative of themselves and the people. Jesus did not need a victim to represent himself in sacrifice. Being divine he had the right to offer his own life and his own blood so that sins might be forgiven. In offering himself for his people he may have appeared to unbelievers as being out of his mind, but his act was the greatest manifestation of love the world has ever seen. Jesus by the shedding of his blood "has cleansed our consciences from dead works to worship the living God."

So that we may identify with this sacrifice and enter into it personally, Jesus in the Mass renews the offering of himself. He declares through the priest, "This is my body given up for you. This is the cup of my blood shed for you and for all men so that sins may be forgiven." Jesus in the Mass does not die again, but he does make the one sacrificial offering of himself a present reality among us. We have the opportunity of sharing directly in this sacrifice which is the source of our forgiveness and the means whereby we can offer pleasing worship to the Father. Nothing was more important to the world than the sacrifice of Christ, and nothing is more important to us than our sharing in the Mass.

Saturday of the Second Week (II)

King Saul's son, Jonathan, was a very close friend of David, and he attempted to persuade his father to give up his plot to assasinate David. The king, on the other hand, was the mortal enemy of David. When both the king and his son were killed in battle, the way to the throne was open to David. His reaction was not one of joy because he was about to become king, but one of sorrow because Saul and Jonathan had died. That he would weep for Jonathan seemed natural since they were close friends. That he would weep for Saul manifested true nobility since Saul was his enemy.

Throughout his life David wavered between greatness and weakness, but in this episode he showed what a really big person he was. Only petty people delight in evil which comes to others even if they be enemies. Later Jesus would set forth his own directives for greatness. He would say, "Love your enemies. Do good to those who persecute you." He himself would also give the example from the cross by forgiving those who had put him to death. As far as worldly values are concerned, his teaching and his example were madness.

We are called to be big people. It is easy to love our friends and those who are good to us. It takes real character to rise above the inclination of sinful human nature to react in kind, to hate those who hate us and to ignore those who ignore us. Such strength cannot come from within us. It comes only from God. Here at Mass we have the source of that strength as we receive the body of Christ given up out of love for all people and his blood which was shed so that sins might be forgiven. Through the Eucharist Jesus wants to transform us into himself so that like him we too can love our enemies and do good to those who hate us.

Monday of the Third Week (I)

Some years ago most newspapers carried a comic strip entitled "Alley Oop," which featured a time machine. With the proper setting of dials, one stepping into the machine could be transported back in time to any period of history. Of course the time machine was only the product of the author's imagination. No device can actually reach back into historical events now long past. We are bound by time. But are we? Is it possible that somehow events of the past are not beyond our grasp, at least by the almighty power of God? After all, God himself is not limited by time, having no past and no future. All is present for God.

In the Mass God uses his almighty power to transcend time. We should not think of the Mass as a time machine. That is much too simplistic and mundane an image. The liturgy does not thrust us back in time, but God in the Mass does make the sacrifice of Jesus Christ present before us so that we may share in it. Jesus died only once and cannot die again as the reading from Hebrews tells us. The Mass in no sense makes Jesus die again. Rather the one sacrificial death of himself which he offered on the cross is now made present for us on the altar.

We are not deprived of sharing in the sacrifice of the cross by an accident of time. The fact that we have been born long after the event makes no difference to God. Nor need we be envious of Mary, our mother, who had the privilege of standing at the foot of the cross and joining her son in the offering of himself. By the power of the Mass we have the same privilege as did Mary, and she is our model as we offer the Mass in this church.

The Mass is not a time machine, but it is the reality of Christ's sacrificial death made present for us on the altar.

Monday of the Third Week (II)

David was first anointed king of Judah, the southern kingdom. In today's reading we see him anointed also king of Israel, the northern kingdom. The two kingdoms remained separate political entities in which the government of the two states was united only in the person of David, their king. In an effort to unite the two as closely as possible, David made Jerusalem the one capital of both. Nonetheless the kingdoms later drew apart completely, having distinct kings, even though they should have been joined by faith in the one, true God. Eventually both kingdoms fell to the Babylonians for, as Jesus said, "If a household is divided according to loyalties, that household will not survive."

Our world is made up of many countries, usually in competition with one another and sometimes in open hostility. Borders are carefully guarded and the right to citizenship rigidly restricted. Frequently national loyalties take precedence over basic human needs. All efforts to form one world have failed, and the United Nations, while deserving of support for its charter, is basically an impotent organization.

Although unity has not been accomplished on a worldwide scale, it must be brought about among ourselves who share one faith. Such is the minimum, but it is not always achieved. We have but one king, Jesus Christ. That Christians are divided is a scandal, but that we as Catholics are sometimes divided is intolerable. We are called to be one in mind, one in heart, and one in affection. In the third Eucharistic prayer we pray, "Grant that we, who are nourished by his body and blood may be filled with his Holy Spirit and become one body, one spirit in Christ." That unity for which we pray is expressed by putting aside jealousy and selfishness and by being absorbed in care and concern for each other.

Tuesday of the Third Week (I)

Gift giving has always been part of human experience. A gift is meant to express a feeling which words alone cannot convey. A gift need not be something practical, something that can be used, because its meaning is symbolic. Flowers as a gift are not practical, but they convey affection and love for another person.

We are called in the Mass to express our love for God through gift giving. And we are fortunate indeed. We do not offer God a gift of flowers, however beautiful. We do not offer God a gift of gold, however precious. And we do not offer God mere bread and wine. Rather we offer bread and wine which have been transformed into the body and blood of Christ, the most beautiful and the most precious gift possible. For a gift to be meaningful, there must be something behind it. For example, if a man gives his wife a gift on their wedding anniversary, no matter how costly the gift, it may mean little or nothing. If she rarely sees her husband at home, if he seems to have little time for her, if they are always bickering and quarreling, then the gift is empty, hollow, and even hypocritical.

And so with ourselves here at Mass. Our gift of Christ to the Father has real meaning in the measure that we try to have time for God, that we think about him and pray to him during the day, and that we are faithful to him. We have to become like the Gift we give, Jesus himself, who declared to his Father, "I have come to do your will." We leave the celebration of Mass in order to live the Mass in union with Christ, our brother. United with Christ and dedicated like him to the Father's will, we are to go in peace to love and serve the Lord.

Tuesday of the Third Week (II)

The Ark, which represented the presence of God among his people, had been housed in various places after its recovery from the Philistines. King David permanently set up the ark in Jerusalem, his capital city. It was a momentous occasion. The people carried the ark with shouts of joy and David himself, in a kind of ecstasy, danced before the Lord with abandon. In one word, it was a celebration.

The Mass is our celebration, not merely of the presence of God among us, but of the fact that God has united us with himself through the body and blood of his son, making us brothers and sisters of Jesus. That is a truth worthy of celebration.

Celebration implies first a joyful experience. That is why music is ideally a part of every Mass. Almost nothing adds more to a celebration than music. People standing around a birthday cake do not merely recite the words, "Happy birthday to you." They sing them. And yet the root meaning of the word, "celebration," in Latin means a gathering of people. Celebration is something you cannot do alone. Think of a person far from home, family, and friends on his birthday. Feeling lost in a strange city, he eats dinner all by himself in a cafeteria. Such can hardly be considered a celebration. A celebration is always festive, and that necessarily includes people. The Mass is not meant to be a private devotion. The presence of people is not incidental to Mass but essential. The Mass is the celebration of God's people.

Celebration centers around an event. You have to have a reason to celebrate. The great event we observe in the Mass is that Jesus in "dying destroyed our death and in rising restored our life." The Mass, no matter what the occasion, is always the celebration of an event, the death and resurrection of Jesus. The Mass is our joyful, community experience of God's love for us.

Wednesday of the Third Week (I)

The preaching of Jesus reached many people, but only some accepted what he proclaimed. The word was there like a seed, but it was necessary for the hearers to be receptive like good soil. Somewhat the same can be said about the forgiveness of sin which Jesus achieved by his sacrificial death on the cross. He shed his blood for all mankind, but people must be receptive to that forgiveness.

The offering made by the levitical priests of the old law had no power to take away sins. God is the one offended by sin, and only the God made man, Jesus Christ, can bring about its forgiveness. It is through the sacraments that this forgiveness is granted to us, first in baptism, through the Eucharist, and especially by means of the sacrament of penance. Our only work, with the help of the Spirit, is to make ourselves open to forgiveness.

We must understand that in no way do we ever make any payment for sin. Jesus alone can do that and he has done it once and for all by his sacrifice. His blood has been shed for the remission of sins. Perhaps in the past we got the idea that the "penance" we receive after confessing our sins is some kind of payment for sin. It is not. God's forgiveness is granted to us without charge because of what Jesus has done. The penance we receive, which is more properly termed "satisfaction," is intended to be the opposite of the sin we have committed. It is supposed to be medicinal for the purpose of healing, not punitive for the purpose of payment. The penance is a way of turning our lives around.

Jesus offered one sacrifice for sins. No other payment is necessary or even possible.

Wednesday of the Third Week (II)

It has been said that the pun is the lowest form of humor. Usually those who do not have the ability to create a pun repeat that statement. As a matter of fact, God himself, through his prophet Nathan, made use of a pun to proclaim an important prophecy. King David was eager to build a house, meaning a temple, for the Lord. Nathan, the prophet, told the King that rather it was God who would build a house, meaning a dynasty, for David. This prophetic pun is of great theological significance. It marks the beginning of a belief that God would send a kingly messiah to his people, born of the house of David.

In fulfillment of this prophecy, Jesus our King, was born of Mary, of the house of David, in Bethlehem, the city of David, about a thousand years after the prophecy had been made. It took a long time for God to fulfill the prophecy. God is very patient because to his "eyes a thousand years are like yesterday, come and gone, no more than a watch in the night" (Ps 90). Through all those years, as in all the years before them, God was working out his plan for the sending of his Son.

The era of the Old Testament is important to us because it reveals the unfolding of God's loving plan. It is our history because the chosen people are our ancestors just as surely as David was the ancestor of Jesus himself. If we receive this word of the Old Testament like a seed falling on good soil, it will lift our hearts in greater love of God. It is quite proper that the Old Testament form part of our scriptural readings at Mass. We can rejoice in the name Christian and be thankful for Jesus as our Savior only because of all that God accomplished in the era of the Old Testament.

Thursday of the Third Week (I)

The Second Vatican Council, in its Dogmatic Constitution on the Church (9), has emphasized a fundamental truth of our faith: "It has pleased God to make men holy and save them not merely as individuals, without any mutual bonds, but by making them into a single people, a people who acknowledges him in truth and serves him in holiness." The Church by its essence is a community with mutual bonds. Because of our mutual bonds, we have obligations toward each other.

Jesus himself makes an application of this truth when he talks about the lamp which is not to be hidden but put on a stand so that its light may be seen. This lamp is our faith. Professing and living the faith helps others to be strong in their faith. It is hard to be the only person who holds a certain position. If you are surrounded by people who take the opposite position, even in a matter as simple as supporting a certain team in sports or a certain candidate in politics, you feel alone and may begin to waver. When it comes to something important like our faith, we should support one another.

In the first reading today we are told that "we should not absent ourselves from the assembly, as some do, but encourage one another." The assembly referred to is the one gathered together for the Eucharist. Seeing others here at daily Mass is a real encouragement. The same is true on a larger scale on Sundays. But this encouragement becomes even stronger when our participation in the Mass is both devout and enthusiastic, not merely passive or indifferent. Externals do make a difference. Singing the hymns and answering the prayers aloud, rather than being quiet or merely mumbling the words, brightens the lamp of our faith for others to see. We should never have to feel alone in our faith. God has called us to be members of a community, the Church, with mutual bonds and mutual obligations.

Thursday of the Third Week (II)

The first reading today is unusual in that it is not a teaching addressed to us but a prayer by David addressed to God. The prayer is, however, a lesson in our relationship to God. David had just received through the prophet, Nathan, a solemn promise from God that he would build a dynasty for David. The promise meant that David's line would not die out and would be the source of the royal messiah, whom we know to be Jesus Christ.

David is filled with thanksgiving and gives praise to the Lord. But the foundation of his prayer is humility. He says to God. "Who am I, Lord God, and who are the members of my house, that you have brought me to this point?" David realized that he was a mere mortal and had done nothing to merit this prophecy. The promise God made was freely given out of unmerited love.

In every Mass we are called to praise and thank God. At the beginning of the Eucharistic prayer we acknowledge that it is right to give God thanks and praise. The foundation of this prayer must be humility. A person who works hard all month at his job has a right to his pay check. He need not be grateful to his employer because his salary is due him in justice. Humility makes us recognize that nothing is due us from God in justice. Everything he gives is a gift.

This kind of humility is not debasing. It does not place us in the position of a beggar who has to seek the pity of others. God does not pity us. He loves us. He wants to give himself and his goodness to us. In return it is right that we give him thanks and praise.

Friday of the Third Week (I)

Memory sometimes plays tricks on us. Years after some difficult struggle, which at the time seemed unbearable, we scarcely recall how trying things were. That is why people can so easily refer back to the good old days. More often than not, they were not really good but memory has mercifully cast its veil over the unplesantries. This is especially true if the struggle was worth it.

The Letter to the Hebrews was written after the original "good old days" of Christianity, probably between the years 80 and 90. Many of the people to whom this letter was addressed had gone through terrible persecutions but had survived. Now for some reason they had grown discouraged and lax in their faith. They needed to recall former times when they were more heroic, not with a sense of nostalgia, but with a realization that old zeal and enthusiasm could be recaptured. We are not sure what their present problem was, but the author of the letter wanted them to recognize that any effort needed to rejuvenate themselves should be put forth. Effort in the present would bring about satisfaction in the future, because God responds to that effort.

Something of this same idea is contained in the word of Jesus in the gospel. The most difficult time of farming is when the seed must be sown. Once that work has been completed, the farmer can look forward to the harvest. And the day of harvest makes him forget all the back breaking work which preceded it.

When we have bad days, we can all look back on some past experience and remember that God got us through. That realization should give us encouragement in the present and hope for the future. The harvest God will grant us is worth any struggle now.

Friday of the Third Week (II)

David was the greatest king of Israel and Judah. Not only had he been chosen by God himself to be king, but God had so favored him that he pledged that the Messiah would be born of his family. Every Israelite thought David the most fortunate person alive and many envied his power and riches as king. Anyone would gladly have traded places with him.

But David, despite his power, his possessions and even his many wives, allowed himself to become desirous of Bathsheba, the wife of another man, Uriah. He committed adultery with her and compounded this sin by murdering her husband. Although a great king, David was no superman. He was very human and very weak.

One of the strangest weaknesses of human nature is that, no matter what we have, we are never satisfied. You look forward to Christmas or some other celebration with great expectation, and the day itself is not quite as fulfilling as you had expected. Or if the celebration is all you hoped for, it is soon over and the memory of it quickly fades. We must not miss the meaning of this restlessness, this continued yearning of the human heart as did David. Nothing short of God himself can satisfy us because we are made for God. We must never be discouraged by the incompleteness of human experience, nor can we allow ourselves to be fooled by unanswered desires. We should take our restlessness and our yearning as reminders that we have a higher destiny than this life can provide. Even the bleakest unhappiness can be a joy if we recognize that the only reason we are unhappy is that perfect life with God alone can make us truly and permanently happy. St. Augustine wrote: "Our hearts were made for you, O Lord, and they will remain restless until they rest in you."

Saturday of the Third Week (I)

A very beautiful trait of most little children is that they have faith in their parents. They believe that their parents can do anything. As a result little children can go about their play with a joy and abandon, all the while knowing that their parents will take care of them. If they are hurt, they go right to their mother. If a toy is broken, they go right to their father. Their faith is not theoretical, merely a belief that this man and woman are their parents. Their faith is practical, a confident assurance that their parents are powerful and loving.

Such is the faith which the Letter to the Hebrews proclaims today. We are told that faith is confident assurance concerning what we hope for, a conviction about things we do not see. We are to be like little children who while at play do not see their parents and yet know that they are there to help. To make sure that we understand that faith is practical, and not merely theoretical, the author gives us the example of Abraham and Sarah. Faith moved them to accept God's promises and to live their lives with confidence in him. The most magnificent act of faith of Abraham occurred when he was willing to sacrifice his own son at God's command. It was a troubled and turbulent moment for Abraham, but faith saw him through it.

We need faith in all the moments of our lives, but it becomes particularly necessary when a storm of confusion threatens us and the waters of life become troubled and turbulent. In the darkness of the storm we cannot see our way and wonder where Jesus is. We cry out, "Lord, does it not matter to you that we are going to drown?" With faith we can hear his powerful and loving words, "Quiet. Be still."

Saturday of the Third Week (II)

Nathan, the prophet, received a difficult mission from the Lord which demanded courage on his part. He was to confront the king himself, and make him realize the gravity of his sins of adultery and murder, and call him to repentance. Prudently, and with a great deal of ingenuity, he prepared the king by telling him the parable of the selfish rich man. David fell into the trap and by condemning the rich man he condemned himself. Imagine his shock when he heard the word of the Lord through Nathan, "You are the man!"

These words were more than a condemnation. They contained within them the grace needed for repentance, to which David quickly responded by admitting, "I have sinned against the Lord." That was all God wanted to hear. He immediately forgave David, even though it was necessary that David be deprived of the fruit of his adultery. David really had no excuse for his sin. He was the favored of the Lord. He had everything he should have ever desired. When his greed led to adultery and murder, it would have been understandable if God had washed his hands of him. But God is not that way.

What this episode tells us is that although God does not ignore sin, he is eager to grant forgiveness. He condemns sin only so that the sinner may repent, no matter how bad the sin may be. The sinner is one who is about to drown in the dark waters of his own selfishness. Does it matter to God that a sinner is about to drown? It certainly does. As surely as Jesus brought peace to the turbulent waters, so will the Father through Jesus bring peace to the troubled heart of the sinner who repents.

Monday of the Fourth Week (I)

They say that misery loves company. I suppose that there are some people who find some kind of consolation in dragging others down to their level of misery. More profoundly it can be said that challenge loves company. Almost everyone takes courage from the realization that others have met much the same challenge and succeeded. It is lonely and discouraging to find oneself in a struggle all by himself.

One purpose of the Letter to the Hebrews was to give courage and support to a community of Christians who had lost heart. First fervor had cooled and a spiritual lethargy had set in. The author jogged their memory about heroes of the past and all that they endured for the Lord. The point was that God was not asking more of them than he had of people of faith in the past, and that what others had done in union with the Lord, they could do too.

We ourselves are in union with the Lord Jesus, a union which is daily enhanced by our sharing in his body and blood. God the Father does not ask more of us than he did of his Son. From our communion with him we should draw strength to be enthusiastic and persevering, for he is the mighty Lord who overcomes the demons which afflict us, whether they be the demons of despair or demons of lethargy.

Our communion is not only with Jesus but with all those who are in union with Jesus. The people we see around us at Mass are sharing in the same struggles and drawing from the same source of strength. In the battles of life we never stand alone. We should see life, not as a misery, but as a challenge, and in facing that challenge we have wonderful company.

Monday of the Fourth Week (II)

Absalom was a son of King David. He had murdered Amnon, his half brother and David's oldest son. David imposed upon him a punishment which was mild in comparison with the crime he had committed: he was sent into exile for two years and then banished from the court. In retaliation Absalom determined to kill his own father and to seize the throne for himself. David fled in fear. When confronted by Shimei, David accepted his threats and insults because he was aware of his own sins. Significantly for us David's flight took him up the Mount of Olives, near the Garden of Gethsemane where Jesus endured his agony.

David and Jesus are similar in that they both had to suffer from their own people. But they are completely unlike in that David was sinful and Jesus was sinless, David was guilty and Jesus was innocent. It was out of a sense of justice that David was willing to accept his affliction, but it was out of pure love that Jesus endured his passion.

The marvel of our redemption is that Jesus, though sinless, freely took upon himself the burden of sin. That burden of sin he accepted not only during the hours of his passion but all through his life. That is why in the gospel today we witnessed his expelling of the demons who were so heinous that not even the swine could tolerate their presence. After Jesus had expelled the demons, he said to the man, "Go home to your family and make it clear to them how much the Lord in his mercy has done for you." We are here in this church, our spiritual home, to praise God the Father for all he has done for us in his mercy through the death and resurrection of his son. Our praise of God here should lead us forth to proclaim the good news of salvation to all we meet. It is right that we give thanks and praise to God and we should be willing to share the news of God's love with others.

Tuesday of the Fourth Week (I)

All the men and women of faith who have gone before us and who remained true to God are models of encouragement and hope. By their lives, and often by their deaths through martyrdom, they manifest the ideals of dedication to God and his people. At the high point of history, one person above all stands out, and that one person is Jesus Christ, the Son of God.

The entire life of Jesus was one of dedication to his Father and to his people. Dedication to his Father was the driving force of Jesus' life. It moved him to spend whole nights in prayer to his Father. And from that dedication and prayer he found motivation and strength to love and serve all of his brothers and sisters in all of their needs. In today's gospel we see that Jesus is as attentive to the unnamed woman in the crowd as he is to Jairus, the official of the synagogue and an important man in the community. We see that Jesus is as concerned about the minor ailment of the woman as he is about the critical illness of the little girl.

This universal love of Jesus found its highest expression in his death on the cross. Jesus died for big people and for little people. He died to forgive big sins and little sins. And from his death comes forth a healing power for all human sorrow and sicknesses. The power of his death will lead all of us eventually to share in the glory of his resurrection.

Whether we are important people or not, whether our problems are large or small, we can take courage from the truth that Jesus cares for us and loves each one of us without exception.

Tuesday of the Fourth Week (II)

It is the most natural thing in the world for good parents to be concerned about and loving toward their children. Jairus in the gospel is someone we can understand. His little, twelve year old daughter was critically ill. No one need explain his feelings, his worry, his desperation. The gospel says that his appeal to Jesus for help was an earnest one. It was an expression of love for his little girl.

David was in a similar, yet different situation. His child, Absalom, was a grown man. No longer was he a little boy dependent on his father, David. In fact, he had turned against David, wanted to murder him and replace him as king. Absalom had become the enemy of his own father. When word reached David that Absalom had been killed he reacted as a father, not as an enemy. The news of the death of a feared enemy would have brought relief, even joy, to David. But his bond with Absalom was so strong that he could view him not as an enemy, but as his son. And so the news of his death did not bring joy, only sorrow.

God has become our Father through baptism. In our time of need he looks upon us with even greater concern and tenderness than Jairus had for his daughter. When we are in sin, he has a greater affection and love for us than David had for Absalom. In every circumstance God reacts to us as our Father. And God is the perfect Father. God is never impatient, never thoughtless, never too preoccupied with other matters to be concerned about us.

We can presume that the little girl in the gospel appreciated her father's love. It is too bad that Absalom did not understand David's affection for him. And we? How right it is that we never forget that God is our loving Father.

Wednesday of the Fourth Week (I)

There is a deep mystery in human suffering. Surely God is not some kind of ogre who takes a twisted delight in seeing his creatures in pain and misery. God is an all good and loving God. In his plan suffering must have some noble and beneficial purpose. In this life we are not in a position to comprehend that purpose.

All of us, no matter what our age or experience, are like little children in relation to God. The point of the first reading today is that little children cannot understand why their parents discipline them. "At the time it is administered, all discipline seems a cause for grief and not for joy." The fact is that parents who fail to discipline their children also in effect fail to love them properly. Allowing a child complete freedom to do whatever he pleases, no matter what the consequences, is not doing him a favor. It is doing him irreparable damage. When children grow up and become parents themselves, they begin to appreciate the training and formation afforded them by loving parents.

In this life we do not grow to the point of fully understanding God. We accept the discipline, the suffering, which comes into our lives only by faith. Our faith can be bolstered, however, by considering the life of Jesus Christ, God's beloved Son. Not only in his passion but all through his time here on earth he endured suffering. The rejection he experienced in today's gospel is only one example of his suffering which reached its climax in the shedding of his blood. God the Father loved Jesus his Son without reservation. In our suffering we must believe that God the Father loves us in the same way.

Wednesday of the Fourth Week (II)

In 1980 the United States government took up a census of all citizens and aliens living within the confines of the country. One of the chief purposes of the census is to determine pockets and concentrations of population for the sake of alloting government services equitably. David's census, on the face of it, seemed normal enough, but it was different from what we experience. His was a military census to determine the possible strength of an army. The results indicated that David could conscript a sizeable army according to the standards of the day.

We may wonder what David did that was wrong. David wanted a sense of political security by relying on military might. Among God's people his approach was a sinful reliance on human means alone without recognition of God. According to the covenant all the people, king included, were to look to God as the means of their support and defense. The words of today's responsorial psalm, besides indicating the repentance to which David eventually came, express the outlook of a faithful person: "(Lord) you are my shelter; from distress you will preserve me."

Jesus did not work miracles when faith was lacking. People without a practical faith in God are precariously on their own. We are joined to God in a new, everlasting covenant, sealed in the blood of Jesus Christ. We are to be a people of practical faith. Practical faith means more than believing that there is a God. It includes a trust and confidence that God guides and directs our lives and that he cares for us. The words of today's psalm must be on our lips and in our hearts as we go through life: "(Lord), you are my shelter; from distress you will preserve me."

Thursday of the Fourth Week (I)

Makers of biblical movies relish the opportunity to depict on film the more extraordinary events of the Old Testament. A favorite scene is that of Moses going up the mountain amid lightning and thunder to receive from God the commandments of the covenant. It was for the chosen people a momentous event, filled with the majesty and power of God.

In contrast is the establishing of the new covenant in the blood of Christ shed on the cross. That moment seemed to be one, not of majesty and power, but of weakness and humiliation. And yet the new covenant is greater than the old as heaven is greater than earth, and as eternity is greater than time. The apparent weakness and humiliation of Christ was a sign that God offers his eternal and heavenly covenant to those who are weak and humble.

The author of the Letter to the Hebrews recalls another contrast, that between Abel and Jesus. Abel's brother, Cain, was jealous of him because Abel in his humility was favored by God. Cain murdered his brother as Jesus was put to death by his brothers. The contrast is that the blood of Abel cried out for vengeance; the blood of Jesus brought forgiveness and access to God.

We are ordinary, humble, weak people. But we are recipients of the new and everlasting covenant with God.

Thursday of the Fourth Week (II)

When a person knows he is about to die, he usually wishes to make sure that as far as possible he has left nothing undone. Often he hopes that there will be someone who will carry on what he has tried to accomplish during his lifetime. When David knew that he was about to die, he called to his side Solomon, his son and his successor as king. He wanted Solomon to understand clearly the conditions he would have to follow if the Lord's promises to David were to be fulfilled. He wanted Solomon to follow the Lord's will.

All through his life Jesus preached the will of his Father, and he sent his disciples on the same mission. On Holy Thursday evening he knew that on the next day he would be dead. His death would accomplish all he had come to do. And yet he called his apostles around him at the supper table and there he made clear to them the one ultimate condition for being his disciples. He declared his great commandment: "Love one another as I have loved you."

All David could do was instruct Solomon. Death would separate them, leaving Solomon on his own. But the death of Jesus did not and does not separate us from him, for Jesus did more than give us a commandment of love on that night before he died. He gave us a supreme expression of love, the gift of his body and blood in the eucharist. That gift makes Jesus present among us always, but it does more. That gift in holy communion is the source of the spiritual strength we need to carry out his commandment of love.

What David could never have done for his son, Jesus has done for us, his brothers and sisters.

Friday of the Fourth Week (I)

John the Baptist was a man who was completely absorbed in the person of Jesus Christ. He had only one mission: to point out Jesus to others. In fact, we cannot even think of the Baptist without thinking of Jesus.

That sounds like a very heroic—even romantic—form of life. What a beautiful vocation! And indeed it was. Nonetheless his heroic, unselfish life ended with what can scarcely be called a bang. His death was almost ludicrous. He was destroyed by a petty ruler, the pawn of an unscrupulous and evil wife, who allowed himself to become trapped by the lewdness of a cheap dancing girl. Such is hardly the stuff of which heroics are made. How could the great herald of the Lord become the victim of such small people? The truth is that even an heroic life is necessarily caught up in the trivia of human existence.

We have been called to be disciples of Jesus Christ. This calling is a great privilege, but we should not allow a false romanticism to obscure our vision of reality. For the most part our lives will be rather ordinary, even humdrum. Unselfish love like that of John the Baptist must mark us as disciples of Christ, but that love is expressed in the simple, practical ways suggested in the first reading today: hospitality, concern for those in need, faithfulness in marriage, detachment from money, and reliance on the Lord. Our lives may never appear romantic or heroic to others, but they can be very worthwhile if they are pleasing to God.

Friday of the Fourth Week (II)

The Book of Sirach was written many centuries after the death of King David. It looked back upon his life in much the same way as we look back upon the lives of our national heroes, such as Washington and Lincoln, whose virtues we remember while forgetting or ignoring their faults. Sirach recalled David's considerable faults with only a fleeting reference to the fact that "The Lord forgave him his sins."

Strangely enough Sirach's attitude about David's sins is not different from that of God. Our God does not brood over our sins. When he forgives, he forgives completely. In the sacrament of penance, speaking through the person of the priest, God declares, "I absolve you from your sins." Some have suggested that the word "absolve" should be changed to "forgive." But such is not a good idea. "Absolve" is an unusual word, one we do not use every day, and God's forgiveness is unusual. It is indeed an absolution.

"To absolve" literally means to set free, or release, as from some obligation. Listen to the word, "absolve." There is a certain ring to it, a ring of finality, a relationship to the word "absolute," which means perfect, complete, certain. When we are truly sorry for our sins and confess them, God does not forgive us as we may forgive each other, grudgingly and partially. God never says what we may sometimes say, "I forgive, but I just can't forget." No, God *absolves* us from our sins.

Having absolved us from our sins, God, like Sirach whom he inspired to write about David, recalls only our virtues and our goodness.

Saturday of the Fourth Week (I)

In today's gospel we hear a touching invitation from Jesus to his apostles, "Come by yourselves to an out-of-the-way place and rest a little." The apostles had just returned from a missionary journey, and Jesus was eager that they enjoy not only a physical rest but a spiritual one as well. He was concerned that the rigors and demands of ministry might so absorb them that they could lose a sense of union with him. He wanted them to spend time alone with him.

In a busy, distracting life we too need time alone with Jesus. Here at Mass we fulfill the exhortation of the Letter to the Hebrews, "Through Jesus let us continually offer God a sacrifice of praise." But the Mass is community prayer and is meant to be a generous, outgoing, largely other-centered type of prayer. As community prayer it cannot possibly cater to the taste of each individual; as other-centered prayer it cannot always satisfy genuine personal needs. For a proper life of prayer we need both liturgical and private prayer, each in its own time and place.

Some people still complain that they do not like "the new Mass" because they can't pray at Mass. What this reflects is that previously they said personal, private prayers during Mass. Now with the return to the vernacular and active participation, they find no opportunity during the Mass for personal devotions and intentions. This opportunity must be found outside the liturgy.

Coming to Mass on a weekday means that you have already made a sacrifice of time and effort, and a very worthwhile sacrifice it is. But even more is needed. In addition to daily Mass, each of us must search for solitude and a time to pray in his own way.

Saturday of the Fourth Week (II)

God was pleased with the prayer of Solomon because it was an unselfish prayer. The gift he asked for, although for himself, was a quality he would use for the benefit of others. He requested a practical wisdom in his task of judging and governing God's people. In the gospel we see an even greater altruism on the part of Jesus. Wearied from his preaching and care for the people, Jesus sought a moment of rest and quiet alone with his apostles in a deserted place. But the people saw where he went and followed. Forgetting himself, despite his fatigue, Jesus immediately turned his attentions once again to the needs of the people.

The liturgy of the Church calls us to an unselfish spirit like that of Jesus and Solomon. While we can and should bring our personal needs to the liturgy—needs which should already have been expressed in private prayer—we will find that in the Mass the Church invites us to broaden our horizons beyond our own individual world.

The Prayer of the Faithful, following the homily, is intended to be intercessions for the benefit of the whole world. As such it is a generous kind of prayer and reflects an expansive spirit which excludes no one from its concern. These intercessions to the Father are prayed in union with Jesus who "opened his arms on the cross" to embrace all mankind and who shed his blood for everyone. They express the "catholic," the universal aspect of our prayer. When we have spontaneous prayers, they should not neglect a universal concern. For example, one may be mindful of a relative who is to be operated on; his prayer could possibly be phrased in this way: "For my cousin who is to undergo surgery tomorrow and for all those who are seriously ill, we pray."

Jesus, together with his ancestor Solomon, is an example of how our prayer should be generous and unselfish.

Monday of the Fifth Week (I)

Today we begin reading the beautifully poetic account of creation. The purpose of the inspired author was not to present a scientific explanation of the origin of the world. His was a religious purpose. No one should attempt to reconcile the story of Genesis with scientific theories, such as that of evolution, because there simply is no point of comparison. Science attempts to unravel the facts of how the world came to be. Genesis presents the meaning of creation. It does so in a picturesque fashion, suited to the mentality of a people far removed from us in time and culture.

The Israelites were surrounded by pagan people who believed in many and varied gods. Some worshipped the sun, others the moon or other created entities as divine. The Israelites were called to worship the one, true God, a personal God of intelligence and love. Their God was not an object, however awesome, but a person. He was to be worshipped, not his creation, for he was the one who created the sun, the moon and the stars, the plants and all living things. All the good things of the world are but a reflection of God's all powerful goodness. Good things should not replace the cause of goodness, God himself.

Scientific language can at times be cold and lifeless. Poetry is intended to be inspiring and uplifting. The simple, but beautiful, Book of Genesis should raise our minds and hearts to God the creator. He is a God who is all powerful and who has given us this magnificent world with its many gifts. From what we see all around us we should be moved to give praise and thanks to God, the creator.

Monday of the Fifth Week (II)

Today's first reading presents a jubilant scene. King Solomon offered sacrifices before the ark of the covenant which the priests had placed in the new temple. The ark represented the presence of the Lord in his new house. The joy and enthusiasm of the people was intense.

No less intense was the eagerness of the people in the gospel to come into contact with Jesus from whom went forth healing power. As Jesus left the boat, the people recognized him and began to bring their sick to him. They were almost frantic in their attempts to come close to Jesus.

In contrast to these two scenes is the atmosphere of our daily Mass which is usually somewhat quiet and reserved. And yet much more is happening here. We do not have an ark which represents the presence of God. We have the reality of the presence of Jesus Christ in the holy eucharist. Although Jesus is not present here visibly in the flesh so that we can touch him as did the people in the gospel, he is active among us in his mercy and compassion. In fact the Mass is much more than his presence. Jesus is present in the Mass, not passively as we are sometimes present to each other, nor is he present as a person asleep in his bed. Rather the Mass is Christ in the act of his sacrifice, his death and resurrection, the greatest sign of love for us. The Mass is an event, a happening, a dynamic reality. It is the sacrificial offering of Christ as a reality among us.

The Mass is a privilege greater than that afforded Solomon or even the people mentioned in today's gospel. We need not leap for joy at the Mass, but in faith we must strive to appreciate the great gift which is ours.

Tuesday of the Fifth Week (I)

In some circles it is considered sophisticated to minimize the importance of our planet and the dignity of the human race in the light of modern findings concerning the universe. Earth, we are told, is a mere satellite of the sun in our solar system and less than a pinhead within the expanse of our galaxy. Human life, we are cautioned, is a frail expression of reality, utterly dependent on a tenuous balance of nature and ultimately insignificant within a constantly expanding universe.

The Book of Genesis tells a different story. It says that God created our world and saw that it was very good. And God created the human race in his own image and likeness, giving it a special dignity above other creatures. Jesus himself not only declared all things on this earth clean by his words in today's gospel, but also gave a special meaning to our world and our life by his presence.

Here it was that the eternal Word of God, through whom God made the entire universe, was born. He walked upon our earth. He was warmed by our sun and nourished by our produce. Here he made his home and consecrated our dwelling place by his presence.

Born of a woman, truly human like us in all things but sin, Jesus has given to the human race a special dignity and worth beyond that of any other aspect of the cosmos. In a profoundly simple

statement the Second Vatican Council declared: "By his incarnation the Son of God has united himself in some fashion with every
man. He worked with human hands, he thought with a human mind,
acted by human choice, and loved with a human heart" (*Church in
the Modern World*, 22).

God was free to send his son into the confines of time and space
at any point within the universe. He chose the planet earth. God
was free to have his son take on material dimensions by means of
identity with any cosmic reality. He chose to make him human. In
creating mankind and the earth God saw that what he had done
was very good. Now he sees us and our planet with a special love
because Jesus was one of us and lived on our earth.

Tuesday of the Fifth Week (II)

Most of us have never been to the Holy Land, the site of the
magnificent temple built by Solomon, which was the symbol of
God's presence. Most of us have never been to Lourdes where the
healing power of God through the intercession of Mary is evident.
And not one of us has been to heaven. But we can and should have
the same realization as did Emily Dickinson, who led a very
sheltered life. In one of her simple but beautiful poems she wrote:

> I never saw a moor.
> I never saw the sea;
> Yet know I how the heather looks,
> And what a wave must be.
>
> I never spoke with God,
> Nor visited in Heaven
> Yet certain am I of the spot
> As if the chart were given.

The point is that God is all around us. Solomon, although
exultant about the temple, realized that it could not contain God nor
limit him to one place. God is everywhere in the work of his creation.
Jesus in the gospel declared all things clean, for all things come
from God and bear his creative presence. All things are sacred.

Even simple bread and ordinary wine are not unworthy to be the signs of divinity, nor are they unfit to make present the great saving act of the death and resurrection of Jesus. God is present not only in the book of scripture, but in the books of men and of nature. He is present not only in his people but in all his creatures.

Even when we leave this church, we will walk on sacred ground, we will breathe holy air, and we will touch and use hallowed things. God is not limited, nor should we limit our vision in a spiritual myopia. In faith we can open our eyes to see the goodness and love of God all around us.

Wednesday of the Fifth Week (I)

When God created the world, he gave human beings a special power which sets them apart from other created things. It is a beautiful power, and yet it is dangerous. This power makes people more like God, and yet its misuse can drive people away from God. Men have fought and died for the right to exercise this power, and others have attempted to suppress it in order to gain complete domination over a nation. This awesome power is freedom.

Although we have instincts like those of the animals, we are not completely controlled by them. We have the ability to choose. A hungry animal confronted with food has no option; he is driven to eat. An equally hungry man can, for whatever reason, choose not to eat. It is no wonder that the Bible presented the problem of freedom within the poetic context of forbidden fruit. We should not envision a literal tree or even a literal apple. The author presents the tree as a symbol of the fact that we human beings are called to choose real good, not apparent good, and that God directs us in what is the real good of life.

When God gave us the gift of freedom, a gift which he did not give to irrational animals, in a certain sense he gambled with us. He ran the risk that we would abuse our freedom. And yet he judged that the gamble was worthwhile. The reason is that God wants us to return his love voluntarily, not by compulsion. He sees value only in love which is freely given. God does not want robots who must respond to the proper command.

The fact that we are at this Mass shows that we have used our gift of freedom well. We could be elsewhere, resting or reading a newspaper or watching television. We have freely chosen to show our love for God through the celebration of this Mass. Love freely given is indeed very pleasing to God, and despite the dangers of freedom, we ought to rejoice that God has given us this marvelous gift.

Wednesday of the Fifth Week (II)

People are generally attracted to celebrities, whether they be movie stars, ball players, or politicians. People are eager to see them, to touch them if possible, and to get their autographs. Solomon was surely a celebrity of his day, and so it is not surprising that the Queen of Sheba was eager to see him in person and to hear his words of wisdom. She was overwhelmed not only by Solomon himself but by the elegant trappings of his royal court.

Sometimes in their eagerness to meet celebrities people miss the really important persons in life, one in particular. That one is Jesus Christ. Jesus has not chosen to surround himself with the elegant trappings of a royal court. Rather he has willed to veil himself under the simplicity of human words in the sacred scriptures and under the appearances of ordinary bread and wine in the Eucharist. He will not give us his autograph, but every day he does give us his wisdom in the scriptures and his nourishment in the Eucharist. Nothing can be more precious than that.

The Queen of Sheba traveled many miles to see Solomon, an effort not unmatched today by some people who seek to contact the celebrities of our times. The sacrifice we make to share daily in the Mass is well worth it, for Jesus is greater than Solomon or any other human person. The effect upon us of this daily contact with Jesus is not fleeting, like a scrap of paper upon which a person writes his autograph. This contact will lead us through our journey of life to our everlasting home in heaven.

Thursday of the Fifth Week (I)

The first reading today indicates in a poetic fashion that sex and its fulfillment in marriage are God's idea, his creation. Sex is not an accident of evolution, nor is marriage a product of social necessity. The reading also indicates that from the beginning God intended marriage to be a lasting relationship between one man and one woman.

Particularly expressive is the statement that "the two of them become one body." This statement, as understood and developed by the long tradition of the Church, means that sexual love between a husband and wife is meant to say something. Sex is intended to express a relationship so profound and so intimate that mere words are inadequate for it. In God's plan sex says, "I love you completely, exclusively, and forever."

Sex says, "I love you completely." This means that a husband and wife give themselves to each other without any holding back, and they accept each other just as they are, with all their excellent qualities and with their shortcomings. "I love you exclusively." This means that people who give themselves honestly to each other through sexual love cannot honestly give themselves in that way to anyone else. There is no one in the whole world to whom they are as committed as they are to each other. "I love you forever." A spouse should believe that his partner is so precious, so valuable that he wants the relationship to last for a lifetime.

We must admit that these ideals of sex and marriage are being eroded in our society. Through God's inspired word, we are called to have God's view of sex and marriage and to uphold his plan by our attitudes and by our example. Sex and marriage are God's idea, and they are a precious gift to the human race.

Thursday of the Fifth Week (II)

Solomon was given the gift of wisdom by God, but he was still free to use the gift or to reject it. Whatever our idea of wisdom may be, it does not seem that Solomon acted in a wise manner in the episode described in today's first reading. In his old age, when he should have been wiser than ever, he allowed his foreign wives to turn his heart to gods other than the Lord, the God of Israel. In effect he abandoned his faith in God. Because of his infidelity, he fell from favor with God.

The woman in the gospel was a foreigner, a Syro-Phoenician by birth, not a Jew, but she is in direct contrast to both Solomon and his foreign wives. She responded to a gift of faith given her by God and approached Jesus to ask that he drive a demon from her daughter. Jesus granted her request because of her faith.

The main point of the gospel is to teach that God gives his gift of faith freely to whomever he wishes. No one has a right to faith either by birth or by merit. A further lesson is that it is faith which finds favor with God. Think about Solomon. He was a great king, a man whose fame had spread far beyond Israel and Judah. Today even school children know his name. The woman in the gospel, on the other hand, would be considered a very unimportant person. Notice that her name is not even mentioned. And yet because of faith she found the kind of approval from God which Solomon in his old age did not.

It does not matter to God whether anyone in this world happens to think we are important. It does not matter to God which position we may happen to occupy in society. It does not matter to God whether we are rich or poor. What really counts with God is whether we have responded to his gift of faith.

Friday of the Fifth Week (I)

Today's first reading in symbolic and imaginative language presents the origin of sin in this world. The serpent is the symbol of all temptations. The two people, who elsewhere are called Adam and Eve, are referred to simply as the man and the woman to indicate that they are really no different from any other human being. In a sense they stand for the entire human race.

This story is indeed a tragic one. The man and the woman attempted to become like God by abandoning him and his will. They actually wanted to put themselves in the place of God. The result was the opposite of what they hoped for: instead of becoming divine they fell from divine favor and were separated from God. Rather than being satisfied with all the gifts God had given them they wanted more, and yet they went from good to evil.

In one sense all of us are that man and that woman. Every temptation which comes to us is basically a drive to abandon God's will, to put ourselves in the place of God, to worship ourselves rather than God. Jesus himself is the antidote to the poison of sin. This antidote was applied to us first in the sacrament of baptism. Jesus reached out to us in our time of need as surely as he reached out to the deaf and dumb man in the gospel. He freed us from sin and gave us the gift of faith which opened our ears to hear the word of God, a word which gives the meaning and purpose of life as well as the grace to follow that meaning and purpose.

The man and the woman allowed themselves to become confused about what life is all about. Our faith, if we are open to it, gives us the proper sense of values. Above all, it teaches us that happiness and fulfillment are found only in God and through devotion to his will.

Friday of the Fifth Week (II)

Jesus loved to tell parables to teach a lesson. The first reading today, from the Old Testament, is a parable not in words but in action. Jeroboam was a minister in the service of Solomon. When the propeht Ahijah tore his cloak before Jeroboam into twelve pieces, he was illustrating that Solomon's kingdom would be divided into the northern kingdom with ten tribes and the southern kingdom with only the tribe of Judah (which by David's time had incorporated the tribe of Simeon, thus accounting for all twelve tribes). From this point on the kingdoms of Israel and Judah go their separate ways, often in open hostility to one another. It is not a pretty picture.

The power of God is such, however, that even amid division and hatred he can work his plan. By divine irony God drew upon this situation to bring his son into the world, born of the house of David and of the tribe of Judah. He sent his son to reverse the movement for separation and to replace hatred with love. On the night before he died, expressing the purpose of his mission, Jesus prayed that all might be one.

The deaf man with the speech impediment is a symbol of disunity. Unable to hear or to communicate properly, he was cut off from those around him, forced to live a solitary life. Jesus cured him. Jesus is also the one who can establish unity among us, a unity whereby we speak and listen to each other with respect and concern. In the Eucharist God our Father gives us a share in the one bread and the one cup and makes us one in Christ. That oneness we all have with Christ must be expressed in our love and care for each other.

Saturday of the Fifth Week (I)

They say that history tends to repeat itself. I suppose that is true mainly because human nature does not change. Our first parents were sinful. When they sinned, they looked around for excuses. They were trying to "pass the buck." Adam said, "Don't blame me; blame that woman you gave me." And Eve said, "Don't blame me; blame that snake in the grass."

Sometimes we are very like our first parents. It is very hard to admit that we are weak, that we are imperfect, that we have faults. Most of us can use a big dose of honesty in admitting that as human beings we are far from perfect. The problem is enlarged by the fact that we are engaged in a bitter struggle against evil. God warned that from the time of the first sin enmity would exist between good and evil. Enmity means all out war to the end. We simply cannot afford to overestimate ourselves any more than we can afford to underestimate temptation in our lives. Making excuses, pretending that we are stronger and better than we are is the pride which comes before the fall.

If we had to fight the battle alone, we would have to give up in despair. But we need not struggle alone, provided we stand before God in honest humility and say, "We can't do it alone; we need your help." Jesus responds to this need as specifically as he did to that of the people who were without anything to eat in the gospel story today. He gives us the nourishment of his body and blood which is a spiritual strength to stand firm in the face of temptation. We need not rely on our own resources. United with Jesus in the Eucharist we have the power we need to remain faithful people.

Saturday of the Fifth Week (II)

After the death of Solomon, the kingdom was split in two. Jeroboam, who had fled to Egypt to escape the wrath of Solomon, returned as ruler of the northern kingdom. Jerusalem in the south had been the center of religious worship. To win the loyalty of his people Jeroboam realized that he had to break their ties with Jerusalem, and so he set up official places of worship within his own territory. Soon the inevitable happened. Worship of the one true God was affected by pagan beliefs and the people fell into pagan practices.

We believe that there is but one God. He is the God who has created us and the God who has given us a share in his own life through baptism. He is the God who provides the resources of this earth whereby we are nourished, and he is the God who feeds us spiritually in the Eucharist. He is the God who looks upon us with compassion in all our needs.

But like the people of the northern kingdom, we are surrounded by pagan beliefs and values. No one of us will fall down in worship before a golden temple of money and influence. Not one of us will offer sacrifices to idols, but we may be tempted to sacrifice our Christian values for what the world has to offer.

Everyone, whether he likes it or not, is influenced by his environment. We need a constant antidote to the poison of materialism and the disease which produces an insatiable thirst for power. That is why the Mass is so important to us. Here we are given the guiding principles of Christian living and a sense of true values by means of the scriptures. Here we are strengthened by the spiritual food and drink of the Eucharist to remain faithful to what we hear in the scriptures. Here we worship the one true God.

Monday of the Sixth Week (I)

Very often we hear the important scriptural message that we cannot love God if we do not love our fellow human beings. If our professed love for God does not overflow into love for his people, we are deceiving ourselves. Today's first reading gives a complimentary and equally important lesson. Revolt against God eventually leads to sins against our fellow human beings. To put it another way, if we do not have true love for God we will not have true love for his people.

For a reason which is not explained in the Bible, Cain did not find favor with God. We do not know what the problem was precisely, but although he offered sacrifice to God, the offering was empty of meaning. Since love for God was not in his heart, it was not in his offering either. Abel, his brother, was pleasing to God because of the sincerity of his worship. Cain became so jealous of Abel that he killed him. Murder is always horrible, but murder of a brother indeed cries out to heaven for vengeance.

Because Cain did not love God, he did not love his fellow human beings, not even his own brother. Trying to lead a good life without love for God is like trying to drive an automobile without fuel or like expecting a bulb to light up without electricity. Those without love for God easily commit atrocities such as murder, rape, assault, and robbery, or readily exploit others through such activities as dope traffic and prostitution.

Through God's gift we have his love in our hearts. The degree of that love directly influences our relationship with others. The Mass is a vital way of deepening our love for God. As we grow in love for God, so we will grow in love for our fellow human beings.

Monday of the Sixth Week (II)

Today we began reading from the epistle of St. James, who was a relative of Jesus. The content of the epistle was probably originally a sermon given during the liturgy. Its main purpose is to insist that Christianity must be practical, that faith must influence the way in which we live. It is a very old writing, dating back to possibly the year 62 A.D.

In his introduction St. James encourages us to pray for wisdom. The word "wisdom" can suggest the image of an elderly man, probably with a long, white beard, rocking back and forth in his chair, and proclaiming wise sayings, such as "A stitch in time saves nine," or "A penny saved is a penny earned." But such is not the scriptural image of wisdom. Rather, the kind of wisdom of which St. James writes should be seen as a person who hears the word of God and acts in accord with it. A wise person is one who, when he has offended someone, immediately tries to mend the situation (that is the stitch in time which saves nine). A wise person is one, who rather than saving his pennies, gladly uses his money to help those who are in financial need.

When we come to Mass we hear the word of God which is intended to give a sense of direction in life. We receive the body and blood of Jesus who wants to transform us into himself so that we may live as he lived. The Mass is beyond doubt the way to true wisdom, the means for responding to St. James' call that we be a wise people. We must allow the Mass to guide and strengthen us in our lives.

Tuesday of the Sixth Week (I)

Yesterday we heard the story of how Cain murdered his brother, Abel. The evil in the heart of Cain was multiplied many times in others, so much so that God determined that something must be done. God's sense of justice called him to remove sinful people from the earth by means of the great flood for the sake of good people who were represented by Noah.

This well-known story of the flood had for its purpose to meet a problem which disturbs good people of any era. Often it seems that evil men are rich and powerful. They oppress and exploit good people to their own profit. Although they live without any faith in God and surely with no concern for his commandments, they seem to prosper while the good continue to suffer. The problem in the minds of many is: if there is a just God in heaven, how can he tolerate such evil. It seems unfair. The narrative about the flood shows that God, in his own good time, rises up to destroy wickedness, while preserving the earth for the sake of people who are faithful to him.

One important principle of the Bible is that what God has done, he will do. We believe that Jesus Christ will come again to right the wrongs of our world. At that time the Lord will bless his people with peace. We do not know the time of that coming. Meanwhile we must continue to work for good. Part of that work comes from seeing that each one of us is a microcosm, the world in miniature. As there is both good and evil in the world, so there is both good and evil within us. With God's grace, especially the grace we receive at Mass, we must struggle to overcome evil within ourselves, no matter how large or small that evil may be. Noah found favor with the Lord. We find favor with him too in our daily struggle against sin.

Tuesday of the Sixth Week (II)

The apostles were confused by the words of Jesus in today's gospel, and maybe we are too. He told them to be on guard against the yeast of Herod and the Pharisees. Jesus spoke of yeast in the sense that it is a symbol of corruption. The apostles thought he was referring to bread, but he was warning them that they must be concerned lest they fall prey to the corrupting influence of evil men. He added that they need not worry about bread because God supplies their needs.

St. James in the reading today says much the same thing. He warns that we must be on guard against temptation. These temptations do not come from God. They come from within ourselves and from persons and things around us. What comes from God is only good. In fact, every genuine benefit comes from God the Father. We need not worry about strength to resist temptations; that strength comes from God as surely as bread comes from God.

The chief source of our strength is the Eucharistic bread. Although God offers his help to us through many means, such as prayers and devotions, nothing can substitute for the power of the Holy Eucharist. We all know that we must have food. A man who is starving can be comforted by consoling words, but what he wants and needs is nourishment.

God does much more than give us consoling words of encouragement as we struggle through life. He gives us the gift of the Eucharist. No one need starve spiritually. Our presence here at Mass indicates our appreciation of God's gift. What we must do is to open ourselves as fully as possible to receive the benefit of this spiritual food. First, we must be humble enough to admit that we need Jesus in the Eucharist. Secondly, we must have a firm faith that he can and will help us. Thirdly, we must tell him that we are willing and eager to respond to the grace he gives us.

We are a people favored by God. Through the Eucharist he gives us the power and support we require in life.

Wednesday of the Sixth Week (I)

Water is an awesome and powerful element. We need only think of the raging waters of a flood to appreciate its devastating force. In the Bible control over water was considered a sign of divinity. God alone could overcome the power of water and bring peace to its turbulence. Water is the central symbol in the story about Noah, but two other symbols are at work. They are the dove and the olive branch, which have long been seen as signs of peace.

They were both a sign to Noah that God by his almighty power had brought the waters under control and had restored peace to the world.

When Noah emerged from the ark, the first thing he did was to offer a sacrifice of thanksgiving to God. He realized that it was God who had granted peace to him and the remnant who had been the inhabitants of the ark. In our own faith we have more than symbols of peace. We have Jesus himself, and he is the one who has overcome the turbulent waters of sin which alone can destroy us. The peace of mind and heart which he grants us are drawn from the conviction that we are right with God, that through his death and resurrection he has reconciled us with the Father. We now have nothing to fear. As members of God's household, we are safe and secure. Anxiety need not hold any grip on us.

The theme of peace is very strong during the communion of the Mass. We pray that God may grant us peace, a peace which comes from our union with Christ in the Eucharist. But peace is something to be shared. That is why we are encouraged to offer each other a sign of peace. This sign is actually a prayer that others may enjoy the peace which Christ brings. Then together we all participate in the one body and blood of Christ, the cause of unity and peace in our lives.

Wednesday of the Sixth Week (II)

St. James is adamant about the truth that our faith must be practical, that it must affect for good the way in which we live. There are of course many reasons why faith must be practical, but St. James today presents a reason which is perhaps a little subtle and could be missed.

He says that a person whose faith is not practical is like a man who knows what he looks like by seeing himself in a mirror but then goes off and promptly forgets what he has seen. In this instance he is worse off than the blind man of the gospel, who had no possibility of knowing what his appearance was. The point of the comparison made by St. James is that faith enlightens us as to our identity. Faith is like a mirror in which we can see that we have become children of God. Our actions should flow from this identity.

The principle that actions should flow from identity is valid in every phase of life. A policeman should maintain law and order, not disrupt it. A doctor should foster and uphold human life, not destroy it. A judge should seek and promote justice, not violate it. And a person of faith, a child of God, should radiate the goodness of God.

So often it seems that people of no religion complain that people of faith are no better, sometimes worse, than others. It is a fair complaint. We know we are not perfect, nor should we pretend to be, but faith should be the guiding light of our lives which motivates us to strive for perfection. Faith teaches us that we have become children of God, and that faith should move us to be more like our Father.

Thursday of the Sixth Week (I)

After God had saved Noah from the flood, he made the rainbow a symbol of his mercy and love. A rainbow is a sign that the storm is over, that the danger has passed. Even after this event we still see clouds of evil gathering around us, and we still hear the distant rumbling of a hatred that wishes to harm us, but God has promised that never again shall all living creatures be destroyed. The covenant from God with Noah is a sign that God considers our world precious and worth saving.

Within this passage is a prescription which became part of Jewish dietary law: although humans were allowed to slaughter animals for the sake of food, they were not to eat flesh with the lifeblood still in it. Among the ancient Semites blood was considered to be the seat of life (somewhat after the manner in which Western philosophy maintains that the soul is the seat of life). The point is that life comes directly from God and is his greatest gift to the world. No one but God has absolute dominion over life, especially over human life.

The truth is that we are verging on a situation which is not unlike the era before the great flood. In our society life is becoming as cheap as it was then. Unchecked violence frightens many people away from being on the streets after dark even to go to church. Abortion, which the Second Vatican Council deplored as an unspeakable crime, is a blight which is reducing us to the condition of an uncivilized country. The drug culture is lowering many to a state but little better than that of animals.

Sometimes it seems inane to speak of love when respect for life, the foundation of love, has been eroded. As people of God we are called to have the most profound respect and regard for all forms of human life. To do otherwise is to ignore God's covenant with Noah, a covenant which is based on respect for life.

Thursday of the Sixth Week (II)

Poor Peter! With the best of intentions, he said the wrong thing. When Jesus predicted his own passion and death, Peter tried to tell him that such a thing could never happen. Jesus' reply was swift: "You are judging not by God's standards but by man's!" Peter did not understand that in God's plan the death of Jesus would lead to the glorious life of the resurrection. Jesus was forceful in his declaration to Peter because it was imperative for any disciple of Jesus to begin to follow God's values, not those of the world.

An understanding of God's standards must influence our way of acting in all circumstances. St. James gives a good example in the first reading. The truth is that in most instances a well dressed, apparently affluent person is going to be given preferential treatment. Such is true in most restaurants, department stores, and doctors' offices. On the other hand, a person in shabby clothes will generally be avoided or ignored. How does God view such matters? He is not impressed by wealth. He does not have his hand out for a tip, nor does he have to hope that a wealthy person will provide him with a handsome profit by purchasing an elegant home in heaven. If anything, God gives special attention to those who have next to nothing in this life. "He has chosen those who are poor in the eyes of the world to be rich in faith and heirs of the kingdom." He does not ask for money. He does not seek the benefits of someone's power or influence. God is eager to help those who are generally ignored by the world.

All of us have been favored with the gift of faith. St. James is urgent about the fact that this faith must move us to abandon the world's sense of values and to adopt God's way. What now is our attitude toward those who are ignored or even despised by the world?

Friday of the Sixth Week (I)

The story of the Tower of Babel is a dramatic presentation of the most basic form of all sin, a wish to be independent of God. It is the same sin as that of Adam and Eve. The men who planned the tower wanted to make a name for themselves by building a tower which would reach to the sky. In other words, they wanted to make a heaven for themselves without God. There is no question of whether they were theoretical atheists, that is, people who denied that there is a god. They were practical atheists, that is, they wanted to live as if there were no god.

The result was disastrous. They brought confusion and disunity upon themselves. From this confusion and disunity, as the sad tale of history reveals, came conflict, dissension, and war. Jesus was sent to reverse the trend. In the gospel he gave his formula for happiness and harmony. He declared that we must forget ourselves and our own selfishness. In complete unselfishness he gave his life on the cross and through that heroic act he won for us the gift of the Holy Spirit, a Spirit of unity and love. With the coming of the Holy Spirit at Pentecost, we see the change begin to take place. The efforts of men to build the Tower of Babel ended in a confusion of the languages of the whole world. The Spirit at Pentecost moved people of many languages to unite in a single voice of praise of God.

What God wants from us is a spirit of harmony and mutual cooperation. That requires unselfishness, a willingness to take up our cross with Jesus whereby we surrender our own interests for the sake of others. That is the way to happiness. It is even the right way to begin heaven here on earth.

Friday of the Sixth Week (II)

We are not saved by our own power any more than a baby is conceived in the womb by his own power. A baby is conceived by his parents, and we are saved by God our Father. In the moment of conception a person comes into being and receives his identity. In the moment of baptism we come into being with a new identity as God's children. Salvation, becoming children of God, is God's work, not our own.

When a child begins to grow up, it is natural for him to respond in love to his parents. In the same way through faith we are expected to respond to God in love by doing his will. It is in this sense that St. James says that faith which does nothing in practice is thoroughly lifeless. Believing in God demands that we respond to God.

Jesus proclaims the same truth in the gospel. He declares that if anyone wishes to follow him, to be his disciple, he must deny his very self, take up his cross and follow in his steps. Crying out, "Lord, Lord," is not what Jesus wants. He desires not words, but actions.

Here in the Mass we use many words in addressing God in our prayers. What we say in words must flow into our lives. We tell God in the Lord's Prayer that we want his will to be done. We are the ones who must seek to do his will here on earth the way his will is done in heaven. When our words are wedded to our actions, we are faithful children in whom the Father is well pleased.

Saturday of the Sixth Week (I)

Today's readings are about three groups of three men. The first three, Abel, Enoch, and Noah, go back to the dawn of history before the time of Abraham, the father of the Hebrews. They form part of the story which leads up to what we call the period of the Old Testament which really begins with the covenant God made with Abraham. In a sense good people, like these three men, because of their faith in God prepared for the covenant with Abraham.

The second group of three are Jesus himself together with Moses and Elijah. Jesus was transfigured in glory on the mountain. Moses represented the law of the Old Testament and Elijah represented the prophets. Together they summed up the entire Old Testament which flowed from God's relationship with Abraham. Their presence with Jesus symbolized the fact that the Old Testament was fulfilled in Jesus. As the earliest times prepared for Abraham, so the Old Testament era prepared for Jesus.

The third group of three are Peter, James, and John. They represent the people of the New Testament. They are symbols of ourselves, a people of fulfillment. They gaze upon the glorified Jesus, not comprehending the full import of who he is and what his glorification means to them. Nonetheless people of faith like them prepare for the second coming of Jesus Christ.

We ought to see ourselves as part of God's overall plan. Although this plan is fulfilled in Jesus Christ, it has not yet reached completion. Through faith we look upon Jesus as glorified through his death and resurrection, and yet we cannot begin to grasp what is yet in store when Jesus will come again. In that coming we will be caught up in his everlasting glory. That is why every Mass indicates that we wait in joyful hope for the coming of our Savior, Jesus Christ.

Saturday of the Sixth Week (II)

St. James is the eminently practical writer of the New Testament. In today's reading he strikes at the heart of a basic human problem: misuse of the great gift of speech. He makes a marvelous comparison in which he likens the tongue to a rudder which, despite its smallness, controls the course of a mighty ship.

And indeed mighty is the gift of speech, even mightier than the face which launched a thousand ships. A person at the Space Control Center in Houston declared, "All systems are 'go,' " and man was reaching for and finding the moon. A young couple says, "I do," and their lives are completely changed, as they reach for and hope to find happiness. A single word can irreparably ruin the reputation of a person, or it can save someone from death.

We begin to appreciate the meaning of speech when we recognize that it is a sharing in the power of God. In the beginning God said, "Let there be light," and there was light. Through the priest Jesus says, "This is my body . . . this is my blood," and bread and wine are wondrously transformed. Our human words are but a faint reflection of the magnificence of God's word but they are a marvelous privilege nonetheless. The power of speech sets us apart from the animals and gives us a share in divinity.

When St. Peter saw Jesus transfigured on the mountain, he hardly knew what to say because he was overcome with awe. Recognizing the awesomeness of speech, we should be conscientious in its use. The positive use of speech is like a transfiguration for us, making us like God himself.

Monday of the Seventh Week (I)

Today we began reading from the Book of Sirach, which was composed approximately two hundred years before the birth of Christ. The author was concerned that some of his people were adopting the customs and outlook of the pagan Greek civilization. He wished to call them back to their own religious traditions and the values they had been taught. In a sense he was like parents today who have raised their children to be good Catholics only to see them abandon their faith as young adults. Such parents often wonder what they have done wrong when the truth may simply be that the culture in which we live has overcome their children without any fault of the parents.

Pressures on young people are often quite strong. It is common for young people to see their peers living together without benefit of marriage. The use of alcohol or drugs has for some become a way of life. A kind of hedonism, self-indulgent pleasure seeking for its own sake, tends to replace purpose in life and care for others. Even good young people are not immune to these pressures.

Devoted parents are often frustrated in trying to deal with these and similar problems. As one father put it, "Talking to my son is like talking to the wall!" There is, of course, no easy solution. But these problems must be the concern of all of us. The father in the gospel brought his possessed son to Jesus after all else failed. We must bring young people back to Jesus, not only by trying to reason with them or even by giving them good example, but through the means emphasized by Jesus in the gospel. That means is prayer. Constant, never-failing prayer is not the least we can do. It is the most we can do.

Monday of the Seventh Week (II)

Today's gospel story about the cure of the young boy is fascinating reading because of the richness of its detail. Listening closely to the gospel, you can easily form a clear picture in your mind of what happened. But we can understand the real significance of the story only by knowing what happened immediately beforehand.

Just before this episode Jesus has been transfigured on the mountain. This magnificent appearance of Jesus was a foreshadowing of the glory which would come to him through his death and resurrection. It was meant as a sign that death would not conquer Jesus. On the contrary Jesus would show that he was the master who overcomes both sin and death. Today's gospel is but a foreshadowing of the power which Jesus will bring to bear upon all of us. The little boy, plagued by a demon, appeared to be dead, but Jesus took him by the hand and helped him to his feet.

We are plagued by sin. It is like a disease which appears to be terminal. Only Jesus, the divine physician, has the power to cure. It is a power to make us whole and healthy like himself. We are already well on the way to a complete cure because Jesus has washed us clean of this disease by the water of baptism. Now he strengthens us in our recovery by means of a marvelous food and drink, the spiritual nourishment of his body and blood in the Eucharist.

One day in a future unknown to us each of us will be pronounced dead. Like the boy in the gospel we will become like a corpse. But in faith we know that Jesus will be there and he will take us by the hand and help us to our feet. With Jesus we will then stand upright in the presence of God forever.

Tuesday of the Seventh Week (I)

The Wisdom Literature of the Bible, to which our first reading belongs, is not concerned with theory but with practice. Wisdom to the Jews was not an abstract way of looking at life but a concrete way of living life. Our present reading considers the problem of human suffering. This passage urges us to accept whatever befalls us and to be patient in crushing misfortune, but one of the most striking statements is this: "Study the generations long past and understand; has anyone hoped in the Lord and been disappointed?"

We must remember that this book was written about two hundred years before Christ. When the author encourages us to look at persons of the past who trusted in the Lord, he is thinking about people like Abraham, Moses, and Elijah. We are in a more advantageous position than those for whom this Book was originally written. We stand at a vantage point of time at which we can look back, not only to persons in the Old Testament era, but to the person of Jesus Christ himself.

Jesus in the gospel today makes a prediction of his passion: "The Son of Man is going to be delivered into the hands of men who will put him to death." No one on this earth had to endure more suffering, both mental and physical, than did Jesus. Over the centuries, devotions like the Way of the Cross, have been developed to help Christians appreciate the intensity of Jesus' sufferings. But we know that Jesus made a prediction of his resurrection as well as of his suffering and death. Both predictions came true. Jesus handed his life over to his Father completely by means of his death on the cross, and the Father responded by raising him from the dead. Jesus went from sorrow to joy, from suffering to glory, from death to life.

In our own suffering and trials, we in faith study the life of Jesus. We see that his hope in his Father was not disappointed. Nor will our complete trust in God be disappointed either.

Tuesday of the Seventh Week (II)

Christianity is an upside down way of looking at the values of life. It is like choosing bread rather than cake, straw rather than gold, death rather than life. There is a divine irony in Christianity which is easy to miss. It was a lesson the disciples of Jesus had to learn.

In today's gospel the disciples can be seen as typical human beings. Ambition like a deadly leech had taken hold of them. On their way to Capernaum, outside of Jesus' hearing, they had been arguing about who was the most important. Each one wanted to be at the top because they thought that Jesus was going to establish a worldly kingdom in which they would be bathed in luxuries as were the Romans occupying their land. Jesus had just warned them that he himself would be put to death, but the message had not sunk in.

Then Jesus tried to make the message explicit: "If anyone wishes to rank first, he must remain the last one of all and the servant of all." Next he exemplified his lesson by embracing the little child, an action not entirely lost upon his disciples. A child in that era was a person of no rights, a person "to be seen and not heard." To welcome a child in this context meant to become his equal, to be like him in humility and simplicity. St. James learned the lesson as we heard in the first reading, for his great advice was: "Be humbled in the sight of the Lord and he will raise you on high."

Christianity is a new set of values. The simplicity of bread, and not the elegance of cake, is what is transformed into the body of Christ. Humility, which is like straw rather than pride which is like gold, is the way to find favor with God. And death to sin, rather than a clutching to selfishness, is the way to eternal life.

Wednesday of the Seventh Week (I)

Today's gospel poses a difficult problem: what to do when nondisciples act in the name of Jesus? The answer which Jesus gives requires the wisdom spoken of in the first reading for a correct understanding.

The specific problem which Jesus addressed was the expelling of demons by those who were not his disciples. His cryptic answer was: "Anyone who is not against us is with us." In our own times we might say that the answer of Jesus addresses a situation in which people maintain that they have the right way to pray, to cure illness, or to spread the gospel. Can we accept the actions of such people merely because it cannot be shown that they are not against the Church? Too quick an answer is not acceptable because almost all of us know people who have been led astray from the Church by those who say they are acting in the name of Jesus Christ.

From other parts of the New Testament, particularly the inspired writings of St. Paul, we find more explicit criteria to judge these situations. Three of these criteria are the most important. The first question to ask is whether a position or action is motivated by love. If the motive seems to be ambition or personal gain or anything other than Christian love, the work is not of God. The second question to ask is whether unity and harmony, the building of the mystical body of Christ, is being effected. If the work by its nature brings about factions and divisions, it is not of God. The third question to ask is whether the stance a person takes is in accord with the teachings of scripture and tradition. If his stance is opposed, for example, to the sacraments and especially to the Holy Eucharist, then his opinion is not of God. Real wisdom is needed to determine whether a person is for or against Christ.

Wednesday of the Seventh Week (II)

Part of growing up is acknowledging that we have responsibilities toward other people. A little child knows that he should not do things without his parents' permission, but more often than not he does not understand that he must be responsible. A husband, on the other hand, knows that he should not invite someone to dinner without first consulting his wife because she may already have other plans for the family.

We are God's children and we act rightly only by his permission, but we are adult children. Maturity means that we recognize our responsibilities toward God. We are more completely in his hands than any little child can be in the hands of his parents. That is why St. James today teaches us that we are not to make plans for our lives as if God did not exist. He guides and controls our lives and we should be happy about that. We could not possibly be in better hands.

St. James sums up what should be our spirit: "If the Lord wills it, we shall live to do this or that." Of course we do not have to use those explicit words. It is their spirit that count. And this spirit is exemplified for us by Jesus himself. His whole life was guided by the will of his Father. His loving obedience reached its climax during his agony in the garden when in the face of his passion he prayed, "Not my will but yours be done."

Every day in the Mass we pray as Jesus taught us, "Thy will be done." This prayer to the Father puts us in union with Jesus for it expresses the disposition he himself had. It is the disposition of an obedient child, but it is even more the disposition of a mature, responsible person.

Thursday of the Seventh Week (I)

Sometimes we exaggerate to make a point and we do not mean that our words be taken literally. A man carrying a heavy object may say that it weighs a ton. Of course the object does not even approach a ton in weight, but you understand the meaning of the expression.

In the gospel today Jesus uses exaggeration, or hyperbole, to make a point. He does not want us to cut off a hand or pluck out an eye. These external organs are not the cause of sin, which originates in our mind and in our heart. But he does wish to make a point and he wishes to make it forcefully. Any sacrifice must be accepted which is necessary to exclude deadly sins from our lives. That we must understand.

His point really makes sense. What is the wisdom in choosing some pleasure or situation which will deprive us of the ultimate goal of life, everlasting happiness with him in heaven? A small child thinks only of the moment. He has neither the experience nor the intellectual development to weigh values. It is impossible for him to understand the consequences of his actions. Unfortunately some adults do not act in a mature fashion. They refuse to accept the consequences of their own decisions.

On the other hand, the wise person sees everything in the light of eternity. He knows that every earthly pleasure can last but a short time and cannot possibly fulfill him. He is a person who turns to God as the source of lasting happiness and perfect fulfillment.

Even as adults we are weak and make mistakes. That is why Sirach in the first reading urges us not to delay our conversion to the Lord. Since this conversion is a never-ending process, we begin each Mass by calling upon God's mercy and forgiveness. The one truth we cannot exaggerate is the importance of our complete dedication to our God.

Thursday of the Seventh Week (II)

St. James in the first reading today sounds much like an Old Testament prophet crying out against the injustices of his day. Apparently similar injustices existed in St. James' era even among the earliest Christians. We should not be surprised since many similar injustices exist among us.

It has never been popular to protest injustices. From the time of the prophets to the present, dedicated people have had to give up their lives in the cause of social justice. In 1980 we witnessed the death of an Archbishop who spoke out for the rights of the oppressed in El Salvador. The wealthy who exploit others usually have the means to retaliate against those who prick their consciences. Often in Catholic circles such retaliation is relatively mild, taking the form of letters of complaint to bishops about sermons.

In any case the practical thing at the moment is for us to examine our own conduct. While we rightly protest abominations in our society, such as abortion, we must make sure we are consistent in the matter of recognizing basic human dignity. What is our attitude toward those held in contempt by some, such as alcoholics, drug addicts, or derelicts? Do we really accept the human rights of those who just happen to be undocumented aliens or who speak a language foreign to our own?

Actually, Jesus calls for much more than strict justice. He expects us to see and love his own person hidden beneath the veils of humanity all around us. That is the meaning he has in mind when he says, "Any man who gives you a drink of water because you belong to Christ will not, I assure you, go without his reward." Do we refuse anyone this drink of water?

Friday of the Seventh Week (I)

Our human lives are intended to reflect the relationship between God the Father and his Son, united by the love of the Holy Spirit. God can rightly be said to be these very relationships. Created as we are in God's image and likeness, we approach the fulfillment of our human personalities through relationships here on earth which are a reflection of God's own relationships and our ultimate relationship with him. God is love, and a loving relationship helps us to become more like him.

Marriage is a profound reflection of God. God intends that it be a commitment for life, not because of an arbitrary law but because marriage is meant to be a reflection of God's own fidelity. We cannot imagine God saying that he no longer loves his Son or that he is bored with him or that he wishes to explore a new way of living. Married people cannot pretend to be equal to God, but they are called to strive to be like him.

Friendships too are meant to mirror the loving relationship which is God. Friendships which are characterized by jealousy, possessiveness, and lack of trust are not true friendships at all. We can all recognize the kind of friend who reflects God's love. He is willing to help at a moment's notice and is always available to listen when we need an ear. He is the kind of person you are comfortable with, and he does not place constant demands upon you and your time. In his love he is generous and unselfish.

Life is a time for growth, a time for living in loving relationships with each other so that we may truly reflect the image of God according to which we have been created.

Friday of the Seventh Week (II)

It goes without saying that divorce today is a serious problem. The teaching of Jesus in the gospel stands, but when we hear the startling statistics about how many marriages end in divorce, we ought to realize that a significant number of fellow Catholics are included. We may not take upon ourselves from God his right to judge them. Judgment belongs to God alone. But there is confusion among many divorced Catholics which you can help clear up.

Divorce by itself without remarriage does not exclude people from holy communion. Of course, the Church does not accept the idea that divorce can void a valid, Catholic marriage, but divorce may be necessary in society for legal effects only. If you know of a divorced Catholic who has not remarried and yet is staying away from Church because of a confusion, you should reach out to that person with an explanation and with an invitation to return to Church and the Sacraments.

If a person may not receive communion because of a second

marriage not recognized by the Church, there is no reason why that person should not join the community in the prayer of the Mass. In fact, we wish to welcome such a person warmly and encourage that person to seek the help needed from God by joining us here at Mass. If you know of such persons, you should seek them out.

St. James warns us that we are not to grumble against one another. Rather in everyway possible we are to help and encourage one another. We must try to act toward each other as God acts toward us, for as we heard in the responsorial psalm, "Merciful and gracious is the Lord, slow to anger and abounding in kindness."

Saturday of the Seventh Week (I)

In some circles it is considered sophisticated to minimize the importance of our planet and the dignity of the human race. Earth, we are told, is a mere satellite of the sun in our solar system and less than a pinhead within the expanse of our galaxy. Human life, we are cautioned, is a frail expression of reality, utterly dependent on a tenuous balance of nature and ultimately insignificant within a constantly expanding universe.

This kind of view, while displaying a specious humility, is not in accord with divine revelation. The Book of Sirach today contains a beautiful hymn of praise to God, the Creator. It exalts the majesty and goodness of God by indicating the marvel of the human race which he has created in his own image. God has enriched the planet earth with seemingly endless species of many life forms. Scientists search in vain for the slightest hint of life elsewhere within the universe while our planet teems with life. Above all these varied expressions of life, God has placed the human race.

The gospel in contrast with the picture of God's majesty in creation as presented by Sirach paints a tender and touching picture of God in the flesh. Jesus says, "Let the children come to me." Few realities are better calculated than this invitation to emphasize God's love for his creature, man. Jesus goes on to say, "It is to just such as these (children) that the kingdom of God belongs." Man is a frail, weak creature, as symbolized in a little child, but God has nonetheless chosen us as the kingly and royal people of his kingdom.

Minimizing the importance of our planet and the dignity of the human race is not an act of humility but an affront to God the creator. In this Mass we praise and thank God for the marvel he has shown in creating the earth and the human race.

Saturday of the Seventh Week (II)

Almost all Catholics think about calling a priest when a loved one is near death. That moment is indeed a significant one, and proper concern should be manifested. The Church, in fact, meets the moment of death with the sacrament of penance, if possible, and with holy communion as viaticum. The sacrament of the anointing, which we used to call extreme unction and which was promulgated in the reading from St. James, is really intended, not for the dying, but for those who are gravely ill.

Actually the primary point by St. James in today's reading is that prayer should characterize all aspects of our lives, and not only the moments of crisis. His words are worth repeating: "If anyone among you is suffering hardship, he must pray. If a person is in good spirits, he should sing a hymn of praise." Grave illness is not the only time to think about the importance and necessity of prayer.

All prayer, whether it be petition or praise or any other form, is a way of expressing our complete dependence on God. God is our Father and we are his children, more dependent on him than even an infant on his mother. When Jesus embraced the little children, he declared, "It is to just such as these that the kingdom of God belongs." Authentic prayer helps to develop the childlike dispositions which Jesus wants: simplicity, humility, and trust.

No matter how old we are, no matter what our responsibilities in life, in relation to God we are like little children. We should rejoice in that relationship. It should give us a great sense of serenity and peace as we go through life. When we have the disposition of a child, Jesus himself embraces us and blesses us by placing his hands upon us.

Monday of the Eighth Week (I)

A camel is an unattractive animal with a large hump on its back. The picture of such an animal attempting to pass through the eye of a needle is ludicrous at best. The picture is a typical form of Hebrew overstatement for the purpose of making a point. The point is that some people bring with them obstacles which make it impossible for them to enter the kingdom of God.

When Jesus spoke to the man in the gospel, he singled out his wealth as his obstacle. Wealth in itself is not a problem; attachment is. Jesus saw in the heart of the man precisely this attachment, which forced the man to walk away from Jesus. He could not accept the challenge of detachment even with the help of God.

Wealth may be a problem for some people, but we should not limit our view by concentrating on the matter of money. The real point is that any obstacle must be given up. If it is not riches, it may be something else. Simply being poor is no guarantee because a poor person may be improperly avaricious. His own life may be directed toward getting to the point of wealth possessed by those whom he envies.

An attachment interfering with our advance to the kingdom may be for a person, an object, or even a way of acting. Each person must examine his own life to determine the obstacle. I cannot tell you what the obstacle is in your own life. You must decide that for yourself. Even small attachments should not be overlooked since Jesus calls us to constant progress in our journey toward his kingdom.

At Mass we celebrate the greatest detachment possible. We relive with Jesus the giving up of his life voluntarily on the cross. From him, especially in holy communion, we can draw the strength we need to remove from our shoulders the bloated hump of attachment. With God, all things are possible.

Monday of the Eighth Week (II)

The First Letter of Peter, which we began reading today, is an important part of the New Testament. One of its main purposes is to explain the meaning of the Christian life in view of the significance of baptism. It may be drawn from an instruction which was given to converts who were preparing for baptism. Baptism in this opening reading is referred to as a new birth.

This beautiful reading is positive and uplifting in tone. It quite appropriately reflects the announcement of a new baby by proud and happy parents, even though it is most likely that the baptism thought of is that of adults. But the parallel is there nonetheless. Devoted parents rejoice in the new life which they have brought into the world by means of the fruitfulness granted to their sexuality by God. Baptism is the begetting of a new life too, the life of faith which leads to an imperishable inheritance. This life comes from an act of love which is fruitful. This act is that great event in which God the Father brought his son through death to the fullness of life, the resurrection.

St. Peter in a classic understatement calmly writes, "There is cause for rejoicing here." Rejoicing indeed! It has been said that the birth of a child is a sign that God has not given up on the human race. Turning things around, we can say that a baptism, our own included, is a sign that we must not give up on God. We may have to suffer the distress of many trials. Jesus in the gospel calls us to supreme detachment. But it is all worthwhile because of the great love of God manifested in the new birth of baptism. We have become God's children and we must have complete confidence in his fatherly love for us.

In this Mass we join in the sentiments expressed in the opening of this letter: "Praised by the God and Father of our Lord Jesus Christ, he who in his great mercy gave us new birth."

Tuesday of the Eighth Week (I)

Gift giving is a beautiful expression of love. The more we love a person, the more valuable we wish our gift to be. And yet a precious gift may be meaningless if it is a mere gesture and not a sign of true love and dedication.

Jesus gave his life as a gift to his Father in sacrifice. No gift could have been more precious nor more meaningful. His sacrifice was the greatest act of the love the world has ever seen. Now Jesus makes that sacrifice a present reality among us in the Mass. Jesus does not die again nor does he repeat his sacrifice. Rather the one unique act of the gift of himself is made present for our benefit. We are not deprived of sharing in this act by an accident of time, simply because we happen to have been born centuries after the event.

The offering of the Mass is always valuable because it is the one offering of Jesus Christ, but it can be meaningless as far as we are concerned. We must bring something to the Mass. We must offer ourselves with Christ to the Father. Peter said to Jesus, "We have put aside everything to follow you." By full participation in the Mass we can say that little by little we are putting aside everything negative about our lives. Here at the Mass we must offer the giving up of sin. Our impatience, our jealousy, our lack of love and generosity, these must be put to death in the death of Christ at Mass.

But there is more. Here we are also to offer our joys and our sorrows, our hopes and disappointments, our successes and our failures. In short we are to join our lives with Christ and pray earnestly to the Father as we say in the Third Eucharistic Prayer, "May he make us an everlasting gift to you."

Tuesday of the Eighth Week (II)

A beautiful custom in our society is that of a baby shower. People bring gifts for the expected baby out of love for the parents to be. The shower is a happy event, full of promise and hope for the future.

Out of love for God the prophets gave the gift of hope that a new era would dawn upon the world, an era awaited by God's promise and longed for with hope. That era has come in Jesus Christ, and we are the beneficiaries. Speaking to us St. Peter declares of the prophets, "They knew by revelation that they were providing, not for themselves, but for you."

By baptism we have been born as children of God and have become part of his family, the family Jesus spoke of in today's gospel. Now we are to live up to the hope and expectation manifested for us throughout the Old Testament era. That is what St. Peter has in mind when he writes, "As obedient sons, do not yield to the desire that once shaped you in your ignorance." We have taken on a new identity as God's children. That is why we are to become holy in every aspect of our conduct, after the likeness of the holy one who calls us.

After a baby has been born, the parents take on the responsibility of feeding and caring for him. After our birth of baptism God the Father feeds and cares for us by means of his inspired word and the Holy Eucharist. In responding to his word and the Eucharist, we have the means we need to live up to his expectations, to become holy in every aspect of our conduct.

Wednesday of the Eighth Week (I)

Today's first reading is unusual in that it is not a lesson addressed to us but a prayer addressed to God. We should note that God is called upon as "God of the universe." It is an expression unique to the People of God. Among the ancients each nation had its own god, and within a nation there were many other gods, such as the god of war, the god of the harvest, and so on in a long list. The God of Israel was considered by his people to be the God of gods, the God who had made the heavens and the earth, the God indeed of the universe. This was the way God had revealed himself to the Israelites.

This God of the universe is our God. We need not placate his wrath nor bargain with him for the food we need, as the ancients thought was necessary with their gods. The reason is that the God of the universe is our Father. He has given us a share in his own life and loves us with a greater love than the most devoted parents can have for their children. As a constant sign of his fatherly concern, he tenderly feeds us with the Holy Eucharist, the body and blood of his Son.

Jesus was eager that we understand and relish our identity as his Father's children. He wanted us to have a certain serenity which would exclude the kind of ambition manifested by the apostles in the gospel today. A child does not have to prove himself. He takes for granted that he is loveable and loved by his parents. And he believes that his parents will take care of him.

Our Father is the God of the universe, almighty and all loving. We can rest secure in his arms, knowing that his almighty power is motivated by his fatherly love for us in all our cares and concerns.

Wednesday of the Eighth Week (II)

Sometimes we say that a person is worth his weight in gold. With the fluctuation in gold prices these days it is hard to say what such a person is worth in this view, but an average adult could be priced at about a million and a half dollars. That is obviously a lot of money. Of course the expression, "worth his weight in gold," is only a figurative way of indicating a person's preciousness.

We may go on, however, to say that God is not on the gold standard. His standard for measuring our worth is something much more precious than gold. St. Peter writes, "You were delivered from the futile way of life your fathers handed on to you, not by any diminishable sum of silver or gold but by Christ's blood beyond all price."

Today in the gospel Jesus made a prediction of his death. He did so because he knew that in the Father's plan the shedding of his blood on the cross would be the price of our salvation. Many spiritual writers have observed that Jesus would have died even if only one person had stood in need of salvation. That observation is valid. Even though God saves us and makes us holy by forming us into a single people, the Church, he does not look upon us as a nebulous crowd of humanity. He knows and loves each one of us as an individual. We can rightly say that what God does for all, he does for each person in particular.

James and John, as pointed out in the gospel, were concerned about their place in the kingdom. They wanted preferential treatment. Such should not have been their concern, nor need it be ours. We ought simply to rejoice in the fact that we are precious in the eyes of God, that our worth has been measured by his standard, the blood of his own divine Son.

Thursday of the Eighth Week (I)

At one time if an astronomer wrote about God, his fellow scientists usually thought he had taken leave of his senses. But today the picture is changing. The essence of recent developments is the conviction that the universe had a sharply defined beginning, and some scientists are daring to ask the question, "What came before the beginning?" The wise man, Sirach, answered the question two hundred years before Christ: "At God's word were his works brought into being; they do his will as he has ordained for them." He reflects the proclamation of faith found in the Book of Genesis: "In the beginning God created the heavens and the earth."

Scientists will, and should, continue to search for an explanation of the origin of the universe from their point of view. The "big bang" theory, current among most astronomers, postulates a beginning which requires a first cause. The picture is incomplete without a first cause, and it is that first cause whom we call God.

Belief in God, however, is not based on scientific evidence. About that we should be clear. The personal, loving God of creation is the object of revelation. The gift of faith, like the gift of sight given by Jesus to the blind man, allows us to get a glimpse of God as he is: not a nebulous, ethereal force, but a personal loving Lord of all reality.

Listen again to the words of the wise man: "At God's word were his works brought into being; they do his will as he has ordained them." The point is that God did not create the universe, wind it up as a child does with a toy, and abandon it to run about at its whim. God controls the fate of the universe as his kingdom and directs the lives of men as the crown of his creation.

Thursday of the Eighth Week (II)

Today the first reading declares that we are a chosen race, a royal priesthood. This is the priesthood of the baptized, whereby we are all called and empowered to worship God in spirit and in truth. In particular this priesthood is exercised by means of full participation in the Mass.

In the earliest days of the Church, the title "priest" was reserved to Jesus Christ. When the term "priesthood" was applied to human persons, it was done so only in the plural, as in the first reading today: "the priestly people." Those whom we call priests today were designated by various titles, usually presbyter, and it was not until the seventh century that the term was applied to the ordained. This fact should help us to realize that Jesus is the only priest of our religion, and that his own priesthood is shared in essentially different ways by the ordained and the baptized.

No one who is a Catholic may deny that the ordained priest is necessary, but this truth does not minimize the importance or value of the priesthood of the laity. In fact, the priesthood of the ordained is one of service. Only an ordained priest can make Christ present under the appearances of bread and wine, but he does so for the sake of the people. In one sense, he makes Christ come alive in the eucharist. He activates Christ. He also activates Christ the priest in you, the people.

A practical application is that here at Mass you must not be passive. You must enter actively into the celebration of the Mass. You must join in the hymns and prayers of the Mass with enthusiasm and devotion. Above all, you must offer Christ and yourselves to the Father through the hands of the priest and in union with him. Your priesthood demands full, active participation in the celebration of the sacred liturgy.

Friday of the Eighth Week (I)

Today's gospel presents us with an unfamiliar picture of Jesus. We are so used to his image of goodness and healing that we may be surprised to see him in a destructive mood as he curses the fig tree and causes it to wither. Actually we must view the scene as a parable in action. Jesus apparently wanted to teach that Israel because it was barren of true devotion would wither and die. The fact that it was not the season for figs heightens the meaning of the parable. Israel was not expected to produce the fruit of sincerity in the ordinary course of events; rather the people had been given the extraordinary grace of God, and so their barrenness was all the more reprehensible.

We should not think that all the people were devoid of true religious devotion. Sirach in the first reading praises the godly men of the past, but he too indicates that for some it was as if they had not existed.

We stand at a vantage point of time in which we enjoy even greater graces and helps than those granted to Israel. First we benefit from God's presence in the inspired word of the Hebrew Scriptures, the Old Testament. Added to that for us is the revelation of Jesus Christ as found in the New Testament. God was present to his people with his grace before Christ, but now he is present in an even more dynamic way through his Son, especially in the Eucharist. We are nourished and strengthened by the Word of God in the scriptures and by the Word of God in the Holy Eucharist.

At daily Mass we find the right means to be fruitful in God's sight: the scriptures and the Eucharist. Despite the aridities all around us and the barrenness of the soil of the world in which we live, God's almighty power can make us bear the fruit of true devotion.

Friday of the Eighth Week (II)

There is an old saying, "Blood is thicker than water." The meaning is that family ties should be more solid than other relationships. A blood relationship, however, is not more solid than the relationship into which we enter by means of the water of baptism. By baptism we enter God's family. We become children of God and brothers and sisters of one another. Actually this spiritual relationship is a blood relationship too, for it is sealed by the blood of Christ shed on the cross.

Our first reading today, which is basically a teaching on baptism, applies the principles of family relationships to our lives as Christians. The ideal family virtues are harmony, mutual help, and thoughtfulness. All these virtues add up to love which makes everyone happy to be at home. Of course no family is perfect, and neither is the family of the Church on this earth since it is made up of imperfect human beings. Nonetheless, Jesus who gave his life so that we might become children of his Father expects that our lives, unlike the fig tree in the gospel, will be fruitful.

Jesus is the model for the whole Christian family. We must never forget the full extent of his love, his death for us, which we celebrate in every Mass. His example should motivate us to try to live together in harmony by being truly thoughtful of, and helpful to, one another. Jesus is also more than a model. He comes to us in communion so that if our hearts are open we may become more and more like him, filled with love, the summit of all family virtues.

Saturday of the Eighth Week (I)

If we could project ourselves back in time to stand in the temple precincts with Jesus, I wonder what our reaction to him would be. Would it be like that of the leaders of the people, a challenge motivated by doubt or rejection? Would it be that of faithful disciples? Of course, we really have no way of knowing, but we can make some guesses.

One reason some people rejected Jesus was that they did not have the gift of faith to see through his humanity to his true identity as God's son. Jesus to them looked like any other man. His humanity was like a veil covering over his divinity.

God has lifted this veil for us. That is the literal meaning of revelation. The correlative of revelation is faith. In lifting the veil, God has given us also a wisdom like that granted to Sirach. In the first reading Sirach states, "I sought wisdom. She came to me in her beauty and until the end I will cultivate her." We too must cultivate our faith so that it may broaden our vision all the more. And this is where we can make a guess about what our reaction to Jesus would have been two thousand years ago.

In faith we embrace Jesus but do we really respond to him in all instances? We know that Jesus is present in the Holy Eucharist. Without that faith we cannot even be a Catholic. Jesus is also truly present in the inspired word of sacred scripture, the Bible. Do we have a proper appreciation and love of Jesus in the word? Jesus is also present in the people all around us. Is their humanity, with all its weaknesses and faults, like a veil which hides the presence of Jesus from our eyes?

Faith is a gift which we cultivate through prayer. We must pray that God will help us to see, to appreciate, and to love the presence of his Son in the Eucharist, in the scriptures, and in his people.

Saturday of the Eighth Week (II)

On his birthday an elderly man, surrounded by members of his family, lay dying. He called for his grandson for whom he had a particular affection since he had been born on this very day twenty-one years ago. Sharing a birthday with the young man, the dying great-grandfather wanted to share his wisdom with him. In a weak voice, he said, "In all you do, seek the truth. Not money, because it cannot last. Not fame, because it will pass. Not love, for in love you can be deceived. Seek truth and you will find God, and in finding God you will find perfect love."

We do not know whether the young man followed the advice of his great-grandfather. More important for us is the fact that Jesus on the night before he died declared to his disciples, "The truth will set you free." The truth does set us free from error and confusion to find God and to love him. But it is no easy task. From the very beginning the Church has been seeking that truth which is God, but in every age it has been beset by error and confusion.

The first reading today, which is more like a sermon than a letter, was addressed to a Christian community as a warning against certain errors. It dates back to about the year 80 A.D. Even at that early date the teachings of Jesus as passed on by the apostles had become obscure for some people.

The Church must ever be vigilant about the truth. There are those who feel that the Church at times has been too inhibitive. It is true that theological scholarship must continue, that new insights are always possible, but there are also limits set by divine revelation, and the Church is bound in conscience to indicate those limits. The Church cannot accept the position that "anything goes." Actually we should be grateful for the teaching authority of the Church because the words of the dying man are valid: "Seek truth and you will find God, and in finding God you will find perfect love."

Monday of the Ninth Week (I)

Today we began reading from the Book of Tobit, the story of a devout Israelite family, forced to live in exile in the pagan city of Nineveh.* Its purpose apparently was to encourage the people of God who were forced to live apart from their homeland to remain faithful. It serves as an instruction for us as well, exiled as we are from our heavenly home.

In the part of the story for today we see the virtue of charity in action. Tobit, the father, is eager that others may share his fine dinner on the feast of Pentecost. Tobiah, his son, is sent to offer

---

* Most modern scholars consider the Book of Tobit to be a religious novel, part of the Wisdom literature of the Bible rather than an historical account. Since the purpose of the Book is to present moral teaching in either case, homiletically it is not necessary to make these distinctions.

invitations but comes across a dead Israelite instead. Tobit, again out of charity, feels compelled to bury his fellow Israelite despite the dangers involved.

Tobit is the kind of man you would like to meet, as well as the kind of person we should imitate. In contrast is the action of the tenant farmers in the gospel parable which vividly depicts the fate of the prophets and of Jesus himself. Jesus was even more heroic than Tobit, for he met rejection with love and accepted death so that others might have eternal life.

The hospitality and the concern of Tobit are models for us, but they, together with all merely human examples of charity, are caught up like so many drops of water into the one magnificent wave of love which is Jesus Christ. The Mass, no matter what its occasion, is the living memorial of the life and death of Jesus. Through the priest he daily declares to us: "This is my body . . . given up for you. This is the cup of my blood . . . poured out for you." We simply cannot have a more forceful example of, and motive for, our own Christian love toward others.

Monday of the Ninth Week (II)

There is an underlying theme to many fairy tales, including the most famous of all, that of Cinderella. A beautiful maiden is hidden in obscurity and poverty. A handsome prince is determined to discover her, and when he does he takes her in marriage and elevates her to his own royal dignity. This theme has something to say about God and ourselves.

Some people, although they would never express it in this manner, think of God as the beautiful maiden and themselves as the prince. What I mean is that they seem to believe that they must go in search of God, that they must take the initiative. Actually the opposite is true. It is we who are lost in obscurity and poverty. God on his own searches us out, unites us to himself in a relationship not unlike marriage, and elevates us to his own dignity.

The fairy tale puts into graphic language the parallel of the basic message found in today's first reading: God's power "has freely bestowed on us everything necessary for a life of genuine piety through knowledge of him who called us by his own glory and power." We have not found God. God has found us.

Of course we must respond to God's loving embrace. We are free and unfortunately we can reject God as did the people represented by the tenant farmers in the gospel. Response is important but we must not overemphasize it to the detriment of the message in today's gospel. Make no mistake about God's initiative in our regard. It is he who out of pure love has called us to share in his glory and eternal happiness.

Tuesday of the Ninth Week (I)

There is a mystery in God's providence which we will never fully understand. That is the lesson in our reading today from the Book of Tobit. Tobit was an outstanding example of devotion and charity, and yet in God's providence he was allowed to become the victim of a freak accident which blinded him.

Despite his misfortune, he remained faithful to God. When he thought that the young goat, which would have made a marvelous feast, had been stolen, he insisted that it be returned. He did not feel sorry for himself and conclude that he deserved something of value, even if it had been stolen. His wife was equally insistent that the goat had been given her as a bonus, and in the frustration of trying to support a blind husband who had become angry with her, she turned against him. She even taunted him: "Where are your charitable deeds now?" She was implying that despite his good works, he had not found favor with God.

It would have been the most natural thing in the world for Tobit to have given up on God. But he did not. He knew what it meant to give to God what is God's. This statement of Jesus in the gospel shocked his questioners. They wanted a settlement of the political question, but adding a religious exhortation Jesus implied that they had asked the wrong question and that they were remiss in their religious duties. The Romans would see to it that they paid the tax, by force if necessary. God asks for a service which is freely given and which never lessens, no matter what.

The "no matter what" is important. Like Tobit we must keep our trust in God and remain faithful to him in bad times as well as in good.

Tuesday of the Ninth Week (II)

Some people have a seriously distorted view of the end of the world. They picture in their minds a terrible cataclysm that will annihilate the universe. This picture is drawn from a misinformed reading of sacred scripture. For example, they read the passage we just heard from the second letter of Peter without understanding its symbolism: "The heavens will be destroyed in flames and the elements will melt away in a blaze." They take this to mean annihilation, but fire is a standard symbol in the Bible to mean purification from sin and imperfection. In commenting on this passage the Second Vatican Council teaches: "As deformed by sin, the shape of this world will pass away, but we are taught that God is preparing a new dwelling place and a new earth where justice will abide and whose blessedness will answer and surpass all the longings for peace which spring up in the human heart" (*The Church in the Modern World*, 39).

God destroys only evil, not good, and his creation is good. He will purify his creation, however, and it is in that sense that the heavens and the earth will be new. This will be the kingdom of Christ come to full perfection. Meanwhile, we must work to destroy sin in our own lives. That is what the reading today has in mind when it says, "Beloved, while waiting for this, make every effort to be found without stain or defilement, and at peace in his sight." Our preoccupation should be to give to God what is God's, in accord with the teaching of Jesus in today's gospel.

For those who are on God's side the end of this world as we know it is not something to be feared, but something to be anticipated. Jesus himself has taught us to pray, "Thy kingdom come."

We should indeed pray earnestly for the consummation of God's plan, for the coming of his kingdom, a kingdom of perfect justice and love.

Wednesday of the Ninth Week (I)

Today Tobit shows his true mettle. Although he had been blinded by a freak accident and although his wife had turned against him, he remained faithful to God. We heard this beautiful prayer: "You are righteous, O Lord, and all your deeds are just; all your ways are mercy and truth."

On the same day Sarah, the daughter of Tobit's relative, Raguel, was also in sorry straits. Incredibly every time she married, her husband died almost immediately, and this had happened seven times. Her maid taunted her as Tobit's wife had taunted him. Near despair she went to her room with the thought of hanging herself. Reconsidering, she thought better of it and instead poured out her heart in prayer to God. Later we shall see how the prayer of both of these people was heard by God: Tobit will recover his sight and Sarah will find a husband who survives.

The lesson taught by this reading is that God does indeed hear the prayers of his faithful people. And yet we know that God answers prayers in his own way and in his own time. In our Christian faith we believe that God responds to our ultimate prayer, the desire for everlasting life. In the gospel today Jesus is not concerned with answering a silly question but with insisting on the truth of resurrection from the dead. He indicates that the question is actually irrelevant since resurrection means an entirely new life, not a mere resumption of this earthly existence.

Of course we would like to have all of our petitions answered here and now. But we must accept God's plan. That plan may not answer needs we think we have, but it does guarantee the final answer to all prayers. In our faithfulness to God we have the assurance that "Christ will raise our mortal bodies and make them like his own in glory." We will share in his kingdom "where every tear will be wiped away."

Wednesday of the Ninth Week (II)

There is an old saying, "You get what you pay for." This statement means, in effect, that you have to pay for quality, that there are no real bargains. Our whole economic system develops within us the attitude that there is a price for everything and that we are responsible people when we accept this attitude as reality. In fact, we are always a little suspicious when something is offered "for free," and we want to know what the catch is.

Unfortunately our economic system can affect the way we look at God. When we think of God we ought not to consider the saying, "You get what you pay for." Rather we ought to remember the words of an old song, "The best things in life are free." We cannot buy God's favor. We do not purchase heaven. These best of all things are entirely free, given us by God out of pure love for us. The first reading today puts it this way: "God has saved us and has called us to a holy life, not because of any merit of ours but according to his own design."

Of course we must respond to God's gift of grace, but it is necessary to emphasize the gratuity of God's love and especially of everlasting life. Resurrection to everlasting life is the greatest gift of all. Jesus in the gospel took the occasion of the foolish question put to him by the Sadducees to insist that resurrection means an entirely new life, not a mere resumption of this earthly existence.

But let the message stand clear: "God has saved us and has called us to a holy life, not because of any merit of ours but according to his own design."

Thursday of the Ninth Week (I)

Some people say of an ideal marriage that it was made in heaven. The marriage of Tobiah and Sarah was made on earth, to be sure, but in a sense it came from heaven for it was in answer to a prayer. According to the story Sarah had seen the death of seven husbands, each virtually on the wedding night. In desparation she turned to God for help and Tobiah was sent to her. They entered into a long and happy marriage.

Tobiah was so grateful for his lovely wife and their mutual affection that on the wedding night he prayed with her the beautiful prayer which is part of today's reading. In it they praised and thanked God for his wonderful plan whereby he joins a man and woman together in marital love. This prayer is so touching that some young couples choose this reading for their wedding Mass.

There is a hint in this reading, written some one hundred and fifty years before Christ, of today's gospel message. It is a realization that all true love is of God. In the Gospel Jesus was asked a single question to which he gave two answers. "What is the first of all the commandments?" he was asked. Jesus responded that we must love God with our whole being and our neighbor as ourselves. What Jesus did was to combine two commandments of the Old Testament, one from the book of Deuteronomy and the other from the Book of Leviticus. In effect, he was saying that the two cannot really be separated. We cannot truly love God if we do not love our fellow human beings, nor can we truly love our fellow human beings if we do not love God.

Marriage is a special form of human love, consecrated for Christians by a sacrament. In a true marriage God is loved as the spouses express love for each other. And their love for each other grows in the degree that they love God.

Thursday of the Ninth Week (II)

St. Vincent de Paul used to say, "I have a single sermon but I twist it a thousand ways." Of course his statement was something of an exaggeration, but his point was that there is a core to our faith, a central message which must be constantly repeated in every possible way. Our two readings today certainly present the core of the Christian faith.

First in the gospel we find the great commandment of love. And we should observe carefully that there is but one commandment of love, not two. Jesus was asked, "Which is the first of all the commandments?" To that question there should have been only one answer. Jesus did indeed respond that we must love God with our whole being, but he refused to stop there. He added that we must also love our neighbor as ourselves.

The command to love God with our whole being is from the Old Testament book of Deuteronomy and the command to love our neighbor is from the Old Testament book of Leviticus. The commandments were not new by Jesus. His contribution, so to speak, was to combine the two separate commandments into one. The truth is that we cannot truly love God if we do not love our neighbors, and we cannot truly love our neighbors if we do not love God.

And that brings us to the second reading and another aspect of the core of the Christian message. True love often demands a dying to self, an unselfishness. Even our physical death is the ultimate act of love by placing ourselves confidently into the hands of God. The message is that death leads to life, the eternal life of the resurrection.

Love in this life and resurrection to eternal life in the perfect love of God: that pretty well sums up the Christian message.

Friday of the Ninth Week (I)

If you heard the readings earlier this week you know that Tobit was blinded by a freak accident. He turned to God in prayer for help. When his son, Tobiah, returned from his wedding he brought with him, at the direction of the angel Raphael, a strange medicine made of fish gall. After he smeared the gall on his father's eyes, the old man's sight was restored.

Ophthalmologists would, I suppose, scoff at the idea that fish gall has curative powers, but the purpose of the biblical story is not to teach a lesson in medical science. Rather the story intends to show that God uses his power in answer to prayer.

God can work directly if he wishes; he can heal without any created intermediary. More often than not, he does work through his creation. That is why in the story Tobiah was shown as using the fish gall. But we should not think that there are two separate forces at work in our world, one human and one divine. It is not as if God is at work when there is a direct cure, and man alone is at work when medicine brings about a cure.

Jesus in the gospel is proclaimed as Lord, and he is Lord of all creation. When scientific research discovers a wonder drug, it is by the direction of Christ. When medicine actually works, that is the power of Christ. Even the skilled hand of a surgeon is guided by the hand of Christ.

When we pray for health or for a cure, we should not do so because all else has failed. Even with confidence in a doctor and in medical science, we should pray that Jesus will indeed consecrate these human instruments so that they may be effective. Jesus is Lord of all creation.

Friday of the Ninth Week (II)

One of the principal causes of the advance of civilization was the development of written languages. That human beings have been able to communicate with each other through sounds is marvelous enough, but the fact that the meaning of these sounds could be permanently recorded and disseminated through writing is astounding. This development is part of God's plan and he has used it to communicate himself through sacred scripture, sacred writings, which he himself has inspired.

St. Paul today tells us that the scriptures inspired by God are useful for teaching, for reproof, correction, and training in holiness. In a sense this is a classic understatement. Next to the Eucharist, the scriptures are our most precious possession.

Words, written or spoken, are the expression of a person's ideas. The words of scripture are God's words, but he has only one idea. That idea is a person, his Son. We say that parents conceive a child, and that people conceive ideas. This double meaning of the word is helpful in understanding that God conceives his Son after the fashion in which we conceive an idea. The Church teaches, then, that Christ, the Word of God, is present in the words of sacred scripture. That is why the Lectionary used at Mass and which contains the word of God, is deserving of respect and honor. But this word is meant to be communicated to us, and we must hear it with much the same reverence and appreciation with which we receive Christ in the Eucharist.

At the dawn of civilization oral communication was rudimentary and a written language did not exist. God saw to the development of written languages so that we could benefit from the permanent record of his revelation.

Saturday of the Ninth Week (I)

In the book of Tobit two people were in need. Tobit needed recovery of his sight after he had been blinded, and Sarah, who had lost seven husbands in death, needed protection for her spouse. Both had their prayers answered by God through the ministry of the angel, Raphael. Not knowing Raphael's identity, Tobit insisted that his son reward him richly for his help. The Angel Raphael informed them both that they were to thank God, not himself, and they were to do so both by prayer and almsgiving.

An angel is a messenger, a servant of God. In our lives there are many angels, not the kind who are of heaven, like Raphael, but the kind who are of earth. Seneca, an ancient Roman philosopher, wrote: "Wherever there is a human being, there is a chance for kindness." We can say in faith: "Wherever there is a human being, God finds a chance to show his love." The people who love us, who care about us, who are always willing to help, are the messengers, the servants of God. To them we must be grateful, but we must not forget to praise and thank God for working through human instruments.

This thanksgiving to God is rightly expressed here at Mass. But there is more. Kindness from others should beget kindness toward others. That is a form of gratitude very pleasing to God. Even the smallest act of thoughtfulness toward others, like the two small copper coins given by the widow in the gospel, will not go unnoticed by God. In gratitude for the angels of love in our lives, God wants us to become angels of his love to others.

Saturday of the Ninth Week (II)

We live in a society in which values that are contrary to the gospel message are canonized. The cornerstone is not Christ but economics. A person's value is measured more often than not in terms of his economic status. The poor are shunted aside as worthless and the wealthy are given every consideration. "Money talks," we say. That is the doctrine of our society but it is not the sound doctrine of our faith.

God has a different set of values from those on which our society is based. When Jesus saw the wealthy putting sizeable amounts of money into the collection box of the temple, he was not impressed. It was not as if the wealthy should not have given large sums, but Jesus was looking for something else. He saw that something in the poor widow who donated only two small copper coins. He explained to his disciples what he saw: "The wealthy gave from their surplus, but the woman gave from her want, all that she had to live on."

It was the generosity of the widow that mattered, not the money she gave. I have to imagine that this generosity was characteristic of her entire life. She must have been the kind of person who not only gave everything to the temple treasury but who also made time to help others in need. She was the kind of person who could always be counted on. Actually the widow is a symbol of Jesus himself. Out of love for us he gave everything he had, his very life. Our model is not an anonymous widow, but Jesus Christ himself.

A donation to the Church is of course welcome, but such does not exhaust the lesson of the gospel or the example of Jesus. We are called to be a generous people, unselfish people in all of our relations with others. God does not value us for our money but for our generosity.

Monday of the Tenth Week (I)

Today's gospel contains declarations by Jesus known as "the beatitudes." "Beatitude" means happiness or even something stronger, perhaps like bliss. In fact, some translations have "Happy are the poor in spirit," rather than "Blessed are the poor in spirit." "Beatitude" is an unusual word, one we scarcely use every day, and it describes statements by Jesus which are unusual indeed.

After all, where is the happiness in being poor, or sorrowful, or hungry or thirsty? Everything in our society is calculated to becoming rich and to eliminating every form of pain and sorrow. We are led to believe that happiness is found in money and everything money can buy. Even though we say that money cannot buy happiness, one cynic expressed his view by saying, "Having money is a pretty good way to be miserable."

Jesus wished to establish a whole new set of values. He insisted that happiness comes, not from relying on riches, but from relying on God. His key statement is "How blest are the poor in spirit." The poor in spirit are those who depend completely on God and see him alone as the source of all good. The cynic would protest that this approach does not work, but the truth is that it has worked for centuries. It has worked for the saints, who like St. Paul truly believe that God "comforts us in all our afflictions."

Jesus in effect says to us: Make your choice; rely on material things which cannot last, or rely on God who never fails.

Monday of the Tenth Week (II)

If you had been in the position of Elijah, the prophet, you would have felt very insecure. He was called by God to face down Ahab, king of Israel. Ahab had married Jezebel, a very evil pagan woman who had total influence over him. As a result Ahab abandoned the God of Israel and had gone over to the worship and veneration of Baal, a pagan god. He even went so far as to erect an altar to Baal in a temple which he built in Samaria. The Bible says of him that he did more to anger the Lord than any of the kings of Israel before him.

Elijah was sent by God to warn this incredibly evil man that as a punishment for his sins a terrible drought would come upon the land. He did his duty but then his life was in jeopardy, to put it mildly. The hazard was so great that God warned him that he must flee from the king's wrath and hide.

It took a lot of courage for Elijah to speak out boldly against the king. I doubt very much that he needed the warning from God that he should escape from the king. Actually the words of God were not so much a warning as they were an assurance. God wanted Elijah to know that he would protect him and he would even see to it that he was fed by ravens.

Elijah as a matter of fact lived according to the beatitudes even before they were proclaimed by Jesus. All the beatitudes add up to one truth: trust in God and you will find happiness.

No matter what we are called to in life, no matter how challenging or threatening our situation may be, we must have trust in God. To be "poor in spirit" means to rely completely on God as did Elijah, the prophet.

Tuesday of the Tenth Week (I)

James Thomson, an author of the 18th century, wrote the famous line: "A penny saved is a penny got." You might guess correctly that Thomson was a Scotchman. Another way of looking at the matter says that a penny spent is a penny used. In other words, the purpose of money is found not in hoarding but in using it to purchase something you want or need.

Faith is a precious gift from God, but it is not to be hoarded. It is to be shared with others. That is what Jesus has in mind when he tells us that we are salt of the earth and the light of the world. Salt is useless until it savors food and a lamp is meaningless until it enlightens the darkness.

Some very committed people believe that they must spread the faith by going from door to door and confronting people. Perhaps you have had experience with people like Jehovah's Witnesses. They are zealous but often they alienate people by their tactics. Jesus has a better way. He tells us that our light must shine before men so that they may see goodness in our acts and give praise to our heavenly Father. It's the old truth that actions speak louder than words. St. Paul in the excerpt we heard today from his Second Letter to the Corinthians reminded his readers that he proclaimed faith in Christ without equivocation, but later in this letter he was compelled to remind them of the example he himself had given of devotion and zeal.

Sharing our own goodness is helpful both to others and to ourselves. When a person spends a penny, it is used up. When a person spreads his faith through goodness, he does not have less faith and goodness. He actually has more. Both faith and goodness grow in the sharing.

Tuesday of the Tenth Week (II)

The prophet Elijah reprimanded King Ahab for his evil ways and had to flee for his life because the wrath of the king had been aroused. But God took care of his faithful prophet through the kindness of the widow who shared food and drink with him. The widow was in a dire situation herself, fully expecting to die because of the famine over the land. Quite understandably, Elijah had to coax her into sharing because she had next to nothing left for herself and her child. The generosity of the widow did not go unrewarded by God, who saw to it that her jar of flour did not go empty until the famine ended. That is the way God is. He is generous with the generous. Jesus appeals to us to be equally generous by not hoarding our goodness as if it were a lamp to be stowed away in a closet. He says, "Your light must shine before men so that they may see goodness in your acts and give praise to your heavenly Father."

The widow was persuaded to share with Elijah on the basis of his promise that she would not lack sustenance during the famine. We have a much greater motive for sharing with others. That motive is the fact that God himself nourishes us, not with ordinary food and drink, but with the body and blood of his own Son. This spiritual nourishment will sustain us throughout this life until we enter the fullness of life in heaven.

An ideal of Christian living is that whenever we are presented with an opportunity to share with others we should not stop to calculate whether we will be deprived ourselves. Rather we should think only of the generosity of God toward us and respond in kind to the needs of others.

Wednesday of the Tenth Week (I)

On December 17, 1903 in Kitty Hawk, North Carolina, Orville and Wilbur Wright accomplished an amazing feat. They actually made a flying machine work. The primitive airplane flew only a short distance just a few feet off the ground, but it was a significant beginning. Wilbur died in 1912 without any idea of how far aviation would progress in this century. Orville lived until 1948 but he did not get to see the huge jets which climb to 35,000 feet and fly from coast to coast in a matter of hours. Much credit is due the Wright brothers, for modern jet aircraft are the outgrowth of their simple flying machine.

The era of the Wright brothers in its relationship to the jet age bears a resemblance to the relationship between the time before Christ and the time after. Jesus protested that he had come not to abolish the law and the prophets but to build on them and to bring them to completion. All that God accomplished with his chosen people was a necessary preparation for the mission of his Son.

That history is important to us, even more important than the Kitty Hawk event is to modern aviation.

Almost always on Sundays and frequently during the week we hear a reading from the Old Testament. We must not let its meaning slip by us. God's special relationship with us did not begin with Jesus Christ, but with Abraham, the father of the chosen people. The events of the Old Testament era were part of God's plan for us. We benefit from all that occurred in God's plan before the coming of Christ. The Wright brothers prepared for the jet age and the Old Testament prepared for the Christian era.

Wednesday of the Tenth Week (II)

The people of Israel were presented with a choice to accept the God of their fathers or to accept the pagan God, Baal. They could not serve both any more than a person can go north and south at the same time. Of course the marvelous event described in the first reading was intended to convince the people that they should follow God and not Baal. God sent lightning from heaven to set ablaze the water-soaked offering upon the altar. That must have been a very convincing sign.

The God of Elijah is our God too, the creator of heaven and earth. It is very unlikely, however, that in a challenge to modern pagans, God would repeat the miracle he performed in answer to the prayer of Elijah. The reason is that God has already given us the greatest sign possible to win our loyalty and our affection. He has not sent lightning from heaven; rather he has sent his own Son. That is indeed a marvel!

Jesus is greater than Elijah, and the offering of himself on the cross is greater than the holocaust consumed upon the altar erected by Elijah. In fact, Jesus is the fulfillment of all the great people and all of the marvelous events of the entire Old Testament era.

In any moment of doubt or temptation, we need to remember God's special sign to us. That is why daily Mass is so important. In the Mass we recall the coming of Jesus among us as man as well as the offering of himself on the cross. In fact, here at Mass we truly relive those mysteries. We should look for no greater sign from God.

Thursday of the Tenth Week (I)

Some people complain that too many workmen no longer take any pride in their work. Few true craftsmen are left. One buys a new car only to find that the doors do not fit properly. A television set goes on the blink only a couple of days after purchase. The fact is that there are people who want to do the minimum, not only at their jobs, but in their religion.

The point Jesus makes in the gospel is that religion cannot be approached as a job to be done in the quickest, most convenient way possible. Minimalism will not work. We cannot ask "What is the least I can do to get by and not end up outside the kingdom of heaven." I am quite confident that none of us thinks that way, but we must take even new determination from today's gospel to be generous with God.

Jesus puts a particular emphasis on the fact that life must reflect worship. He does so in startling fashion, saying that we must leave our gift at the altar if we discover that our brother has something against us. It is another way of saying that we cannot love God if we do not love our neighbor. In one sense, it is easier to make the effort to come to church than it is to make the effort to love everyone we meet. Coming to church without really trying to live a life of love for others is a form of minimalism. Worship must be reflected in life.

St. Paul says that "God has shone in our hearts, that we in turn might make known the glory of God shining on the face of Christ." Our contact with the love of Christ here at Mass must be reflected in the way in which we live.

Thursday of the Tenth Week (II)

God had sent a serious drought over the land of Israel to purify the people from their sins. Elijah had called for prayer and fasting as a sign of repentance. When he was convinced that God would end the drought, he went to the king and announced that he could now eat and drink. Both the drought and its conclusion marked by a heavy rain were signs to Israel of God's sovereign power, but the king did not learn the lesson. As the story goes on, Ahab allowed his pagan wife, Jezebel, to turn him against God and his prophet, Elijah, once again. It was a strange reaction. One wonders what it would have taken to convert Ahab. He had seen God's power at work in Elijah, and yet he allowed himself to be influenced by Jezebel rather than by the man of God.

We have signs of God's power all around us. All the forces of nature operate, not by accident, but by the wonderful design of God. It is he who maintains the marvelous balance of nature by which we survive and who keeps constant the laws of the universe upon which we depend. God uses his almighty power out of love for us. The great sign of his love, however, remains the Holy Eucharist. He himself transcends his own laws so that bread becomes the body of his son and wine becomes his blood.

Our belief in God's actions among us should motivate us to be faithful, as King Ahab was not. Our experience of his love should inspire us to be generous as the Pharisees were not. We often hear about people with no religion who lead very good lives. Jesus tells us that our holiness must exceed that of those who do not share our faith.

Friday of the Tenth Week (I)

St. Paul lived a very difficult and challenging life. After his conversion he was called by God to preach the gospel, but he met much opposition as did Jesus himself. And as Jesus was opposed by the Pharisees, so Paul was opposed by those who preached a gospel other than his own and disclaimed him as a fake. It was a bitter pill for Paul, but he continued in his zeal, going from place to place on long, arduous missionary journeys to proclaim the truth. Eventually he was arrested and suffered a martyr's death.

What kept Paul going? He did indeed act out of pure love for Jesus and his people, but he also believed that Jesus held out a promise to him that made everything worthwhile. He states in our reading today: "We believe and so we speak, knowing that he who raised up the Lord Jesus will raise us up along with Jesus and place both us and you in his presence." Paul's faith was so strong that he really believed that God the Father loves us as he loved his own Son, and that as the Father raised his Son from death to life so will he do for all the faithful followers of Jesus.

Jesus in the gospel today wants us to know that anything is worth sacrificing to preserve the treasure of God's love which will raise us from the dead. The laws of marriage are difficult. Jesus knows that. The laws of purity of heart are difficult too. Jesus knows that also. But he asks us to think of higher values, to be like Paul, a man whose motive is love and whose strong incentive is the promise of resurrection for those who are faithful.

Friday of the Tenth Week (II)

Elijah, the prophet, thought of himself as a failure because he could not convert his people from idolatry. In his disappointment he yearned to die because God seemed far from him. Then the Lord told him to go to the mountains because he, the Lord, would pass by. Elijah apparently expected a marvelous manifestation. But he did not find God in a mighty wind, or a great fire, or even an earthquake. To his amazement Elijah felt the divine presence in a breeze so gentle that it seemed like a whisper. The lesson was that without great fanfare God would work his will for Israel in his own way.

Sometimes we may want God to intervene dramatically in our human affairs. After all, why should he not use his power to prevent people from destroying millions of innocent human lives through abortion? Is he not concerned enough to give us a miraculous cure for the terror of cancer? Why does he not prevent horrible natural disasters, such as earthquakes and hurricanes?

Thinking of less momentous but more personal problems, we

may wonder why God does not seem to answer our prayers, especially when through those prayers we are attempting to keep a marriage together, to rear children properly, or to make ends meet financially in order to live a more tranquil life.

To these and similar questions we have no humanly satisfactory answers. We are in much the same position as was Elijah. We may think that God ought to do things our way, but we must accept the fact that he will do things his way. Such an acceptance takes not only faith but a real humility. Faith moves us to believe that God is in control, but humility helps us to realize that his form of control is for the best.

Saturday of the Tenth Week (I)

When a man and a woman are married, they begin a whole new way of life. Their union will affect their whole future, a future which is hidden from their eyes. Their lives will be filled with hopes and disappointments, successes and failures, joys and sorrows. They take each other, not knowing what is before them, for better or for worse, in sickness and in health, until death. It is their love for each other which moves them to approach the future with confidence. They will live for each other.

Our reconciliation with God by Christ is somewhat like a marriage. Sin separates us from God but reconciliation unites us with him again. It is a whole new way of living: "The old order has passed away; now all is new!" There is a driving force which should motivate our new life. St. Paul expresses it by saying, "The love of Christ impells us." That love should move us to accept with equal devotion both hope and disappointment, successes and failure, joy and sorrow.

In secular society marriage is referred to as a contract, but the sacrament of marriage is more aptly termed a covenant. A contract is an agreement based on law; a covenant is a union between people based on love. God entered into a covenant with his people in the Old Testament. Jesus has given us a new covenant with God, sealed by the greatest sign of love, the shedding of his blood.

This covenant of love with God is renewed every day at Mass. Jesus says to us, "Take and drink . . . this is the cup of my blood, the blood of the new and everlasting covenant." As we partake of the cup, we should pledge ourselves anew to God in love.

Saturday of the Tenth Week (II)

Elijah was a great prophet of the Old Testament. In fact he is sometimes presented as representing the essence of prophecy in Israel. When he was about to die, he was moved by God to appoint Elisha his successor. Elisha was apparently rather well off financially, if we may judge by the fact that he owned twelve yoke of oxen. When Elisha was called by Elijah, he was at first somewhat reluctant. He asked for a moment with his parents and Elijah grudgingly granted his permission in a rather enigmatic way by saying, "Go back. Have I done anything for you?"

Jesus may have had this incident in mind when he said of the demands of discipleship, "No one, having put his hand to the plow and looking back is fit for the kingdom of God" (Lk 9:62). Elisha, however, immediately repented of his hesitation. His slaughter of the oxen and his burning of the plow marked his complete break with his old manner of life. Now he was ready to accept his office of prophet, which was symbolized by his receiving the cloak of Elijah.

In baptism we received a white garment, the sign of our complete dedication to Christ. In a sense, it too was a cloak of prophecy. A prophet is a witness for God, and through baptism we are called to be witnesses to the truth by word and action. Jesus in the gospel tells us that we are to speak the truth openly and to live honestly. There must be no hesitation in bearing witness to our faith or in living according to the gospel. Once we have committed ourselves to Christ, there must be no looking back, no compromise with values and principles which are contrary to the teachings of Jesus.

Monday of the Eleventh Week (I)

We usually do not like people who brag about their accomplishments. Their boasting leaves us thinking that they are very conceited. St. Paul in today's first reading is quite frankly boasting before the Corinthians, but his purpose is not to inflate his own ego but to put the Corinthians back on the right path.

The problem was that after Paul had preached the good news in Corinth and founded the Church, some false preachers came along to turn Paul's converts from the true faith. Their ways were winning and their words were persuasive. Paul was so disturbed that he felt compelled to present the Corinthians with his credentials as a true apostle to whom they should return in docility. By all that he had endured Paul demonstrated his love for Christ and for the Corinthians as the false apostles could not.

The Church in her liturgy boasts, not about herself, but about God. In fact, one main purpose of the liturgy is to make present before us during the liturgical year all the loving, saving acts of God from the conception and birth of Christ, through his life of ministry, and to the high point of his death and resurrection and the sending of the Spirit. And every Mass centers around that high point since every Mass is the living memorial of the death and resurrection of Jesus.

The liturgy, constantly recalling all that God has done for us, wishes us to appreciate that all God's actions show his wisdom and love. We must not abandon God to follow the false apostles and prophets of our time. Participating in the liturgy should help us to turn all the more in love and devotion to God.

Monday of the Eleventh Week (II)

Ahab was an evil king and he was exceeded in his wickedness by his pagan wife, Jezebel. In fact, the name "Jezebel" has entered our language to refer to a wicked or bold woman. Ahab, not satisfied with all he possessed as king, wanted the vineyard which belonged to Naboth. When Naboth, fully within his rights, refused to sell, Ahab apparently was willing to back off. But not Jezebel. She perpetrated the terrible murder of Naboth and told her husband that he could now take the vineyard without even paying for it.

People like Ahab and Jezebel arouse our wrath. When we hear in the news about terrible crimes, such as the hideous rape and murder of a little girl, we wish that God would follow the old way of an eye for an eye and a tooth for a tooth. Tomorrow's reading will show us how God relented in the punishment due Ahab because he repented. There is a temptation for us not to go along with that kind of mercy. But Jesus came to reveal that God does not will the death of the sinner but that he repent and be saved.

God is different from us. He sees the whole picture in a unique light, and he views human activity as a loving Father who is eager to have all his children return to him, no matter what they have done. It is not that God fails to give justice. He does, but his sense of justice is entirely different from ours.

Rather than being upset with God that evil people are apparently "getting away with murder," we must learn to leave the matter of judgment and punishment in his hands. Rather than calling down his wrath, we ought to pray that those who do evil will repent and return to the Lord.

Tuesday of the Eleventh Week (I)

The story is told of a man and wife who in their travels attended Mass in a Catholic church of the Eastern Rite. The ceremonies were quite different from what they were used to in their home parish, but at one point the ushers began to take up the collection. At that the man turned to his wife and whispered, "Now I know we are in a Catholic church."

Some Catholics complain that there are too many special collections during the year, for the foreign missions, the home missions, and so on in a long list. And most priests will tell you that they hate to talk about money. St. Paul, however, did not hesitate to urge the Corinthians to contribute generously to a collection which was being taken up for the poor in Jerusalem. He even presented to the Corinthians the motive that the Philippians in Macedonia had not only given generously beyond their means to this collection but had even begged him for the privilege of helping the less fortunate members of the Church.

Then Paul presented to the Corinthians the ultimate motive for generosity. He reminded them that the Lord Jesus for their sake made himself poor though he was rich so that they might become rich by his poverty. Jesus, so to speak, had to give up the riches of his divinity to enter the poverty of humanity so that they and we might enjoy the wealth of his divinity.

Our generosity must exclude no one. In Jesus' day love of neighbor was of the essence of the law, but neighbor meant only those of one's country and religion. Jesus indicated that neighbor means everyone without exception. Because of the generosity of Jesus toward us, we must always be generous in helping those who are in need.

Tuesday of the Eleventh Week (II)

Yesterday we read how Jezebel, the wife of King Ahab, murdered Naboth so that her husband could take over Naboth's vineyard. Ahab was guilty with his wife by complicity and all the more responsible since he was the king. Elijah presented himself before the king to impose the sentence of God for his evil deeds. In a somewhat surprising reaction, Ahab repented. What should not surprise us is that God delayed his sentence in order to give Ahab a chance to get his life in order.

The truth is that God loved Ahab despite his terrible sins. God yearned for the complete and final repentance of Ahab. God preaches what he practices. Through his Son, Jesus, we heard the teaching that we are to love our enemies and pray for our persecutors. Jesus goes on to say that "this will prove that we are sons of our heavenly Father." It is the old idea: like father, like son.

As children of the Father, we are to become like him. We see what we should be in his only begotten Son, his perfect image in the flesh, Jesus Christ. And what did Jesus do? He died for us while we were as yet sinners (cf. Rm 5:8-9). He did not wait until we could somehow be counted worthy of his death. As for those who were physically putting him to death, his persecutors, he prayed for them from the cross.

It is no easy task to love our enemies and to pray for our persecutors. But we should not complain that God is asking us to do something which he himself does not do. We have heard the teaching of Jesus. We also have before us the perfect example of his teaching which should be a sufficient motive for us to be even heroic in the love of our enemies.

Wednesday of the Eleventh Week (I)

Some of the most admired and sought after people in our society are movie and television stars. In many instances this is really a personality cult, not an appreciation of acting ability, since a number of the most popular stars really play themselves, no matter which role they may have been assigned. But every actor in his role performs in order to be seen and heard by an audience. An actor without an audience is like a baseball pitcher without a catcher.

Acting is just the opposite of what Jesus wants from us. In living our Christianity we do not play to an audience in order to be seen and heard. We should not have the motive of drawing fans to ourselves who will applaud us, ask for our autograph, and pay us homage. The Christian life is not an onstage performance.

Jesus gives three examples of Christian acts upon which we should not shine the light of publicity: giving alms, praying, and fasting. These examples are not exhaustive. They are meant to bring home the point of not doing anything to seek the admiration of others. Actually very few people will brag directly about how generous they are, or how hard they pray, or how much mortification they practice. More often, it seems to me, we are tempted to let others know subtly how much work we do, or how tough life is for us, or how busy we really are.

Actually we need be concerned with only one person who sees all things. And he wants to see within us a generous but humble heart, a love which is unselfish and sincere. It is not what others think of us that counts. The only thing that matters is what God knows about us.

Wednesday of the Eleventh Week (II)

Elijah was an important figure in the Old Testament. In fact, he was thought of as having epitomized the prophetic office in Israel. A prophet was the representative of God, one who spoke and acted in his name. For a long time God dealt with his people chiefly through prophets. And so when Elijah died, God saw to it that his place was taken by Elisha.

God can act in anyway he chooses, but for the most part he still wishes to communicate his truth and love through human beings. That is what you see at Mass. When you look to the altar you see a man, human like yourself, whom God has called to be a priest. The priest presides at the Eucharist and makes our worship possible through the power granted him in ordination. But there is more. You should also see that God is acting through the lector who proclaims God's word and through the special minister who gives you holy communion. Notice especially that receiving holy communion, God's great communication of himself to us through his Son, is never something you do for yourself. You always receive communion from a minister, be he bishop, priest, deacon or special minister.

What God does for you through others here at Mass, he wishes you to do for others outside Mass. You are to be the instruments of his truth and love. As a matter of fact, by means of your baptism you have been constituted a prophet, one who is to give witness to God. Your role will not be as dramatic as that of Elijah or Elisha, but it is real. It is more in accord with the spirit taught by Jesus today, quiet and unassuming.

We should not think that we are unimportant, no matter how hidden or simple our roles may be. Jesus is present within us to guide us and to accomplish the good that is possible for us as ministers, modern prophets, of his truth and goodness.

Thursday of the Eleventh Week (I)

I suppose that we have all heard of some Catholics, especially young people, who no longer consider themselves to be Catholic. They have been attracted by another group, often one which preaches a simplistic approach to the Bible as if one could pick it up and understand it fully as one might a cheap novel written a few months ago.

Paul faced much the same problem with his converts at Corinth. After he had preached and founded the Church in Corinth, some false apostles came in and perverted the faith of the people. When Paul was informed, he was more than distressed; he was incensed. He admitted that perhaps he was not as persuasive a speaker as were his opponents, but he protested that he had proclaimed the truth.

He also presented a strong motive to the Corinthians for return-ing to their original faith in Christ. Paul looked upon the Corinthian Church as his daughter whom he had presented to Christ as his spouse. Their union with him was to be what a marital union should be: complete, exclusive, and unbreakable.

We share the faith which has been handed down through Paul and the other apostles. It spans the centuries back to the day of Christ and includes a countless number of men and women before us who remained faithful. Let nothing ever separate us from Christ in his Church. Our union with him in our Catholic faith must be complete, exclusive and forever.

Thursday of the Eleventh Week (II)

Today's first reading is a poem in honor of Elijah, the prophet.

Elijah was truly a great man, the representative of God to his people, who spoke in God's name. When Jesus was transfigured on the mountain, there appeared with him Moses, who represented the Law, and Elijah, who represented the prophets.

Great though he was, Elijah did not have the privilege of praying to God in the manner in which Jesus has taught us to pray. To Elijah, God was the Lord, the creator of the heavens and the earth and all they contain, the protector and guide of his people with whom he had entered into a covenant of fidelity and love. But Elijah had no revelation that God is actually a Father. It was left for Jesus, the eternal Son of God, to reveal that God is literally his Father, and that we have been called to enter into a relationship with the Father through Christ which makes us God's children.

It should be noted that the word which Jesus used for "Father" was not the formal expression. Jesus used the Aramaic word, "Abba," which was the term a little child used in speaking to his father. It is the equivalent of our word, "papa," and even sounds a little like it. The word "Abba" is intended to convey all the tenderness and love of a devoted father toward his little child. Our response should contain all of the affection, trust, and simplicity which characterizes a loving child.

In teaching us to pray Jesus did more than leave a formula. When he invited us to address God with him as "Our Father," he opened up a whole new vision of God for us. We should see that God views us as very precious and loveable simply because we have been made his children. And we ought to realize that we can approach God with the confidence of knowing that we are truly his children.

Friday of the Eleventh Week (I)

Financial institutions these days do a lot of advertising to get people to invest their money in savings accounts. Since the amount of interest they may pay is controlled by law and usually identical with every institution, they resort to all kinds of gimmicks to get people to save with them. There is a certain prudence in saving, no doubt, but how much real security can we find in money?

Jesus says, "Do not lay up for yourselves an earthly treasure. Moths and rust corrode and thieves break in and steal." The words of Jesus are verified by an economy characterized by recession and general instability. We need not say that many people are out to rob us, and not all of them wear masks and carry guns. The truth is that money has no intrinsic worth; it only represents values other than itself.

Jesus is eager that we store up treasures which cannot depreciate in value or be lost by theft. Ironically these permanent treasures come not from saving, but from giving, not from being selfish, but from being generous in the dedicating of ourselves to God and to others. Jesus wants us to be generous with our money, but he includes in his exhortation all forms of generosity to others. The first reading is a cataloguing of some of the things Paul endured in his generosity to his people.

With a savings account you can earn an interest on your money, a fraction more than it is worth in itself. Jesus has promised that our generosity in love will gain much more interest than that. In fact, he says that we will be given a hundredfold. No savings company can make or keep a promise like that.

Friday of the Eleventh Week (II)

Today's first reading sounds like the plot of a movie or one of Shakespeare's plays, especially *Richard II*. Athaliah was the daughter of Ahab, the evil king of Israel, the northern kingdom. She had married Jehoram of Judah and fully expected that their son, Ahaziah, would become king of Judah. When he was assassinated, she violently usurped the throne of Judah for herself and introduced the worship of the pagan god, Baal. After seven years she was overthrown and executed. The temple of Baal was destroyed, and Joash, the legitimate heir of King David, was installed as king.

Athaliah reflected what Jesus preached in today's gospel. He said that "where your treasure is, there your heart is also." Athalia's treasure was the power and luxury of the court, and she sought it with all the ambition of her heart. It was indeed an earthly treasure, one which endured for a mere seven years. There was no lasting value in the power and luxury which she had taken to herself.

That which lasts forever is really much more humble than all the trappings of royalty and all the heady wine of political power. That which lasts forever is really much more simple than all the searching after fleeting pleasure and passing luxury. Jesus tells us to lay up heavenly treasures.

Heavenly treasures come from a humility which makes us look to God as the source of all life, all holiness. Heavenly treasures come from a simplicity which makes us realize that lasting values are found in goodness, and love, and unselfishness. Athaliah is an example to us. We must not make the mistake of basing our lives on a search for false treasures.

Saturday of the Eleventh Week (I)

In today's first reading we heard Paul "boasting" again about all that he had endured for the gospel. Remember that his motive was pure; he wanted to convince the Corinthians that what he had preached was from Christ. Then in this reading he went on to another point. He admitted that he was weak, not a very impressive person, not possessed of the marvelous rhetoric of his opponents. But in this weakness he rejoiced because in his weakness the power of Christ was more manifest.

Weakness is rarely considered a virtue. At one time we believed that the United States was the most powerful nation on the earth. We thought that our unlimited natural resources coupled with our famous American know-how made us completely independent of any other nation. We have learned a different story. We have seen the value of our currency dwindle on the world market and we have had to recognize that we are dependent for energy sources on other countries. This situation is considered a calamity. And yet some observers believe that our present situation will lead the United States to a greater sense of cooperation with, rather than exploitation of others.

Leaving aside the national scene, we should recognize that admitting our personal human weakness is not only realistic but healthy. Those who are weak must learn to depend on someone else. That someone else for us is God. With a healthy sense of dependence on God for everything, we can go about our lives with the serenity of the birds of the air and the flowers of the fields. God will take care of his faithful people.

Through St. Paul today God tells us that his grace is sufficient for us. Unlike a supply of oil in the ground, his grace will never be exhausted. His grace is not only sufficient; it is more than abundant for all our needs.

Saturday of the Eleventh Week (II)

Joash was the legitimate heir to the throne of King David, and the priest, Jehoida, saw to it that he was rightly installed as king (see yesterday's reading). The king began his reign well, but when the priest died, things started to fall apart. Evil princes persuaded Joash to allow a return to pagan practices. When the priest's son, Zechariah, admonished him, the king ordered him stoned to death. As a result of his perfidy, God permitted the Arameans to invade Judah and to bring disaster upon the land.

Joash is a perfect example of what Jesus says in today's gospel: "No man can serve two masters." He wanted to be king of Judah, which meant that he was to be totally dedicated to God since kingship was essentially a religious role, but he also wanted to please the powerful princes who were pagan at heart. As a result he was attentive to the princes and despised God.

If one does attempt to serve two masters, a tension develops since a person is thereby pulled in opposite directions. Perhaps we have experienced something of that tension as we try to rely on God, all the while finding it difficult not to worry about our livelihood.

We do have responsibilities. We do have to make ends meet. To some, the message of Jesus may sound very simplistic: "Do not worry about what you are to eat or drink or use for clothing." It can easily be observed that he did not live in the economic rat race of the twentieth century. But we must not so lightly dismiss this message.

In this life we will not be perfect. We must, however, try to grow in that trust which makes us like the birds of the air or the flowers of the fields. Those who move in this direction develop a great serenity and peace. They do not worry about tomorrow or its needs. The Lord is their one Master and they are quite content to leave everything in his hands.

Monday of the Twelfth Week (I)

Today we began reading from the twelfth chapter of the Book of Genesis. Actually it is the beginning of the story of our salvation. All that had gone before in Genesis, the story of Adam and Eve, the Tower of Babel, the flood, all of that was a prelude which painted the picture of the need for salvation. In a sense the first eleven chapters set the stage for the beautiful story of salvation which begins with Abraham, who was first called Abram.

God gave Abraham the gift of faith to embrace him as the one God, the creator of the heavens and the earth. God set him apart for a purpose, to be the father of a people whom God would favor with his revelation. This people, despite their weakness and their many failures, preserved the faith and handed it down.

Faith is not an abstraction, floating somehow in the air to be absorbed by a kind of spiritual osmosis by anyone who comes into contact with it. Faith is found within the lives of people. With the Hebrews it became a living tradition which was handed down from one generation to another. Even when that faith became a written record in the biblical books, it found life and vitality only in people who lived according to the message of the books.

The Church today, in its first Eucharistic prayer, refers to Abraham as "our father in faith." He is such because he is the father of a people, God's people. We are their descendants in the faith. In the words of Pope Pius XI, "We are all spiritually Semites."

In this Mass we praise and thank God for what he has accomplished through his servant, Abraham. The story which began with the call of Abraham is our story. We are part of God's plan to form a people for himself, a people of faith.

Monday of the Twelfth Week (II)

In a brief passage the Bible today sums up a terrible tragedy which had been brewing for many years. It was the destruction of the northern kingdom, Israel, and its capital, Samaria in 721 B.C. by the mighty Assyrian armies. The conquered people were deported in disgrace. The northern kingdom was never the same. The disaster was really their own making because of their infidelity to God despite the repeated warnings of the prophets.

Only Judah remained. It was to be the birthplace of the Messiah, the scene of much of his preaching, and the place where he died and was raised to life. Jerusalem, its capital, became the first center of Christianity. All had worked out as God had planned for he was not to be frustrated by the infidelity of the northern kingdom of Israel or by the rejection of his son by the leaders of the southern kingdom of Judah.

It would be an easy thing for us to look harshly upon all of these people. The Bible makes clear God's judgment upon them, but God's judgment is filled with mercy. Even though Jesus came later in time, he died for all of the people who had gone before him. He shed his blood for us and for all men so that sin might be forgiven.

The biblical accounts of infidelity are preserved for us as a warning against complacency. Some of the Old Testament people thought that all would be well no matter what, since they had been chosen by God. They did not realize that God's choice of them demanded a response on their part.

We need not live by fear since the Bible does not teach fear.

And yet we cannot naively think that all we need is to be a Catholic. We must live in accord with our faith. And the call to faithfulness is a call which we must never tire of hearing. We can always grow in our faith and our dedication to God.

Tuesday of the Twelfth Week (I)

Some people work on the principle that you have to look out for yourself, for number one, because if you don't, nobody else will. Abram, later known as Abraham, was not of that mind. When his herdsmen and those of his nephew, Lot, quarreled over grazing rights for their flocks, Abraham allowed Lot to take his choice of the land. Lot elected what was obviously the richer portion of land. He seemed to have gotten the better of the deal, but God had other, greater plans for Abram. God promised him that one day all the land of Canaan would belong to his numerous descendants.

Abram's actions were in accord with the principle enunciated by Jesus in the gospel: "Treat others the way you would have them treat you." Not many people are really willing to follow that principle. And it is no surprise. Practically everything in our society is based on the idea that you do indeed have to look out for yourself. It is weak and foolish, we are told, not to be assertive, not to stick up for your rights, and to let someone take advantage of you.

Sin makes us selfish, turning the focus of life upon ourselves. Jesus in a way admits that orientation within us, but then he urges us to turn that orientation around. He tells us that our inclination to want the best of ourselves, to seek our own convenience, is to be used as an indication of how we should treat others. We should give to them what we want most for ourselves.

In following this "golden rule," we will be considered foolish by many. But the story of Abram illustrates for us God takes care of those who are generous and unselfish. Abram allowed Lot to take the better portion of land, but God showed Abraham that his descendants would possess the entire land of Canaan. God grants to us even more than we give away.

Tuesday of the Twelfth Week (II)

Sennacherib, the king of Assyria, had destroyed the northern kingdom of Israel and led the people off into slavery. He intended to do fully the same with Judah and so informed Hezekiah, king of Judah. Hezekiah knew that Judah was no match for Assyria. It would be like an infant trying to defend himself against a giant, or perhaps like Afghanistan trying to ward off a Russian invasion. So Hezekiah did the best of all things. He turned to God in earnest prayer. That night a large portion of the Assyrian army was mysteriously destroyed in its camp. Sennacherib gave up and returned to his capital.

There are two ways of looking at this extraordinary event. One could say it was just a lucky break for Judah, but one could also say that God had intervened to protect his people. The Bible deliberately does not tell why so many enemy soldiers suddenly died. Perhaps there was some terrible plague, but the Bible wants to make the point that it was God who had defended his people.

Lord Byron, the English poet, has sculptured the scene in poetic images in his narrative entitled, "The Destruction of Sennacherib." His opening stanza borrows from the biblical picture of God as shepherd: "The Assyrian came down like the wolf on the fold, / And his cohorts were gleaming in purple and gold." The wolf came but the shepherd was there. Byron's concluding couplet sums up God's action: "The might of the Gentile, unsmote by the sword, / Hath melted like snow in the glance of the Lord."

God is indeed the observer of human events. His mere glance has the power to protect his people. We do not live by chance or lucky breaks. We live by the loving providence of our God.

Wednesday of the Twelfth Week (I)

If there is anything we look for in human relationships, it is trustworthiness. We want to be able to depend on a friend's word; we want someone who will keep his promises.

God made extraordinary promises to Abram, later known as Abraham. He told him that his descendants would be very numerous and that, despite his old age, he would have a son from whom all these people would come. God was very pleased that Abraham took him at his word, but he understood the human heart and the need we feel for a sign of trustworthiness.

God was willing to submit himself to a strange ceremony which was in use at the time as a way of sealing a contract. Animals were cut in two, and the contracting parties walked between the halves as a sign that they were willing to suffer the fate of the animals if they broke the covenant. Such a sign was not necessary from God, but out of love for Abraham he gave it anyway.

We are the beneficiaries of the new covenant, not a promise of continued life through many descendants, but the pledge of everlasting life. God has given us a sign of this new covenant. God, so to speak, stands on one side and we on the other. Between us he has placed his son upon the cross. This new covenant is sealed in the death of his Son. That death is the pledge of his everlasting love.

Today there are many false prophets who promise happiness from money, power, prestige. But they can give no sign of their trustworthiness. God alone has given the ulitmate sign of his fidelity, the death of his own Son upon the cross.

Wednesday of the Twelfth Week (II)

Imagine that one day when you open your mail, you find a letter from an attorney. A distant relative whom you have never met has died and named you in his will. You have inherited a fortune! After the shock of disbelief has worn off, you begin to plan what you will do with all the money.

Something like this happened to King Josiah of Judah. The Book of the Law (probably parts of Deuteronomy) had been abandoned and forgotten during the reign of Josiah's predecessor, Manasseh. When the high priest Hilikiah found the book in the temple, he sent it to the king through one of the scribes. Receiving the book was for the king very much like receiving a fortune by inheritance. He was overjoyed but he also knew that his fortune was to be shared. He summoned all the people to the temple and had the contents of the book read out to them.

The title, "Book of the Law," is somewhat misleading to us. Its contents actually told again in a very profound way God's saving action which established a covenant with the people, and this book made it clear that the covenant was not only for those who lived in the past but for those who were alive at that moment. To this covenant the people were called to be faithful as all of their ancestors had been called.

We have become used to the story of Christian salvation and of the new covenant sealed in the blood of Christ. Consider how thrilling it would be to hear this story as adults for the first time. How moving to think of God's love for us in the sending of his son! How impressive to realize that this son died for us and established us in a loving relationship with the creator of the universe as our Father! This wonderful story is our inheritance from the evangelists. It should be the motivating force of our whole lives. It should make us become the tree, spoken of by Jesus in the gospel, which produces the good fruit of complete dedication to our loving God.

Thursday of the Twelfth Week (I)

The first part of today's reading (long form) reflects the marriage practices of the day whereby a husband was allowed to take a concubine. Jesus later was to insist on the original plan of God, one man and one woman in marriage. The inspired author of the story takes for granted the marriage practice of that time without comment on its correctness. He had an entirely different purpose in relating the incident, for he wished to show the universal love of God.

Abraham was to become the father of the chosen people, the Israelites, through his son, Isaac, who would be born of his wife,

Sarah. The Bible shows how the Israelites were the beloved of God, but that does not mean that other people were excluded. Hagar's son by Abraham was named Ishmael, and he became the father of the Ishmaelites as Isaac became the father of the Israelites. Both people spring from Abraham, who represents God himself.

The Israelites would later come into conflict with the Ishmaelites as Sarah came into conflict with Hagar, the mothers here representing two distinct people. When Hagar ran away from Sarah's persecution of her, the Lord's messenger assured her that her descendants would be very numerous, a sign of God's favor.

In the Christian era there is no longer a people chosen because of their physical birth. Rather all people of every nation are invited to enjoy the new birth of baptism which brings them into God's one family. Baptism becomes our dedication to God whereby we pledge to do the will of the Father in heaven. Those who keep this pledge no matter what their national, racial or ethnic origin, will indeed enter the kingdom of God. Our God is the God of all peoples.

Thursday of the Twelfth Week (II)

Today's first reading records a tragic event, the fall of Jerusalem on March 16, 597 B.C. God had protected Judah under Josiah who had instituted religious reforms, but after his death internal corruption became so rampant that the tiny kingdom no longer enjoyed God's special protection against the mighty Babylonian forces. Judah had become a sham.

Judah was a religious kingdom. Its king ideally was not merely a political figure but the representative of God. That ideal had been lost. The spiritual foundation of the kingdom had been destroyed. Judah was no longer built on rock. It was now a house built on sandy ground. Its fall under the Babylonian forces was inevitable.

Jesus in the gospel declared: "None of those who cry out, 'Lord, Lord,' will enter the kingdom of God but only the one who does the will of my Father in heaven." Pretending to be religious without dedication to God's will is to be like the corrupt kingdom of Judah.

Jesus taught us to pray, "Thy kingdom come." That is the first petition of his prayer. To it he immediately joined a second petition: "Thy will be done on earth as it is in heaven." God's kingdom comes to us in the degree that we strive to do his will. In the very act of teaching us to pray Jesus instructs us that prayer must lead to action. Devotion to God must affect the way in which we live.

Jesus is more than a teacher. He is also the perfect example. His whole life was lived in accord with the will of his heavenly Father, even to accepting death on the cross. To be true christians we must listen to the words of Jesus and then we must follow his example.

Friday of the Twelfth Week (I)

It is always fascinating to watch people peering at newly born babies through the glass in the maternity ward of a hospital. If a man doing so is in his twenties or thirties, you suspect that he is the father of one of the infants. If a man doing so is in his fifties or sixties, you suspect he is a grandfather. If a man in his nineties is doing so, you are not quite sure what to think except that he is certainly not the father.

People who knew Abraham were amazed, to put it mildly, to see him swell up with pride in looking at an infant born to him when he was ninety-nine years of age. They were even more amazed to know that his wife, Sarah, had become a mother at the age of ninety! Of course anybody today would say such a thing is impossible. And that is just the point. It was out of the realm of human possibility for Abraham and Sarah to become parents at their age. The conception and birth of their child, Isaac, was so obviously God's special work that anyone should have seen clearly that this little boy had a special destiny from God.

Isaac was to become the father of the twelve tribes of Israel. From one of these tribes, that of Judah, would come the Messiah. His birth would be even more clearly the work of God, for he would be the eternal Son of God born in time of a virgin.

322 / Friday of the Twelfth Week of the Year

God wants us to know that he is the one who works out our salvation. Salvation is not something we can do for ourselves, any more than in the ordinary course of nature an ancient couple can become parents or a virgin can give birth to any child, let alone the Son of God. We are completely in the hands of God. Actually we should be grateful that we are not the ones who must accomplish our own salvation. With God at work we know that our salvation is assured.

Friday of the Twelfth Week (II)

The city of Jerusalem surrendered to the Babylonians in the year 597 B.C. About ten years later Zedekiah, a mere puppet king, foolishly rebelled against the Babylonians and a second siege followed. The temple and much of the city were destroyed and more Jews were deported to Babylon.

The devastation was something which Judah had brought on itself because of its blatant infidelity to God. Judah was to have been a country religious by essence, dedicated to the one true God. Without the practice of religion Judah was like a river without water, an orchard without trees, a marriage without love. By abandoning God the country had lost its identity. It was no longer Judah but an area masquerading under that name.

And yet all was not lost. Subsequent prophets would preach a message of hope. They would call for a return to the Lord, a real repentance. Such was still possible for God had not abandoned his people; they had abandoned him. The hope of the future was realized in the person of Jesus Christ. He was the great healer, as we saw in today's gospel. The leper was an outcast, like the Jews who had been deported. Jesus cured the man out of a motive of compassion, but the cure was also a sign that Jesus had come to heal the world of the wounds of sin. His form of healing was to reconcile man with God.

Sin wounds, but reconciliation heals. Sin separates, but reconciliation unites. In the words of absolution in the sacrament of penance, we hear these words: "God, the Father of mercies, through the death and resurrection of his son has reconciled the world to himself." We, the new people of God, are the beneficiaries of this marvelous reconciliation.

Saturday of the Twelfth Week (I)

Today's first reading is another way of telling the story which we heard read yesterday from the Book of Genesis. Both are concerned with the extraordinary intervention by God which brought about the birth of Isaac when Abraham and his wife were both far beyond the age when people can become parents in the ordinary course of nature.

Today's story, one might say, has a little more flesh and blood to it. God sent representatives, or angels, in the form of three visitors to Abraham. (We should not think that these three represented the persons of the Trinity, for the revelation of that truth had not yet been made.) One of the visitors spoke in the name of the Lord and his message was that Abraham would have a son by his wife, Sarah, despite their advanced old age.

This message is the point of the story, but we should also notice the admirable hospitality offered by Abraham before he knew the identity of his guests. The Epistle to the Hebrews, in reflecting on this passage, urges us: "Do not neglect to show hospitality, for by that means some have entertained angels without knowing it" (Heb 13:2).

The complete fulfillment of the promise to Abraham brought about the human birth of the Son of God. In becoming human Jesus put himself into a human state whereby he could be offered hospitality by people like Martha and Mary. But Jesus continues to live in the members of his body, the Church. In showing hospitality or any other form of love to them, we are showing hospitality and love to Jesus. That is something we should know, and we should act in accord with the truth that Jesus is present to his followers.

Saturday of the Twelfth Week (II)

Jesus was a Jew among Jews, a descendant through Mary of those people who, as we have been reading this week, brought destruction upon themselves through infidelity. The prophets of the exile held out hope for the people that all would yet be well. And indeed they were correct, but the fulfillment of their hopes went far beyond their expectations. They thought only of salvation for their own people, which was natural enough. Little did they know that a descendant of this people would open his arms on a cross to embrace the whole world in his love.

The gospel story today is important for indicating the full scope of the salvation brought about by Jesus. The point to notice about the centurion who asked Jesus to cure his servant is that he was not a Jew. The centurion was a Roman, a member of a hated and conquering race, and a military leader on top of that. Did Jesus refuse to help because the man was a Gentile? No, but Jesus' fellow Jews were shocked that he would reach out to favor such a man. Jesus responded to the man's faith and even alluded to the lack of faith in Israel.

Connected immediately to this event is the scene at Peter's house. Peter had, of course, a Jewish mother-in-law, but it was not funny at that moment. The lady was in bed with a fever. Did Jesus refuse to help her because she was a descendant of a faithless people? By no means. Jesus had come for all peoples of all times and places without exception.

Every day at Mass we hear these saving words of Jesus: "This is the cup of my blood . . . shed for you and for all men so that sins may be forgiven." Physical birth and ancestry no longer matter. Whether born Jew or Gentile, rich or poor, black or white, all of us are the specially favored people of God.

Monday of the Thirteenth Week (I)

God had determined that the city of Sodom was to be destroyed because of its wickedness. Abraham, in an act of boldness, attempted to reason with God. He protested, "Far be it from you to make the innocent die with the guilty." Then, as we heard, he went on to bargain with God, trying to convince him that he should spare the city even if he could find only ten innocent people. As a matter of record, there were not even ten innocent people in Sodom, and so the city was destroyed.

The scene between God and Abraham is painted in very human (anthropomorphic) tones. This picturesque presentation has a point. No, God does not condemn the innocent with the guilty. Yes, good people can somehow save the guilty.

Pope Pius XII expressed the same teaching in more theological terms. In writing on the Church as the Mystical Body of Christ, he gave us these memorable words: "Deep mystery this, subject of inexhaustible meditation, that the salvation of many depends on the prayers and voluntary penances which the members of the Mystical Body of Jesus Christ offer for this intention" (*Mystici Corporis Christi*, 46). Each one of us by our prayers and goodness can be a savior to others.

When we hear about terribly evil people, the rapist, the dope peddler, the child abuser, we can do one of two things. We can condemn them and lament their conduct. Or we can do something to help them repent. We can offer prayers, backed up by goodness, for the sake of others in a generous spirit with a willingness to leave judgment to God. God indicated to Abraham that he was willing to spare an entire city because of only ten innocent people. Will we be counted among those who pray earnestly for the salvation of the world?

Monday of the Thirteenth Week (II)

The prophet Amos was a southerner, from Judah, who was sent by God to the northern kingdom of Israel. At the time Israel was prospering and all seemed well. Ordinarily a move north would have been desirable, but not for Amos. He knew that amid the affluence of the northern kingdom there was much corruption. God called him to preach repentance there, no pleasant task. He had to proclaim to the people that their injustice and their oppression of the poor made a mockery of the faith to which they were committed. They looked upon themselves as God's chosen people, but Amos, had to remind them that their election was meaningless without a life in keeping with God's law.

Amos arrived on the scene about 670 years before the birth of Christ, but he is indeed a prophet for our times. Even amid recession we are by any standard an affluent society. Affluence can make for comfortable religion. Why not be religious when everything seems pretty comfortable? Affluence can also make for self-protection. Once one has tasted the comforts of what is called the good life, one does not want to surrender that. Sometimes self-protection goes as far as exploitation of others.

It is very likely that you do not think you fit this picture of the affluent, and I am no Amos to proclaim otherwise to you. But rich or poor we must hear the message of Amos as a challenge to us about our attitudes and our actions. How much value do we place on the comforts money can buy? Where is our heart? Are we satisfied with simple necessities or do we look always for more? If necessary are we willing to be like Jesus who had nowhere to lay his head?

The words of Amos are good for us to hear. We will never be guilty of injustice or oppression if we live according to his basic message which is that following God's law and his will is the only way to live.

Tuesday of the Thirteenth Week (I)

Divine justice demanded that the sinful cities of Sodom and Gomorrah be destroyed. Because of his great love for Abraham, God spared his nephew, Lot, and his family. Only Lot's wife made a terrible mistake by failing to obey the command not to look back.

We have no clear idea of the nature of the calamity which destroyed those fated cities, nor is such information important. This narrative has been included in the Bible to give witness to God's justice and mercy. In his justice God will destroy evil, not always by a natural calamity but in his own way and in his own time. In his mercy God will save the good, and that too he will accomplish in his own way and in his own time. Especially from our Christian revelation we know that God rescues us, not from a natural death but from eternal death. God wished to save Lot and his family out of his love for Abraham. He will save us from eternal death out of his love for his son, Jesus.

The apostles, as we saw in the gospel, feared death by drowning. Jesus appeared to be unconcerned, mysteriously sleeping at the height of the storm. He was disappointed that the asposltes did not have complete trust in him, but even so he did calm the winds and the waves. In the Bible the waters are often a symbol of ultimate destruction, as for example in the great flood of Noah's time. The real storms of life which we must fear are not those of nature but those of an evil which can bring us everlasting death.

We have a savior, one greater than Abraham, one whom God loves even more than he did Abraham. Faith in this savior, even when he seems far away or asleep, will save us from the violent forces which can bring eternal death.

Tuesday of the Thirteenth Week (II)

It has been said that marriage is a fifty-fifty proposition, a two-way street. These expressions, devoid of any romanticism, are an attempt to indicate that marriage brings mutual responsibilities. It cannot be one-sided. In fact, each partner must be willing to give as much love and devotion as possible. But the truth remains that unrequited love does not make for a successful marriage.

This is pretty much the point Amos made with the people concerning their relationship with God. God had entered into a covenant of love with them, but they were expected to respond in kind. In fact, God had given much more than they could ever match in response, but when virtually no response came, the relationship, as Amos saw it, was doomed to failure.

We see much the same reality in the gospel story. Jesus was looking for a return of faith for all the signs of love which he had manifested. Could not the apostles trust him in the midst of a storm, even when he was sleeping? There is a ring of deep disappointment in the words of Jesus, "How little faith you have!"

There is a thin, but important, line between complacency and faith. The Israelites were complacent. They thought God would do anything for them despite their infidelities. What Jesus wanted from the apostles, and what he wants from us, is the conviction that God takes care of his devoted people. Jesus brought peace to the storm on the lake, and he wants to bring peace to us in the storms of life. Anxiety and worry bring disappointment to God. We pray in the Mass after the "Our Father" that God may keep us free from sin and protect us from all anxiety. A people who strive to overcome sin and be faithful should feel no anxiety about life. Peace should be the fruit of our faith in a loving God.

Wednesday of the Thirteenth Week (I)

Most Americans rightly take pride in our country, despite its imperfections. After the second world war the United States emerged as the most powerful nation on earth, with a much better record for respecting human rights than its chief competitor, the Soviet Union. America has been known as the land of the free even though the beauty of freedom has been tainted by racial discrimination and some questionable immigration laws. The political rhetoric of candidates for national office emphasizes the greatness of the country and contains only those admonitions which are considered necessary for insuring continued greatness.

It would be a rare politician indeed who would run for office on a platform which advocated respect for countries upon whom we are dependent for oil, rather than disdain, and which promoted open policies for immigration rather than selectivity. The people for whom today's story from Genesis was written took great pride in their national origins from Abraham, and who, for the most part, considered their neighbors unworthy of God's favor. And yet the point of the story, in showing God's protection of Ishmael, is to illustrate God's love for a people other than the Israelites. It was not political rhetoric.

For us the point is that God never uses the word "foreigner," as some do with connotations of condescension if not disdain. God loves all the people of the world and so must we. The two men in the strange gospel story for today were not Jews, and yet Jesus came to their rescue. Love of country is one thing, but any form of nationalism or ethnic pride which fails to recognize the dignity and worth of every human being is not what God expects from us.

Wednesday of the Thirteenth Week (II)

A Christian king in medieval Europe was making a tour of his kingdom when he came across a very elderly man working in a vineyard. "How old are you?" the king inquired. The man replied, "Your majesty, I am four years of age." The king laughingly protested that this was impossible, so the man explained, "Your majesty, I count only those moments when I have faithfully served the Lord."

The Israelites to whom Amos preached would have had a hard time reckoning the time they had spent in faithfully serving the Lord. They would have wanted to include all the hours absorbed in worship, in prayer and the offering of sacrifice. But Amos discounted all that. He proclaimed that liturgical celebrations without a good life are an abomination to God. He emphasized that worship must lead to a truly religious life in which one shows respect for the rights of others. The psalm which we prayed following this reading reflects the same point.

Many here today attend Mass daily or almost daily. This time is well spent before God, and yet we are called to recognize that the Mass must have an effect upon the way in which we live. God does not expect us to be perfect even after many years of daily Mass, but he does want effort at growth.

330 / *Thursday of the Thirteenth Week of the Year*

Time is a precious gift given us by God to serve him. Time is so precious that he gives it to us only moment by moment, and when one moment is gone it can never be recovered. When we come before God in death, he will want to know "how old" we are in his service. Let us hope that he can count more than the time we have spent in prayer and worship.

Thursday of the Thirteenth Week (I)

Faith means much more than believing that there is a God. Faith means turning one's whole life over to God with complete confidence. Abraham is the biblical man of faith.

God had made extraordinary promises to Abraham. He had told him that he would be the father of a great people through his legitimate heir. Even after he and his wife were long past the time for becoming parents there was no heir. Then Isaac was born. Trust in God was rewarded. But just when it appeared that the promises would indeed be fulfilled, Abraham received the conviction that God was requiring the sacrificial death of his son. That death would render impossible the promises made by God.

It was terrible enough for Abraham to think that he must kill his own son. What was almost unbearable was the thought that all the promises must meet with failure. Heroically and with blind trust, he proceeded to carry out the sacrifice of his son. We know how the story ended. God did not require the death of Isaac, only a sign of Abraham's faith.

God deserves our faith because he is all powerful and all loving. Abraham believed that, for he was willing to accept the fact that God could do what seemed impossible. The scribes in the gospel did not have that kind of faith. They could not believe that sin could be forgiven through the humanity of Jesus. But God can do anything and he brings his almighty power to bear on us because he is all loving.

Abraham is our father and our model in faith. Like him we are called to turn our lives completely over to God.

Thursday of the Thirteenth Week (II)

Amos was considered obnoxious because he preached the need of repentance by all in Israel, including the king and the priests. Amaziah tried to persuade the king to get rid of Amos not only because he took his preaching as an insult but because he held Amos in contempt. He considered him a "nobody." And indeed in comparison with Amaziah, the priest of Bethel, Amos was a nobody. He admitted that he was not a prophet in his own right nor did he belong to a company of prophets. He was nothing more than a shepherd and a dresser of sycamores. On top of that he was not from Israel but from the hated south, Judah.

Despite appearances, Amos had credentials of the highest order. It was the Lord himself who had taken him from the south and his previous work to be a prophet to the northern kingdom. His worth was not due to his own sagacity but only to the call of God.

Jesus was in much the same position as Amos. Judging by appearances many considered him to be nothing more than a carpenter's son who had suddenly turned rabbi. When he forgave the sins of the paralytic, he was accused of blasphemy by arrogating to himself an authority which belongs to God alone. But beyond appearances lay divinity. Jesus is God in the flesh.

God acted through the humanity of Amos and Jesus, Son of God, acted through his own humanity. This providential movement of God continues. No priest forgives sins on his own in the sacrament of penance. He does so by the power of Christ granted him by ordination. It is really Christ who forgives. But God goes even further. He uses not only humanity but even simple substances such as bread and wine, for despite their appearances bread and wine become the body and the blood of the Lord.

We do not judge by appearances. By the light of faith we see God at work among us through his chosen instruments.

Friday of the Thirteenth Week (I)

The death of Sarah was mourned by Abraham, her loving

husband, and by Isaac, her devoted son. Abraham knew that he was soon to follow her, but he also believed that God's plan would be carried on through Isaac. That is why he was so specific about the kind of wife he should have. His was not the attitude of an overbearing father but of the Lord's faithful servant who wanted to make sure that God's will would be done.

The story of Isaac and Rebekah is beautifully told in the Bible. Here at Mass we have only an abbreviated version, but the message is clear. The promises of God continue. Isaac and Rebekah will have a son, Jacob, who will be the father of the twelve tribes of Israel. One of these twelve tribes will be that of Judah, the Jews from whom the Messiah will be born.

God was very patient in unfolding his plan. He knew the right moment in history for the coming of his Son, born of the house of David of the tribe of Judah. Through the human arms of his divine Son God the Father would reach out to embrace the whole world in his love. The Pharisees in the gospel did not have the mind of God. They were petty where God was big, exclusive where God was all loving. That is why they could not comprehend the actions of Jesus whereby he welcomed even those considered to be sinners and outside the law.

The Messiah came into the world through a long line of descendants reaching back through David, Judah, Jacob, and Isaac to Abraham, the first to receive God's promises. Now regardless of our human genealogy, we are the beneficiaries of those promises. It matters not what our ancestry is. Jesus has shown us that God is our true Father who embraces us with divine love.

Friday of the Thirteenth Week (II)

Tax collectors among the Jews were a despised group. They were Jews themselves but they acted on behalf of the occupying Roman government. As such they were considered traitors. They received no pay from the Romans. They made their living by overcharging their fellow countrymen; what was over and above the required tax they were allowed to keep for themselves. For that they were considered thieves. As traitors and thieves, they were treated with hatred and contempt. But not by Jesus.

In a way one cannot blame the Pharisees for objecting that Jesus ate with tax collectors. After all, Amos the prophet had condemned those Israelites who had cheated at business deals and taken advantage of the poor. What the Pharisees failed to understand was that Amos meant his words of condemnation as an admonition which would lead to repentance. He was like a doctor who warns a patient that his way of living is so injurious to his health that if it continues it will prove fatal.

Jesus stated his identical concern clearly: "People who are in good health do not need a doctor; sick people do." Jesus associated with known sinners to offer them the medicine of repentance. But then he turned the tables on the Pharisees by saying, "Go and learn the meaning of the words, 'It is mercy I desire and not sacrifice.' " This too was a message from Amos. The Israelites of his day were exact, if not devout, in observing the prescriptions of the law about worship but they were unmerciful in their dealings with others, especially in business matters. The Pharisees considered themselves observers of the law but their hearts were not filled with mercy and compassion toward their fellow men.

Jesus has called us to repentance. He has bathed us with the medicinal waters of baptism and strengthened us with the nourishment of the Eucharist. What he wants in return is a true love for others. The love we have received is to be shared.

Saturday of the Thirteenth Week (I)

Jacob took advantage of his father's blindness and with the connivance of Rebekah, his mother, deceived the old man. As a result Jacob benefited from the blessing which Isaac intended for his older son, Esau. The blessing ensured Jacob that his descendants would enjoy the possession of fertile lands.

St. Augustine in commenting on this passage states that the

deception by Jacob was not a lie, but a mystery. It is a kind interpretation. Modern scholars say that there is no need to defend Jacob. He was guilty of a lie. And yet there is a ring of truth to Augustine's words, for although there is a lie in Jacob there is a mystery in God. The mystery is that God could take an evil act and turn it to his own good purposes. It was his will that the Messiah would be born, not from the descendants of Esau but from those of Jacob. God writes straight with crooked lines.

The lie by Jacob and his mother was serious enough but it does not compare with the monumental evil we see all around us. The traffic in dope which reduces humans to a state little better than that of animals, the persecution of religion and the enslavement of people meant to be free, the injustices perpetrated on the poor and defenseless, the blatant destruction of innocent human life by abortion: these are serious evils. We may wonder why God does not in one strike of his almighty power, destroy such wickedness.

Today's reading tells us that God has a plan which he is working out with patience and wisdom. We ought indeed to struggle to overcome the injustices of our age, but all the while we must not lose faith in God. He is still in charge and will bring good from evil. Herein lies a great mystery indeed, but it is a mystery we accept if we really believe in God.

Saturday of the Thirteenth Week (II)

Sometimes Amos has been referred to as a prophet of doom. Certainly his warnings about the infidelity of the people toward God were strong, even ominous. But since he was truly God's prophet he could not leave the people without hope. God, he says, will bring about a new age for his people. In order to emphasize the magnanimity of God's love he paints a picture in terms the people can understand. The new age will be like the situation in which the earth is so fertile that the planter of the seed can scarcely keep ahead of the one harvesting the crop. Although the image is not to be taken literally, there is a promise of the great abundance of God's love.

Some people—the Pharisees seem to have been like this— have a picture of God as a miserly old man. In return for some good work, he carefully unties the strings of a small money bag, reaches in for a tiny coin which he places very carefully in the person's hand and says, "Now, don't spend this all in one place." Amos, with his exaggerated agricultural image, wishes to indicate that God is not like that. God is generous beyond our powers to imagine.

In the gospel Jesus charged the Pharisees to change their way of thinking about God. They could not absorb his message about God if they persisted in trying to limit God by the old wineskins. God is so great that he would burst those wineskins of old ideas. The new wineskins really are without limit for God's love is infinite.

We cannot comprehend God. But in faith we should believe that he is more forgiving than we suspect, more generous than we hope, and more loving than we can possibly know.

Monday of the Fourteenth Week (I)

Isaac did not want his son Jacob to marry a Canaanite woman and sent him off to Mesopotamia to find a wife. When he stopped for the night, Jacob had a strange dream of a ladder or stairway reaching from earth to the heavens, upon which God's messengers, his angels, were going up and down. The meaning of the dream is not clear but it would seem to indicate a continuing interaction between God and Israel, an interaction of which Jacob was to be an important part. Jacob did not yet understand that he was a man of destiny in God's plan of salvation.

The dream aroused an awareness in Jacob, especially as it continued with the voice of the Lord promising him that the land upon which he slept would become the home of his descendants. The words of the Lord went back to the covenant he had made with Jacob's grandfather, Abraham. Fulfilling those promises through

Jacob and his descendants was part of the long, often shaky, history of the chosen people from whom the Messiah would be born.

Was this long, complex history, often calling for supreme patience from God, worth the outcome? By all means! No need now for symbolic dreams of angels going back and forth from heaven to earth to show God's concern. Jesus is God himself in the flesh. A woman could reach out and touch his cloak and be healed. A little girl is roused from the sleep of death by the touch of this person's hand. These touches were contact with divinity.

For us the reality of contact with divinity is just as real. When Jesus walked this earth, people came into contact with divinity through his humanity. Now we come into contact with this divinity through sacramental signs. Only faith is needed for us to realize that we are as fortunate as the woman who touched his cloak and the little girl who touched his hand.

Monday of the Fourteenth Week (II)

We can never fully appreciate the depth and intensity of God's love for us. The reason is that all we can do is to compare his love with what we already know about love from human experience, and that experience can never match the reality of God's love for us.

In the first reading the prophet implies that God's love is like that of a husband for his wife. He has God say to his people, "I will espouse you to me forever." But we know that even the most ideal human marriage is imperfect. In God's love there is simply no imperfection.

We get a better picture of God's love by observing the actions of Jesus, who is God in the flesh. We see his concern for the synagogue leader whose daughter had died. It was a sad, serious situation. In contrast, the woman with the hemorrhage was really a "nobody" as compared with the important leader of the synagogue. And her malady was scarcely a critical one since she had lived with it for twelve years. And yet Jesus showed just as much concern for her and was unwilling to ignore her. Jesus loves all his people, big and small, and he appreciates human problems, both critical ones, like the death of the little girl, and less serious ones, like the illness of the woman.

Very often the purpose of a scriptural passage is to help us appreciate God's love for us. We must never tire of that vital message because in this life we must constantly be striving to see a little more deeply into the infinite love of an infinite God.

Tuesday of the Fourteenth Week (I)

Yesterday's reading showed that Isaac did not want his son Jacob to marry a Canaanite woman and sent him off to Mesopotamia to find a wife. The Lectionary omits the long, involved story of his adventures there and today takes up the narrative with Jacob on his way home. The strange incident of his wrestling with a man who eventually is shown to represent God accounts for the origin of a new name given to Jacob by God. That name is Israel, which seems to mean "struggle with God." It is this name which is given to the people descended from Jacob. The change in name indicates that he owed his position as father of the Israelites to God alone.

It can be said that this name sums up much of the relationship between God and his people. It was a struggle for God to keep his people close to himself as they twisted and turned to get away to follow false gods. Despite the struggle God constantly blessed his people as he blessed Jacob.

The meaning of the name "Israelite" applies to us also, for we are in a constant struggle. God is always calling us to himself for an embrace of love, but his invitation is free, not one of force. All the while there are factors pulling us in the opposite direction. We are drawn by our own selfishness, by the allure of false gods of money and pleasure, by the hollow values proposed as the means to the good life. God sometimes seems distant while we are tempted to embrace temporary attractions. Life is a struggle, and this struggle produces tension in our lives.

Think of a rubber band. When you pull from the ends in opposite directions, you produce tension. When you let go of one end, there is no more tension. Faithfulness to God means letting go of whatever pulls us away from him. When we learn to let go, the struggle ends and we find peace in the loving embrace of God.

Tuesday of the Fourteenth Week (II)

Hosea is known as the prophet of love. Yesterday we heard him, speaking in the person of God, saying, "I will espouse you to myself forever." It must have been difficult for this prophet of love to pronounce the warnings found in today's reading. The warnings, on first hearing, do not have the ring of a lover's voice. And yet his words are motivated by nothing other than love.

The people had abandoned God for the worship of pagan idols. Hosea, through his admonitions, wanted only to call the people back to the loving embrace of God. True love often demands saying and doing what is best for people, even though that form of love may hurt at first.

When Hamlet in Shakespeare's play admonished his mother, Queen Gertrude, for her immorality, she complained about his cruelty with bitter tears. Hamlet replied, "I am cruel only to be kind."

In today's gospel we saw Jesus curing sickness and disease. That was what the people needed at the time. On other occasions we have seen Jesus warning the people and condemning improper practices. On these occasions Jesus was no less loving than he was when he was curing sickness. True love means saying and doing what is best for people.

In our own lives there are times when we may wonder whether God really loves us. When everything seems to be going wrong, it is difficult to believe that there is a loving God who is directing our lives. Now at this Mass is the time for us to grow in accepting the truth that whatever God does, he does out of love, and what he does is best for us.

Wednesday of the Fourteenth Week (I)

The story of Joseph in the Old Testament is one of the most fascinating narratives in all literature. It begins in the thirty-seventh chapter of the Book of Genesis and should be read in full. The Lectionary for Mass, however, can give us only brief excerpts. This story shows how God guides the course of human events despite the evil intentions of men.

The story of Joseph images the life of Jesus himself. Joseph was sold by his brothers into slavery and was taken to Egypt. There, after many difficulties and a threat to his life because of a false accusation, he eventually rose to a position of prominence in which he had much power and authority. He was a prudent administrator who had made provision for an expected famine.

When Joseph's father and brothers suffered from the widespread famine, they went to Egypt looking for help, never realizing that God, through their evil designs upon Joseph, had sent him ahead to Egypt to save them from starvation. Even when the brothers saw Joseph, their memory of him dimmed by years of separation, they failed to recognize him.

Doesn't even this summary remind you of the life of Jesus? His own people failed to recognize him, a people who ultimately betrayed him. Despite their betrayal, Jesus did not turn against his own. Rather it was precisely through this rejection which led to his death that salvation came.

Jesus could never abandon the human race. He recognized us as his brothers and sisters in a situation much worse than that brought on by a famine. We were starving spiritually and very near death. He has given us a spiritual food so that we may never need be hungry again. He has given us a spiritual drink so that we may never need be thirsty again. He has given us his own body and his own blood.

Wednesday of the Fourteenth Week (II)

Today's first reading presents a bleak picture of the kingdom of

Israel. The more luxurious the life of the people became, the more altars and shrines they built to pagan gods. The more affluence increased among them, the more did the people wander from faithfulness to God. Hosea tried to warn them, but the fact is that in 732 B.C. part of the northern kingdom was destroyed by Assyrian armies and the rest fell to these forces ten years later.

But God never gives up on his people. In the gospel we saw Jesus choosing the twelve and sending them out to recover "the lost sheep of the house of Israel." He wanted them for the moment to confine their attention to their own people, to give them the first opportunity. Ultimately, however, the gospel was to be communicated through the apostles to all peoples.

Removed though we are by two thousand years from the time of Jesus and by thousands of miles from the holy land, we are the recipients of the gospel. The apostles and all ministers of the gospel are but the instruments of God. It is his almighty power which has been responsible for the spread of the faith. And it is his grace which has opened our hearts to accept that faith.

By most standards we live in a luxurious, affluent culture. The power of God which spread the gospel can also protect us from the pitfalls of our culture. We need to acknowledge that our receiving of the faith as well as our preserving of it are both dependent on the almighty, loving power of God. He will never give up on us. We must never give up on him.

Thursday of the Fourteenth Week (I)

When famine spread across the land, Jacob sent his sons to Egypt to look for food. There Joseph, their brother whom they had sold into slavery and whom they presumed to be dead, had risen to prominence. He supplied them with food, even though they did not recognize him. But Joseph yearned to see his father and his younger brother, Benjamin. As we heard in today's reading, Joseph could no longer control himself before his brothers. He broke down in tears of joy and revealed his identity.

The brothers were at first apprehensive. Knowing how shamefully they had treated Joseph, they feared that he would now have revenge upon them. Little did they understand Joseph's holiness or the plan of God. Joseph explained to them that the whole episode of his being sold into slavery was part of God's plan to place him in Egypt where he could save many people, including his own family, from starvation.

In his holiness Joseph did not want revenge. He only wanted to help because he knew that God had favored him greatly. In Egypt he had risen to a position which made him practically the equal of Pharaoh himself. He knew that this favor from God was not for his own benefit. He lived the words which Jesus would proclaim centuries later: "The gift you have received give as a gift."

We rarely, if ever, have as clear a perception of God's plan as did Joseph. And yet we must in faith see how blessed we have been by God. "Count your blessings" is good advice. But we must not count as does a miser who only wishes to be a hoarder. The gifts we have received must be given to others as a gift. Love and service freely given to others is part of the lesson from the story of Joseph. It is also both the command and example of Jesus himself.

Thursday of the Fourteenth Week (II)

Today's reading from the prophet Hosea is one of the high points of Old Testament revelation about God. Hosea is the prophet of God's love despite the infidelity of his people. He is famous for his image of God as a husband who continues to love an adulterous wife and who searches for her to bring her back home. Today's reading in a sense is even more beautiful because it prepares for the teaching of Jesus that God is truly our Father.

Hosea presents God as a devoted Father who lifts his infant to his cheek. The image reminds me of the picture of the Pope embracing a little child in Brazil, a smile on his face as he holds the child close to himself. God is seen as nourishing his child and teaching him how to walk. Perhaps the impact of one sentence can easily be missed. God declares, "Out of Egypt I called my son."

This statement refers to the Exodus when God led the Israelites out of the slavery of Egypt and formed them into his people. It was the great, central saving event of the Old Testament, comparable to the death and resurrection of Jesus in the Christian era.

Although Israel has been unfaithful, God protests that he will not give vent to blazing anger. Notice that he then says, "For I am God and not man." For any human parent there is a limit. Human nature can endure only so much. But with God there is no limit to his love, to his forebearance, to his power to endure. God's love never fails (cf. 1 Cor 13:7-8).

The central message of Jesus is that God truly is our Father from whom all life, all holiness comes to us. He taught us to call upon God as Father in prayer, and every day at Mass we follow his teaching. How blessed are we in the knowledge that the Father of Jesus Christ is our Father too!

Friday of the Fourteenth Week (I)

The story of Joseph in the Old Testament reveals God's plan at work. A terrible famine came upon Jacob (renamed Israel) and his family. Joseph had been sold by his brothers into slavery and was brought to Egypt where he could supply food for his family. When Jacob realized that his son Joseph was still alive he set off for Egypt, despite his advanced age, to lay eyes upon him once again. It was a meeting filled with tears of joy. Because Joseph was so prominent and in such favor with Pharaoh, Jacob brought his whole family, all his descendants, with him to Egypt.

This event accounts for the presence of the Israelites in Egypt. It would later seem an unfortunate move for them because when a new Pharaoh who did not know Joseph came to power, the Israelites no longer enjoyed royal favor. In fact they were completely deprived of their social status and put to work as slaves. What had been a dream of fortune come true turned into a nightmare of oppression. It seemed that God had sent them into Egypt like sheep among wolves.

But God's plan was still at work. In his wisdom he saw this purifying experience as necessary for the Israelites as a preparation for the extraordinary experience of the Exodus. Previous to the Egyptian sojourn, they were a nomadic people, wandering about from place to place with no sense of identity. By means of the Exodus God formed them into his own special people and through Moses, the leader of the Exodus, he made his covenant with them.

The authors of the Bible, inspired by God, saw the meaning of these events only after they had taken place. It was spiritual hindsight. The meaning of our individual lives may seem vague at times. We do not yet have the benefit of hindsight. But we do have the gift of faith. And in faith we must believe that God is forming and shaping our lives according to his wisdom and love as surely as he did for the Israelites.

Friday of the Fourteenth Week (II)

Hosea is the prophet of God's love. Yesterday his reading was touching and tender. He presented God as a Father who scoops his child, Israel, into his arms and presses him against his cheek. Today, fully aware of Israel's disobedience, he cries out: "Return, O Israel, to the Lord, your God." His words easily make us think of the parable in which Jesus shows the young, prodigal son returning to his Father. That too is a touching and tender scene, an image of how completely God loves us despite our failures.

The knowledge that God is our Father should give us courage in life, especially when things are difficult. Jesus in the gospel warned his disciples that they would be like sheep among wolves, that they would be hated because of him. The particular problems faced by the disciples may not be identical with ours but there are parallels nonetheless. There is no point in trying to cite examples since difficulties and trials are different for each one of us and we know our own problems well enough.

The point is that as we go through life we are not all alone. We have the help, the guidance, and the protection of a loving Father. God is especially present to us through his Son in the Eucharist.

That is the most important help of all. But when we pray in the Lord's prayer for our daily bread, we should understand that this daily bread includes not only the Eucharist and our natural food but everything we need to continue as faithful, loving children of God. Even when we sin, God calls us to return to his fatherly embrace. With God as our Father we can and should lead lives of joy and peace.

Saturday of the Fourteenth Week (I)

The magnificent story of Joseph has a happy ending. Jacob and his family have been saved from starvation through the ministry of Joseph. Before he dies Jacob has the joy of seeing his son Joseph whom he presumed to have died long before. And Joseph is happy to be reunited with his family. Only one discordant note remains. After the father dies, Joseph's brothers fear that he is going to take revenge on them because they sold him into slavery. "Suppose," they say, "that Joseph has been nursing a grudge against us and now plans to pay us back in full for the wrong we did him?"

They were fearful only because they did not understand their brother Joseph. It seems that they were judging him by their own standard, thinking that if they were in his position they would want revenge. But Joseph was a true man of God, reflecting his goodness.

Sometimes we mistakenly judge God by our own human standards. We find it very difficult to forgive serious offenses, and it would have been no surprise to us if Joseph had taken revenge on his brothers. But God is not like that. Jesus in the gospel tells us to fear God, not men, because only God can destroy both body and soul in Gehenna. But notice that he cannot let matters rest there. He seems to be in a hurry to assure us that God does not want to harm us. He says, "Every hair of your head has been counted; so do not be afraid of anything." It is an emphatic way of saying that we are precious to God. He wants only the best for us.

Joseph did not hold grudges against his brothers, and God does not hold grudges against us, his children.

Saturday of the Fourteenth Week (II)

God has revealed to us that he is not some nebulous, cosmic force, far removed from us and disinterested in our well-being. Rather God has shown us that he is a tender, loving Father. We can approach him with the simplicity and confidence of a little child. But we must never forget that he is God. We should not want to make him less than he is. The more exalted we see God, the more significant to us is the reality of his fatherhood. We love our heavenly Father, but we see that he is also worthy of respect, even of awe.

The great prophet Isaiah fully appreciated God's majesty. He has recounted for us the vision he had of the magnificence of God. He heard the angelic hymn of praise: "Holy, holy, holy is the Lord of hosts. All the earth is filled with his glory." The Church has rightly incorporated this hymn into every Eucharistic prayer at the conclusion of the preface. It is a constant reminder of the respect we must have for our heavenly Father.

Isaiah felt unworthy to be in the presence of the mighty Lord. He was humble before God because of his sinfulness. God, through one of the seraphim, removed his wickedness and purged him of his sins. Every day at Mass we come before the throne of God to sing his praises in union with the angels, but we always begin Mass by acknowledging our unworthiness. We ask for God's mercy and pardon so that we may be prepared to celebrate the sacred mysteries. God responds by drawing us even closer to himself through his mercy and pardon.

The Mass gives us a perfect balance in our relationship with God. We approach him with confidence and love as his children but we do so with a sense of reverence and awe.

Monday of the Fifteenth Week (I)

Today we began reading the book of Exodus from the Old

Testament. We will continue to hear readings from this book for the better part of three weeks during daily Mass. The book describes the providential events which form the foundation of Israel as God's chosen people. Today's reading prepares for the story of Moses who was destined by God to lead his people to freedom.

Some may wonder why the Church is so attached to the Old Testament, especially the book of Exodus. The basic reason is that the God of Israel is the God of Christians. There are not two Gods, one for the Jews of the past and one for us today as Catholics. We must remember that Jesus did not come to destroy the past but to bring it to fulfillment.

God's providential movements in the history of the chosen people are important to us in the Christian era. Pope Pius XI pointed out that we are all spiritually Semites. Abraham, as we proclaim in the first Eucharistic prayer, is our father in faith. The coming of Jesus Christ is the fulfillment of the covenant made with Abraham, and the entire Old Testament is a saving action of God which reaches its climax in the person of Jesus Christ.

Our spiritual roots go back farther than to ancestors whom we may have had in Germany, Mexico, Ireland, Africa, Italy, Poland, or some other country. Our spiritual roots reach back through the centuries to the chosen people of the Old Testament. Their story is our story.

During the coming weeks we will all do well to listen attentively to the readings from the book of Exodus.

Monday of the Fifteenth Week (II)

There is a big difference between a bribe and a gift. A bribe is some kind of payment given with the view of perverting the judgment or corrupting the conduct of a person in a position of power. A bribe, rather than being a generous act, is really a selfish one. A gift is an expression of love with no strings attached. One who gives a gift in the proper spirit does not do so in order to receive something in return.

The people to whom Isaiah preached looked upon God as

someone with a lot of power whom they could bribe. Despite their lack of genuine piety, they expected to win favors from God by bribing him with meaningless prayers and sacrifices. You may wonder how the people could have so deceived themselves. The answer is that they had allowed themselves to be influenced by the approach of their pagan neighbors to their gods.

Isaiah was warning the people that they must be different from the pagans and their perverse view of religion. The blunt, almost shocking, words of Jesus in the gospel have much the same purpose. His point about coming to spread division, even within families, was his way of stating emphatically that his followers must not allow themselves to be influenced by anyone who would turn them away from sound religion.

Every day here at Mass we offer the gift of Christ and ourselves wtih him to our heavenly Father. This act must not become a bribe. We do not worship God with the hope of buying him off. We offer worship to God because he is deserving of it. The Mass must be the expression of our unselfish love for God.

Tuesday of the Fifteenth Week (I)

The fascinating story of how Moses while an infant was rescued from death illustrates God's providential care of his chosen one. Despite the machinations of an evil ruler in Egypt, God was powerful enough to bring his plan for Moses to completion.

This story also explains how it was that Moses, a Hebrew child, received an Egyptian education (cf. Ac 7:22). The Egyptians were a highly cultured people, and God made use of their erudition to train his servant, Moses. Moses, however, had to come to a realization of his own identity and his mission. God began to accomplish this realization in Moses, again providentially, through the unusual episode in which Moses defended a fellow Hebrew against the attack of an Egyptian. The subsequent misunderstanding and flight of Moses were all part of God's plan.

As these events transpired, it is hardly likely that Moses understood what was happening to him. Only upon later reflection under the guidance of the Spirit could Moses have come to an awareness that God's hand was at work in his life.

As we go through life many ordinary and some extraordinary things happen to us. Some make obvious sense and others appear to have no reason behind them. In this liturgy God calls us to look up to heaven with a faith that everything about our lives is guided by his great wisdom and according to his magnificent love for us.

Tuesday of the Fifteenth Week (II)

We all like to hear good things about ourselves. We even go to a doctor with the hope that there is nothing seriously wrong with us, but a doctor would be doing a great disservice if he were to pretend that we are in good health when actually we are not. His real kindness and concern are manifested in telling us the truth and indicating what we must do for our health.

I suppose that many people have a picture of Jesus as a very kind and gentle man, the Good Shepherd. But Jesus is also the Divine Physician, and so we should not be surprised to hear some rather stern warnings from him in today's gospel. He is like a conscientious doctor who warns us that unless we change something about our diet or way of living we will end up with a fatal illness. Jesus is concerned about our spiritual health.

Isaiah, under God's directive, acted sternly toward King Ahaz. God was deeply disturbed about the spiritual illness of Israel, and he sent Isaiah to warn the king and his people.

The scripture readings today do not contain specifics upon which we can examine ourselves, but they should give us pause and move us to reflect on our spiritual health. I cannot give you ideas suitable to each of you any more than a doctor can give the same diagnosis to each patient. An old practice of the Church is still a very good idea, and that is the habit of examining our consciences every night before retiring. This does not have to be a deep, painful, searching experience. Humble honesty in the presence of God is all that is required. A nightly examination of conscience is a practical means toward a healthy spiritual life.

Wednesday of the Fifteenth Week (I)

Moses had become a shepherd, working for his father-in-law. His life was simple and unassuming, and he could not be counted among the learned and the clever of this world. He was like the merest child, spoken of by Jesus in the gospel, to whom God offers his revelation.

At first Moses was curious about the burning bush. When he heard the voice of God, he was stupified. He did not know what to do. He had to be reminded that a sign of respect and humility was in order. That sign, according to the custom of the time, was the removing of his sandals. It was a gesture, but its purpose was to help Moses realize that he was in the presence of the almighty God.

We do much the same as Moses shortly after each Mass has begun. We are asked to acknowledge our sinfulness, to express our need for God's mercy, to humble ourselves out of respect for God's presence among us. The penitential rite is not an examination of conscience. Rather it is spiritually removing our sandals before God.

After Moses had humbled himself before God, he was given the favor of his revelation. God spoke to him intimately and shared himself with him. After the penitential rite, God speaks to us through the scriptures; he shares himself with us through the gift of his Son's body and blood.

When we become simple and humble like a child, God reveals to us what he has hidden from the learned and clever.

Wednesday of the Fifteenth Week (II)

Today's first reading from the Prophet Isaiah has a strange, bellicose ring to it. We must understand its background. In Isaiah's time Assyria was the great military power bent upon conquering all its neighbors. You might say that it was the Soviet Russia of that day. Moreover, there was no country like the United States to counterbalance its power. The Assyrians were haughty and in their pride they attributed their victories to their own power and their national god, Ashur. But Isaiah knew and proclaimed that Assyria was but an instrument in the hands of God to purify sinful Judah, and that God would in time humble Assyria.

Of course the Assyrians would have scoffed at Isaiah's message if they had heard it and would have considered the great prophet to have a childish approach to the hard, cruel world of politics and war. The truth was that Isaiah was the really wise person, not because he was childish, but because he was childlike in his openness to God's revelation. He had a simplicity born of wisdom.

Jesus in the gospel approves of Isaiah and all those like him. In fact, he gives praise to his heavenly Father for his love of the simple and the humble, those who are childlike. He prays: "Father, Lord of heaven and earth, to you I offer praise, for what you have hidden from the learned and the clever you have revealed to the merest children." We have been made God's children by baptism. Now we must respond to him as children with their openness, their trust, their simplicity. We come to deep understandings not by our own efforts but by the grace of God. And that grace is granted to those who are childlike.

Thursday of the Fifteenth Week (I)

There is something special in a name. A certain intimacy is included in calling someone by his first name. It is virtually impossible to feel close to a person if you do not know his name.

"God" is actually a generic name and is applied even to Greek or Roman deities. To Moses God revealed his personal name. One problem is that it is uncertain what the original Hebrew, Yahweh, really means, even though it is usually translated as "I AM," or more precisely "I am what I am." The text in the Bible is rather complicated, but it does seem that the best opinion is that the expression is properly understood to mean that this God is the cause of all that comes into existence, in short, the Creator. The God of Israel is not the sun or the moon, as was the god of some pagans, but rather the God who created the sun, the moon and everything else.

The final import of this name is that God is a personal God, not an inanimate object or a vague, nebulous force in the universe. In giving his name through Moses to his people, God wished to show that he was entering into an intimate, personal relationship with them. Although God is transcendent, far above his creation, and one worthy of awe and respect (remember yesterday Moses had to take off his sandals in the presence of God), he is close to his chosen people.

This intimacy of God and men is even more evident in the person of Jesus Christ, the God made man, who invites us to come to him for refreshment and rest. Though far above us as God, Jesus Christ in his human nature has become part of the human scene, part of our own lives.

We do not have a God who is far removed from the sorrow and joy of our everyday existence. Rather we are blessed to have as our God one who is close to us, one who guides and directs our lives with love and concern.

Thursday of the Fifteenth Week (II)

A loving husband and wife who really want children look forward to the birth of their first child. The thought of the child, snugly wrapped in the warm security of the womb, preoccupies all their waking thoughts and maybe their dreams as well. Imagine that a wife is convinced that she is pregnant. She and her husband are overjoyed. The wife goes to a doctor to confirm her pregnancy only to discover that she has been mistaken. Conception has not taken place. It is a bitter disappointment, but they know that they still have hope that a child will be theirs in the future.

This is the picture which Isaiah paints of the people of their day. They had heard promises of salvation and they were convinced that the time had come for the birth of a new era upon the earth. But that era had not come. It was a bitter disappointment, but Isaiah wanted to encourage the people to keep up their hope in the future.

We are in a different position. We believe that salvation has come in the birth of a child and that a new era of salvation has opened for the whole world. And God has accomplished this salvation in a way so tender and so touching that it was not envisioned by the prophets of old.

Our salvation has come in the birth of the eternal Son of God, made human like us in all things but sin. God always had a tender love for his people, but how much more touching it is to experience this love in the human heart of Jesus Christ. Living fully a human life, with all of its burdens and difficulties, Jesus says "Come to me, all you who are weary and find life burdensome, and I will refresh you."

Jesus here at Mass invites us to come to him and be refreshed with spiritual food and drink. His heart is so loving that he wishes to share his own body and blood with us. That is a salvation worth waiting for.

Friday of the Fifteenth Week (I)

Today's first reading explains the origin and meaning of the feast of the Passover. This feast was to become a yearly celebration of Israel's deliverance from the slavery of Egypt. As the event of the Passover was the greatest one in the history of the people, so the feast of the Passover was the greatest celebration of the year.

Jesus in his death and resurrection, the Christian Passover, gave a new meaning to freedom. Ours is a freedom from the slavery of sin and its effect which is eternal death. In dying Jesus destroyed our death and in rising he restored our life. That is the greatest event in all of history.

At the Last Supper, which took place within the context of the Passover celebration, Jesus also gave a new meaning to that feast as he changed bread and wine into his body and blood. The Eucharist, his body given up for us and his blood poured out for us, is the living memorial of our redemption, our freedom from sin.

We celebrate the Christian Passover in a special way once a year at Easter time. But what Jesus did for us is so vital that we are called to celebrate it also once a week on Sundays. And if we wish, we may celebrate it even daily. Every Mass, no matter what the occasion or feast may be, is principally an offering of praise and thanks to God for our salvation in Christ.

The Israelites were told that they must never forget what God had done for them in the passover. That was the reason for their yearly celebration. What God has done for us is so marvelous that once a year is not enough to commemorate it. Even every Sunday can fall short of a proper remembrance. We are quite right in celebrating the Christian Passover by means of daily Mass.

Friday of the Fifteenth Week (II)

The Jewish law regarding rest on the Sabbath was very strict. There were, of course, different interpretations but in the strict view of the Pharisees the disciples by pulling off the heads of grain to eat were violating the law which forbade harvesting on the Sabbath. It was one of thirty-nine works which the rabbis counted as violation of the Sabbath rest.

When the Pharisees objected to what the disciples were doing, Jesus came to their defense. He pointed out that when David was in danger of his life from King Saul, he begged food of the priest Ahimelech. The priest, having nothing else to offer them, gave them the showbread of the sanctuary which ordinarily was reserved for sacred purposes alone. The point Jesus was making was that in God's mind human needs take precedence over ritual law.

A careful examination reveals a still deeper point. When he reminds his hearers that God desires mercy and not sacrifice, he is not condemning the act of ritual sacrifice. Rather he wanted them to understand that since the purpose of sacrifice is to bring us into closer union with God, worship should make us more like God.

And what is God like? Today's first reading shows us one aspect of God, his compassion and mercy. King Hezekiah deserved to die because of his sins. God could have abided by strict justice but in answer to the fervent prayer of the king he relented and allowed him to live.

Our worship of God at Mass should make us more like God. It is not Godlike to turn aside from someone in need because we judge that he does not deserve help. It is not Godlike to look with contempt upon people who are slaves of alcohol or narcotics. God wants us to be compassionate, understanding, and merciful as he is. Being like God in this way should be the fruit of our worship.

Saturday of the Fifteenth Week (I)

Four hundred and thirty years is a very long time, much longer than the life span of any human person. It was for that length of time that Israelites lived in slavery in Egypt. All the while God had a plan to free the people. He was very patient in carrying out his plan, since to God even four hundred and thirty thousand years is a brief period in light of eternity.

God is responsible for the totality of human history. In that realization we may perhaps feel rather insignificant, as if we really do not count for much in the overall picture. Nothing could be less in accord with the truth of God's goodness.

Each one of us is very important in God's eyes and even in his overall plan for human history. The world may take but little or no note of our existence, but we are precious in God's estimation. The words of Isaiah the prophet, "Here is my servant whom I have chosen, my loved one in whom I delight," were fulfilled in Jesus.

They are also fulfilled in each one of us for we have been called to be like Jesus, children of the Father. We are indeed his loved ones in whom he takes delight.

Saturday of the Fifteenth Week (II)

Some scholars have referred to the prophets of the Old Testament as being the conscience of the people of God. Micah, a contemporary of Isaiah, was one of these men. In today's reading he attacks the wealthy landowners who have been dispossessing the poor by illegal means. He condemns exploitation of the underprivileged.

When the prophets speak out boldy and courageously against injustice, they do so for two reasons. They wish to protect the rights of God's poor but they also wish to call those who have sinned to repentance. In other words, they are not intent on destroying those who are guilty of injustice. They wish to save them as well as to uphold the rights of others. But because they stirred up the conscience of the guilty, the prophets often suffered persecution, even death. The same thing happened to Jesus. Today's gospel tells us that the Pharisees began to plot against Jesus to find a way to destroy him.

In 1980 the Archbishop of San Salvador and a number of his priests were murdered because they opposed oppression of the poor. Usually the reaction to the preaching of social justice is not so violent. But in our own country people have been known to walk out of church or to stop contributing to the collection because a priest has pricked their consciences regarding social matters.

Some people protest that the Church should stay out of economic and social matters. While it is true that these areas can be complex, the biblical tradition, both Old and New Testaments, gives witness that God's ministers are called to try to right injustice. Religion does not end in church. It only begins in church and must influence the way in which we live. In our conduct there must not be the slightest hint of prejudice, injustice or exploitation. God wants our worship but he also wants us to act in justice and love toward all his people.

Monday of the Sixteenth Week (I)

There are some people in this world who are never satisfied. No matter what you may do for them they are unhappy.

In a sense the Israelites mentioned in the first reading were that way. After 430 years of slavery in Egypt, God was leading them to freedom and a promised land. And yet they found something to grumble about. Much the same was true of the scribes and Pharisees in the Gospel. After all that Jesus had said and done, they were not satisfied. They wanted something more and something different.

We are called to accept God's plan for our lives, and we are called to do so, not with grumbling, but with joy. That joy is the fruit of a real faith and trust in God's power, wisdom, and goodness.

Every day in the Mass we place ourselves together with Jesus in God's hands. As we share in the sacrificial death of Jesus, we should have his sentiment, "Father, into your hands I deliver up my spirit." In his turn God the Father gives us the strength to carry out that sentiment as he nourishes us with the body and blood of his Son.

I hope we all can be very well-satisfied with God's plan for us.

Monday of the Sixteenth Week (II)

The scene of today's first reading is a lawcourt of cosmic dimensions. All of nature is called to be a witness in this trial of the people in which God is both prosecutor and judge. Despite all that God has done for them, the people have been unfaithful, thinking that external religious rites could substitute for a life of true devotion. The people have no case. They deserve to be condemned.

But God is an unusual judge. He is not intent upon condemnation. He passes no sentence because he prefers repentance to punishment. He dismises the case with an admonition which is so gentle that there is scarcely any sting to it. He reminds the people: "You have been told what is good and what the Lord requires of you: only to do the right thing and to love goodness and to walk humbly with your God."

This admonition is the constant message of the prophets. "To love goodness" is a key phrase. The Hebrew word (hesed) is difficult to translate, and our English word, "goodness," cannot convey the full meaning. "Goodness" here refers to a response to God made not out of duty but out of love. "To walk humbly with God" means to live in union with God and to serve him in love.

When the Pharisees asked Jesus for a special sign, in effect he told them to follow the teaching of the prophets, such as Jonah, in their call for repentance. Repentance is a change of heart, a turning away from false values, to walk humbly with God, to love goodness. The Christian message is basically the same and just as simple. We are called to respond out of love to God because of all the love he has shown us.

Tuesday of the Sixteenth Week (I)

The Israelite community reflected on the events of its history in the light of faith. They could have looked back on the episode recounted in today's first reading and said, "Boy, were we lucky," or even "Gosh, those Egyptians were pretty stupid." Rather, they saw that the hand of God was at work in their destiny. The story we have just heard was composed in such a way that any reader of faith should quickly conclude that God alone was responsible for the freedom of the Israelites.

In his famous play Shakespeare has Hamlet say to his friend, Horatio, "There's a divinity that shapes our ends / Rough-hew them how we will." We are called to a faith which sees that no matter how roughly we may seem to be shaping our own lives, God has a plan for each one of us, a plan that makes us brothers and sisters of Jesus, God's own children.

In the gospel Jesus indicates that we must be open to his Father's will. That openness is the corrective for any mistake, the antidote for any poison. Today we pray with Jesus to the Father, "Thy will be done on earth as it is in heaven." We must pray with a confidence that God is responsible for our lives, and that it is his divine plan which shapes our ends.

Tuesday of the Sixteenth Week (II)

Today's first reading is a beautiful prayer asking God to shepherd his people. From an early period in the Old Testament era God as Shepherd was a warm and heartening image for the people. Of course Jesus used that image for himself, and for centuries later it still held much meaning while society continued in a simple, agrarian form. With the industrial revolution and our own era of modern technology the image of shepherd has lost something of its richness. Shepherding is not within our direct experience.

If Jesus were preaching today, he would undoubtedly use some other image to indicate the tenderness of his loving care for us. Actually in today's gospel we heard a declaration which should touch our hearts: "Whoever does the will of my heavenly Father is brother and sister and mother to me." Jesus indicated that as his disciples we enjoy a personal relationship with him. We have been taken into his family and we are to feel at home with him.

Someone had told Jesus that his mother and relatives (for such is the meaning of "brothers" here), wanted to speak with him. Jesus did not ignore his mother. Rather he wanted the crowd to know that she enjoyed a relationship with him which was more profound than the one they thought of which came from physical birth. Mary went beyond being the physical mother of Jesus. She was actually his perfect disciple, the one who in everything followed the will of God, who was Father of both Jesus and Mary.

Every day at Mass we pray as Jesus taught us and we ask that God's will be done by us on earth as it is in heaven. In striving to do God's will in everything, we become more like Mary, the perfect disciple. And as disciples we are brother and sister and mother to Jesus.

Wednesday of the Sixteenth Week (I)

God continually cares for his people, and he responds to human need. Even if a "natural" explanation may be offered for the presence of manna and quails in the Sinai Peninsula where the Israelites were wandering, it is clear that the Bible wishes us to know that God himself was the provider.

That the Israelites grumbled and complained should not be surprising. They had reached a point at which they were starving. Their mistake was that they complained to the wrong people. Moses and Aaron were powerless to help them. Their complaint could easily have been turned into a prayer of faith to God.

When we are in need, we should without hesitation turn to God for help. Prayer of petition need not be a complaint, or even a selfish act. Prayer of petition should be an expression of our faith that God is all powerful, and so he can help us, and that God is all loving, and so he will help us.

God gives us sustenance for our daily lives as surely as he gives us spiritual nourishment through his inspired word (the seed spoken of in the gospel) and through the body and blood of his Son. When we come to recognize that all good things come from God, then we will know to whom we should look in time of any need.

Wednesday of the Sixteenth Week (II)

Today the liturgy begins a series of fifteen readings from the prophet Jeremiah, who was called by God in the year 626 B.C. He was reluctant to accept the call because of his youth, but God told him, "Before I formed you in the womb I knew you, a prophet to the nations I appointed you."

The first part of Jeremiah's ministry occurred during the reign of the devout king Josiah who in the year 622 began a series of religious reforms. During that era Jeremiah's words were like the seed, spoken of by Jesus, which fell on good soil and yielded a rich harvest. But then things changed.

King Josiah died in 609 B.C. and under his successor the religious reform was abandoned and Jeremiah, witnessing the corruption of the people, feared that the northern kingdom would inevitably fall. From then on Jeremiah preached repentance but with very little apparent success and at the cost of much suffering on his part. His words became like the seed which fell among thorns, which grew up and choked it.

We have been called as surely as Jeremiah was. We were in the mind of God even before the world began, and his plan for us is an eternal one. Like Jeremiah, we find that some aspects of our lives are pleasant and others are discouraging. We meet with both success and failure, joy and sorrow, hope and disappointment. Even in the most disheartening times of his ministry, Jeremiah persevered and proclaimed a message of hope for Israel which sprang from his intense faith in God.

Our faith in God must move us to overcome any reluctance we may have about accepting his will for us. Through the bad as well as the good, God is guiding us with the loving hand of a Father.

Thursday of the Sixteenth Week (I)

God is master of all his creation. Creation is his own personal communication system.

God manifested himself to the Israelites in the awesome movements of nature described in the first reading. For our part we must learn to see God's beauty in a sunset, his power in a mighty wind, his loving care in life-giving rain.

God also continues to act through people as he did through Moses. Here at Mass we must see that it is God who is acting through the priest who presides at the Eucharist, through the lector who proclaims the word, through the special minister who gives you communion.

And what God does at Mass, he continues during the other moments of our lives. His love is in the embrace of a husband and

wife, his healing and care in those who nurse the sick, his genuine-
ness in the response of a little child, his joy in the mutual delight of
friends.

God is active all around us. How blest are the eyes which see
him and the ears which hear him.

Thursday of the Sixteenth Week (II)

It is a rare marriage indeed which does not begin with great
promises of fidelity and love undying. Of course the real test of love
comes over the long haul of day in and day out living. God spoke
through his prophet, Jeremiah, to his people about their relationship of love: "I remember the devotion of your youth, how you loved
me as a bride." It was a great beginning when at the time of the
exodus from Egypt God shaped a formless, enslaved humanity into
his own people, whom he united to himself in a spiritual marriage.

The honeymoon did not last forever, or even anything like
forever. After they entered their home, the promised land, the
people began to drift away from their love for God and turned to
other, pagan gods. It was like an act of adultery. When we see the
marriage of friends break up because of infidelity, we are dis-
mayed. God calls upon the heavens to witness the infidelity of his
people: "Be amazed at this, O heavens, and shudder with sheer
horror," said the Lord.

Through Jesus we have entered into a union with God even
more intimate than that of the initial chosen people. It too is like a
marriage. Some people say that a marriage begins to break up the
moment that two people start to take each other for granted. We
must never take for granted the new covenant of love, the new
marriage, between God and ourselves. That is what Jesus meant
when he said, "I assure you, many a prophet and many a saint
longed to see what you see but did not see it, to hear what you hear
but did not hear it." How blest we are in the union with God which is
ours through Jesus Christ.

Friday of the Sixteenth Week (I)

There are different ways to receive God's word. We can receive it fruitfully and joyfully or with resentment and frustration. That is the meaning of the gospel parable.

The ten commandments are God's word to his people, part of his covenant. He was to be their God and they were to be his people. He would guide, protect, and love his people; they in return were asked to follow his will as manifested in the commandments. Throughout the Old Testament people responded to the command-ments in different ways.

Those commandments are still God's will for us today. How do we respond? Even very good people at times yearn for what they think is a greater freedom, to have the liberty to do what they want rather than what they should.

I am reminded of the astronauts who walked in space. What an exhilarating experience of freedom that must have been! And yet for survival they had to be confined within a space suit, which was a protection against a hostile environment, and they had to be tethered by a lifeline to the ship. Rather than inhibiting freedom, the space suit and lifeline were indispensable for allowing it.

God's commandments are not an inhibition. Rather they are a condition for the true freedom which allows us to fulfill our destiny. They are more than a protection against a hostile environment. They are a real lifeline from God himself. God's commandments are revealed to us so that we may respond fruitfully and joyfully.

Friday of the Sixteenth Week (II)

When the part of Jeremiah's prophecy which we heard today was written, Jerusalem had already been destroyed and the ark of the covenant had disappeared, never to be replaced. The loss of the ark was a depressing blow since it symbolized God's presence among his people. The word of the prophet was that the people were not to lose heart. The new era to come would be even greater than that of the former. Jerusalem itself would be the Lord's throne, and there all the nations would be gathered to honor the name of the Lord.

The prophets, even though moved by God to speak in his name, did not often realize the full meaning of what they proclaimed. Nor do we really, since the truth of God is beyond our understanding. More often than not, the promises of the prophets were fulfilled in a way far beyond their expectations.

The Christian era fulfills the prophetic vision. As a matter of fact, all the nations, and not merely the Israelites, now know and worship the one true God. But their worship is not confined to a building, such as the temple in Jerusalem, for Jesus has declared that he in his person is the new temple of worship. He is not limited in time or space. Those who are in union with him by faith and love, no matter where they may be found throughout the world, worship the Father in spirit and in truth. Where Jesus is, there is a magnificent temple of worship.

The Mass is the greatest fulfillment of the words of Jeremiah. Here Jesus is present in the eucharist, in the inspired word, in his people, and in his priest. Even at a weekday Mass, with only a few of us present, this church becomes the new Jerusalem, the city of the living temple, Jesus Christ.

Saturday of the Sixteenth Week (I)

Today we have heard how God ratified his covenant with his people. The covenant was sealed when Moses sprinkled the blood of the sacrificed animals on the altar, which represented God, and then on the people. In this way God and his people were symbolically united. The covenant was like a contract and the blood was like the signatures which make a contract legal.

One big difference between a human contract and God's covenant is that a contract is binding by law and God's covenant is binding by love. Love, not law, is the unifying force of the covenant.

We do not live under the old covenant described in today's first reading. We live under a new covenant, the one established by Jesus Christ. It too has love as its binding force. The old covenant was sealed in the blood of animal sacrifices, but the new covenant is sealed in the blood of Jesus Christ. As the blood of Christ is more excellent than that of animals, so is the new covenant more excellent than the old.

The blood of Christ, present on the altar of God, is not sprinkled upon us. Rather we are invited to drink of this blood of Christ from the cup. The Father offers us the cup as a means of renewing his covenant of love with us. As we receive the blood of Christ today we should in faith see that our act is a response to God's love, a sacramental and real way of affirming again our covenant with God.

Saturday of the Sixteenth Week (II)

Jeremiah condemned the superstition of the people of his time. Some of them believed that simply because they possessed the temple in Jerusalem, God would favor them. Their triple invocation, "the temple of the Lord, the temple of the Lord, the temple of the Lord," was the indication of their superstition. It was as if they were saying, "With the temple of the Lord in our midst, what more need be done?" Jeremiah's response was that the more to be done was to live an upright life.

We Catholics have not always been immune from superstition. In most places after Vatican II there has been a lessening of reliance on certain practices which were supposed to guarantee getting to heaven or at least being released quickly from purgatory. Please note that the practices were not bad; thinking that the practices without a good, moral life would be beneficial was bad. Perhaps what we need these days is not so much a warning against superstition as a proper understanding of our relationship with God.

We should never think that the purpose of a good life is to buy or purchase or merit heaven or good things in this life. God grants his grace freely. There is no way in which we can offer anything to God which would be the proper price for his gifts. The reason we should live good lives in accord with God's will is simply that it is the right way for children of a loving Father to act. A deliberately evil life is our way of excluding ourselves from the family. God does not reject us; we reject him.

In the Gospel Jesus says that at harvest time the weeds will be burned, but the good wheat will be gathered into the barn. We will be gathered into the loving arms of God, not because of some superstition, but because God loves us and we have chosen not to reject that love.

Monday of the Seventeenth Week (I)

The Israelites had just concluded a covenant of love with God. After Moses had left them for only a short time to commune with God and to receive the tablets of the law, the people reverted to pagan practices. Their actions bespoke a betrayal of God.

When Moses came upon the scene, he was disappointed, but disappointment soon turned to shock, and shock to outrage. I think some people readily understand how Moses felt. Those people are parents who have been disappointed, shocked, and even outraged at the behavior of their children who have become young adults. So often these days it seems that young adults stop going to church, abandon their faith and live as if they never heard of the commandments of God. Parents, who have tried to bring their children up as good Catholics, ask themselves, "What did we do wrong?"

Often the wrong is not with the parents at all. Young people, like everyone else, have freedom, a gift from God which he will not take away. Because they are free, children may choose to abandon all that the faith of their parents stands for, as the Israelites abandoned what Moses stood for.

But notice what happened to Moses. His outrage turned to compassion. He went before God in prayer to plead for the people, and offered to give his own life for them.

Such should be our response. We all know people, whether relatives or not, who have abandoned the practice of their faith and who perhaps are living apparently godless lives. Prayer for them, which can begin in this Mass, is the reaction God wants from us. God wants not disappointment or shock but compassion, not outrage but loving concern.

Monday of the Seventeenth Week (II)

These days much use is made in schools of audio-visual materials. Long before these pedagogical techniques became popular, God commanded Jeremiah to use a very visual, if somewhat revolting, means to illustrate the decay in the people's relationship with God. The rotted loin cloth, no longer fit for use, was a symbol of Israel's corruption.

But God is not thwarted by human betrayal. All along his plan was at work. With the coming of Jesus he made all things new. The kingdom of God broke upon the world with that coming. The renewed presence of God's love and life in and among us started with one person, Jesus, and his small band of followers. It was a small beginning, as tiny as the mustard seed, but it has spread throughout the whole world. A new people, the Church, now worships God in spirit and in truth.

And yet we realize that we ourselves are not immune from corruption. All around us are forces which would lead us to betrayal. Our life in God is a constant challenge to be a yeast in society, to be a means, not for corruption, but for growth.

Jeremiah was sent by God to admonish the people, to call them to repentance. We have that same message before us constantly in the holy scriptures. And we have even more. We have a means for strength in the body of the Lord to overcome evil. We have a means for preserving the good in the blood of the Lord. The holy eucharist is more than the presence of Christ among us. It is a spiritual nourishment for a people who need this source of vitality to continue living in God.

Tuesday of the Seventeenth Week (I)

It is very likely that along the line somewhere most of us have heard it said that the God of the Old Testament is a God of judgment and the God of the New Testament is a God of compassion. The implication is that somehow God changed his mind about dealing with people, that he decided to change from being a God of wrath to being a God of mercy. Simplifications are usually dangerous, and this one is downright erroneous.

Both the Old Testament reading and the gospel today reveal that God is just in punishing evil, but that he is overwhelming in his mercy. There could scarcely be a more beautiful description of God than that of today's Old Testament reading: "The Lord, the Lord, a merciful and gracious God, slow to anger and rich in kindness and fidelity. . . ."

In complete accord with the attitude of that reading is the responsorial psalm. One word in the psalm needs some explanation, and that word is "fear." The word in Hebrew which is translated as "fear" does not denote anxiety or trepidation. Rather it refers to a spirit of humble reverence, filled with awe, not unlike the attitude of a little child who believes that his parents can do anything. The person who "fears the Lord" acknowledges his total dependence upon God who is both all powerful and all loving. Without hesitation we can proclaim in the words of the psalm: "As a father has compassion on his children, so the Lord has compassion on those who fear him."

There is but one God who is a God of love at all times.

Tuesday of the Seventeenth Week (II)

Today's first reading is an indication of what our reaction should be during the time of any serious adversity. The particular circumstances are not clear but apparently Judah was suffering from war and drought. Human nature being what it is, it is not inconceivable that some of the people simply gave up on God. But not Jeremiah. Others probably decided that someone other than themselves was to blame for the calamity and were indignant that in their innocence they had to suffer. But not Jeremiah. Still others believed that they had better find someone other than God to help them. But not Jeremiah.

In Jeremiah's prayer we can see several elements which are important to us when things go wrong. Jeremiah's first thought was to turn to God. It is true that he queried God as to why such terrible things were happening. But his questions reveal that he believed that God is in charge and therefore is not to be abandoned. Secondly, he admits that he and the people are far from perfect. He says, "We recognize, O Lord, that we have sinned against you." He does not pretend to be the innocent person who is treated unjustly. Finally he recognizes that God alone is the source of hope as he cries out, "Is it not you alone, O Lord, our God, to whom we look?" There is still one more element suggested by the gospel. We must be patient. God in his own time and in a manner best for us will remove the weeds from our lives. This, then, is how we should pray about our serious problems. We should turn to God, admit our own sins, and call out for mercy. Then we must be patient as we await God's action.

Wednesday of the Seventeenth Week (I)

After his forty days in the presence of God, Moses' face reflected the glory of God whom he had been privileged to see. Moses was so affected by what he saw that his face became radiant. Sometimes when two people are deeply in love, their love is apparent in a glow on their faces. Something like that happened to Moses.

It is impossible for us to imagine how awesomely beautiful and wonderful God really is. Some theologians refer to heaven as a beatific vision, a vision which brings unspeakable happiness.

The words of Jesus in the gospel about the reign of God, his kingdom, can rightly be applied to God himself. God is a treasure so precious that no sacrifice is too great to make in order to enter into his presence. God is a pearl so beautiful that we should gladly leave behind all other attractions so that we may be absorbed by his splendor.

Heaven is still before us. Continue on we must in this present life until God calls us to himself. But all the while we should go about our ordinary occupations with a glow, if not on our faces, then in our hearts. This glow is the reflection of our faith that our God is a God of beauty and wonder, our treasure and our joy.

Wednesday of the Seventeenth Week (II)

Jeremiah had a difficult and frustrating mission in trying to call the people of his time to repentance. He could have identified with an expression we use these days: "It is like beating your head against a stone wall." Nor did Jeremiah hesitate to complain to God. He felt abandoned by God who had given him his mission, and he let him know how he felt. But God remained serene. He told Jeremiah that he must repent of this unworthy rebellion. God then renewed his promises of help and promised that he would give Jeremiah strength to withstand opposition. Jeremiah thought of the people as a stone wall, but God said, "I will make you toward this people a solid wall of brass."

As time went on, things as a matter of fact, got no better for Jeremiah. But he did find strength from God. At first he failed to see the value of remaining faithful to God. This value was like a treasure hidden in a field. Then his view changed. The treasure was no longer hidden, and he realized that any sacrifice was worth remaining loyal to God.

Most of us are not called to condemn an evil generation and urge it to repent. And yet we meet with opposition to our faith all the time. That opposition can come from people who think that our faith is foolish or even the enemy of a society bent on self-destruction through abortion, euthanasia, drug abuse, and the pursuit of pleasure as a god. That opposition can come within us; it is our discouragement, our frustration, or our laziness.

God says to us: "I will make you a solid wall of brass against any opposition." Our strength lies not in ourselves, but in God. It was a lesson Jeremiah had to learn and it is a lesson we must live by.

Thursday of the Seventeenth Week (I)

People who love each other hate to be separated, even for a short time. During a time of separation, they keep some reminder of the other, a picture or a gift. This reminder is a way of making the loved one present in affection though absent in body.

The tent or tabernacle mentioned in the first reading was the place of God's invisible presence among his people. It was also called the meeting tent because there God met his people. The ark, a small box, was placed within the tent. It contained the two tablets of the law, God's gift to his people. The whole arrangement was a way of making God present to his people in a symbolic and affectionate manner.

We have given to an object in our churches the name, tabernacle. Within it is not a symbol of God's presence, but the very body of Jesus Christ. The Eucharist must be understood to be primarily the sacrament of the death and resurrection of Jesus Christ. The Eucharist is first and fundamentally an action, the reality of the sacrifice of Jesus Christ, and only secondarily a permanent presence. And yet Christ is truly present in our tabernacles.

To have a proper understanding of this presence, we must realize that Jesus is present specifically as the victim given up in sacrifice to effect our union with the Father. The ark was a sign of God's covenant with his people. The Eucharist is the means of the new covenant of God with us, a union more profound and complete than that enjoyed by the chosen of the Old Testament. As we visit the blessed sacrament in the tabernacle, we must appreciate the truth that through Christ we have entered into an intimate union of love with God our Father.

Thursday of the Seventeenth Week (II)

Historians will have a difficult time giving a label to the twentieth century. It could be called the atomic age, the space age or simply the scientific age. Amazing progress has been made in applied science and one of the most fascinating developments is that of the robots, not the still imaginary kind one sees in movies but the kind which work, calculate and remember.

"Robot" is derived from a play by Karel Capek, who died in 1938. It was the name he gave to artificially manufactured persons in the play which were mechanically efficient but devoid of any human feelings. He took the name from a word in his native Czech language which means compulsory service. Robots are the creatures of men as men are the creatures of God, but with a big difference.

God does not fashion human beings as men fashion robots. God has instilled within our incredibly efficient body a mind and a heart. God does not program us. We can think for ourselves. We have been created free, so that our service of God is not compulsory as is that of robots. We can also respond to our creator with our hearts. We cannot only serve him; we can love him.

The image of the potter found in the reading from Jeremiah today is admittedly inadequate. No image from human experience can represent the manner in which God has created us. In fact, the image of the potter seems even less accurate than that of the scientist who builds a robot. But there is another way to look at the image of the potter.

The potter shapes the clay as he pleases. Out of love and freely we can place ourselves into the hands of God to allow him to shape our lives as he sees fit. That is the best possible use of freedom, not to turn away from God, but to turn back to him, our creator, so that our lives may freely match the plan he has for us.

Friday of the Seventeenth Week (I)

The first reading is a summary of the liturgical year observed by the Chosen People. Feasts were established so that the Israelites might never forget the great events of their history whereby God saved them and established them as his own people. These events are important to us, not only because they are part of our own salvation through our oneness with the people of the Old Testament, but also because they are the foreshadowing of our own feast days. The liturgical year of the Old Testament set a precedent for our own.

Within the cycle of a year the Church unfolds for us the whole mystery of Christ, from his incarnation and birth until his ascension, and as reflected in the day of Pentecost, and the expectation of a blessed hoped-for return of the Lord (cf. *Constitution on the Liturgy*, 102).

Jesus was rejected by the people of his own town. Even worse than being rejected is to be accepted and then forgotten. We are the people, not of Jesus' town, but of his Church. Through the faith granted us in baptism, we have accepted him and all that he has done for us. The Church, under the guidance of the Holy Spirit, is eager that we not forget any of the great events of the life of Christ, events which are our salvation.

In our own lives we want to be remembered on important days, such as birthdays and anniversaries. In the same way, throughout the course of the liturgical year we are called to remember and to celebrate the great events of the life of Christ. To forget is ugly, but to remember is beautiful.

Friday of the Seventeenth Week (II)

When Jeremiah preached he had no idea that all of his work was really going to bear fruit in one person. Nor did he even suspect that there would be similarities between that person and himself. Had he known, perhaps his mission would have seemed easier and his burden lighter.

That one person was, of course, Jesus Christ. Jesus, like Jeremiah, preached a message of repentance but with little of his harshness. His message was really overladen with the love which was at times submerged in that of Jeremiah. But Jesus too met with rejection and rebuff as had Jeremiah.

Why was Jesus rejected? Ultimately the answer is found only in the eternal wisdom and plan of God. On one level we can see a lack of faith. When Jesus preached in the synagogue of Nazareth, those who reacted against him thought of him as only a carpenter's son. But why did they not have faith? One answer is that faith is a gift from God, freely given and freely received or refused.

We can go still further and wonder why now, twenty centuries after the events of the life of Jesus, he is still rejected by many. Perhaps in this question we reach a deeper level. The kingdom which Jesus preached and established has not yet come to full flowering. That will happen only when Jesus comes again in glory.

Meanwhile we as people of faith stand between two moments of history, the first and the second comings of Christ. An important mission which we have as members of the Church is to give witness to that kingdom, a kingdom of love and harmony where all will be happy with God. Our witness to the world is intended to bring about a conviction that this kingdom is worthwhile, something to hope for and work toward. That is one reason why Christian love for each other is important. It is also why the love of God within us should be reflected in the joy of Christian living. Through our union with Christ we are called to build up his kingdom here on earth.

Saturday of the Seventeenth Week (I)

Every fifty years the Israelites observed a year of jubilee. It was not only a celebration but also a profession of faith. In the jubilee year farms were left fallow, land that had been sold was restored to its original owner, and slaves were set free. These observances were an expression of the people's belief that the land and the people of Israel belonged to God alone. Only God has the right of absolute dominion.

In the gospel we see that Herod flew in the face of this great truth. He violated God's absolute dominion not only by his blatant murder of John the Baptist but also by his supposing that he was free of God's law. Murder was Herod's response to John's reminder that he too was subject to God's dominion regarding his relationship with his brother's wife.

Every Mass is a jubilee year within the span of a few minutes. The Mass is fundamentally an act of thanksgiving through Christ to the Father, proclaiming that all life and all gifts come from him. No human person has an absolute right over life or property, only God.

We don't own slaves and we are not expected to return our property to those from whom we bought it. But perhaps we do need to reflect on whether we really respect other people and use our own things with the realization of God's dominion. The truth that all life and all gifts come from God is to be more than a motive of thanks and praise offered to God. It must be a guiding principle of our lives.

Saturday of the Seventeenth Week (II)

Sometimes nothing seems quite right in this world. Not only do the rich get richer and the poor get poorer, but the powerful become more powerful and the weak become weaker. Evil appears to triumph and good is defeated.

Jeremiah was a good man, dedicated to God and to his people. Through his preaching he was trying to call especially the rich and powerful persons of his time back to the Lord through repentance. He was actually doing them a favor, but their response was to persecute him and eventually to exile him from his homeland. John the Baptist tried in vain to turn the rich and powerful King Herod from his evil ways. The result of his efforts cost him his head. And Jesus? Despite the fact that he did nothing but good throughout his entire life, he died on the cross in weakness and poverty.

In our situation we can easily, though painfully, observe that the poor person has a pretty hard time of it. He cannot become a "free agent," as do modern athletes and demand millions of dollars as salary and a long term contract which guarantees security. Even a few days off work without pay can mean financial disaster to him and his family. The weak of this world without political or social influence will never receive preferential treatment as do the powerful figures of our times. Why not then seek after money and power by any means?

God looks at things differently and we must embrace his values. Think about it this way. Would you rather be Jeremiah or the people who persecuted him? Would you rather be John the Baptist or King Herod who saw to his murder? And would you rather be Jesus or the officials who plotted and achieved his death? Better to be poor rather than rich and have God on our side. Better to be weak rather than powerful and have God on our side. Better to be like Jesus than anything else.

Monday of the Eighteenth Week (I)

Poor Moses! He had a very difficult time in dealing with his own people. All their complaints, their unhappiness, their discontent came to rest on his shoulders. The weight was so overwhelming that he felt he could not bear it and turned to God almost in despair.

Do you know how Moses felt? Have you ever felt that your children, other relatives or friends have been a burden, expecting much from you that you could not deliver? If so, then you can appreciate Moses' situation. If not, you ought to consider that we are all responsible for the welfare of all people thoughout the world. As Christians we are called to carry each other's burdens. That is one reminder which should be ours in the prayer of the faithful in which we are supposed to pray in a generous, unselfish spirit for others, even people whom we do not know personally.

In any case, we need to know how God responded to Moses' plea, a response which is not included in today's reading. The story goes on and shows that God transferred some of Moses' responsibility to seventy elders who were to help him in dealing with the people.

In our responsibilites we have more than seventy elders as a help. We have the whole Church throughout the entire world. Just as we share a responsibility, so do we share the goodness and prayers of all of our spiritual brothers and sisters. We are all one in the Church through Christ. We are never alone. And we should be uplifted in knowing that our help comes from a worldwide people of faith.

Monday of the Eighteenth Week (II)

People in this life who want "to get ahead" usually learn to tell others what they want to hear, especially if they are influential. It often takes much courage to tell others what they need to hear. Jeremiah was one of those with courage, whereas his contemporary, Hananiah, was intent upon not upsetting anyone, especially at the king's court. That is what was behind the incident related in the first reading today. A conscientious person says what has to be said and does what has to be done.

Perhaps an everyday expression of this principle is the relationship between a mother and her children. They would like to eat nothing but "junk food." If the mother were to give in, they would think her the best possible mother in the whole world. But the mother insists that the children eat good, substantial food because she knows it is the proper nourishment. They do not appreciate now what she is doing for them, but they will later in life.

When the people in the gospel were hungry and had nothing to eat, Jesus fed them. It was good, substantial food, but Jesus wanted to give to all of his followers a nourishment which would be even more beneficial. Jesus wanted to give a food and drink which would not merely sustain natural life, but which would make us grow toward spiritual adulthood and eventually to everlasting life. That nourishment is his body and blood in the Eucharist.

It takes only a moment of thought to recognize that the Eucharist is not nearly as palatable or as humanly desirable as the dinners which are our everyday fare. Some people might even wish, if Jesus wanted to give us a gift, that he would have given us something which could have made life more comfortable or more fun. That, of course, is a childish way of looking at things. Jesus wants to give us, not necessarily what we may want, but what we really need. And his gift of the Eucharist, as we will appreciate fully only later, is a precious gift which we really need.

Tuesday of the Eighteenth Week (I)

What a bad mistake Aaron and Miriam made! They attacked the authority of Moses because a personal action of his did not please them. Whereas Moses was obliged to give good example and live a correct life, his personal conduct had nothing to do with his authority, which came from God and not from himself.

The mistake of Aaron and Miriam is the same one which we can make in the Church today. All the authorities in the Church, from the Pope, down to me as a priest, are human. We are weak and we have faults. Like everyone else, authorities in the Church must strive to lead good lives, but authority does not flow from personal worthiness. God is not pleased with attacks upon or rejection of legitimate authority. (By the way, however, God did relent in his punishment of Miriam and within seven days restored her to the community in good health.)

When we are tempted to complain about authority, we should follow the example of Moses. When he was rebuffed by Aaron and Miriam, he prayed for them. When you feel rebuffed or let down or disappointed by someone in authority, complaint will accomplish nothing. But prayer to God will help to bring good out of a bad situation.

Tuesday of the Eighteenth Week (II)

The dark, mysterious depths of the ocean are terrifying and suggestive of death. It is no wonder that in the Bible, power over the vast waters is seen as a mark of divinity. Only God has such power.

When Jesus walked on the water, it was no theatrical gesture. It was a sign of his divinity. The day before Jesus had fed the hungry thousands with bread. Now he wanted to show that he had power over the great, primal force which can bring death. He was the sign of hope.

Jeremiah held out a hope to his people in the face of military forces which were bent on their destruction. Their hope was to be found only in God. Sometimes in life we may suspect that all elements are conspiring against us. We may feel that the fatal waters are about to engulf us.

A man who felt that way was an Englishman of the nineteenth century. He was a failure at everything he tried. For four years he managed to survive by selling matches on a street corner in London, but he inevitably sank under the weight of poverty and was starving. He was rescued by a prostitute who took him to her room, fed him, and gave him shelter. A friend later found him and brought him to a Franciscan priory. There he returned to God. His name was Francis Thompson and he is famous for his poem written while he was with the Franciscans, "The Hound of Heaven." In another poem, "In No Strange Land," he thought of today's gospel and wrote these lines: "yea, in the night my soul, my daughter, / Cry—clinging Heaven by the hems; / And lo, Christ walking on the water / Not of Gennesareth, but Thames!"

A man as desperate as Francis Thompson was amost compelled to turn to Christ. But how beautiful was his faith. He did not see Christ as a distant figure of history, but as a loving God present with him there in London and with the power to walk on water, the power to save him from eternal death.

Wednesday of the Eighteenth Week (I)

The Israelites in the face of their opposition protested that they felt like mere grasshoppers. It is too bad that they did not act more like grasshoppers. As does any insect, a grasshopper has three simple eyes in its forehead by which it sees straight ahead. On the top of its head it has two complex eyes, which give it peripheral vision; it can even see somewhat behind itself.

The Israelites were expected to have faith and trust in God by looking back upon all the marvels God had worked for them in the Exodus. But seeing only the present with its obstacles, they lacked trust in God, and as a consequence were condemned to wander in the desert for forty years. Those who had been freed from slavery in Egypt never entered the promised land.

In contrast is the Canaanite woman in the gospel. Her faith in Jesus was so strong that she refused to give up in her pleas that her daughter be cured. Jesus responded, "Woman, you have great faith. Your wish will come to pass."

In our faith we need a rear vision, whereby we can look back upon all the marvels God has accomplished for us, especially through the death and resurrection of his Son. In dying Jesus destroyed our death, and in rising he restored our life. Now we are expected to have complete trust in God, to believe that he knows what he is doing and that what he has planned for our lives is for the best. It is especially when we are confused, when the odds seem stacked against us, when everything appears to be going wrong, that we need to trust God. It would be a terrible thing to wander through the desert of this life and to fail to enter the promised land of heaven because of a lack of faith.

Wednesday of the Eighteenth Week (II)

When the Israelites entered the promised land after the exodus, they encountered the Canaanites, whom they considered to be a sinful race which embodied all that was wicked and godless, a race which was to be exterminated. This outlook persisted until the time of Jesus. In the gospel today Jesus indicated that this outlook was no longer to be held by his followers.

The woman in the gospel was a Canaanite. She had enough faith in Jesus to come and ask him to release her daughter from a demon. The apostles represented the mentality of their time when they urged Jesus to get rid of the woman. Then Jesus said a shocking thing to the woman: "It is not right to take the food of the sons and daughters and throw them to the dogs." These words do not represent his own sentiments. He is merely quoting what the Jews of the day would say to the woman. His own response to the woman was one of love as is seen by the fact that he granted her favor.

The story is not specifically about Canaanites. The woman stands for anyone who is disliked, hated, or despised. Jesus constantly preached that love is not exclusively for those who are dear to us. He proclaimed that we must love our enemies and pray for those who persecute us. Our love for others is to be like his own, all inclusive. This teaching has an application on both the national and personal level.

Some people consider it patriotic to hate Russians and Iranians. They think it is only right to look with contempt upon those "puny, little countries," as they call them, which have brought us to our knees in the oil shortage, as if other countries exist only to keep us supplied with our needs and luxuries. "Those dirty dogs," some say. But Jesus cannot approve of such attitudes.

On a personal level the same lesson applies. We may not turn away from anyone no matter how much we may dislike the person, and no matter what they have done against us. If we do not love everyone as Jesus does, we are in big trouble.

Thursday of the Eighteenth Week (I)

It is said that one can survive longer without food than he can without water. Water is absolutely necessary not only for humans but all living things on this earth.

I think we can appreciate how the Israelites felt without water, especially in the desert. Miraculously God produced the water needed for life from a rock and they survived. St. Paul, in commenting on this passage, sees the rock as a sign of Christ himself, the source of our life (1 Cor 10:4).

There is no similarity between Christ and a rock, however miraculous. The point is that St. Paul understood that the favors and blessings of God upon his people in the long history of Israel reached a fullness in Jesus Christ. Water from the rock in the desert gave the people renewed life, and we ought easily to think about the water of Baptism whereby Jesus Christ has given us a share in his life and made all of us members of his Father's family, the Church. Jesus did not end with giving us life. He also gives the means of strengthening this life through the Holy Eucharist wherein he nourishes us with his own body and blood.

We cannot survive without water anymore than could the Israelites in the desert. God cares for us in our human needs, but he has also called us to a fuller, higher life. This is a gift which will lead us, not to a promised land, but to a destiny: an eternal life of happiness with him in heaven, our ultimate home.

Thursday of the Eighteenth Week (II)

During the great depression of the 1930's, the outlook was pretty bleak. Hollywood came to the rescue of the American public. They produced many movies based on the theme of going from rags to riches. And every movie, no matter how much the plot needed to be manipulated, had a happy ending.

Jeremiah was very much a prophet of doom. He had to be because the religious condition of the people had seriously deteriorated. And yet even though he was not a Hollywood movie maker he could not bring himself to end his story on a note of tragedy. He had too much faith in God for that. Speaking the name of the Lord he painted a beautiful picture of a new age to come. It was to be the age of a new covenant with God.

That new covenant came to be through the person of Jesus Christ. Peter acknowledged that Jesus was the Messiah, the Son of the living God. In that he was correct, but he failed to understand the plot. When Jesus said that he had to die, Peter felt like those audiences at one of the old time movies. Boy meets girl, they fall in love, but then they are separated or fall into a misunderstanding.

The audience reacts by saying, "Oh, no!" They want a happy ending. Peter wanted a happy ending for Jesus but he could not see what death had to do with that. He did not understand the grand plan of God that Jesus himself would go from "rags to riches," from death to life. Jesus passed through the poverty of death to the riches of everlasting life. In dying he was not leaving us, the poor girl, in the lurch. Rather he came into riches which he is more than eager to share with us through an eternal union of love, the new covenant.

Everybody loves a happy ending, even God. We must have the faith that he will lead us through all the difficulties and disappointments of this life to an eternal embrace of his Son when he comes again in glory to claim us as his own.

Friday of the Eighteenth Week (I)

We have a saying that actions speak louder than words. More often than not this statement is correct. Words are cheap, but actions require sincerity.

The Israelities, through a realization of God's actions on their behalf as presented in today's first reading, were called to respond to God in praise and love. God did not merely tell the people of his affection for them; he demonstrated that affection by means of all the wonderful things he accomplished for them.

What is true of the Old Testament era is also true of the New. In the gospel Jesus gives us a formula of Christian living, the taking up of the cross and following him. These are not hollow words. They are backed up by his actions. Jesus himself not only took up the cross; he died upon it. That was the greatest act of love the world has ever seen.

When we contemplate this act of Jesus Christ, we should be willing, even eager, to respond in kind. Can we really think that the price of discipleship is too high, that it is too much for us to accept the cross we find in our own lives? We should not think so if we appreciate what Christ has done for us.

Love calls out for love, not a love expressed only in mere words but in actions. The measure of our love is found in how willing we are to accept whatever trials or frustrations come to us from the hand of God. We want our words of acceptance to be sincere, but there will be no doubt about sincerity if our actions are generous.

Friday of the Eighteenth Week (II)

The mighty Assyrians were for a long time the relentless oppressors of the Jews. Nahum, the prophet, foresaw the impending destruction of this feared adversary and proclaimed a message of hope to the people. As a matter of fact, Nineveh, the capital city of Assyria, was destroyed in 612 B.C. by the combined forces of Babylon and Media. The Jews thought it was the end of misfortune but Assyria's place was taken by Babylon and later by the Roman Empire, both of which conquered the Jews. The relief afforded by the demise of Assyria was only temporary.

In our own century the First World War was hailed as the war to end all wars, but it was followed by an even more terrible Second World War. And that war did not end hostilities, as we have seen by the conflicts in Korea and Viet-Nam, to mention only two incidents. Now wholesale destruction in an all out nuclear attack is fully within the realm of possibility.

War is terrible, but death by any means is the inevitable lot of all human beings. Death is certain. What is uncertain in the minds of many is the meaning of life and death. Is life nothing more than what Macbeth said it is, "a tale told by an idiot, full of sound and fury, signifying nothing?" Is there a prophet bold enough to proclaim a message of hope for mankind? Yes there is. It is Jesus Christ. He says to us today, "Whoever loses his life for my sake will find it."

Only Jesus has the answer to death, whether it be brought on by war, disease, accident, or old age. The Preface for the Mass of Christian Death proclaims our faith: "In Christ who rose from the dead our hope of resurrection dawned, and the sadness of death gives way to the bright promise of immortality. When the body of our earthly dwelling lies in death we gain an everlasting dwelling place in heaven."

Saturday of the Eighteenth Week (I)

There is a familiar ring to the words we have just heard from the Old Testament book of Deuteronomy about loving God with one's whole being. The reason is that the words are quoted by Jesus in the gospel. The familiar verses form part of a prayer or profession of faith which every devout Israelite recited daily. Many took the words of Moses literally, wrote out the words on a small scroll, and placed it in a small box which they wore on their foreheads.

The whole idea was that the love of God was to be the guiding principle of their whole lives. It is instructive for us to note that the Israelites consider these words to be a profession of faith. Faith in the Bible is understood as being something practical, not merely theoretical. In other words it was more than a matter of believing in God as the supreme being and the creator of the world. People can actually believe this truth without its having much effect on their lives. Faith in the Bible means a response to God. Perhaps a good word for this kind of faith is trust. Trust means turning your whole life over to God, having complete confidence in him. It is like the attitude of a little child who depends completely on his parents for everything. He will never say to his parents, "I believe in you and in your love for me," but his actions express that belief.

This kind of trust is an exquisite expression of love. It is the kind of response we should have toward God.

Saturday of the Eighteenth Week (II)

A woman was diagnosed as having terminal cancer. She prayed for a cure but her condition only worsened. One friend told her that it was foolish to pray because prayer accomplished nothing. Another friend told her that the only reason she was not cured was that her faith was not strong enough. She said that anyone who had enough faith will be cured. Both friends were wrong.

The gospels give ample witness to the power of prayer. Today we have seen Jesus respond to the prayer of faith of the man who asked him to take pity on his son. When Jesus told his disciples that they could not cure the boy because they lacked trust or faith, he meant that they had failed to recognize the source of their power, which was himself.

On the other hand Jesus did not choose to cure every sickness or heal every disease, and he does not choose to do so in our own time either. To say that every sick person lacks sufficient faith is to be guilty of rash judgment of the person and to be presumptuous of God. St. Theresa, the Little Flower, died of tuberculosis at the age of twenty-four. There was nothing wrong with her faith. To say that God should have cured her and prolonged her life is to presume that we know more about it than God.

There is a mystery about life and its suffering. The prophet Habakkuk could not understand why God would allow Judah's enemies to punish her because if Judah was sinful they were more so. The only answer to be found is that "the just man, because of his faith, will live." Faith is necessary, not to bring about cures and alleviate suffering, but to live with God and to accept his will in our lives.

Monday of the Nineteenth Week (I)

The first reading today can be summed up by saying that God wanted his people to be like himself. As he was dedicated to them, so they were to be dedicated to him. As he had freed them when they were aliens in Egypt, so were they to befriend the alien in their own land. As he treated everyone with fairness and justice, so were they to treat others.

In Jesus we see the perfect reflection or image of the Father. He personified the response which should have been that of the chosen people. And yet with Jesus a change had taken place. He was willing to pay the temple tax, as was the duty of any good Jew, but he was quick to point out that a new era of mankind's relationship with God was dawning. The prediction of his death and resurrection in connection with the matter of the temple tax was a latent proclamation that the temple would soon cease to be the center of the community. By means of his death and resurrection, his paschal sacrifice, Jesus himself would replace the temple. The Jews gathered in the temple for the worship of sacrifice. In the new era the community would gather in union with Jesus, like a new temple, for worship through the sacrifice of the Mass.

Our worship is not limited to one place or even to one kind of building. Where two or three are gathered in the name of Jesus, especially at Mass, he is in our midst. What has not changed is that God still wants us to be like himself. As Jesus is our temple, so is he now also our model. To be like God means to be like Jesus, who is God in the flesh. The Christian life is summed up in our living the life of Jesus Christ.

Monday of the Nineteenth Week (II)

The Jews thought of their temple as very precious to them, not because it was laden with valuable stones and metals, but because they saw it as the special abode of God on earth. It was, therefore, the supreme place for the worship of God. All Jews had to contribute by means of a temple tax to the upkeep of this magnificent edifice.

When Peter was asked whether Jesus would pay the temple tax, he did not hesitate to answer in the affirmative. Jesus, however, took the occasion to teach an important lesson about himself and the temple. He observed that kings do not take tax from their own sons, and he thereby implied that he was not a subject of God, but his son. Only gradually did the earliest Christians grow in a realization of the full extent of this truth. Jesus is the unique son of God, equally divine with him, appearances to the contrary notwithstanding.

His humanity was the new temple wherein dwelt the fullness of divinity. We have been given a share in what Jesus is. We too are temples of God.

There was a hint of this marvelous communication of God to men in the vision which Ezekiel saw. This vision came to him in the land of the Chaldeans, a pagan land far from the temple in

Jerusalem. Ezekiel realized that God's presence is not limited to any one place.

As we must appreciate the identity of Jesus, so should we also appreciate our own. We are the living temples of God, more precious to him than any building, even the Jerusalem temple, could possibly be. His life and love are within us since we are his children, made sons in the Son. Because we are his temples, he does not exact tribute from us, only the free response of love.

Tuesday of the Nineteenth Week (I)

There is a certain sadness about today's first reading. Moses had been the great hero of his people. He had resisted Pharaoh to his face, demanding the release of the people in the name of God. He had led them out of slavery from Egypt. In the desert he was God's instrument for a covenant with the people. He had endured the rebellion of the people and had interceded for them with God.

Now near death he knew that it was not to be his joy and privilege to lead the people into the promised land. That destiny was to fall to Joshua. Moses needed profound humility to accept the plan of God. Somehow he understood that God's plan, although not in accord with his own preference, was best. Not concerned with being recognized as of the greatest importance among God's people, like a little child he was docile to God's will.

In the Church, God has a plan for each one of us. At times we may wish that we could have a different vocation, perhaps one more in the limelight or in contrast one less demanding. But it is God's choice which counts. Even the Pope must accept his exalted position with a childlike docility to God's will, not with ambition to be the most important person in God's kingdom. Think about Pope John Paul I. Pope for only thirty-three days, with no opportunity to lead the Church forward, he was like Moses who was not privileged to lead the people into the promised land. Such, for his own good reasons, was God's choice.

Who we are and what we do in life is God's choice, his plan. And it is that choice which makes everything worthwhile.

Tuesday of the Nineteenth Week (II)

Ezekiel, like many of the prophets, was sent by God to proclaim a message of warning to the people. The scroll represented this message from God. When Ezekiel ate the scroll, it was a sign that he had assimilated God's word. It became part of his being. The word was sweet as honey to him, meaning that he found joy through his insight into God's word. And yet when he proclaimed this word to the people, they found it so bitter that they rejected it.

In one sense it is the old principle that one man's meat is another man's poison. God through Ezekiel was inviting the people to renew their covenant of love with him, but that renewal called for a complete change in their lives. It was this change which they were unwilling to accept.

The command of Jesus that we become like little children is, you might say, a message as sweet as honey. Whether this command is really sweet or bitter depends on how it is received, or it too calls for change. Becoming a little child in the sight of God is not as easy as it sounds. It means living a life of simplicity and trust, for humility and meekness. This is a bitter message for those who believe in getting ahead, in being assertive, in allowing no one to take advantage of them, in taking care of number one.

You know how teenagers do not like being treated as children. That is understandable because they are still reaching for adulthood and are not yet secure in adulthood. For the person who is spiritually mature it is a delight to live like a child under God as our Father. We need to assimilate this command of Jesus, to make it part of our being. With the faith of a child we will find that this message adds both a sweetness and a serenity to our lives.

Wednesday of the Nineteenth Week (I)

Moses, who had led the people out of slavery and who had struggled with them to keep them faithful to God, died before he had the privilege of entering the promised land.

Some speculate that Moses was denied this final privilege as a punishment from God, but the evidence to that effect in the Bible is not at all clear. Last Thursday the reading had God saying to Moses, "Because you were not faithful to me in showing forth my sanctity before the Israelites, you shall not lead this community into the land I will give them." What this unfaithfulness was we simply are not certain, and commentators have differing opinions.

It seems that the matter is contained in the complaint that Moses did not sufficiently show forth the sanctity of God. What this problem means is that Moses had failed to make the people realize that the great marvels accomplished for them were the work of God and not of Moses himself. Moses was but God's instrument, freely chosen by him. God did not need Moses. With him dead God immediately selected Joshua as the leader of the people. This interpretation may sound harsh, but any form of pride, taking credit away from God, is a terrible affrontery to God's power and his love.

Death, over which we really have no control, manifests that God is in charge. When Pope John Paul I died prematurely after only thirty-three days in office, all Catholics were stunned and many were fearful about the future. But God immediately raised up a great man to succeed the dead Pope. We too one day will die and be replaced among those who gather in the name of Christ.

We should not have a somber reaction to God's providence. Rather we should rejoice in knowing that he is in charge, that the progress of the Church and the welfare of individuals is dependent, not on human powers, but divine.

Wednesday of the Nineteenth Week (II)

The prophet Ezekiel was God's messenger to proclaim a warning that the city of Jerusalem would be destroyed because of the appalling sins of its people. In effect the prophet told the people that God was not to be blamed for their coming misfortune since they were bringing punishment upon themselves. As a sign of God's good will, the innocent would be spared, marked with an X. Actually the mark upon their foreheads was to be the last letter of the Hebrew alaphabet, Tau, which only resembles an X.

Ezekiel's visions were all highly symbolic. It may be that the use of the last letter of the alphabet was intended to mean that the innocent would find salvation only on the last day, that though they would die they would be saved on the Great Day of the Lord. That day of the Lord has already arrived with Christ and yet is also to come in the future. This Day is not a period of twenty-four hours, but the era for the unfolding of the kingdom of God which will reach its perfection with the second coming of Christ.

Meanwhile we pray, "Thy kingdom come." But we must also work for the realization of the kingdom, a kingdom of peace, harmony and love. That is why Jesus preached that his followers must seek reconciliation with each other. He calls upon us to point out a wrong that may have been committed, especially one which destroys harmony and peace. Correcting others is a hazardous duty and must be done with humility and meekness. We must also keep in mind the proper motive, which is to make present among us Christ's kingdom of unity and love.

Jesus also urges us to pray together. Individual prayer is indispensable, but it can never substitute for that community prayer where Jesus is present to unite us in his love. The highest form of this community prayer is, of course, the Mass. We all bear the mark, not of a Hebrew letter, but the baptismal sign of oneness with Christ. According to that oneness we must pray and work for the final coming of the kingdom.

Thursday of the Nineteenth Week (I)

We come to know God by comparing him with our human experiences. We just cannot get away from the principle that we learn by going from the known to the unknown. God is far above us, beyond our human experience. As such, he is unknown to us. But God has revealed himself to us in human terms, in accord with what we do know.

Until we reach heaven and see God as he is, we simply will not appreciate how magnificent he is. We must remember that all human comparisons fall short of the mark, that God is far above what we can know or even imagine.

Is it possible to take a group of weak, simple people, devoid of weapons and other resources, and lead them from slavery in a powerful country to a promised land? No human leader could have accomplished this feat. And that is the point of many of our recent readings from the Old Testament. It is God and God alone who accomplishes good things for his people. The story of the parting of the waters in today's reading is so unusual that it should immediately make us realize that God has been at work for the benefit of his people.

Whereas the first reading is about God's power, the gospel is about his forgiveness. God is like the king who wiped out the huge debt owed him by his servant. Well, that kind of thing does not happen in human affairs. People want their money, and it seems the wealthier they are, the more demanding they are that every debt be paid. Wiping out the debt is a symbol of forgiveness. God's forgiveness, like his power, is beyond our powers to imagine. He absolves us, that is, he completely wipes out the debt of sin. And he does so in a superhuman way. He forgives us by the blood of his Son, shed for the forgiveness of sins. The giving up of his Son is also beyond what humans are willing to do.

How blest we are that our God is far above us humans.

Thursday of the Nineteenth Week (II)

(Note: Some translations of the lectionary have printed an incomplete version of the first reading. The typical edition of the lectionary indicates that the reading should be from Ezekiel, 12:1-12. This homily is based on the correct version.)

There are two ways to punish a child. One makes the parent feel better, the other makes the child become better. People who write books about rearing children advise parents never to correct a child when they are angry with him. An immediate response to a misdeed ventilates anger but probably does little to help the child and tends to make him resentful. A correction made later in a calm manner and with an explanation can be "medicinal," that is, it can help the child to change his behavior for the better. At least, that is the theory.

As a matter of fact, this is the theory followed by God in dealing with his people. Through the prophets, like Ezekiel, he gave explanations for his corrections. In one instance Ezekiel, as we read today, acted out for the people the fact God would send them into exile, like a disobedient child who is sent to his room. God made it clear that the purpose of the exile was to bring about their conversion. God is not one to hold grudges or to punish others for his own satisfaction.

God is the king who wipes out the huge debt owed him. He is not petty like the official who refused to forgive his fellow servant and who demanded payment in full. God does not exact payment from us in any form. He is eager to forgive and any correction he brings to bear is medicinal. His desire is that we change our behavior for the better.

A little child cannot always understand the actions of his parents even with an explanation. Nor can we understand all of God's actions toward us. In faith, however, we should be prepared to believe that whatever happens to us is somehow part of God's plan. And God's plan is always for our ultimate benefit.

Friday of the Nineteenth Week (I)

They say that repetition is the mother of learning. Many teachers tell students, who complain that they have heard all about the subject before, that it won't hurt them to hear it again.

Joshua, as a teacher of the people, decided that it would not hurt them to hear again the story of God's marvelous deeds on their behalf. And it does not hurt us either. All of God's actions throughout history manifest his wisdom and his love. That is a subject we must never grow weary of.

All of these marvelous deeds of God reached a climax in the death and resurrection of his Son. It is the central event of all history because in dying Jesus destroyed our death and in rising he restored our life. No one can have a greater love than to lay down his life for others. Jesus laid down his life so that we may live forever.

If we could fix in our minds that God's actions all manifest his love, then maybe we could come to a better understanding of his laws, even difficult ones like the one about divorce in the gospel. If we are convinced that everything God does is out of love, then we can see that his laws are not an affliction. Of course life is never simple or easy. But how we approach it is important.

We cannot afford to tire of hearing about God's love for us. If we are attentive, we will see that every scripture reading ultimately comes down to the same thing: God loves us and asks us for our love in return.

Friday of the Nineteenth Week (II)

Every young man has an image of what he considers to be the perfect woman. And every young woman has an image of what she considers to be the perfect man. These pictures are taken from experience but touched up considerably by imagination. One thing people cannot do is to create someone according to this image. They must search for their ideal person.

Such is not the case with God. He does not love people because they are beautiful. Rather people become beautiful because God loves them. God has the power to create people according to the image he has for them. Literature has a fancy which only approximates what God does. In a fairy tale the rich and handsome prince comes across a peasant girl. She appears disheveled in a tattered dress. The prince takes her to the palace, sees that she is attired in a magnificent gown and adorned with rich jewels. He introduces her at a royal ball where everyone stands in awe at her beauty. Of course her beauty was always there. All the prince did was to reveal it.

Ezekiel in the straightforward image of today's first reading struggles to show how it was God who made his people beautiful. They had nothing of their own to give them charm or appeal. God did it all. Then forgetting from where their beauty came, the people gave themselves over to harlotry, a symbol of their abandoning God for pagan idols and disgraceful living.

And yet God did not abandon his people. Divorce is not in his vocabulary. One reason Jesus condemned divorce is that Christian marriage is a human expression of God's love for his people. Leaving aside any discussion of today's problems involving divorce, we should acknowledge that we have been made beautiful people by God. What we do does not make us lovable. It is his almighty power which makes us worthwhile. That we must never forget, for we must respond to God's love by the complete devotion of our lives.

Saturday of the Nineteenth Week (I)

Many people hate to make decisions, whether large or small. They may spend as much time deciding what they will wear to a party as they do deciding which kind of car they will buy. And there are those who are perfectly happy to let others make their decisions for them. For everyone any hesitancy involved in making decisions stems from the fear of making the wrong choice.

In the first reading a day of ultimate decision had come for the people. Joshua put it to them quite clearly: "Decide today whom you will serve." He was equally clear about where he stood: "As for me and my household, we will serve the Lord." Joshua had no fear of error in his decision; his faith in the Lord was firm.

A big decision was made for most of us by our parents when they brought us to the church to be baptized. At the time we had no say in the matter. Our parents and godparents professed faith in our name. As we grew up we gradually made their decision our own. The process was amost imperceptible. The grace of God was at work in us, and as we progressed toward maturity our faith slowly grew. There are times when we more explicitly affirm the faith for ourselves, such as before first communion, confirmation, or marriage. One very special time is at Easter when we renew our baptismal vows.

Daily Mass is another very important opportunity to affirm our faith for ourselves. Even without a creed as part of the Mass, we profess our faith in God by our very presence and in a particular way through the Eucharistic prayer. All of us here, without fear of error, can rightly say, "As for me and my household, we will serve the Lord."

Saturday of the Nineteenth Week (II)

Almost every culture has its share of proverbs. A strange proverb among the Jews to whom Ezekiel wrote stated that, "Fathers have eaten green grapes, thus their children's teeth are on edge." It sounds a little like the genetic theory, rejected by most scientists, which maintains that acquired characteristics are passed on by heredity. In particular, the proverb means that children inherit the sinful ways of their fathers, a proverb which was applied to an entire generation of people and not to a single family.

Ezekiel as God's spokesman rejected this proverb. Directly he was indicating that each person is born free to follow or abandon God, but indirectly he was implying that children have a certain dignity and self-determination. This implication had a long way to go before it sank in.

Later in the Jewish society in which Jesus lived and preached, religion was considered to be chiefly a matter for grown men, not women and children. In fact, it was generally acknowledged that a woman should not be the student of a rabbi, and even that such a role was impossible since women were thought to be incapable of learning the Law. Children were indeed put into a position in which they were to be seen and not heard. Jesus by word and action wished to reverse those views.

Yesterday in the gospel Jesus condemned divorce. His

reasons were many, but one of them was to establish the dignity of women. At the time a woman had no rights. Her husband could divorce her almost at his whim. Such action was always unilateral: no woman could divorce her husband. Jesus in particular wanted to make a point about the dignity of a woman. She could not be thrust aside like an unwanted piece of furniture.

Today in the gospel Jesus intended to affirm the dignity of children. The disciples, respresenting the outlook of the time, scolded the children for bothering Jesus, but he admonished the disciples by saying, "Let the children come to me. The kingdom of God belongs to such as these." It was an astounding statement. In God's eyes all of his people, regardless of age or sex, are precious and valuable.

Monday of the Twentieth Week (I)

The first reading today is a sad recital of infidelities on the part of the people. Again and again they abandoned the God who had saved them to turn to false gods. Precisely what their problem was is difficult to say, but it does appear that they failed to heed the repeated biblical message that humility is needed. This humility recognizes that all depends on God, that we cannot do anything worthwhile without him.

The young man in the gospel turned away from Jesus to rely on the false god of possessions. He was very wealthy and he was willing to depend on riches rather than on Jesus for happiness in this life and in the life to come. Although he appears to have been greedy, his basic flaw was that he was not humble enough to admit that everything comes from God and not from himself or his financial abilities.

I think it can be said that each of us has a false god in our lives to whom we are tempted to pay allegiance. It may be money or it may be a number of other things, even persons. We alone can answer the question. Whatever or whoever we are tempted to depend on rather than God is a false god.

But we are doing the right thing by our practice of daily Mass. Here we profess that God comes first in our lives, and we pray before communion in the Lord's prayer that we may not fall into temptation. In receiving the body and the blood of Christ we should wish to express our belief that Jesus is the true source of all our strength, that we simply cannot get along without him.

Monday of the Twentieth Week (II)

Ezekiel the prophet witnessed the death of his wife and he saw her death as a foreshadowing of the destruction of the temple and the exile of the people. All individuals must one day die. The famous people of history and the unremembered multitudes all lie in their graves. Nations eventually fade from power. The once mighty empires of Assyria and of Rome are no more. All things human are but temporary.

There is nothing like death to put human life and its values into perspective. Even before death we taste the impermanence of pleasure and satisfaction. At this time of the year many people take their vacations. They save and plan all year and look forward with great eagerness to a trip as a time of relaxation. And yet the most pleasurable and satisfying of all vacations seems to be over all too soon and we are left wondering where the time has gone.

As we go through life we need times of respite, even just plain fun. We should see wholesome pleasure and the joys of living as God's gifts to us. We must never, however, substitute the gift for the giver, or think there is nothing more to the meaning of life than alternating between work and play, pleasure and pain.

A man saved for a very long time to buy the expensive car of his dreams. It cost him almost thirty thousand dollars and he told his friends that it was worth every penny. And yet deep down he had to admit that an automobile could not bring him the true happiness for which we all yearn. Jesus tried to give a somewhat similar man a sense of proper values. That man asked the right question, "What must I do to possess everlasting life?" In effect Jesus told him that he had to free himself from dependence on material things and turn his life over to God. As long as his heart was divided between temporary and eternal values, he could not be open to the Spirit of God. God alone can give us the everlasting happiness for which we were created.

Tuesday of the Twentieth Week (I)

If you would like some delightful, as well as profitable reading, I suggest that later today you read the sixth, seventh, and eighth chapters of the Book of Judges from the Bible. It is the story of Gideon.

Gideon was a simple farmer. Part of his charm is that he spoke to God as if God were a fellow farmer who lived nearby. Gideon did not hesitate to tell God about his doubts concerning him. But the remarkable thing about Gideon is his humility. When he was called by God to be a leader of the people (judges were more like army generals than a court magistrate), he protested that he had none of the qualities necessary. He was also concerned about the odds of the enemy against him. God told him that he should not worry and added, "I will be with you."

Humility was just the quality God was looking for. He wanted it to be clear to Gideon and his people that it was he, God, and not military power or astuteness, which would win the victory. Jesus in the gospel gave a stern warning about the danger of possessions. It is very tempting for a wealthy person to trust in riches rather than in God.

God wants us to be humble enough to depend on him completely. When things are particularly difficult and we say to God in prayer, "I simply can't do it. This is too much for me," he will reply, "Now you get the message. Rely on me."

Tuesday of the Twentieth Week (II)

One of the greatest sins a person can commit is to put himself in the place of God. The king of Tyre, an island off the coast of present day Lebanon, thought of himself as almighty. He was not an atheist. Unfortunately the god he worshipped was not the creator of the heavens and the earth but himself. Ezekiel courageously condemned this powerful but foolish man in unmitigated terms.

A twentieth century counterpart of the king of Tyre on a much larger scale was Adolph Hitler. From being a mere corporal in the army he rose to be the Chancellor and Führer of the Third Reich with absolute power. He became a perfect example of the axiom, "Power corrupts and absolute power corrupts absolutely." He too was not an atheist. He was his own god.

Jesus does not want us to fall into the trap of false independence which leads to self worship. The sense of self-sufficiency and power which wealth and power can create tends to make a person deify himself. When he feels that his wants are satisfied by his possessions he can think that he does not need God. That is why Jesus says that it is easier for a camel to pass through a needle's eye than for a rich man to enter the kingdom of heaven.

Jesus does not praise poverty as an intrinsic god, as is unselfish love. Rather he sees a sense of detachment from material riches as the necessary condition for believing in the great riches of everlasting life. Complete dependence on God, rather than on ourselves, is the expression of true faith.

The Mass is the great prayer of faith. Here we identify with Jesus in that most profound act of dependence, the giving of his life into the hands of his Father. We acknowledge that all life, all holiness come from God. This profession of faith must overflow into the way we live. Our lives must say in clear tones, "Father, we need you. We cannot get along without you."

Wednesday of the Twentieth Week (I)

Today we have heard two parables: one obscure and the other difficult. The obscure parable from the Old Testament belongs to an era when God had not yet established kings in Israel. Abimilech persuaded the leaders of Schechem to murder all his brothers and proclaim him king. Jotham, wishing to warn the people about this terrible mistake, presented the parable. The point is that all the productive trees and vines, which gave forth olives or figs or grapes, refused to become king. They already had a useful role to play. The dried up thorn bush, useless for men and dangerous to the forests as an easy source of fire, eagerly assumed the role of king. Abimilech, since he was not chosen by God, had nothing to offer the people; on the contrary he would only bring them harm. He was the thorn bush.

The difficult gospel parable revolves around the truth that God chooses to give his gifts gratuitously, not in accord with any imagined merit, but always without any injustice. All the workers received a just wage, which they had agreed to accept. The late comers received more out of generosity by the owner of the estate. Being generous to them in no way infringed on the rights of the early workers. God is more than just; he is generous.

God it is who calls each of us to our particular vocation in life. Pope John Paul II is pope not because he merited the office, but only because he was freely chosen by God. It is God's choice which makes him suitable. The same is true of us. Whatever we do in life is of worth only if it be in accord with God's will. We can insist on following false values of money and prestige, but we will thereby become thorn bushes. We can also embrace God's will and be assured, not of mere justice from God, but of supreme generosity.

Wednesday of the Twentieth Week (II)

God is so different from us that it is impossible to find language and images to describe him. Sometimes we can take the wrong impression from human examples about God, such as today's parable, unless we examine them closely. Many people feel that the workers who labored all day in the vineyard got a raw deal. It surely looks like they should have received a greater pay than those who did only an hour's work.

An important element in the story is the fact that the first workers agreed on the usual daily wage. Since they received this wage, no injustice was done them. But the key to the parable is found in the words of the owner of the estate, "I am free to do as I please with my money. Are you envious because I am generous?" The story is not about justice or the lack thereof. The story is about generosity.

The truth is that we cannot earn anything from God as if our actions deserve a payment from him. God's gifts come from his goodness, not his justice. All that God gives us is not payment but a gift, not a reward but a favor. Thinking that we can earn or merit something from God is like trying to buy the Hilton hotel chain with play money, the kind they use in the game called Monopoly. After all, how much does the death of Jesus cost? What is the price of his body and blood? How much do you have to pay to purchase everlasting life?

Ezekiel condemned the kings and princes, the shepherds of Judah. The reason is that as representatives of God they were to reflect his generosity. Instead they thought only of themselves. God expects us to be unselfish in our love for him and in our service of others, but first we must understand as best we can what God is like. Justice means giving in proportion to what has been received: a day's wage for a day's work. That is not God's principle. Rather he is generous with his goodness, giving freely and abundantly to us simply because he loves us.

Thursday of the Twentieth Week (I)

Today's first reading is one of the most shocking in all the Bible. Jephthah, chosen by God to rescue the Israelites from the attacks of the Ammonites, made a vow, the result of which was far beyond his expectation. Even though he was horrified at the thought that he must sacrifice his own daughter, an only child, he went through with what he believed to be God's will for him.

The biblical story expresses no judgment on Jephthah's action, but elsewhere in the Bible human sacrifice is condemned (cf. Lev 18:21 and Dt 12:31). There is something admirable in the docility with which both Jephthah and his daughter carried out the vow, but they were mistaken in thinking that God required this death. You will remember that Abraham believed that God wished him to sacrifice his son, Isaac, but all God wanted from Abraham was a sincere expression of his willingness to do anything for God.

The marvel of our Christian revelation is that we come to see that what God did not require of Abraham or Jephthah he did require of himself. He gave up his own Son, his only begotten, to death on the cross for our salvation. That great act is so important that we celebrate it in every Mass. Jephthah in his later years no doubt looked back in great sadness upon the death of his daughter. We look back upon the death of Jesus with great joy because his death brought about our redemption. We even call the Friday on which he died "good." And good indeed it was for us.

In the best times and in the worst we ought to realize what we celebrate in each Mass, the sign of God's magnificent love for us. That realization should add a special brightness to our happiest days and it should be a beacon to lead us through the bleakest days of our lives.

Thursday of the Twentieth Week (II)

One of the Bible's favorite images to illustrate the relationship between God and his people is that taken from the union of husband and wife. The gospel speaks of a wedding banquet and the prophet Ezekiel proclaims that God's people will have a new heart, the symbol of love. Here at Mass before communion we hear the words, "Happy are those who are called to his supper." These words do not refer to the Last Supper but are taken from the Book of Revelation (19:9), which speaks of the wedding supper of the Lamb of God. This wedding celebration, as do the other images from marriage, symbolizes the intimate union of Christ with his people.

There was a time in many cultures when spouses did not select each other. Marriages were arranged by parents for social, economic, and sometimes political purposes. Love and freedom of choice were generally considered irrelevant. The wisdom of matchmakers, which was sometimes really cunning, was the determining factor in who married whom. Cynics say that having the freedom to choose a partner based on love does not work any better than the old idea of arranging marriages. But it is not so with God. He forces no one to accept his proposal. The people in the gospel who refused to go to the wedding banquet were foolish, but they were no more foolish than those who refuse to live with God. God, however, is undaunted. He continues to offer his invitation to everyone.

We too have been invited. We have been given the wedding garment of baptism which makes us welcome in God's loving presence. We can and must grow in the fullness of our response. We are free to do that, just as free as we are to come forward or not to receive the Lamb of God in the wedding supper of the Mass. God will not force our love because love which is not freely given is no love at all. His invitation is always there for us. All we need do is respond.

Friday of the Twentieth Week (I)

I suppose that mother-in-law jokes are as old as the institution of marriage itself, and yet in the Bible we find the story of the marvelous relationship between a young widow, Ruth, and her mother-in-law. Ruth was not Jewish (she was a Moabite), but she had married a Jew, the son of Naomi.

After the death of her husband, rather than return to her own country, Ruth decided to stay with Naomi because she believed that Naomi needed her. It was a double decision for Ruth: she attached herself in devotion both to her mother-in-law and to the God of Israel. Neither decision was easy for Ruth. In effect she was leaving behind her other relatives and their religious customs. Although she had lived with a Jewish husband for ten years, she was now embarking on a new way of faith as part of a new family.

Ruth stands as a beautiful and touching model of one who follows the two great commandments, the love of God and the love of neighbor. She is indeed an example for us to follow. In baptism we were embraced by God our Father and made his children. We entered a new family, God's family. There is no need for us to leave behind our blood relatives, but we should realize that what happened to us in baptism calls us to complete devotion to our heavenly father and all his children. In particular we may need to expand our vision to recognize that God's family includes a vast number of brothers and sisters throughout the whole world.

One way in which we try to express our relationships in God's family is by means of the prayer of the faithful. This prayer is to be a universal prayer, a broad, expansive prayer which reaches out to include all who are in need. Through this prayer we express some of the devotion which we see in Ruth, a truly dedicated woman.

Friday of the Twentieth Week (II)

The remarkable vision recorded by Ezekiel took place in Babylon where the conquered Israelites were in exile. The people felt that their nation was as good as dead, like the bones of corpses fallen in battle and allowed to rot and dry in the sun. The Israelites thought their situation was hopeless, as hopeless as a person who had been reduced to dry bones. There is no comparative degree for the word "dead," but one is tempted to say that there is nothing "deader" than dry bones.

The word to Ezekiel was one of hope. In his vision he saw the bones joining together and flesh coming over them. God's spirit breathed on those who had died and they came to life again.

This passage is not about resurrection from the dead. It is a symbol that Israel will be freed from bondage and restored to freedom. But of course this passage easily makes us think of the Christian doctrine of resurrection, nor is it unrelated to that doctrine. The truth is that the restoration promised by God is realized fully for all people of faith in the resurrection on the last day. We know that we will die, but we also believe that though we be as dead as dry bones God will raise us, body and soul, to the fullness of life. He who loves God and his neighbor as Jesus teaches is promised everlasting life. We must believe that.

In Ezekiel's vision those who had been slain and reduced to bones came alive and stood upright. When we stand upright to pray we express our faith in the resurrection. In particular we stand to receive communion to proclaim our faith in the resurrection for Jesus said, "He who feeds on my flesh and drinks my blood has life eternal and I will raise him up on the last day" (Jn 6:54).

Saturday of the Twentieth Week (I)

Yesterday we saw that Ruth attached herself to Naomi, her mother-in-law, and became a follower of the God of Israel. Her touching declaration to Naomi was: "Wherever you go I will go, your people shall be my people, and your God my God."

Eventually Ruth married the Jew, Boaz. Through this marriage, which was occasioned by her devotion to Naomi and her conversion to Judaism, she became the great grandmother of David, from whose family line was born in Bethlehem the Savior, Jesus Christ. Ruth was an ancestress of Jesus Christ himself. Ruth could have lived out her life in obscurity without any memory of her left to subsequent generation. Instead her name has been indelibly etched in the pages of salvation history.

I cannot guarantee that history will preserve the memory of any of us, but the fact is that we have already been rescued from obscurity by God himself. It was God, through the circumstances recorded in the Bible, who chose Ruth, and it is God who has chosen us to be members of his Church, the mystical body of Jesus Christ. We make Christ present in the world, not as his ancestors, but as members of his body. He truly lives, loves, and prays within us. Through us he wishes to continue to praise his Father and to show his love to others. We can declare to Jesus Christ: "Wherever you go I will go, your people shall be my people, and your God my God."

Saturday of the Twentieth Week (II)

Ezekiel promised that God would restore the people to their homeland and their temple. He used the image of the flowing water as a sign of God's gift of life to a people who were near extinction. The people were to look to God and his gift of life as the source of their continued existence.

All life, especially, human life, is the extraordinary gift of God. Worship acknowledges that God alone is the source of life and that his gift must be valued and safeguarded. Everyone is familiar with the story of the novel, *Frankenstein*, by Mary Shelly. Although the book was written in 1817, the plot has lost none of its fascination for people today. Dr. Frankenstein attempted to create the spark of life in his laboratory. The result was a monster out of control. His mistake was trying to play God.

Our society is also making a serious mistake in wantonly destroying human life through abortion. Equally monstrous is the movement toward the extermination of the elderly and terminally ill by means of so-called euthanasia. But any stance which places oneself or another in place of God must be condemned. Jesus was upset with those leaders who abused their God-given authority by not practicing what they preached and by imposing impossible religious requirements on the people. In effect these men were placing themselves and their own views ahead of God. In the following part of the gospel Jesus was not opposed to having a child call his male parent "father," nor would he be opposed to the priestly title today. What he objected to was an attitude which denied that God is the Father of us all, the giver of life.

The Mass is concerned with life. Here we acknowledge that God alone is the giver of life. We join Jesus in the offering of his life to the Father in order to profess that all life comes from God and from him alone.

Monday of the Twenty-first Week (I)

Today we were privileged to begin reading from the earliest

book of the New Testament, Paul's first letter to the Thessalonians. This book is as much as twenty years older than the first written gospel. Paul had already preached to the Thessalonians, and his letter manifests the pastoral concern of a man very different from those Pharisees condemned by Jesus in today's gospel.

Even in this brief section from Paul's letter we see a profound and yet simple theology which emphasizes the great virtues of faith, hope and love, the principal characteristics of the true Christian life. Paul commends his converts for the way in which they were proving their faith, laboring in love, and showing constancy of hope in Jesus Christ.

Many centuries later we are called to be like the Thessalonians, who were among the first to hear and respond to the good news of Jesus Christ. Times have changed over two thousand years, but not the essence of Christian living. First is faith, a gift from God which we cannot in any way merit. All depends on faith, which is more than an intellectual assent. Faith must shape our conduct by which we look to God as the source of all life and holiness. Second is hope, a confident trust that God loves us and will lead us in our journey to the fullness of life which he has planned for us. Third is love, which must be the motive and guiding force of all we do in our relationship with God and with each other.

We are no doubt very different from the Thessalonians in our language, our culture, and our way of life. And yet we are exactly the same as these early Christians in what really matters: our faith, our hope, and our love.

Monday of the Twenty-first Week (II)

Anyone who has had to deal with the Federal Government knows that matters can become very complicated. In April of 1977 the Department of Health, Education and Welfare mailed a form to Grove City College in Pennsylvania. The Department required that all colleges receiving federal aid sign the form giving assurance of compliance with the law which forbids discrimination against women. The college refused to sign because they received no federal

408 / Tuesday of the Twenty-first Week of the Year

aid and because their record regarding discrimination was spotless. The department was unrelenting in its demands and the college stood firm as a matter of principle. After two long court battles, the college won.

In this case the college was clearly exempt, but bureaucrats wanted to apply a law blindly with no view to the purpose of the law. It was a matter of law for the sake of law. Such abuses have not been unknown in religion. In fact, it was just this kind of abuse which Jesus roundly condemned in the gospel. Jesus was harsh with those who were harsh, and intolerant of those who were intolerant.

It is true that there is another extreme in which people have contempt for rules and regulations, whether religious or civil. That extreme is equally wrong, but the point of today's gospel is that true religion aims to make us free to worship God and to love our neighbors. Love is the supreme law which admits of no exceptions. That is the clear teaching of Jesus Christ.

Many Catholics have been disturbed in the era following Vatican II because they feel that all laws have been either laid aside or ignored. Nothing could be further from the truth. What the Church has tried to do is to recapture the spirit of the gospels. Abuses on both extreme sides continue because the Church is made up of fallible human beings. What is important for us is our attitude. Are we more interested in following the letter of the law than we are in loving God with our whole being? Are we more concerned with imposing regulations on others than we are with loving them as we love ourselves?

Tuesday of the Twenty-first Week (I)

I suspect that at times we may get a picture of the apostles, especially St. Paul, which suggests that they were men of overwhelming presence and extraordinary powers who were irresistible in their apostolate. Such was not the case.

Paul today talks about his humiliation at Philippi. There was a slave girl there who had some kind of clairvoyant spirit and brought a substantial profit to her masters by fortunetelling. For several days she followed Paul around, apparently making fun of him. Becoming annoyed, Paul commanded the spirit to leave her, which it did, and the girl's masters were left without a fortuneteller. These men were not about to tolerate this interference by Paul. Angered at losing their source of income, the men trumped up charges against Paul, had him beaten and thrown into prison. It was indeed a humiliation for Paul. After escaping from prison, he left for Thessalonica to preach there.

From this experience Paul seems to have learned how much he had to depend on God and not on himself. With that realization he found courage from God to continue to preach in the face of any opposition. He realized that the word he was called to preach was not his own, but God's.

As we look back on the saints perhaps we feel that we could never possibly be as heroic or as brave or as holy as they were. Actually they were ordinary men and women, just as human as we are. The difference in them is that they learned to depend on God and to recognize that any talent they possessed or any good they accomplished was a gift from God. They were humble.

As we receive the body and the blood of Christ today, we should acknowledge in our hearts how much we need the strength which he alone can give us through this spiritual nourishment. Of ourselves we are weak, but with Christ we can be like the saints who have done the Father's will throughout the ages.

Tuesday of the Twenty-first Week (II)

Among the Thessalonians to whom St. Paul wrote there was a certain obsession, almost hysteria, about the second coming of Christ. That kind of outlook continues today. There are people who have given up their homes to live in some remote area where they were convinced Christ would momentarily arrive in a flying saucer to take them to the planet Saturn where they believed heaven to be. Such reactions are not what God has in mind. And yet some people continue to devote themselves to dire threats of the doom Christ's imminent coming will bring upon a sinful world.

Paul wrote his second letter to the Thessalonians because his first letter did not allay their fears. The truth is, he insisted, that though Christ will come again we do not know the time or the manner of that coming. His advice was that the Thessalonians were to hold fast to the traditions they received. That advice is sound for us too. But what is the tradition to which he referred?

Paul summed up the traditional message by briefly indicating what God's relationship is to us and what our relationship to him should be. First, God our Father loves us and in his mercy has given us eternal consolation and hope. To console someone means to soothe and comfort him in sorrow or distress. Consolation is the word from a doctor which assures a patient that he will pull through a serious illness. God assures us that his son, the divine physician, has overcome the disease of sin within us. Such assurance gives us confidence that all will yet be well.

Secondly, Paul tells us what our relationship should be with a loving God. He says, "Strengthen your hearts for every good work and word." That means living the Christian life as Jesus has taught us by word and example. When a certain saint (many names have been given in this context) was asked what he would do if he knew he were to die in a moment, he replied that he would go on doing what he was doing. The reason was that in everything he was trying to do God's will.

There is no need for some extraordinary preparation for the coming of Christ. Believing in God's love for us, we should each day strengthen our hearts for every good work and word.

Wednesday of the Twenty-first Week (I)

Communication is absolutely necessary in human relationships. Without personal communication, a revealing of one's true self, friendships cannot develop and marriages cannot endure.

Without communication from God, which we call revelation, we cannot develop a relationship with him. In his love God has chosen to reveal himself to us, and in his wisdom he has chosen to do so in a human way. That is what Paul had in mind when he commended the Thessalonians for having received his message, not as the word of men, but as it truly is, the word of God. The revelation found in the Bible, both the Old and the New Testaments is the word of God in the words of men.

The Church has always cherished the Bible as a special gift from God. In the very earliest days of the Church, shortly after the death of Jesus, the Old Testament and even the traditions which now form the New Testament, were part of its essential worship, the Eucharist. The Church has never abandoned the practice of combining word and sacrament.

We who are daily Mass-goers obviously value the holy Eucharist. I know people who feel that their day is incomplete if they do not receive communion. The Eucharist is the Eternal Word of God under the appearances of bread and wine. The Bible is the Eternal Word of God under the appearances of human words. In appreciating the gift of the Eucharist we must also appreciate the gift of God's inspired word.

Every day here at Mass we are privileged to hear portions of the bible read to us. This is God's communication to us, his way of developing and deepening our relationship with him. We must hear this communication for what it truly is, the Word of God.

Wednesday of the Twenty-first Week (II)

Many people look forward to retirement and a time when they no longer have to work. Some of the Thessalonians looked forward to retiring from this world in the second coming of Christ. They were so convinced that Christ was to come very soon that they gave up working. After all, if Christ were coming, they thought, what was the point of plowing and planting and harvesting? St. Paul tried to convince them that nothing had happened to foreshadow this coming, and he gave himself as an example of how they should continue to work.

Now almost two centuries after St. Paul wrote we still have no idea of when Christ will come again to bring the kingdom of God to perfection. All we know is that God's kingdom is still in a period of growth and we, as are all God's people, are called to contribute to its upbuilding. Work, however, must be understood. The Catholic Church does not promote a work ethic, the idea that labor is by necessity linked with goodness. Nor does the Church sponsor the view that God helps those who help themselves and that material prosperity is a sign of God's blessings. These notions lead all too easily to a false sense of independence from God and others and actually foster materialism as a way of life.

The Second Vatican Council in its *Constitution on the Church in the Modern World* has much to say about the authentic meaning of work in God's plan. Time allows only a couple of brief quotations. The Council states that "while providing the substance of life for themselves and their families, men and women are performing their activities in a way which appropriately benefits society. They can justly consider that by their labor they are unfolding the Creator's work . . . contributing by their personal industry to the realization in history of the divine plan" (34). In speaking of the improvements which human talent have brought to civilization the Council declares, "Rightly understood, this kind of growth is of greater value than any external riches which can be garnered" (35).

As we await the second coming of Christ we can contribute to the growth of his kindgom here on earth by the use of our minds, the work of our arms, and the sweat of our brows.

Thursday of the Twenty-first Week (I)

There are some things in life which are very difficult to do by yourself. Say that you are traveling alone by car in a strange part of the country. You have car trouble on some deserted stretch of highway. What a lonely, abandoned feeling that is. Just to have someone along, even if he cannot fix the car, is a great consolation.

It is not that misery loves company; rather it is that we all need support, even if it is only moral support.

On this earth we are on a journey to meet the Lord in his final coming, as the opening words of today's gospel remind us. There are many hazards along the way. That is the reason for the warning from Jesus which we just heard. But we should not and need not be alone on this journey.

Paul confessed to his converts that throughout his distress and trial he was consoled by their faith. They were a source of strength to him. And he prays that the Lord will make them overflow with love for one another so that they may be a source of consolation and of strength to each other.

We are saved by God not as individuals but as membe' ʒ of a community, a family, the Church (cf. *Dogmatic Cons   on the Church*, 9). Through our union with Christ we have a b nd with each other. In our journey we are called to be a support to one another, a support through prayer, interest, and action. We cannot please God or achieve our salvation without a relatioship of love with all our spiritual brothers and sisters. We should expect and we should receive support from others, and we must freely and eagerly give that support in return.

Thursday of the Twenty-first Week (II)

St. Paul founded a Christian community in the sea port city of Corinth around the year 50 A.D. It was really "Sin City," and Paul admitted that he approached his work there with trepidation because of the city's moral depravity and its pagan worship which included religious prostitution. He was able to win converts from among the people of Corinth, but later when he was preaching in Ephesus he received disturbing news about them. They had fallen into serious errors both in doctrine and in practice.

St. Paul was never one to pull punches. Throughout the letter he was uncompromising in his correcting of doctrine and his insistence on right practice. And yet he began his letter on a note of optimism based, not on the ability or goodness of the Corinthians, but on the grace of God. He was convinced that they could become like the good and faithful servants spoken of in today's gospel. He wrote: "God will strengthen you to the end so that you will be blameless on the day of the Lord Jesus. God is faithful, and it was he who called you to fellowship with his Son."

This optimism was typical of St. Paul. He did not despair of human nature, but he knew that truth and goodness were the result of God's grace and not of human industry. In fact he delighted in pointing out that God chooses the weak and poor of this world to manifest his power and goodness.

Many people are confused in this matter. They think that virtue is their own accomplishment and they consider themselves better than others because they believe that they work harder at their religion. Actually everything is a gift from God. We pray because we are weak and need God. We receive the Eucharist as spiritual nourishment because we require God's strength. We do not depend on ourselves. We rely on God because he is always faithful.

Friday of the Twenty-first Week (I)

One aspect of the Christian life is that we should never become completely satisfied with ourselves. Complacency means the end of progress. Humility allows us to recognize our never-ending need for growth.

St. Paul complimented his converts on the way in which they were pleasing God by their holiness, but he immediately urged them to make still greater progress. That is a message for us today, but the question is how do we make this progress in holiness.

Humility teaches us that we must continue to grow. It also makes us realize that we do not have the means within ourselves to make progress in holiness. We cannot lift ourselves up by our own boot straps, or by our shoe strings, or whatever the expression should be these days. God is the one who makes us holy.

What we do almost every day at Mass is the correct approach. Here we receive the body and the blood of Jesus Christ, our spiritual nourishment. A child cannot grow without a proper diet. We are all children of God, and without the nourishment of the Eucharist we cannot expect to grow spiritually. Also proper food is needed so that the cells of our bodies may regenerate themselves, especially after an illness or injury. In the same way we need the Eucharist to repair damage caused by sin, which is the real obstacle to growth in holiness.

One big difference between ordinary nourishment and the Eucharist is that ordinary nourishment works automatically, so to speak, without any conscious effort on our part. The Eucharist does not work automatically. We must approach communion with an openness to Jesus Christ, with a prayer in our heart that he will accomplish his work within us. With the proper disposition from us the Eucharist will do wonders in our lives, for the body and the blood of Jesus Christ are real food and real drink, a true means to holiness.

Friday of the Twenty-first Week (II)

The city of Corinth where Paul founded a Christian community was a cosmopolitan center. It was the kind of place where you would find anything as in New York or Los Angeles today. There was some influence of Greek philosophy but mostly the populace was worldly wise, the kind of people who would not easily take to the gospel. It was a miracle of grace that Paul could win even a few converts there and it is not surprising that some of them, under the pressure of neighbors, began to fall away. After all, Christianity is not a doctrine which appeals to the worldly wise.

St. Thomas Aquinas commented that people generally consider anything they do not understand to be foolishness. Imagine someone in the nineteenth century telling people that one day men in space ships would fly to the moon. Such a person would have been labeled as looney indeed. St. Paul's doctrine seemed even more absurd. What is the sense in following a leader who was jeered and spat at by a frenzied crowd and who was put to death by the puny governor of a contemptible outpost of the Roman Empire? Roman soldiers who were sent to Judea considered their mission as a demotion or a punishment. Could any good come from that insignificant country? And yet no matter how absurd it seemed, Paul insisted, "We preach Christ crucified."

God's ways are different from ours. He brings strength out of weakness and life out of death. Here at Mass we have an example of how God works. Jesus takes two of the simplest things possible, ordinary bread and wine, and transforms them into his body and blood. Only God has that power. Then he gives us his body and blood as our spiritual nourishment. Only God could think of something like that. And most marvelous of all, we do not assimilate this food and drink to ourselves, but Christ assimilates us to himself. He transforms us so that for us suffering will turn to joy and death will lead to everlasting life.

Saturday of the Twenty-first Week (I)

One of the reasons that St. Paul wrote his letter to the Thessalonians was that they had some mistaken notions about the second coming of Christ. They thought that since Christ would come again soon to gather them all up in glory there was no need to do any work. (This problem was so serious that it became an even more urgent topic in his second letter to the Thessalonians).

Even though we do not know when Christ will come again, there is nothing wrong with looking forward to his coming. In fact we should "wait in joyful hope" for this coming of our savior. How we wait in joyful hope is what is significant.

Think about something pleasant, such as a vacation, perhaps a trip you have always wanted to take to some south seas island. It really does not make much sense just to sit around for months waiting for the day of departure. You must go on living in your everyday routine. In addition, you make plans for your trip. You save up money, you make reservations, you consult a travel agent, and you probably get some brochures describing the place of your dreams. The truth is that the expectation involved in the planning is a great pleasure itself. And thinking about the trip in the future helps to make life in the present more enjoyable.

Life itself is a journey to meet the Lord in his coming. Jesus himself tells us that we must be ready. He is like the man in the gospel who has gone away for a while, leaving his funds in the hands of others. He will return and he will expect an accounting. In coming to this earth Jesus has given us the great gift of faith and a share in the life of his Father. While he is away we are to grow in these gifts, rather than idly wasting our lives. We are to live in accord with the life he lived, a life of love and generosity. Our calling to faithfulness is often difficult, but we know that through faithfulness we will be like the servants who were given silver pieces and increased their number. We can look forward to the coming of the Lord with joyful hope.

Saturday of the Twenty-first Week (II)

In an expensive restaurant the prime table goes to those people who give the head waiter a handsome tip. But it is not that way with God. In a department store the person who is smartly dressed will get waited on before people who appear less affluent. But it is not that way with God. The label, "VIP," very important person, applies only to those who are considered to be prominent citizens. But it is not that way with God. You will never find God running after a movie star or a professional athlete to get his autograph.

St. Paul makes it quite clear that God favors the weak, the lowborn and despised, and those who count for nothing in this world. Those who are powerful, wealthy, and looked up to in society think they do not need God. They judge that they can get along very well by themselves. Of course they may not say these things in so many words, but by their reliance on themselves, their money and their position they speak very loudly by their actions.

The reason that God favors the weak and the lowly is that they generally are in a better position to recognize that they depend completely on God. God simply cannot brook any competitor. If he were to do so, he would be untrue to himself and would deny that he alone is the source of every good gift. The parable in the gospel makes a point that we must use well the talents we have, but the reason for that, which is the principal lesson of the parable, is that the talents come freely from God. Notice that the man called in his servants and handed his funds over to them. This was no payment; it was a gift. Forgetting from whom the gift came is the biggest mistake anyone can make. Mankind must do no boasting before God.

Actually no Christian, no matter what his status, should have an inferiority complex. God has given us the greatest gift possible. He has given us life in Christ Jesus whom he has made our wisdom, our justice, our sanctification, and our redemption. In God's sight we are all VIP's.

Monday of the Twenty-second Week (I)

The Thessalonians were overcome with sadness because of the death of a number of their fellow Christians. This was not the natural sadness caused by the death of loved ones; it was a supreme regret that those who had died would be deprived of sharing in the glory of Christ's second coming. Their sorrow was somewhat like that which the fathers of our country must have felt when they saw some of their devoted compatriots die before the declaration of independence could be made a reality in a free country.

St. Paul wrote to the Thessalonians to clear up the matter for them and thereby help to overcome their grief. The Thessalonians had become thoroughly convinced that the second coming of Christ would indeed be a marvelous event. What had not become as dominant in their thinking was an understanding that salvation meant that Christ himself would raise the dead to life at his coming. Salvation concerns not only the immortality of the soul, as we may sometimes think, but the glorification of the body as well. In other words, it is the whole person, body as well as soul, who has come under the saving power of Jesus through his death and resurrection. As Jesus died and was raised to fullness of life, so we too will be raised on the last day.

That will be a glorious day for us all, even if we died before it occurs. Jesus himself will announce the glad tidings to us and will proclaim liberty to our bodies held captive in the earth by death. The declaration of our independence from death he has already signed in his own blood. That full freedom will be ours when he comes again.

That is why our memorial acclamation in this Mass, a profession of our faith, will be: "Dying you destroyed our death; rising you restored our life; Lord Jesus, come in glory."

Monday of the Twenty-second Week (II)

The initial reaction to Jesus by the people in his home town synagogue was favorable. When they realized, however, the full implication of what he was saying, that he was the fulfillment of prophecy, their favor turned to incredulity. How could the son of a carpenter be all that he claimed to be? Their incredulity then turned to open hostility. If Jesus had had better credentials, such as wealth, grandeur and prestigious parents, he probably would have been readily acceptable to the populace. As it was, everything about Jesus was too simple.

Paul faced much the same difficulty. In his preaching he did not resort to the philosophical sophistication of the day. He was but a tent maker who spoke a simple message with reliance on the power of the Spirit, not human ingenuity. The result was that some of the Corinthians were being led astray by specious arguments and shallow reasoning.

God's ways are different from our own. Some people wonder why God does not make use of his omnipotence to crush evil with a mighty show of power. Others yearn for Christ to come again in majesty and splendor in order to convince all the skeptics that Christianity is right after all. God prefers the simple unassuming approach. He is like the confident person who is aware of his authority and ability and does not feel that he must prove it to anyone.

We do not understand all the reasons why God chooses to do things the way he does. One reason is that displays of power and majesty leave little room for faith. God wants us to accept the simple words of sacred scripture as his inspired words. He wants us to see through the veil of bread and wine to the reality of the eucharist, despite its ordinary appearance. And he wants us to accept that the son of a carpenter is actually his own divine son. Faith—a complete, fully accepting kind of faith—is the mark of one who is truly devoted to God and to his way of doing things, not our own.

Tuesday of the Twenty-second Week (I)

The thought of the second coming of Christ was more prominent in the minds of the early Christians than in our own. The Thessalonians were eager to know the exact day and hour of that coming so that they could be prepared. Apparently their idea was that, knowing the time of Christ's coming, they could do other things or idle away their time until a few days before the event. They were somewhat like those people who, knowing that Christmas is December 25, put off their shopping until the last minute.

Paul's teaching was that we simply do not know when the second coming will occur. Christ, he said, will come like a thief in the night. The point of this comparison is to emphasize unpredictability, not fear. Christ will not come to rob us of anything, quite the contrary. But just as one does not know when a thief will strike, so we do not know when Christ will come again.

These days we probably do not think much about the second coming but we should. The Church indirectly teaches us what our attitude should be through a prayer which is part of every Mass: "In your mercy keep us free from sin and protect us from all anxiety as we wait in joyful hope for the coming of our Savior, Jesus Christ."

The word "anxiety" sums up modern man. We are often filled with tensions and uneasiness about inflation and recession, about the future of children, about the energy crisis, and an almost endless list of modern problems. In the midst of all these problems we should not abdicate responsibility, as apparently the Thessalonians wished to do, but we really ought to develop a peace of mind that all will be made right when "Christ will raise our mortal bodies and make them like his own in glory." On that great day "every tear will be wiped away . . . and we shall see our God" face to face. Despite our problems and responsibilities, we should "wait in joyful hope for the coming of our Savior, Jesus Christ."

Tuesday of the Twenty-second Week (II)

In looking around at almost any gathering of people, it is surprising to note how many are wearing glasses. Actually the number is even larger than we can observe since in any group several people will be wearing contact lenses. As middle age approaches, bifocals usually become a necessity. They are an inconvenience, but as one man remarked, "They sure beat not being able to see clearly."

If we are to make sense out of human existence, we need to see clearly, not with the help of glasses, but with the aid of the spiritual vision which comes from faith. St. Paul writes, "The Spirit we have received is not the world's spirit but God's spirit, helping us to recognize the gifts he has given us." There are two ways of looking at almost every reality, one fuzzy like the vision of a person who needs glasses and one clearly like that of the person who has received corrective lenses.

The Israelites of old could have thought that it was by chance that a strong east wind dried up the water of the sea for their successful passage in the exodus, but they believed instead that it was the work of God. Roman soldiers looked up at the corpse of a Jew upon a cross as one more sign of their supremacy, but Mary despite her tears saw clearly that her child was God's son and that his crucifixion revealed God's supremacy over sin and death. An unbeliever at Mass sees only ordinary bread and wine, but in faith we perceive that we are in contact with divinity.

The Spirit we have received helps us to recognize God's gifts. In sorrow and joy, in success and failure, we should see God's loving hand at work. Nothing is either too great or too small in our lives to escape the guidance and direction of God's providence. In faith we are called to see everything in the light of the truth of today's responsorial psalm: "The Lord is faithful in all his words and holy in all his works. The Lord lifts up all who are falling and raises up all who are bowed down."

Wednesday of the Twenty-second Week (I)

Today, if you will excuse my saying so, I feel like St. Paul. I do not mean that I am foolish enough to think that I have his holiness, or his wisdom, or his zeal. Rather with him I believe that I can say to you as he wrote to the Colossians: "I give thanks to God, the Father, of our Lord Jesus Christ, in my prayers for you because I have heard of your faith in Christ Jesus. . . .You have heard the message of truth, the gospel, which has come to you, has borne fruit, and has continued to grow in your midst. . . ."

I see no reason why I should not commend you for being good people. Your presence here at Mass, every day or almost every day for most of you, is a beautiful sign of your faith.

My commendation, however, is not a cause for self-satisfaction. We must recognize the source of the goodness which is within us. In the gospel we saw Jesus cure Peter's mother-in-law of the fever. We saw him heal the people sick with a variety of diseases. We saw him drive out demons. Jesus is indeed the healer, not only of the body but of the whole person. He is our healer. Wounded and weakened by sin, we are restored to health by him. We must give credit where credit is due.

Nor is my commendation a cause for complacency. We are constantly being healed by Jesus, especially through the eucharist, because we are still weak and we still make mistakes, despite our best intentions. That is why before communion we say, "Lord, I am not worthy to receive you, but only say the word and I shall be healed." And say the word Jesus does. That word is, "Come to me."

Wednesday of the Twenty-second Week (II)

St. Paul was very disturbed by the fact that factions had developed among the Christians at Corinth. One reason for the division was attachment to the human ministers of the gospel. Some converts pledged allegiance to Paul and others to Apollos. A similar situation today would be that in which a Catholic would say, "I like and follow the teachings of Pope Paul VI, but not Pope John Paul II." Such comparisons are not only divisive but irrelevant. Human ministers are but instruments of Christ and their authority and effectiveness are due to his Spirit working within them.

We must constantly remind ourselves that Jesus Christ is the center of our faith. He is such because of who he is, the Son of God, not because he or his ministers happen to satisfy our taste. The demons driven out by Jesus had more insight than many people today. They declared to Jesus, "You are the Son of God." The identity of Jesus is the crucial question of the gospels and of our faith.

Think of it this way. Jesus cured Peter's mother-in-law of a severe fever, but there were more people similarly ill in Palestine whom he did not cure. Jesus laid his hands on those with various diseases and healed them, but there were many more sick people throughtout the world at the time with whom he never came in contact. Jesus worked his miracles out of a motive of compassion, but he was even more concerned with drawing people to himself in faith. The response of faith is much more important than a cure or a healing. Our eternal future, not just a lifetime, depends on the proper response of faith.

We cannot put ourselves into the position of accepting Jesus only if he pleases our sense of need or values. We must not limit him to our view. He is the Son of God and that truth of faith should be enough for us to attach ourselves to him without condition.

Thursday of the Twenty-second Week (I)

St. Paul did not found the Christian community at Colossae. That was accomplished by Epaphras, who represented Paul as a faithful minister of Christ, a fellow spiritual fisherman. Paul wrote to the Colossians, perhaps at the urging of Epaphras, because they were being confused by some false doctrines. His ministry toward them took the form of the letter from which we have been reading yesterday and today.

Paul was not satisfied with merely writing a letter. He states, "We have been praying for you unceasingly and asking that you may attain full knowledge of his will through perfect wisdom and spiritual insight." Paul was a man of action, but he was not so foolish as to think that his efforts alone could win converts or correct those who were in error. He understood that it is God who accomplishes everything, and that God wishes to respond to need in answer to prayer.

What this means to us is that we must never underestimate the value of prayer. Most good people rush to someone in need, such as helping out when a mother of a family is in the hospital. We know that we should visit the sick. At times we find ourselves talking to someone who has left the Church and we do our best to try to get them to come back. And this is as it should be. But we must never forget prayer in all these and similar situations.

St. Paul was a great apostle, one chosen to be like the men in the gospel, a fisher of men. He coupled his ministry with prayer because he realized that human effort without God is useless. His example of prayer is a model for us in Christian living.

Thursday of the Twenty-second Week (II)

Even if we are not fishermen I think we can sympathize with Peter in today's gospel. Peter was a professional fisherman. Knowing the waters of the lake and the suitable time for fishing as well as understanding the best techniques were essential to his livelihood. Having done everything right and having tried all night long during the proper hours for fishing, he and his companions had caught nothing.

Then along came Jesus, the carpenter who knew nothing about fishing. He told Peter to put out into deep water, not the best spot in the lake, after the sun had risen, not the proper time. Peter began with a protest, "Master, we have been hard at it all night long and have caught nothing." A struggle then took place within him. He was on the verge of telling Jesus that what he had suggested was nonsense, but a sudden realization came over him. Perhaps it was wise to do what this man said. After a pause, which seemed an eternity to Peter but was only a moment, he responded, "But if you say so, I will lower the nets." We know the result. The miraculous catch of fish was the beginning of Peter's faith in Jesus as well as of his call to ministry.

We must always remember that God's ways are not our ways. St. Paul was adamant about that, insisting that what seems to be nonsense is God's wisdom and what seems to be weakness is God's strength. That is why he wrote, "If any one of you thinks he is wise in a worldly way, he had better become a fool." It is not for us to tell God how to run the universe or our lives. Others may feel that it is foolish for Catholics to struggle to keep a marriage together when divorce is so easy. They may judge the Church heartless in its opposition to abortion when others cry out for the freedom of a woman to do as she pleases. They may think it naive to believe that bread can become the body of the Lord and wine can become his blood. But the ways of God are wise. And they work, as they did for St. Peter.

Friday of the Twenty-second Week (I)

In all of history Jesus Christ stands apart. He is unique. There is simply no one else like him, nor will there ever be. As the eternal Son of God, he exists before all of creation. As man he was born in time but continues now in a glorious form of human existence. These are profound truths, difficult to grasp.

The reason St. Paul addressed these great truths is that there was confusion among the Colossians. They actually thought it possible that something created, especially the angels, could be superior to Christ. Paul says a resounding "No" to that thought. Christ, existing before all else that is, is actually the cause of all creation together with his Father. He is the head of all creation. As human, Christ is the head of the Church.

These days I doubt that we are tempted to think that angels could be superior to Christ or that anyone in the Church could possibly be more important than he. Maybe we need to think of new forms of temptations, modern values which could be seen as superior to Christ.

The question comes down to, what are our values in life? How much worth do we place in money, power, prestige, popularity, even just getting our own way all the time? Are we perhaps falling prey to the myriad of commercials on TV which are designed to make us always want something more or something better. An automobile ad proclaims that we should buy their car because "After all, life is to enjoy." Are material things the source of our real joy?

We should not hesitate to think that we are good people. But we are surrounded by temptations to put Christ in second place at best. Today we are called to give a resounding "No" to anything that could possibly be held to be superior to Jesus Christ.

Friday of the Twenty-second Week (II)

Few people like changes in their way of doing things. A man at a service station was very disturbed to discover that he was getting gasoline, no longer by the gallon, but by the liter. The attendant tried to explain that the United States was finally starting to use a system followed throughout most of the world. The man's response was, "I think they should have to change, not us."

Jesus faced much the same difficulty in his own day. For many of the Jewish leaders religion had become a legalistic formalism with little heart. For them it was more important to abide by minute fasting regulations, for example, than it was to help a neighbor in distress. Law had pretty much replaced the law giver himself. Jesus met opposition in trying to change all that. He wanted to show that love is the essence of religion and that regulations were valid only if God's purpose were served. What he asked was really much more demanding. It was actually easier to be precise about fasting than it was to love God with one's whole being and to love one's neighbor as Jesus did.

The response to Jesus required a new, bigger way of thinking. The same is required today. The Second Vatican Council, the providential movement of God's Spirit upon the Church in our time, was an effort to return to the teachings and practices of the pristine Church. Full and active participation in the liturgy was restored. There was an insistence on the responsibility of the laity under the guidance, not the dominance, of the clergy. Emphasis was restored to the importance of the Church as a community, a family under God as Father.

It took a long time for the decrees of the Council of Trent to become fully effective, and we are still far from the full implementation of Vatican II. New wine cannot be put into old wineskins. We need to pray that God will open wide our hearts, and the hearts of all the people of the Church, to accept and adopt the providential movement of the Second Vatican Council.

Saturday of the Twenty-second Week (I)

Sin is the greatest possible evil for one main reason: it separates us from God. That is what St. Paul had in mind when he wrote, "You yourselves were once alienated from God." So abstractly stated, sin does not sound very bad. But imagine that you are living on an island, which is connected to the mainland by a single bridge. You are completely dependent on the bridge to get supplies from the mainland. It is your lifeline.

Then one night in a terrible storm, this link is completely washed away. Barely surviving the storm which lasts all night, you awaken to discover that you are completely cut off from all means of help. You know that somehow a new bridge must be built, but the island is so barren that there simply are no materials with which to construct a bridge. Lost in despair you do not know where to turn. Later when the clouds have blown away and the sun is shining brightly, you return to the edge of the island and are amazed to see that someone in a miraculously short period of time has constructed a bridge. You know that you are saved.

Sin, like a terrible storm, severed our link with God, the source of all life and holiness. No mere human resources are capable of restoring that link. God had to do it. And do it he did by building a bridge, not made of steel or wood, but of flesh and blood, his own Son, Jesus Christ. Through his death Jesus became the bridge by which God restores to us the gift of everlasting life. That is what it means when St. Paul wrote that Christ has achieved reconciliation for us.

In the gospel Jesus proclaims that he is Lord of the Sabbath. The Sabbath was that sacred, special day for communion with God. Jesus is indeed Lord of the Sabbath, for he is our link, our reconciliation with God the Father.

Saturday of the Twenty-second Week (II)

Religion is always open to extreme views, from both the right and the left, and these extremes are divisive. Some people think that religion must be rigid and unbending—the stricter the better. Others feel that anything should go as long as you believe that you are not hurting anybody. Jesus opposed both extremes. In the gospels there are many examples of how Jesus resisted laxity. Today's episode shows how he wanted law to be interpreted with compassion.

Some of the Pharisees judged that the apostles were in violation of the law of the Sabbath rest by pulling off the grainheads, shelling them, and eating them. Their attitude was, "Let them starve; the law is more important than their hunger." Jesus pointed out that what the apostles were doing was reasonable, not without precedent, and certainly not against the purpose of the law.

It is very difficult to keep the balance between rigidity and laxity. Some of us favor rigidity, as long as we are not affected. A couple once said to a priest who had just preached a sermon condemning the evils of our times: "That was a powerful sermon, Father. We're glad it was nothing personal." Still others of us may favor laxity when we do have something personal at stake.

The problem of extremes illustrates why authority is needed in the Church. We can be led astray by ourselves or by individuals. The people in Corinth were led astray by pretentious preachers who boasted in their own clever words and powerful deeds, but they lacked the authority of St. Paul. Paul was saddened by the infatuation which the Corinthians developed for these men whom he labeled "pseudo-apostles."

Today apostolic authority is found in the Pope and the Bishops. In following the official teaching of the Church from the Pope and the Bishops we will not be led astray nor will we fall into an extreme of either rigidity or laxity.

Monday of the Twenty-third Week (I)

It is surprising to realize that Jesus had to suffer. I am referring not only to the moments of his passion. Actually Jesus suffered much throughout his ministry, as he went about proclaiming the truth and doing good. Witness today's gospel. The scribes and the Pharisees were on watch to find a charge against Jesus. When he performed the cure, they were infuriated. Such reactions hurt Jesus. And that is only one incident among many in the gospel.

The followers of Jesus who proclaim the truth and try to do good should expect the same treatment Jesus received. St. Paul understood this truth. He accepted it and even found joy in his suffering. He explains in today's reading his motive: "I fill up what is lacking in the suffering of Christ for the sake of his body, the Church." That sounds very strange. Could anything be lacking to the sufferings of Christ as if they were inadequate? Certainly not. St. Paul wrote in Greek, and the verb he used means precisely to complete something in the place of someone else. In other words, it is proper to understand this sentence as meaning that Paul continued in his ministry where Jesus left off in his existence on this earth. Paul was acting in the name and in the person of Jesus Christ. He could expect nothing different from what Jesus himself endured for the sake of his ministry.

All of us are called to be witnesses to the truth and to be examples of what is right. In this way we too continue the ministry of Jesus, and we too, at least at times, should expect to suffer for what is true and what is right. In this kind of suffering we really ought to find joy, as did St. Paul, since this kind of suffering makes us more like Christ himself.

Monday of the Twenty-third Week (II)

St. Paul used very harsh language about the fact that a Christian in Corinth was living with his stepmother. Such unions were condemned even in ancient Greece and both Roman and Jewish law forbade them as incest. St. Paul strongly opposed the relationship but what really upset him was his realization that the Corinthians not only tolerated the situation but actually boasted about their liberal view of sexual morality. He must have felt a little like a policeman who has arrested a criminal only to find that bystanders are jeering at him for having done so.

Some commentators have seen a contrast between the harshness of Paul and the compassion of Jesus in somewhat similar situations, such as that of the woman caught in adultery. The comparison is neither fair nor just. Jesus showed mercy toward repentant sinners but he never approved of laxity. He was like a parent who is always willing to understand weakness and who offers forgiveness and yet continues to insist on discipline.

The distinction is not specious. Catholics must not be haughty toward a person who feels trapped in a second marriage, but we cannot pretend that divorce and remarriage are acceptable. We must try to be helpful toward a woman who has been led to believe that her only choice was abortion, but that does not mean that abortion is anything but a heinous crime. We should even be patient with our own failures but we must not allow ourselves to develop a hardness of heart or a distorted conscience.

God will always be merciful to a repentant sinner. He would, however, be untrue to himself if he were to pretend that sin does not exist or that evil is not wrong.

Tuesday of the Twenty-third Week (I)

Our God is good, He is not a remote God, distant and ethereal. "In Christ the fullness of deity resides in bodily form." Through the humanity of Jesus Christ God has become very close to us. Jesus was human like us in all things but sin, and it was through his humanity that he saved us from the death of sin.

Jesus wanted his work to continue through the humanity of his followers. Long ago he called Peter and Andrew, James and John and the other apostles. What he did in the past he continues to do in the present. As surely as he called the apostles, he has invited us to be his followers. In baptism, through the priest, he called us each by name. And what he does in the present he will also do in the future.

We stand at some midpoint in time between the past and the future. We should look back on the past with a realization that the faith has been passed down to us through the centuries by men and women of faith like ourselves. Our religion did not start the other day up the street. It has a history, which is a history of humanity transformed by faith.

But we must also look to the future and recognize that those who follow us will have to look back upon our era for a witness to the faith. The kind of people we are as followers of Christ will have an influence not only on those with whom we live but also on those who have yet to be born.

We should never think that anyone of us is insignificant in God's plan. We are part of the history which he himself shapes. And he wants each of us to be a part of that history as living witnesses to faith.

Tuesday of the Twenty-third Week (II)

Historians like to speak about men of destiny: Aristotle, who helped shape western thought, Shakespeare, the greatest artisan of the English language, George Washington, the father of our country. These names are indeed memorable for their contributions to society. And yet how much more exalted to have been called by name to be an apostle by the Son of God himself. We know much about Peter and John, less about the others, and only infamy about Judas. And yet all shared in the honor of having been selected by Jesus.

We need not be envious of these apostles. At baptism Christ himself, speaking through the person who baptized us, called each of us by name. Perhaps we shared an apostolic name, but whatever our name it became ours and served to identify us. There is something very personal about being called by name, and when we are recognized and singled out in this manner by a person of prominence we are thrilled. The use of one's personal name shows recognition, often affection and respect.

We should have a proper sense of our dignity through baptism, and we must recognize that dignity in others. People of dignity do not stoop to actions below them and they understand how to treat others with respect. That is why St. Paul was disappointed that the Corinthians descended so low as to hail one another into court over squabbles and disagreements. Some people might say that St. Paul was idealistic and naive about the hard realities of life, but that is only because they do not have his sense of the dignity possessed by anyone called by Christ.

As we look around this gathering today we see people called and selected by Christ as surely as were the apostles. Can we not live and act in accord with the Christian dignity which is ours?

Wednesday of the Twenty-third Week (I)

Jesus was at the time of his birth prophesied by the wise old man, Simeon, to be a sign of contradiction. He was such in his identity, a man who was human like us in all things but sin and yet truly divine. His humanity, was in a sense, a veil which hid his divinity. But if Jesus was a sign of contradiction, or better a paradox, in his identity, he was such also in his teachings.

He declared that the poor, the hungry, and the sorrowful are the truly blest people of this world, that is, those who are really happy. In blunt contradiction to his teachings are the values of our society, which says that happiness comes from wealth, affluence, and freedom from pain in any form. Note that Jesus is not against happiness; his quarrel is with what constitutes happiness. Nor is Jesus against money, sufficient food, or comfort. The problem is that it is too easy to make gods of such things and to pursue them as a source of happiness.

We cannot afford to deceive ourselves about the source of happiness. That is why St. Paul declares that we must set our hearts on what pertains to higher realms where Christ is seated at God's right hand. Jesus lived a human life according to a set of values different from those of society. As a result he has been exalted in heaven at his Father's right hand. It is by considering his life, as well as his teachings, that we can come to see true values. The entire life of Jesus was directed to the Father, and his teachings were intended to point us in the same direction.

Jesus calls us to worship not wealth or food or comfort, but the God who alone can grant all good things.

Wednesday of the Twenty-third Week (II)

The first reading today may seem to be based on a prejudice against marriage. While we hear St. Paul extolling the values of virginity, we must also remember that he has shown that marriage is a symbol of the union between Christ and his Church. That comparison reflects a very elevated view of marriage. But the point of the reading is not the superiority of one state over another but single mindedness in the service of the Lord. Paul's advice is that we are not to become involved in anything that will distract us from the ultimate purpose of life.

There is an urgency in his message because the early Church apparently thought that the second coming of Christ was imminent. Although that idea was not correct, and we still do not know when Christ will come again, the message is still valid. Paul thought the time was short before the second coming and that was his motive for taking life seriously. Actually the time is short for all of us in this life, whether Christ comes before we die or not.

Jesus, without any reference to the brevity of time, taught a sense of values according to which we should live, values which are challenging because they are so different from what the world takes for granted. He declared that those are blest who are poor, hungry, sorrowful, and hated. It is a strange set of values, but his point is that the people in these conditions are those who turn to God for help in their lives and as the source of their happiness.

Today we must ask ourselves what we want from life. Do we really want to be rich and carefree, devoid of responsibilities and the need to care for others? Or do we want to live simple lives, humbly dependent on God and each other, our only wealth being the love of God in our hearts which we are eager to share with others? The time is indeed short, for our lives are passing away with every moment.

Thursday of the Twenty-third Week (I)

Jesus, we saw yesterday, is a sign of contradiction. He is not a wolf in sheep's clothing, that kind of contradiction; rather he is God clothed in humanity. Through his words and actions he brings a divine wisdom to us, a wisdom which is at odds with many merely human standards.

For example, Jesus says, "Love your enemies." But the world

says, "Don't let anybody take advantage of you; get even with people who offend you." Jesus says, "Give to all who beg from you." But the world says, "Welfare is bad; let them work for their living." The world is harsh but Jesus is gentle.

One of the immediate advantages of following the way of Jesus is that it begets a peace and serenity in our hearts. We refuse to let ourselves become upset over injury and insult. We reject that inner tension which comes from demanding revenge and recompense. We avoid the bitter feelings which are the fruit of judging others harshly.

St. Paul certainly captures the spirit of Jesus' message. Even his words in today's reading breathe forth a spirit of peace and serenity: "Because you are God's chosen ones, holy and beloved, clothe yourselves with heartfelt mercy, with kindness, humility, meekness, and patience."

It is difficult for us to capture this same spirit because opposite pressures are very strong. As we open our ears to hear the message of Christ, we must also open our hearts in prayer to ask for God's strength. If we hear God's word and cooperate with his help, then indeed from this Mass we can go forth in peace.

Thursday of the Twenty-third Week (II)

Sometimes parents have to caution their older children not to speak of certain subjects or to avoid some expressions in the presence of younger children. The topics may be innocent enough and the expressions may be acceptable, but they are not suitable for the ears of little children.

Something like this situation was a problem in the Christian community at Corinth. Animals were sacrificed to pagan gods. The meat was then consumed in temple banquets or made available in the markets for purchase. To partake of the meat was understood to be a sign of fealty to the pagan gods as well as union with them. Sometimes this food was the only meat available to the Christians, and they wanted to know whether it was permissible to consume it. St. Paul's answer in the affirmative was based on the fact that the eating of this meat was actually without religious significance because the gods were a fiction.

But a problem still remained. Some of the Christians who lacked a proper understanding of Paul's principle were shocked to see fellow Christians eating this meat, and in some cases were led to do what they considered to be sinful. Then a different question arose: did those who understood the situation have to give up their right to eat this meat lest they scandalize others? St. Paul urged that charity must be the supreme norm. He made it clear what he himself would do: "If food causes my brother to sin I will never eat meat again."

St. Paul reflected the kind of love taught by Jesus in the gospel today. Paul asks that out of love we give up things we have a perfect right to do so that others may not be offended. His principle is valid but difficult to apply. For example, a parish should not abandon certain liturgical practices approved and even urged by the Church simply because some members are rubbed the wrong way. What is right is right. And yet somehow we must find a way to follow Paul's principle and Jesus' command of perfect love. In the end love will win out over all problems.

Friday of the Twenty-third Week (I)

(*Note to the homilist: Scholars do not all agree that St. Paul was the immediate author of the pastoral epistles, but since they are written according to his spirit and doctrine it is homiletically proper simply to refer to Paul as the author.*)

St. Paul admits that at one time he was a blind guide of blind men. His intentions were good when he persecuted the Christians, but his actions were wrong. He recognized that it was only by the grace of God that his blindness was removed and he was given the gift of faith in Christ Jesus. Once filled with faith his zeal for helping others to come to Christian truth or to deepen it was almost an obsession.

All of us have responsibilities toward others. Parents obviously are obliged to help develop faith and morality in their children. Spouses should be a support for each other. True friendship demands that we come to the aid of others.

Rather often we are not sure what to do. Should parents force children to go to Mass on Sundays, especially if those children are eighteen or nineteen years of age? How do you tell a spouse that he is giving a bad example to the children? Many friends have parted ways when one tries to correct the other. How do we dare to correct anyone when we know that we are far from perfect ourselves? And we see from Paul's own experience that good intentions alone are not enough.

There are no easy solutions to these problems. But we do know that the source of clear vision for St. Paul was God himself. When we face a problem in personal relationships, the very first thing we must do is pray for guidance and help. We can do other things, such as to seek advice, but above all we need to see that it is God upon whom we must depend. In answer to prayer the grace of our Lord Jesus Christ will be granted to us as it was to St. Paul.

Friday of the Twenty-third Week (II)

Sports in many forms have been a part of human life for at least as long as history can record. The city of Corinth during Paul's time hosted Olympic-type games every two years. The prizes were not money or even gold medals but only honorary crowns made of pine branches. Paul reflected on how much discipline and effort were required to win a mere wreath destined only to wither. Even if he had known of the millions of dollars paid to professional athletes these days, he would have considered the sum as nothing compared with the imperishable crown granted by the Lord Jesus to his faithful followers.

His conclusion is obvious. If athletes are willing to sacrifice so much for something which is ultimately without significance, how much more should we be willing to give everything for Christ!

If Paul were living in our times, he would have many more

examples. He could speak of the business man engaged in the rat race of struggling for advancement whose reward turns out to be a severe case of ulcers or perhaps a nervous breakdown. He could refer to the politician stepping over other people to get to the top only to find his ambition cut short by a heart attack.

The question at the moment is: would St. Paul find a similar kind of example in our lives? We must constantly ask ourselves: what are our goals, where are we headed, what are we dedicated to in life? Even granting there are many things which we must do in the ordinary course of daily life without any thought of false ambition, we need to consider the motive behind these things. Are they done out of love for God and because they are his will for us?

Daily Mass is the best means to keep us on the right track. The word of God instructs us. Our prayers help us to keep God and his will in mind. And the Eucharist strengthens us to reach for the crown which is imperishable.

Saturday of the Twenty-third Week (I)

St. Paul saw himself as a living example of the gospel message of God's merciful understanding and forgiveness. We may feel that Paul was exaggerating when he declared that he was the worst of sinners. It is not for us to debate the accuracy of his judgment because his point was not to emphasize his sinfulness but God's forgiveness. It was revealed to Paul that Jesus came into the world to save sinners. His feeling was that if God could forgive him, God could forgive anyone.

Just as we do not judge Paul's sinfulness, so the Church does not judge our personal guilt. Guilt is a matter of conscience for each one of us. The Church does declare, however, that we are all sinners in one way or another. We ought to see that we have received God's mercy and that it is because of his forgiveness that we have entered into a relationship of love with him which we celebrate here in the Eucharist.

At the beginning of Mass we are invited, in varied ways, to acknowledge with Paul that we are sinners who have received God's mercy. This is the purpose of the penitential rite. It is not a time for an examination of conscience. That we should do every night before retiring (cf. the directive at the beginning of official Night Prayer in the Liturgy of the Hours). In the few moments alloted to the pause during the penitential rite, we should not be trying to think of specific sins. Rather we should acknowledge in our hearts that as sinners we have been dealt with mercifully by God, and we ought to rejoice that God has sent his Son as savior so that we may enter into a union of love with our heavenly Father. It is this union of love which we celebrate in the Eucharist.

> (*Note to the homilist: Unfortunately "agnoscamus peccata nostra" has been translated as "Let us call to mind our sins." That suggests an examination of conscience. A correct translation would be "Let us acknowledge our sinfulness."*)

Saturday of the Twenty-third Week (II)

A man owned and operated a delicatessen all of his adult life. He and his family lived in the back of the store. Now on his death bed he called for his wife, his daughters and his sons. His wife assured him that everyone was there. In a last supreme effort, he raised his head from his pillow and asked, "If everyone is here, who's out front watching the store?"

A man who knows that he is about to die thinks of many things. Uppermost in his thoughts is whatever is closest to his heart. Jesus on the night before he was to die prayed earnestly to his Father, but he also thought of us, his followers. His heart overflowed with love and an intense desire that we be united with him and each other. He wanted this union to be more than mere sentiment, unlike that which a youngster might feel for a sport hero. He wanted the union to be real, like that which exists among the parts of a human body.

And so on the night before he died Jesus left us for all time the gift of his body and blood in the Eucharist. The Eucharist is called the effective sign of the unity of the Church, which is to say that its purpose is to form us into one body, one spirit in Christ. His body makes us one body, filled with his life granted us by his blood. Before receiving communion we hear the minister declare, "The Body of Christ." These words are a serious, theological pun. They refer to Christ in the Eucharist and to Christ in us, his mystical body, the Church. We speak of receiving the Eucharist as communion, and that is quite accurate, for through the Eucharist we come into communion with him and each other.

To be true to the meaning of the Eucharist, we must love Christ and one another. In another context St. Paul observes a truth which applies, not only to spouses but to members of the Church: "no one hates his own flesh; he nourishes it and takes care of it" (Ep 6:29). The Eucharist calls us to a life of unity and love, for through the Eucharist we all become one body, one spirit in Christ.

Monday of the Twenty-fourth Week (I)

In the liturgy the Church heeds the command of the Holy Spirit as found in the first reading through the words of St. Paul: "I urge that petitions, prayers, intercessions, and thanksgivings be offered for all men. . . . Prayer of this kind is good, and God our savior is pleased with it, for he wants all men to be saved and come to know the truth."

The Prayer of the Faithful, following the homily, is intended to be intercessions for the benefit of the whole world. As such it is a generous kind of prayer and reflects an expansive spirit which excludes no one from its concern. These intercessions are prayed in union with Jesus Christ who "opened his arms on the cross" to embrace all mankind in his love. They express the "catholic," the universal aspect of our prayer. When spontaneous prayers are offered, they should not neglect this universal concern. For example, one may be mindful of a relative who is to be operated on; his prayer might possibly be phrased in this or a similar way: "For my cousin who is to undergo surgery tomorrow and for all those who are seriously ill, we pray."

This prayer expresses not only our concern but also our faith. Ours should be a faith like that of the centurion in today's gospel, who believed that even a word from Jesus was sufficient to cure his servant.

I think we can all admire mothers of large families who never seem to have a moment for themselves. No doubt they long for a little peace and for precious time in which to be alone, but how beautiful is their unselfish dedication to those who need them. The Church like a good mother is filled with deep love and care for all her children. In the liturgy we are called to share in this love and care of the Church, for God wills that all men be saved and come to know the truth.

Monday of the Twenty-fourth Week (II)

Today's first reading contains the oldest written account we have of the institution of the Eucharist, older even than that found in the gospels. Ironically the account was occasioned by the fact that the Corinthians were abusing the meaning of the Eucharist. There is no suggestion that they doubted the reality of Christ's presence; rather they violated the purpose of his presence.

First there were factions among the Corinthians, cliques of favorites which brought about divisions in the community, despite the fact that receiving the Eucharist was intended to make them one in Christ. In the meal which preceded the Eucharist at that time some ate and drank too much, in contrast to the sacrificial spirit of Jesus manifested by his death which they were commemorating. Finally some were not willing to share their food with others who were in need even though they were celebrating the generosity of Jesus who gave everything, even his life, out of love for his brothers and sisters.

The Eucharist demands much more than external devotion in its celebration. Its meaning requires a response in life, a response which is manifested by love, unselfishness and generosity. In fact, one reason Jesus has given us the Eucharist is that it is so difficult for us to rise above the weaknesses of human nature in order to achieve these ideals.

It is necessary that we recognize our weakness and our need for the strength which Jesus alone can give. That is why the Church has adapted the words of the centurion in today's gospel (more precisely the version found in Mt 8:8) for our use just before communion: "Lord, I am not worthy to receive you, but only say the word and I shall be healed."

These words acknowledge not only our need. They also express faith that union with Jesus and each other can and should lead to a life of love, unselfishness and generosity.

Tuesday of the Twenty-fourth Week (I)

Jesus as Savior was a man not only of power but of sensitivity and compassion. When he saw the funeral procession leaving the city of Naim, he sized up the situation in a moment. Here was a widowed mother about to bury her only child. Jesus realized that the most difficult time for the mother was not at this moment of burial. The really difficult time would follow when she must return to an empty house alone.

His compassion, then, went out not to the boy who had died, but to the mother who would be left all alone. It is not far-fetched to imagine that he saw in his mind another widow about to bury her only son. That woman was his own mother. It is no wonder that he was moved with pity. The high point of the gospel occurs, not when Jesus raises the boy to life, but when he gives him back alive to his mother.

The large crowd participating in the funeral witnessed the compassionate act of Jesus. They were struck with awe, and they gave praise to God. These people are models for us in our worship, especially here at Mass.

God the Father has given us in his Son a savior who is not only powerful, but compassionate. Jesus understands our human feelings and needs. He himself has shared in them. Like the crowd we are called to give praise and thanks to God for the great gift of his Son.

Tuesday of the Twenty-fourth Week (II)

Almost everyone is familiar with the story of the conversion of St. Paul when he was on his way to Damascus to persecute Christians. He was thrown to the ground by a blinding light and he heard a voice say, "Why do you persecute me?" Paul asked, "Who are you, sir?" And the voice of the Lord responded, "I am Jesus, the one you are persecuting" (Ac 9:5). Paul had been persecuting Christians, but Jesus identified himself with his followers.

This event shaped Paul's thinking and understanding. It gave him a deep insight into the relationship between Christ and Christians. In fact, when in his writings he used the name, "Christ," he almost always meant Jesus, not in isolation, but in union with his followers, the Church.

Some of the Corinthians had taken pride in their charismatic gifts and entered into rivalry with one another to determine who was the more important. To Paul these reactions made no sense. He asked the Corinthians to consider that a human body was made up of many parts which formed a single whole. One part is not more important than another since all work together for the good of the whole body. He then declared that it was so with Christ. Remember that by "Christ" he meant the Church, the union of Christ and his people.

In the Church it does not matter whether one is Jew or Greek, slave or free, a prophet, a healer or a speaker in tongues. All have become one in Christ, united by his one Spirit, just as all the parts of the body form one whole. We are the body of Christ. It is he who acts within us. It is he with whom we are in contact when we are in contact with each other.

No one should have an inferiority complex in the Church. No one need compare himself with another. We are important to God and loved by him because Christ lives within us.

Wednesday of the Twenty-fourth Week (I)

Today's gospel breathes forth frustration on the part of Jesus. He felt that no matter what he did he could not please some people—no doubt a feeling we have all had at some time. The problem was that, although Jesus was divine, his humanity was a stumbling block for many of his contemporaries.

By the time the letter to Timothy was written, many people had overcome any stumbling block. Was it merely that with the passage of time Jesus somehow loomed larger in their view than he had in the eyes of those who saw him in person? That kind of thing has happened with some national heroes, such as Washington and Lincoln. Such is not the explanation given in the letter to Timothy.

This letter quotes from a composition which had apparently become an early Christian hymn. Two of the verses state that Jesus was "vindicated in the spirit . . . (and) believed in throughout the world." To vindicate means to clear someone completely. It also refers to a judgment which has been borne out by subsequent events. This is the work of the Holy Spirit in relation to Jesus. The Holy Spirit helped the Church to reflect on the life of Jesus, especially his death and resurrection, in the light of faith. His coming into the world and all the events of his public ministry are understood only through the subsequent events of his death and resurrection, the paschal mystery.

In the paschal mystery God the Father exalted Jesus in glory and proclaimed his true identity as his divine Son. In faith we are called to believe that the man who died is manifested as the true Son of God in the glory of his resurrection. This is God's wisdom, which is vindicated by all who accept it.

Wednesday of the Twenty-fourth Week (II)

Probably more words have been written about love than any other reality. It is the constant subject of poems and songs and the theme of novels and movies. And yet few things are more elusive. St. Paul was determined to put love into practical terms.

The situation was that the Corinthians were taking pride in the charismatic gifts such as speaking in tongues, prophesying, and healing. He urged the Corinthians to seek the greater gifts which are included in Christian love. Then he became practical. By love he did not mean some ethereal and nebulous feeling. Nothing could be more down to earth than his words, "Love is patient; love is kind. . . .There is no limit to love's forebearance, to its trust, its hope, and its power to endure."

It has often been observed that where Paul wrote the word "love," the name of Christ can be inserted: "Christ is patient; Christ is kind. . . .There is no limit to Christ's forebearance, to his trust, his hope, his power to endure." This substitution is in accord with Paul's thinking. For him a Christian is one in union with Christ. When a Christian acts, he must act as Christ does—with love. One might even say that the Christ within us yearns to have us allow him to love others through our humanity. He wants to love with our hearts, to embrace others with our arms, and to serve his brothers and sisters with our hands. He wishes to continue to go about doing good through us, the members of his body.

Our love must be practical in the down-to-earth manner described by St. Paul. And yet a life of love will lift us even now above mere human existence. Here on earth our lives will already share with Christ in the blessedness of the heavenly kingdom.

Thursday of the Twenty-fourth Week (I)

There are many touching events in the gospel, and the one we have just seen is surely among them. At first it is hard to know whether one is more impressed by the humility and faith of the woman or by the warmth and compassion of Jesus. In contrast to both the woman and Jesus is the Pharisee in his self-righteousness.

We know that we must not be self-righteous as was that Pharisee. We also know that, like the woman, we can humbly approach Jesus with faith that he will always welcome us, no matter what our sin may be. We are assured that he will offer us forgiveness. Perhaps it does not occur to us that we are called to be like Jesus in his welcome of the woman.

In the first reading Timothy is urged to be a continuing example of love, faith and purity. St. Paul could just as easily have told Timothy to be like Jesus in the gospel today. Although Timothy was a bishop, the message is applicable to all of us. We do not pretend to be saints, but we are good people who are constantly trying to come closer to God by means of daily Mass. God hopes that people like us will be living examples of his Son's love and forgiveness, especially toward those who do not regularly have this Son presented to them in the Scriptures. If people do not hear of Christ through the scriptures, they can come to know him through our example. We must be living signs to others of the goodness of God which we ourselves believe in and have experienced. Like Timothy we are called to be a continuing example of love, faith and purity.

Thursday of the Twenty-fourth Week (II)

Today and for the next two days our first reading is from the fifteenth chapter of St. Paul's letter to the Corinthians, the high point of his presentation to them. The resurrection is at the very heart of the Christian message. The reason is that the resurrection was the culmination of the whole life of Jesus on this earth, the meaning of his coming not only for himself but for us.

Life is the most precious gift we have. Everything depends on it. We can begin to appreciate life by reflecting on its opposite, which is death. Death means an end to all activity. Lips which smiled and spoke words of life are stilled in death. Hands which formed and shaped the gifts of the earth for useful purposes become stiff and cold. The human brain which could reach toward infinity is suddenly reduced to nothing more than a mass of corrupting tissue. How awesome and fearful is death! But is it really the end?

God created us to be immortal, but sin caused death. The only way to overcome death is to overcome sin. Now the Son of God enters the human scene. What Jesus did for the woman in the gospel is an example of what he does for all of us. Forgiving her sins, however, was only the beginning. She did not realize that by wiping out her sins Jesus was granting her the gift of everlasting life. Jesus became the conqueror of sin by vanquishing its effect, which is death. He triumphed over sin and death in his resurrection. His struggle against sin seemed to end in failure when he died, but the fact that he rose to the fullness of life manifested that he had actually conquered death. Death could not hold him. Nor will it hold us. Though we will die a physical death, we will rise with Christ to the fullness of life.

Friday of the Twenty-fourth Week (I)

The early Church faced problems from two main groups of people. On the one hand were Jewish converts, who were the first to believe in Christ. Some of these converts made the mistake of thinking that to be a Christian one had to observe all of the old Jewish customs and laws. On the other side were Gentiles, most of whom had been pagans. Some of these people were tempted to return to their former way of life which was not in accord with Christian doctrine or practice.

St. Paul was absolutely adamant that all Christians, whether Jews or Gentiles, hold to the sound doctrines of Jesus Christ. He was so insistent that some found him annoying or even unreasonable. But he refused to back down.

Today we face similar issues in the Church, and most of them are extremely delicate. Some people want to harp back to older practices and approaches which they knew as children. Others seem to think that the Church still has not caught up with the modern world and is hopelessly out of date.

The Second Vatican Council, an authentic and official source of the sound doctrines of Jesus Christ, wished to do two things: it wanted to have the Church return to the pristine doctrine and practice of the Church, while making that doctrine and practice meaningful for people of our own times. Some Catholics have ventured to call into question the authority of the Council, whereas others have dared to abuse the Council for their own purposes. In a few moments I cannot establish what is the heart of the matter, but I can urge all of us to pray that we may be docile to the authentic teaching and directives of the Church.

With this docility we can be devoted, as were the women in today's gospel, to the person of Jesus Christ.

Friday of the Twenty-fourth Week (II)

In the days when railroad travel was common, people would go to the station to await the arrival of loved ones. They would look down the track with eagerness and when they saw the light of the locomotive in the distance they would cry out, "Here she comes." With no need to think about such an obvious thing, they knew that if the locomotive was arriving the coaches would be right behind it.

Although railroad trains were unknown to St. Paul, this illustration exemplifies what he had in mind in today's reading about the resurrection. Some of the Corinthians had fallen into the error of denying that people would rise from the dead. St. Paul warned them that their position was untenable as Christians. He insisted: "If there is no resurrection of the dead, Christ himself has not been raised." Belief in the resurrection of Christ is essential to the Christian faith, but in Paul's mind to deny our resurrection is to deny Christ's resurrection. The reason for his stance is that the two resurrections are inseparably bound. The Risen Christ leads us to resurrection as surely as a locomotive draws the coaches into the railroad station.

Paul's position is in accord with his fundamental doctrine that Christ and his followers form one body. We are part of Christ, members of his body, his mystical body, the Church. Paul's own analogy is that Christ is the first fruits of those who have died. In Jewish worship the offering of the first fruits of the harvest to God was the symbol that the entire harvest was dedicated to God. God sees all of us as dedicated to himself through Christ, and the love which moved him to raise his son from the dead will reach out to us as well on the day of resurrection.

The coach which somehow becomes uncoupled from the rest of the train will indeed not arrive. Jesus gives us the means to remain joined to him, and this means is his body and blood. The eucharist is our pledge that we will not become separated from Christ, that we too will rise from the dead as he has done before us.

Saturday of the Twenty-fourth Week (I)

Today's first reading is basically a call to perseverance. We are urged to keep God's commands without blame until Christ comes again. A compelling call to perseverance is a rather constant theme of sacred scripture, and necessary it is. It is part of human nature to grow weary, to tire of doing good, to wish for some relief from constant effort.

Our own particular age seems to be one in which a sense of perseverance is singularly lacking. We are always looking for something new, something different, with little patience for sticking to both large and small commitments. In another era, for example, people had difficulties in their married lives but the last thing they thought of was a divorce. Now with many people it is the first thing they think of. In a former age people went to Mass Sunday after Sunday without expecting any variety. Now many people quickly become bored despite efforts to make a Mass more interesting. And in the long run the idea of persevering for a whole lifetime in accord with the teachings of Christ strikes many as not only undesirable but impossible.

Actually it is here in the Mass that we find the strength we need. Daily we hear the word of God, a seed which we hope is falling upon good ground. That word daily gives renewed meaning and purpose to our lives. Here in the Mass we also receive a nourishment for God's word, the body and the blood of Jesus Christ. That nourishment helps God's word to grow within us so that it can become a guiding force in our lives. That guiding force is the push we need to persevere until Christ comes again.

Saturday of the Twenty-fourth Week (II)

What resurrection from the dead will mean for us we are not absolutely certain. Some people wonder how God will restore to life a body which has corrupted in the grave, or which has been reduced to ashes by cremation, or which has been lost at sea and has been devoured by the great fish of the deep. In fact some skeptics scoff at the idea of resurrection as an impossibility.

St. Paul encountered this kind of skepticism and answered it. His answer did not completely solve the problem, which is truly a mystery of God, but he put the question into perspective by appealing to human experience. He asked the Corinthians to think about a seed which is planted in the ground in a form of death like a person who is buried. That which rises from what can be called the grave of the earth is not just a seed, but a full blown plant, There is an identity of the plant with the seed, but the differences are much greater than the similarities. Nourished by water and soil and energized by the sun the seed undergoes an amazing transformation. We take the facts of agriculture for granted, but the first person to plant a seed must have found it difficult to believe that a beautiful, magnificent tree was the result of an insignificant, tiny seed.

Resurrection for us will be something like that. Nourished by the body and blood of the Lord and energized by his life-giving spirit, we will rise to a new life, body and soul. We will be the same person, but the differences between what we are now and what we will then be are beyond our powers to imagine.

Some people believe only what their minds can grasp. God is much greater than the human mind. It is not foolish to believe in the resurrection. It is foolish to confine God's power to the petty limits of our human imagination.

Monday of the Twenty-fifth Week (I)

In the sixth century before Christ the temple in Jerusalem was destroyed by the Babylonian armies and the people were sent off into exile, far from their homeland with all its promise of God's love and protection.

It was a bleak period for the people, a time in which they were severely tempted to abandon God completely. Then, in his own unique way God acted. Cyrus, the king of Persia and himself a pagan, conquered Babylon in the year 539. The Jews in an agony of anticipation waited to see what their fate would be under the new king. Much to their surprise the following year King Cyrus not only permitted but actually encouraged the Jews to return home and rebuild the temple.

This extraordinary action of the king was due not to his munificence but to the intervention of God. The first reading declares that the Lord inspired King Cyrus to issue the proclamation of freedom.

The point of the reading is that God is in charge. He directs the course of world events. And he does so according to his own wisdom. We may wonder how God allows atheistic communism to attempt to blot out religion in places like Russia and Poland. We may well be confused as to how God permits a government to sanction, and in some instance financially support, the atrocity of abortion.

Today's reading calls us as those who hear the word of God to have faith that he is very much in control. In his inscrutable wisdom he grants freedom whereby some choose evil rather than good, but through evil he somehow works his will for ultimate good. Even the personal evil and suffering which we experience in our lives should not turn us away from faith in the goodness of God. God came to the rescue of his people of old through King Cyrus, a pagan, and he is always directing our lives toward good by means best chosen by himself.

Monday of the Twenty-fifth Week (II)

A man's car simply went dead on a busy street. He raised the hood and began a fruitless search for the problem. Motorists swerved around him, blowing their horns and hurling verbal unpleasantries at him. The man insists that he counted over one hundred cars which passed him by before someone paused, rolled down his window and asked if he needed help.

Apparently the drivers of the cars which passed by had not heard the word of God from the book of Proverbs, "Refuse no one the good on which he has a claim when it is in your power to do it for him." Perhaps they felt they were too busy to stop, but in that case they needed to heed these words of God, "Say not to your neighbor, 'Tomorrow I will give,' when you can give at once."

Jesus in the gospel implies that we are like a lamp. Obviously a lamp is useless if it lies hidden under a bushel basket. Its purpose is to give light so that people may see in the darkness. Jesus does not want us to hide our goodness. He wants us to reach out in love and service of others. Of course there are many more examples than that of the man with the dead car, and we probably need not look far for those who need our help.

What we should remember is that goodness toward others is expected of us in response to God's goodness toward ourselves. Our situation was much more serious and frightening than having a car stop on a busy street. We were dead in sin. Unable to recover or even to cry out for assistance, we were completely helpless. But God did not pass us by. He was not too busy or cold hearted to come to our aid. He sent his own Son to restore us to life. What God has done for us should motivate us in our love and service of others.

Tuesday of the Twenty-fifth Week (I)

I think it is difficult for us to appreciate the jubilation reflected in today's first reading. After the Jews returned to their homeland from exile in Babylon (yesterday's reading) in the year 538 B.C., things were not immediately glorious for them. Particularly lacking was the temple which had been destroyed by the Babylonian armies. It was not until twenty-three years later, in 515 B.C. that the construction of the new temple was completed.

The temple was the very heart of Judaism. It was the political and social, as well as the religious, center of life. It was like a combination of Washington, D.C., New York City, and the Vatican all rolled into one. The temple was also a sign of God's presence and his providential care of his people. Above all the temple had become the only place where the supreme, official act of sacrificial worship could be offered to God.

Jesus Christ replaced the building which was the temple with his own person. He became the Christian temple. Authentic worship of God is not confined to a building in the Christian era. It is offered through, with and in the person of Jesus Christ. To himself Jesus calls those who hear the word of God and act upon it. They enter into a union with him which enjoys the intimacy one has with his mother and his brothers and sisters. People of faith offer a worship in spirit and in truth through Jesus Christ. That worship is the Mass.

Whether the Mass be offered amid all the splendors of St. Peter's Basilica in Rome by the Pope himself, or here in our own parish church, it is the same Mass, the same worship, because Jesus Christ, and not a building, is our temple.

We ought to experience a real jubilation that we are privileged, even daily, to offer the worship of the Mass to our heavenly Father in union with Jesus Christ.

Tuesday of the Twenty-fifth Week (II)

Sometimes a wife will complain to her husband, "You never say you love me any more." The husband usually responds, "You know I love you. I work hard at my job for you and the kids. That shows that I love you." And yet the wife quite rightly would like to hear it in words. On the other hand, the situation is much worse when a man uses words of love which are hollow because he does not back them up by action.

The people of the Old Testament for the most part were pretty faithful about their acts of worship. In other words, they reverently expressed their love for God through prayers and ritual. But often their lives did not reflect their worship of God. That is why the prophets frequently had to admonish the people that external worship was not enough. That sentiment is expressed in the book of Proverbs today: "To do what is right and just is more acceptable to the Lord than sacrifice." Jesus had much the same idea in mind when he said, "My sisters and brothers are those who hear the word of God and act upon it."

To participate in the Mass is to tell God that we love him and wish to dedicate ourselves to doing his will. We need a sound relationship between worship and life. Worship must lead to Christian living. We must also recognize that participation in the Mass is the source of strength for Christian living. A husband and wife who sincerely show love for one another find strength to live for each other. Expression of love is their lifeline for a good marriage and the Mass is our lifeline for a happy relationship with God.

Worship and Christian living go together. The one is incomplete without the other.

Wednesday of the Twenty-fifth Week (I)

Today's first reading may sound negative and depressing. Ezra felt like the wretch mentioned in the song, *Amazing Grace*. With shame he listed the failings of his people and admitted guilt before the Lord.

Actually this reading breathes forth a spirit of both faith and trust in God. Imagine the difference in the situation of a man accused in a court of law. He has enlisted a lawyer to defend him at no small fee. Surely the lawyer will not admit the crimes of his client before the judge. He will be at pains either to excuse his client or to protest that there is no proof against him. As long as there is the slightest hope of not being judged unfavorably, he will plead that he is not guilty. In a court of law one can expect not mercy but only justice. Proven guilt is met with a sentence in proportion to the crime committed.

Think now of the contrast between the lawyer in court and Ezra, the representative of his people, in the presence of God. Although ashamed, he did not hesitate to admit guilt and to plead for mercy.

He approached God with an optimism born of previous experience. He recalled how God had shown mercy to his people by rescuing them from bondage in Babylon.

We can approach God with the same optimism. Each one of us has in his own way experienced God's mercy, but all of us look back upon the great event we celebrate in the Mass, the shedding of Christ's blood so that sins may be forgiven. Our God is a God of mercy and compassion. No matter what our failing, we can approach him with faith and trust.

Wednesday of the Twenty-fifth Week (II)

Today's first reading contains a very brief prayer. Half of it is easy to say and mean; half of it is very difficult. That brief prayer is: "Lord, give me neither poverty nor riches." Nobody wants to live in poverty, but riches may be another matter.

The wise author of the book of Proverbs asked that God provide him with only the necessities of life. Riches frightened him and for good reason. In fact, Jesus himself gave stern warnings about the danger of riches. For the affluent it is much too easy to think that they can be independent of God. When Jesus sent the disciples on a missionary journey, he did not want them to take all kinds of provisions with them. His intention was that they should learn complete dependence on God.

Some people maintain that it is easy for a priest to preach about the danger of riches. After all, he does not have a family to support. But the message is not really mine or that of any priest. It is the message of God through his inspired word in the Bible, and we must take it seriously.

Today we joined with the psalmist in protesting to God, "The law of your mouth is to me more precious than thousands of gold and silver pieces." Do we really mean that? The expression, "Law of God," in the Bible means God's will. We are called to place ourselves, as Jesus did, completely in the hands of God and to say and mean with Jesus, "Not my will, but yours be done."

God does not want us to live in destitution so that we must

literally wonder where our next meal is coming from. That way of surviving is not his will. But he does want us to recognize that he is the source of every good gift. He is happy to respond to our sincere prayer, "Lord, give me neither poverty nor riches."

Thursday of the Twenty-fifth Week (I)

Today and tomorrow we have readings from the prophet Haggai. He was concerned with the reconstruction of the temple and the renewal of authentic religion after the people returned from exile in Babylon.

A certain lethargy and disinterest concerning the temple had overtaken the people. Particularly distressing to Haggai was the fact that those who had material means refused to contribute to the building of the temple. He felt that they were more concerned with their own comfort than they were in providing a suitable place for the worship of the Lord. Filled with indignation Haggai accused the people of being preoccupied with fleeting pleasures, which he graphically presented in images such as that of eating without being satisfied and of putting earnings in a bag with holes in it.

One is tempted to say that the lesson for us is to see the necessity of contributing to the Church. And that would indeed be a valid lesson. On the other hand, our faith tells us that Jesus Christ has replaced the temple. Our faith also teaches us that what is done to the members of the mystical body of Christ is done to Christ himself. The temple of Christ's body in a real sense is made up of living stones—people. We are called to be concerned about those people who are in need.

We should take Haggai's words as another challenge to practical Christianity. We are not hedonists, people who make pleasure their God. But is it not true that we are surrounded by strong influences, such as the commercials we see on TV, which would make hedonists of us all? Have we succeeded sufficiently in defending ourselves against the spirit of consumerism? Have we allowed ourselves to be convinced that we are interested in only the necessities of life when perhaps we have made a necessity of luxuries? Are we willing to contribute generously to the temple of Christ's body, his mystical body, those people who need what we can give?

Thursday of the Twenty-fifth Week (II)

The first reading today is the bleakest and most pessimistic passage in the entire Bible. Although the author believed in God, he was of the view that it is impossible to make much sense of life. A blind trust in God is needed. He saw life as vanity. The Hebrew word which he used means a breath. By this word he wished to say that life is something unsubstantial, fleeting or transitory. There is, in other words, nothing to life.

We can best understand this passage by seeing it as a view of life without God, especially without the revelation of Jesus Christ. A great truth has come to us about human existence not only by the teachings of Jesus but simply by the fact that, though divine, he chose to become human like us in all things but sin. By becoming human Jesus showed that there is a deep value to human existence.

Most of us lead rather simple lives. We can make no pretense to having an effect on the course of history such as do presidents and dictators. We do our work, eat and sleep, have a little free time for the honest pleasures of life, and before we know it our allotted time on this earth will have passed. Our names will not be recorded in history books. But we are in God's mind and in his heart.

During the half time of an NFL championship football game there was a punt, pass, and kick competition for young boys. Most of the fans were bored. What the children were doing could not compare with the play of the professionals whom the fans had come to watch. To one young couple the actions of an eight year old on the field were vastly more important than the outcome of the game. The eight year old was their son.

We are God's children, made like his divine Son who became human. He loves us as only devoted parents can love their children.

He takes delight in us as he took delight in the life of Jesus. What really counts is not what we do, but who we are.

Friday of the Twenty-fifth Week (I)

Haggai, the prophet, was deeply concerned about the rebuilding of the temple because it was the sign of the relationship between God and his people. He promised great blessings for those who would generously take part in the noble work of restoring the temple to its pristine splendor.

We surely should be concerned about our places of worship, and yet, as we saw yesterday, the Christian temple is a person, Jesus Christ. And Jesus as the temple of God has drawn to himself living stones, who are his people. In answer to the question of Jesus, "Who do you say that I am?" we can respond, "You are the Christ, the Son of the Living God, united with all your people."

If there be a single idea of supreme importance to come forth from the Second Vatican Council, it is that the Church is a body of people united with Jesus Christ. We cannot be truly dedicated to the glory of Christ without a concern for him as he is found in people, especially people who are in need.

The building up of the Christian temple means coming to the help of people. Do we not all know friends or relatives who are no longer practicing their faith? We must do what we can to join them once again to the temple of Christ as active Catholics. Is someone seriously ill? We must pray for such a person, but we should also take the time to visit him in order to pray *with* him and to help him in any way possible. Does a friend need only an ear willing to listen to a deep, personal problem? Putting aside our own schedule or convenience for such a person is a way of contributing to the temple of Christ's body.

In caring for the people who form with Christ a living temple, we will receive blessings from the Lord.

Friday of the Twenty-fifth Week (II)

We say that time heals all wounds. When we are uncertain about the outcome of some event, we reluctantly admit that time will tell. The author, Thomas Mann, wrote that time cools and clarifies our moods. Of course time does none of these things, but it is the condition in which they happen.

Time is God's gift. Many of us complain that we do not have enough time, but for at least some of us nothing would get done if we had all the time in the world. How we use time is more important than how much time we have. Jesus in a relatively short span of life founded the Church and accomplished the salvation of the world.

The fact is that we almost always find time for what we like or want to do. We should consider how many hours a day we consume in reading the papers or in watching television. Some of that time is needed to keep up with events and to enjoy needed relaxation, but we must judge whether we are using time well.

In a fast moving, noisy world most of us need time for peace and quiet to pray and to reflect on life and its values. For at least some part of the day we need to shut off the radio and the stereo and the television. We need to lay aside our newspapers and magazines and other distractions. We must make time to be alone with God.

The most important moments of the day are those here at Mass, but even the Mass does not exhaust our relationship with God. The Mass is worship by and with the community. It is God's family at prayer. But each of us is an individual with particular needs. Alone with God we should tell him of our personal failure and success, our joys and our sorrows, our worries and concern. And we need to listen, to open our minds to hear God speaking to us in quiet.

Life is short. It would be a shame to waste it on meaningless activity. The book of Proverbs tells us that there is a time for everything, but time by itself accomplishes nothing. It is an opportunity, nothing more. It is up to us to use our time well for what really counts in life.

Saturday of the Twenty-fifth Week (I)

The prophet Zechariah was deeply impressed by the rebuilding of the temple as a sign of God's favor toward his people. He was convinced that the Lord would not only be the true protector of his people but also that a day was coming when many nations would join themselves to the Lord.

We are the people of that new day. When Jesus Christ was delivered into the hands of men and underwent death on the cross, he shed his blood for all men of all times and all places. When his life ended a new era began. Now the true faith is not limited to one people or one place. All the nations revere the name of the Lord.

At this weekday Mass we are but a small number. And yet we should never forget that we are joined with a vast number of faithful people throughout the world. Though we never see them all or even know their names, though their languages and customs differ from ours, we are all one through our faith in Christ Jesus. What we hold in common by means of faith is much more profound than any differences of language or culture.

Our union is not only with the living, but with all those who have gone before us in faith, both those in heaven and those in purgatory. In the Eucharistic prayer, following the consecration, we pray in union with the Church throughout the world, in purgatory and in heaven.

We are never alone. In faith we must lift our minds and hearts to the consoling realization that we are united as one people of God back through the centuries in space and time, up to heaven and back again to the whole earth. We are so united because we have one Lord, one faith, and one baptism, one God and Father of us all.

Saturday of the Twenty-fifth Week (II)

The meditation we heard today on the span of life is not unusual. Shakespeare in his play, *As You Like It*, wrote a similar meditation which begins with the familiar lines, "All the world's a stage, and all the men and women merely players. / They have their exits and their entrances; / And one man in his time plays many parts, / His acts being seven ages." He then goes on to describe the seven ages from infancy to old age and death. There is a feeling of hollowness about life in this passage, a quizzical attitude about its meaning.

Even Qoheleth, the author of the book of Proverbs, does not sound optimistic. The reason is that, despite his belief in God, he lived in an era when there was no clear understanding of an afterlife. The notion of a blessed immortality was not part of his thinking. If death is the end even the greatest accomplishments are but a fleeting satisfaction, lost forever in the darkness of the grave. The truth is that Jesus by his own death has overcome death. Through Jesus God the Father calls us to everlasting life.

The promise of immortality not only holds out a comforting hope for us; it also gives meaning to our present existence. We live in a "disposable" age. People use a paper plate and a plastic knife and fork at a picnic and then throw them away. Many drinks come in a disposable bottle to be used once and never again. After a disposable item has served its purpose, it is forgotten.

In God's eyes we are not disposable. The meaning of human life is indeed something of a mystery. At times it is hard to understand what the value is in getting up each morning to face another day of work. What is the worth of it all? It is when we wonder about the values of our lives that we must remember that God has a clear view which at best is obscure to us. If the meaning of human existence were not lasting, God would indeed dispose of us in death. But such is not the reality. We go to our rest in the hope, the conviction, of rising again. We believe that Christ will bring us into the eternal light of his presence (cf. Second Eucharistic Prayer).

Monday of the Twenty-sixth Week (I)

Zechariah preached during difficult times for the people, when they were discouraged and disheartened regarding any future for them as a nation. Nonetheless Zechariah saw in the rebuilding of the temple a sign of hope for the future.

To be a person of faith is to have hope in the future, based on a trust in God's goodness. Everyone likes to have something to look forward to. It may be the expectation of a long awaited vacation or something as simple as a nice dinner at the end of the day. Having something to look forward to adds zest to life and gives us the courage to carry on. Such should be the Christian attitude. We should look forward to better times in our personal lives and for the whole world. Ultimately the best times are to come in heaven.

Little children have something to teach us in this regard. Jesus wanted us to welcome children, which means not only to respect and love them but also to imitate them. Little children by necessity live lives which look to the future for the simple reason that childhood is a period of growing toward adulthood. Children, usually stimulated by questions from adults, think about what they want to be when they grow up. At times they may even daydream about being a fireman or a policeman or even a movie star.

Through all their dreams about the future most children live a life of serenity and patience. They are usually in no hurry to grow up. In fact, they tend to take it for granted that when they do grow up everything is going to be just fine for them. That attitude is not far from what should be our attitude, for it is an outlook which is filled with hope but free from anxiety.

In every Mass after the "Our Father" we pray that God will deliver us from all anxiety as we wait in joyful hope for the coming of our Savior, Jesus Christ. Peace and serenity should be ours as we look for something better to turn up for ourselves and for the whole world.

Monday of the Twenty-sixth Week (II)

Suffering is one of the most perplexing of human experiences. If only bad people suffered as a punishment for their badness and if good people were rewarded in this life for their goodness, there would be no problem. Justice would be served. But the fact is that often it seems that the good suffer while the bad do not.

The book of Job addresses this apparent injustice. Job represents all good people. His story is not factual. Rather it is like the parables which Jesus told and is intended to have a universal application. The details of Job's trials are not important. The author intended that we should identify ourselves with Job and adjust the specifics of the narrative to our own circumstances.

The book is a fascinating drama and has been converted into a successful play in modern circumstances by Archibald MacLeish. Generally it ruins a plot to tell the ending, but to appreciate the readings thoughout this week we ought to know how it turns out. After suffering almost every form of devastating adversity, Job does not arrive at a clear understanding of or a neat solution to the mystery of human suffering. Under God's promptings he comes to a blind act of faith. He concludes that he, a mere mortal, does not have the right to call into question the wisdom or the justice of an all wise and all good God.

His conclusion is all the more striking when we realize that this book was composed at a time when the revelation of a perfect life after death was not part of Israel's religion. We are called to less of a blind trust in God than was Job. Even though we must accept God's wisdom and justice, we have come to believe that through Jesus Christ we have the promise of everlasting life where every wrong will be righted and every tear washed away. Suffering is part of God's plan, a plan we cannot fully understand, but we do know that for us, as it did for Jesus, suffering leads to unending happiness with God.

Tuesday of the Twenty-sixth Week (I)

Zechariah looked forward to a day when Jerusalem would be a source of blessing not only for the Jews but for pagans as well. That hope has been fulfilled through the person of Jesus Christ in the Church.

Some people may think of the Church as a storehouse of graces to which we go in somewhat the same way in which a person goes to a larder or a refrigerator for food. While the Church has been given the great gift of the sacraments as a means of spiritual life, today we need to realize also that the Church as a source of blessings is to be identified with the people of faith. We are called to be a source of blessings to the whole world. To be a Catholic is to have a universal outlook, to go beyond the desire "to save my soul" to a concern for all of God's people.

Pope Pius XII, in his encyclical on the Church as the Mystical Body of Christ, wrote these stirring words: "Deep mystery this, subject of inexhaustible meditation, that the salvation of many depends on the prayers and sacrifices which the members of the Mystical Body make for this intention."

We should never underestimate our importance in God's plan. He wants to make us, through our prayers and sacrifices, a channel of his grace to the whole world. As good people we pray for our loved ones in need, but we should expand our vision. The needs we see in those who are close to us are multiplied many times over. Our concern for a family which has suffered a severe tragedy in the premature death of the father or mother should move us to pray not only for them, but for the untold numbers of people who are suffering from the same tragedy. When we see a friend who is confused and frustrated, one who has no faith or hope, we ought to pray not only for him but for all those in similar circumstances.

This is a deep mystery, but a great truth of our faith, that the salvation and well-being of many depends on our prayers and sacrifices.

Tuesday of the Twenty-sixth Week (II)

The meaning of words is conditioned by the circumstances in which they are used. In labor relations the word "strike" means that workers have refused to go to their jobs, but in baseball that same word has a completely different meaning. In contemporary world politics "Jerusalem" refers to a city surrounded by controversy and conflict. In St. Luke's gospel "Jerusalem" indicates not so much a city as it does the destiny of Jesus.

Throughout his story of Jesus' public ministry St. Luke pictured

Jesus on a relentless journey toward Jerusalem for it was there that through his death and resurrection he would achieve the salvation of the world. The mission of Jesus was an arduous one, requiring suffering and death, but Jesus eagerly looked forward to its completion. He struggled with and overcame any reluctance because he was filled with a sense of purpose.

Job, on the other hand, felt that he already had two strikes against him. He was so miserable in his misfortunes that he was tempted to go on strike against God. He was near despair because he could see no reason or purpose in his sufferings. It was through only a desperate and blind act of faith that he continued to cling to God.

Life is easier for us than it was for Job. Because Jesus has gone before us we have a clearer vision of the meaning of suffering and death. The Vatican Council teaches us that "Jesus blazed a trail and if we follow it, life and death are made holy and take on a new meaning" (*Church in the Modern World*, 22). With Jesus we too are on a journey. But our destiny will not be fulfilled in the earthly city of Jerusalem. It will be fulfilled with Jesus in the heavenly Jerusalem in union with his Father, our Father, who will grant us the gift of everlasting life.

Wednesday of the Twenty-sixth Week (I)

Nehemiah was a Jew who had risen to some prominence in the court of King Artaxerxes of Persia, but his heart was in his beloved city of Jerusalem. He received permission from the king to return to Jerusalem where practical problems needed to be solved.

Nehemiah was not a man of mere sentiment. He was a man of action, a person who had the kind of complete dedication called for by Jesus in the gospel. He saw to the rebuilding of the walls of Jerusalem, a construction necessary for the protection of the city and the temple. He also introduced administrative reforms for the purpose of inculcating the values of the Jewish religion. Perhaps most significant of all about Nehemiah is the fact that he was a layman. He stands as a magnificent example for all lay people today. He was generous in the dedication of his talents and his energies to the service of God and his people.

At one time in the Church it was supposed that the priest would do everything, and what he could not do, religious sisters or brothers would do. The climate since the Second Vatican Council is changing in this regard, and rightly so. Baptism is a strong commitment to be a follower of Christ, and it calls for the kind of total dedication which Jesus demands in today's gospel.

Involvement in ministry has been taking many forms. People have been devoting themselves to visiting the sick and as special ministers of the Eucharist bringing them holy communion. Others act as readers at Mass and perform other liturgical functions. This is as it should be. The truth is that all Catholics, by virtue of their baptism, should be involved in the service of God and his people. Such is the example of Nehemiah which is still valid for us today.

Wednesday of the Twenty-sixth Week (II)

In the midst of his suffering Job could have said, "With the kind of friends I have, who needs enemies?" Three of his friends came to console him but gradually consolation turned to accusation. They insisted with Job that he had to be guilty of some terrible sin to deserve such punishment from God. Job equally insisted that he was innocent and could not understand why misfortunes had overcome him.

The point made by Job's friends was that God is just; he rewards good and punishes evil. They were so sure of themselves that they were not willing to allow some aspect of mystery about God. They wanted to make life fit their own understanding. An important lesson of the story of Job is that God has other purposes than merely the exercise of strict justice, even though we may not fully understand what those purposes are. God asks that we trust him.

Some people find it difficult to trust anyone but themselves. For example, some people simply cannot trust a driver even if he is every bit as concerned about safety as anyone in the car. His being a good driver makes no difference. The untrusting person warns him to look out for a car on his left, urges him to slow down for a stop sign still in the distance, and in general is constantly telling him how he should be driving. This lack of trust annoys the driver, but a lack of trust in God is devastating to our relationship with him. God knows what he is doing and what he does is for the best.

Jesus called people to abandon everything and to follow him in complete trust as his disciples. What he demanded did not always appear to make sense, such as insisting that a man should leave the burial of his father to others. Job's suffering made no sense to him and many things about our lives make no sense to us either. Our faith in God is not complete if we do not trust his wisdom and his goodness.

Thursday of the Twenty-sixth Week (I)

After the return of the people from exile in Babylon, those parts of the Bible known as the Law of Moses, the first five books of the Bible, were discovered after a long loss. Ezra, the scribe, was a man who by his calling was devoted to the law. He was overjoyed that he could once more proclaim the authentic word of God to his people. The people heard this word with a sense of awe as well as enthusiasm.

Every day here at Mass we hear the word of God. During one part of the year the readings are from those sacred books discovered after the exile, but we are privileged to hear at weekday Mass many portions of the Bible from both the Old and the New Testaments. The readings we hear are sacred for they are the inspired word of God.

In one sense the priest is like Ezra. It is my privilege to unfold the word to you in these brief, simple homilies. Note, however, that a lay person proclaims the first reading as the lector. This is a sign that spreading the word of God is an office which is not confined to the priest alone. In fact, by virtue especially of the sacrament of confirmation, all lay people are commissioned to bear witness to God's word before others. All of us should be like the seventy-two in the gospel who were sent forth by Jesus to spread the good news. We are precious few here at daily Mass. From us who hear the scriptures should go forth a witness to God's word. This witness is by word and example. We will be like the seventy-two in the degree that we capture the spirit of enthusiasm manifested by Ezra in the first reading. If the word of God is sacred and meaningful to us, we will want to make the word come alive for others.

Thursday of the Twenty-sixth Week (II)

Probably one of the most depressing of all human experiences is to feel all alone. I do not mean being physically alone. Sometimes that is a sought after opportunity for a little peace and quiet. I refer to a situation in which there seems to be no one who understands and who cares about us. Three friends came to see Job in his time of suffering. Rather than console him they condemned him as guilty of some terrible sin which had brought God's wrath upon his head. Job was pushed to cry out to them, "Why do you hound me as though you were divine, and insatiably prey upon me?"

From the depth of his despair Job responded to a grace of God and rose to a supreme act of faith. Despite all that had befallen him and regardless of the accusations of his friends, he put his faith in God's goodness and said, "I know that my Vindicator lives." He was confident that God, like a wise and just judge, would announce his innocence.

Through all this Job had no clear vision of God. Rather he was like a blind man who senses, rather than sees, the presence of someone in a room. He was sure that his present blindness would be overcome and that he would see God. He came to believe that God had not abandoned him even for an instant.

Jesus sent his disciples on mission to preach in his name. Although they were physically separated from him, he was still with them. They were not alone. Nor are we alone, not even for an instant. It is not as if God sits upon a throne in the heavens, looking down upon the world with a bemused and distant interest in our affairs. Father, Son, and Spirit, have made us their living temple.

We may be blind to this divine presence within us, but like Job we have received the gift of faith which overcomes blindness. Alone? Never! Let us lift our hearts in faith to the caring presence of God within us.

Friday of the Twenty-sixth Week (I)

Trust in another person can take several forms. We may have confidence in a physician that he knows the proper way to treat an illness. With some people we are sure that we can always rely on their judgment to be sound and wise. With others we are certain that they would never betray us or talk behind our backs. All of these situations reflect trust, but perhaps the most profound form of trust is that which allows us to ask pardon from someone whom we have offended deeply. We believe that we can approach that person without fear of being rebuffed. We trust him.

The first reading today manifests a profound trust in God. The author, speaking in the name of all the people in exile, candidly admits guilt before God, a guilt which was the cause of the exile. There is no hesitation, no fear that whatever is said may be held against the people, no terror as if God were some implacable judge who is all too eager to impose the most dire sentence possible. His prayer is a beautiful testimonial of trust in God's goodness and compassion.

Frequently at the beginning of Mass during the penitential rite we recite the "I confess." It is a prayer like that of Baruch. We admit that we have sinned through our own fault. We make no excuses. If we have trust in God we need no excuses. We believe in God's goodness and compassion.

This same sentiment of trust should be ours whenever we celebrate the sacrament of penance. We need no fear, no apprehension. We ought never to think that God will rebuff us or treat us harshly.

There are many ways by which we show our trust in God, but one of the most beautiful is to ask his forgiveness when we have sinned.

Friday of the Twenty-sixth Week (II)

Rearing children is indeed a most difficult art. Modern experts in the subject urge parents to give explanations even to small children for the rules and regulations of the home. Children should receive, in accord with their ability to understand, the reasons why they are told to do or not to do something. And yet the fact is that the adult world is often so complicated that it is impossible for children to understand all that their parents require of them. One favorite word of most children is "why." To this one word question frequently there can be only a one word answer, "because"—because daddy or mommy knows best.

Job looked up to God in heaven and wanted to know why he had to suffer all that had befallen him. He simply could not accept the fact that he was sinful as were the evil cities which Jesus condemned in the gospel today. And so the persistent question continued, "Why?" After allowing Job to search for an answer as best he could, God finally spoke to Job. In essence God told Job that the answer to his question, "why," was "because"—because God knows best. There simply was no way in which Job, a mere mortal, could comprehend the actions of God who was responsible for the guidance and direction of the universe. God's domain, like the adult world for little children, is too complicated for us to comprehend.

Job in the end was moved to accept in faith the wisdom and the goodness of God. We have much more to go on than did Job. When we recognize that God not only created us out of love but actually sent his own son to lead us to eternal happiness, it should be easier for us to believe in his goodness. God does not change. He is not at one moment loving and hateful in the next. The love that is clear in the sending of his son is the same love by which he guides and directs all the aspects of our lives.

Saturday of the Twenty-sixth Week (I)

One of the most difficult things for us, especially as adults, is not to hold a grudge. Sometimes we continue to have enmity toward a person over a very long period of time, perhaps even after we can no longer clearly remember what the cause of the rift was. Little children are rarely that way. They can be fighting with one another one minute and the next minute they are playing together as the best of friends.

Jesus says that the Father has revealed to the merest children what he has hidden from the learned and the clever. Perhaps little children, untainted by adult practices, are open to receive God's own spirit of forgiveness, the ability to forget and so to forgive. God does not hold grudges. He is too big to do that. Sometimes we as adults imagine that God is like ourselves when we find it hard to forgive. We ought to realize that his spirit is found in the simplicity of a little child.

The reading from Baruch today reflects a beautiful appreciation of God's eagerness to forgive. The people had been guilty of abandoning God, no doubt about that. The prophet proclaims to the people: "Fear not, my children; call out to God!" His exhortation to repentance is devoid of any fear tactics. Rather it breathes forth a deep faith in the overwhelming goodness of God: "As your hearts have been disposed to stray from God, turn now ten times the more to seek him."

The God of forgiveness is worthy of thanks and praise. It is right that in this eucharist we lift our hearts to him in joyful recognition that in his forgiveness we experience what our God is truly like.

Saturday of the Twenty-sixth Week (II)

Most of us spend a lot of time in looking to the future: a vacation in the summer time, a few days off at Christmas, or just the relaxation at the end of the day. These times are something of a reward for all the long hours of work which we put in. Sometimes what we look forward to turns out to be a disappointment. A vacation is tainted by bickering and disagreement, Christmas is marred by an illness, and the end of the day means facing some family problems. Perhaps most discouraging of all is that a time of rest or pleasure to which we have looked forward for a long time passes in what seems to be an instant. It is over and gone, never to return.

Jesus today puts things into perspective by saying, "Rejoice that your names are inscribed in heaven." Now that fact really gives us something to look forward to. We have no clear idea of what heaven will be like. The truth is that heaven will far surpass anything we can imagine. There will be no disappointments. Best of all heaven is eternal. The goodness of the love of God which will fill us with joy will never fade.

Job, despite all his mysterious sufferings, came to accept God's will. He realized that he had dealt with great things he did not understand and repented of any resistance he had shown to God. The story ends with a restoration to Job of even more than he had lost. When the book of Job was written, there had been no clear revelation of a life after death. The author of the book, working with a limited degree of revelation, thought that temporal reward was the most a person could hope for.

We are in a better position. We have much more to look forward to. Because of the revelation of Jesus Christ, "we look for the resurrection of the dead and the life of the world to come."

Monday of the Twenty-seventh Week (I)

The Book of Jonah in the Bible, like the parable of the good Samaritan, is a story told to teach a lesson. We need not be concerned with what type of fish swallowed Jonah, or whether such a thing is possible, any more than we need be concerned with the name of the Samaritan who stopped along the road to help the person in distress. And the point of both stories is not dissimilar.

The Ninevites were not Jews, as was Jonah. They were pagans. Jonah was commanded by God to preach repentance to the people of Nineveh. Jonah tried to escape from his mission because he was actually afraid that the people would listen to his message and receive mercy from God. He did not want them to repent. He wanted God to limit himself to the Jews, and above all he did not want God to show any favor to the Ninevites, who were enemies of the Jews.

Jonah represents the narrow attitude of those Jews who could not bear the thought that God would favor pagans, but he stands for all people who are prejudiced against others, who want to make of religion a narrow circle of intimates. As we shall see tomorrow, God would not allow Jonah to remain a bigot. And in today's gospel Jesus holds up as a model the Samaritan who befriended his natural enemy, a Jew.

Some people seem to wonder why the Church gets involved in matters of social justice or human rights. They wince when they hear a sermon which calls them to love all peoples without exception. And they seem to hope that somehow it is not true that all men are called to salvation.

The paradoxical fact is that if there be one thing God is intolerant of, it is intolerance. We are expected to be like Jesus, who opened his arms on the cross to embrace all peoples of all times and places. We cannot truly love God if we do not love all of his people.

Monday of the Twenty-seventh Week (II)

Today's parable is among the best known of those preached by Jesus. The point is abundantly clear. Jesus wished to show that no one may be excluded from our love. The early Church fathers clearly understood the meaning of the parable, but some of them were interested in finding an answer to the question, "Who is the Good Samaritan?"

Their answer is that Jesus himself is the Good Samaritan. Implied in this answer is the idea that the Jew in need represents the entire human race. We are the ones on the journey from Jerusalem to Jericho. Along the way we were robbed of our friendship with God through sin and we lay along the roadside, stripped, beaten, and half dead. It was Jesus who entered our journey through his incarnation and who passed by our way during his own journey. He saw us lying alone by the roadside and responded to our need.

Jesus embraced us, dressed our wounds, and brought us to the inn, the Church. The price that he paid was not merely the two pieces of silver mentioned in the parable but his own life. That is what it means to say that Jesus is our Savior. It is to say that he is our personal Good Samaritan.

What Jesus did for the entire human race during his lifetime, he does for each of us living today through the Church. He continues to offer us the healing of the wounds of sin through the beautiful sacrament of penance. He knows that we need more than ordinary food and drink. And so in every Mass he gives us the magnificent gift of his own body and blood to strengthen us on our journey. As we eat his body and drink his blood, we should appreciate how generous and self-sacrificing the love of Jesus really is. He provides us with the nourishment which cannot be bought by any sum of money. His body is our real food and his blood is our real drink.

The Good Samaritan was the hero of the story. Jesus is more. He is the Savior the Father sent to redeem us.

Tuesday of the Twenty-seventh Week (I)

What a marvelous God we have! In today's reading we experience two aspects of his great love. Yesterday we saw Jonah's reluctance to preach to the pagans of Nineveh lest they be converted and find favor with God. God refused to let Jonah abandon his ministry and through very extraordinary events practically forced him to preach to the Ninevites. The response of the entire population was overwhelming. It was a mass conversion. God's love reaches to all people. That is the first aspect of his great love.

The scene in the gospel is quiet and intimate by contrast with the episode described in the first reading. Jesus does not disapprove of Martha as if he were ungrateful for all her efforts. Rather he wanted her to realize that there are times when the duties of ordinary life should be put aside or at least simplified in order to spend time with him personally. In Jesus we see that God loves each one of us individually and not merely as part of a large group. That is the second aspect of his great love.

Liturgy, even our small weekday Mass, is community worship. As a group we form a small segment of God's worldwide family, and in liturgy we worship God as the Father of us all. Liturgy is incomplete without personal prayer, for the liturgy, indispensable as it is, is not meant to express our complete relationship to God. In addition to liturgical prayer, there are times when we must put aside or at least simplify the demands of everyday living in order to find time to be alone with our God.

God loves us as members of his worldwide family, the Church. But he also loves each one of us uniquely as individuals.

Tuesday of the Twenty-seventh Week (II)

Weary from his mission of preaching and teaching, Jesus sought a few moments of rest and relaxation with friends who had been particularly kind to him. After his arrival, Martha complained that all Mary wanted to do was sit and talk with Jesus while she had to do all the work. This story is one of the most charming in all the gospels because it is so human, and yet it contains an important lesson for us.

Many people, especially housewives, symphathize with Martha. They know how she felt. In fact, Martha was much like the Good Samaritan, the hero of yesterday's gospel, for she showed practical hospitality to Jesus as the Good Samaritan did for the Jew lying beaten and wounded on the roadside. By no means did Jesus disapprove of what Martha was doing. He found fault only in her attitude toward her sister as if Mary were being selfish in dedicating herself to listening to Jesus.

When St. Luke recorded this episode in his gospel, his intention was to establish a balance in the lives of Christians between the need for practical charity and the importance of hearing the Word of God. This Word is a nourishment for our spiritual lives, more important than the food which sustains our natural lives. St. Paul tells us that after his conversion he went off to the deserts of Arabia to dedicate himself to communion with God in prayer. His mission was to be a very active one, but he realized his own need to digest and assimilate God's word.

The point of the gospel story is that Martha and Mary together form the ideal disciple of Jesus. A disciple must hear the Word of God and put it into practice. Since people lead very busy lives and are tempted to give but little time directly to God in prayer, Jesus emphasized the example of Mary, an example of prayer and listening. This emphasis on prayer and listening is one which is probably needed in the lives of most of us.

Wednesday of the Twenty-seventh Week (I)

If Jonah's being swallowed by the fish seems unreal to some people, his attitude seems even more unreal. Why is it that Jonah is displeased that God would show compassion and love toward the Ninevites? Why would he be jealous? His problem was that even though he knew that God is gracious and merciful, he did not come close to understanding God and his values.

God used the withered plant to teach Jonah a lesson. Jonah was disappointed that the plant had died. God's point then was that if Jonah had some form of pity for the plant, why should not God the creator show pity toward the people of Nineveh whom he had made?

Jonah today finds a parallel in those people who think that God's favor is something people ought to earn as if some price could be paid to God for his mercy and love. They judge God by those human standards which say that you are entitled only to those things for which you work and work hard. As a consequence they become indignant when they hear of a deathbed conversion or the like. They fail to understand that God loves people gratuitously because they are his creation.

We should see another reason why God gives his love freely. That reason is implicit in the gospel. When Jesus teaches us to call God "Our Father," it is clearly implied that we have become God's children. Good parents love their children, not because of accomplishments, but simply because they are their children. It is a love freely given. God loves us in much the same way. We are much more than God's creatures. We are his beloved children, and he loves us freely because of who we are.

Wednesday of the Twenty-seventh Week (II)

In the early Church all of the first converts were Jews, as were the apostles themselves. When Gentiles began to enter the Church, many of the Jewish Christians had the mistaken notion that they had to become Jews first in order to be Christians. St. Paul's mission was mainly among Gentiles whereas that of St. Peter was spent principally with Jews. St. Peter understood that faith in Jesus as the Christ was the necessary mark of a Christian, not the observance of the old Mosaic law, but he was under pressure from Jewish converts to make everyone follow that law. When Peter showed some weakness about enforcing the correct principle, Paul admonished him. It was vital that Peter, the visible head of the Church, give good example.

St. Paul's understanding, as we shall hear from his own words on Saturday of this week, was that national origin or one's previous religion did not matter. He insisted that "All are one in Christ Jesus." To become a Christian was to take on a new identity, to share with Christ the wonderfully good news of being a child of God.

When his disciples asked Jesus to teach them to pray, he taught them what we call the Lord's prayer. By this prayer Jesus indicated that the God who is his Father is our Father as well. With Jesus, and not only with each other, do we call upon God as "Our Father." Jesus is part of the word, "Our." The Father of Jesus is our Father as well because we are one with Jesus, part of his body, his mystical body which is the Church.

These days some take pride in their national origin, or maybe shame. Converts may regret that they were not Catholic from the time of their infancy. But all that does not matter. The only thing that matters is that Jesus has taken us to himself and transformed us into his likeness so that God is truly our Father. We have a brotherhood in Christ and form but a single family because God is the Father of us all.

Thursday of the Twenty-seventh Week (I)

The first reading today could not be more appropriate for us for the simple reason that the circumstances of the times match our own so closely. It was an era in which the poor were becoming poorer and the rich, richer. Family life was disintegrating through divorce and unfaithfulness. The natural resources needed for that society were in low supply. It seemed that only the dishonest were the ones who were getting ahead. Morale was low and many people were throwing up their hands and saying, "What's the use of trying to be good?"

Through the prophet Malachi God replied to those who had lost heart. He assured the people that they were still his own special possession, dearer to him than children to their parents. He asked for patience, assuring them that in time justice would prevail.

That kind of answer is not very satisfying unless we have faith, real faith that God's wisdom is greater than ours and that his love for us surpasses anything we can imagine.

The gospel tells us to pray, to ask for what we need. That is exactly what we should do. But all the while we must remember that God's view is broader and deeper than our own. In answer to prayer he will give what we need, not necessarily what we ask for. He is like the good parent who listens to the requests of his children, but he is also like the wise parent who insists on giving only what he knows to be best for his children.

We live now a life of faith. That necessarily involves some darkness, an inability to see values as God sees them. Our prayer of petition should be an act of faith that our God is a Father who is both all loving and all wise.

Thursday of the Twenty-seventh Week (II)

Sometimes we hear the advice that we ought to get away from prayers of petition, "gimme" prayers as they are called. We are reminded that we should concentrate on prayers of praise and thanksgiving. And yet today in the gospel Jesus strongly encourages prayers of petition: "Ask and you shall receive, seek and you shall find, knock and it shall be opened to you."

Rather than abandon or even minimize prayers of petitions, we ought to understand the true nature of these prayers. Think of it this way. God the Father has made us his beloved children. He looks upon us in somewhat the same way in which devoted parents look upon their little children. Devoted parents, even if they must struggle to keep their patience, are pleased when their children ask them for favors or for help. The request of their children shows that they have faith in their parents. First they have faith that their parents have the power to help them, a power which they themselves do not have. Little children believe that their parents can do anything. Secondly their request shows that they have faith in their parents' love for them. They believe that their parents will use their power to help them because they love them.

We should understand that our prayers of petition can and should be a beautiful act of faith. God really can do anything. He does indeed have power which we do not. Prayers of petition are an act of faith in God's power. We should also recognize that God's love for us far surpasses any form of human love. Prayers of petition are an act of faith in God's love.

Rightly understood, prayers of petition are not lower on the scale than any other kind of prayer. St. Paul emphasized for the Galatians that faith is what counts. Our prayers of petition can and should be a beautiful act of faith in God's power and God's love.

Friday of the Twenty-seventh Week (I)

The background of today's first reading is that the crops had been devestated by a plague of locusts. Food was practically nonexistent and people literally did not know where their next meal was coming from. The prophet saw the plague not only as a punishment for sin but also as a warning that one day God would come in judgment. On that great day all evil would be destroyed.

Even as the people were starving the prophet was bold enough to warn the people to have a broader view of reality. He was so courageous and so convinced of the truth that in effect he was telling the people that starvation was not the great evil. The great evil was to be against God. That is why he called them to repentance, to turn once again toward God and to be his faithful people. Learn a lesson, he said, from the plague of locusts. If you think it is bad, he was saying, to suffer from starvation, it will be much worse to suffer alienation from God on the last day.

We are here at Mass every day because we want to be good people. I suppose we would like to think that we do not need what might be called scare tactics to keep us faithful. But we too have a lesson to learn from the prophet Malachi. It is a lesson of perspective. Sometimes we are tempted to be a little nearsighted, to become absorbed in problems we face every day, perhaps even to the point of discouragement. It is then that we need to realize that the ultimate evil is that kind of sin which separates us from God. In the light of this perspective most of our problems, none of which is as bad as starvation, ought to appear less significant. What really counts is to be on God's side, to live as his trusting and loving children.

Friday of the Twenty-seventh Week (II)

Some people are very proud of their family roots. In the east they may boast that their ancestors came over on the Mayflower, whereas someone in the west may lay claim to being the descendants of a Spanish family which was among the first Catholics in what is now the state of California. The truth is that as people of faith we all share a common ancestry which dates back to long before the birth of Jesus himself.

The liturgy in the first Eucharistic prayer reminds us that Abraham is our father in faith. This extraordinary man lived in an era when he was surrounded by people who believed in many gods and who worshipped created objects such as the sun and the moon and the stars. To Abraham God revealed himself as the one, true God, the creator of the heavens and the earth. He showed that he was not some inanimate object or a nebulous force. Rather he manifested to Abraham that he was a personal God, one who wished to foster a loving relationship with his people.

God entered into a covenant with Abraham, a promise that

Abraham would be the father of innumerable descendants. These descendants would be linked to Abraham not by physical descent but by the unity of faith. In order to fulfill his part of the covenant God sent his Son, Jesus Christ. The Savior was born to bring the covenant made with Abraham to completion.

St. Paul insisted that salvation comes, not from the observance of the law which was of necessity only until the coming of Christ, but from faith, a faith like that of Abraham. Abraham was God's chosen instrument for the transmission of this faith. We give praise and thanks to God for having given us Abraham as our father in faith.

Saturday of the Twenty-seventh Week (I)

There was a lot of evil in Joel's day, and there is a lot of evil in our own. Such it has been from the beginning and so will be until God's plan is fulfilled. A human way of looking at the first reading today leads to the impression that one of these days God is going to say something like "All right, I am fed up with all this evil. Evil has pushed me as far as I will go, and now I am going to end it all for good." Such is not the case.

There is a mystery in God's plan. It is not as if there are two almost equal forces in the universe, one good and one evil, in a struggle that will last until one manages to eke out a victory. In the gospel Jesus demonstrates his mastery over evil. Yesterday's gospel is a good example. There can be no doubt in the mind of a person of faith about God's power as manifested in Christ Jesus. And yet for his own inscrutible purposes God chooses to allow evil to continue in the world even after the coming of his Son.

Where do we fit in and what are we to do? It seems a simple answer to say that we are to hear God's word and keep it. And yet it is ultimately the only answer for us. We can surely help to overcome evil by our efforts, but the result will be minimal in the face of many problems. Part of God's plan is that he will come in final justice when those who follow his word have built up the kingdom in the manner he has forechosen. Our preoccupation must be to make sure that we are among those who hear and keep God's word.

Saturday of the Twenty-seventh Week (II)

It is probably true that only a mother can appreciate how Mary felt about being the mother of Jesus. The woman in the crowd who praised Mary must have been a mother herself. She called out to Jesus, "Blest is the womb that bore you and the breasts that nursed you." That was a Semitic way of saying, "Your mother must be really proud of you." Jesus replied, "Rather, blest are they who hear the word of God and keep it." His reply was not a reproof of the woman or a denial of what she had said. It was Jesus' way of saying that there was something more important about Mary than the fact that she had given physical birth to him. Actually no human person has more fully heard the word of God and no human person has kept that word more completely than Mary.

Mary was more than the mother of Jesus. She was his perfect disciple. In fact St. Luke, the author of today's gospel, viewed Mary as the model of all Christians. The Second Vatican Council expressed this truth in these words, "She is hailed as the preeminent and altogether singular member of the Church, and as the Church's model and excellent exemplar in faith and charity" (*Constitution on the Church*, 53).

Children inherit physical traits from their parents and usually take on some of their characteristics. The opposite is true of Jesus and Mary. Mary was created in the image of Jesus and as his disciple took on his characteristics. St. Paul teaches that each one of us is a child of God because of our faith in Christ. Because of her faith in her own son, Mary is the most favored daughter of God.

If we want to know what it means to be a disciple of Jesus, we should look to Mary. Her faith in Jesus and her love for him, her humility and her eagerness to serve Jesus, above all the fact that Jesus was the center of her life, these are the virtues which we must imitate to be true disciples.

Monday of the Twenty-eighth Week (I)

Most people are fascinated by celebrities. If they happen to see a movie star or professional ball player, perhaps in a restaurant, they become very excited. Part of the ritual of response to a celebrity is to ask for his autograph. Just what the value of the autograph is, I am not quite sure, and I often wonder where the scrap of paper bearing the "sacred" signature ends up.

Today Jesus mentions two people who could have been considered celebrities, Jonah and Solomon. The latter was without doubt held in high esteem by the people. Jesus, with an honesty which is blunt and to the point, proclaims that he is greater than both Jonah and Solomon; in fact he is greater than any figure in the Old Testament.

St. Paul in his letter to the Romans, which we began reading today, explains why. Jesus is the only source of salvation—not the following of the law nor of any person other than himself. Paul was most emphatic about that for the people of his own day and his message is quite appropriate for our times. Some people these days seem to be willing to put more faith in television news commentators or writers in magazines and newspapers than in the teachings of Jesus Christ. Others will indeed go out of their way to catch a glimpse of a celebrity but not spend one extra minute with God in prayer. They devour magazines which do little more than spread gossip about movie stars, but rarely if ever open the Bible.

This kind of spirit can influence us as well. It is very salutary that we call ourselves back to reality, to a realization that we have in Jesus Christ the source of all wisdom and happiness. Nor do we need an autograph as a memento. We have Jesus among us here. He is present in the word we hear and in the Eucharist which we receive.

Monday of the Twenty-eighth Week (II)

When we think of religious freedom, perhaps we reflect by contrast on the persecutions suffered by our fellow Catholics in communistic and other totalitarian countries. St. Paul had a different notion of freedom in mind when he wrote the first reading for today. He presented his idea by means of a somewhat complex allusion to Abraham. Abraham had two sons, one born of a free woman, his wife, and one born of a slave girl. The point he wanted to make is that we are like the son born of the free woman so that we enjoy freedom from the Mosaic Law.

Jesus has given us our freedom. The real value of our freedom is not that we may do whatever we want, but rather that our salvation does not depend on what we do. We are not saved by observing a set of regulations. Jesus has given us salvation free of charge. We do not pay for our salvation. In fact, we cannot pay for it since no human action can match the value of what is granted us. Salvation means the gift of eternal life and we simply do not have the means to purchase that any more than a small child with play money can purchase a house. Our heavenly home is God's gift to us.

On the other hand we should not think that freedom means we have no duties toward God. If someone presented you with a magnificent home, you would be deeply grateful to that person. You would understand that this expensive gift was a sign of the goodness of the person and the greatness of his love for you. Scarcely, then, would you accept the gift and ignore the giver.

Our effort to lead a life pleasing to God is our response to his goodness, but it is not a way of earning salvation. Trying to love God with our whole being is the right reaction to his love for us, but it is not a payment. God's salvation is free and the dedication of our lives is a return gift to him.

Tuesday of the Twenty-eighth Week (I)

You can always learn something about a person from the things he produces. This is true of artists and composers, and equally true of cooks and carpenters. It is also true of God. St. Paul insists that we can come to know God from what he has created. The world, indeed the entire universe, is the creation of God. There may have been an evolution, as modern science teaches, but even such evolution must be understood as the gradual unfolding of God's creative work.

This work of creation is a magnificent gift from God to us. The harmony and the inner workings of the universe as well as of the human body are no accident. Never can any aspect of creation be taken for granted. The person of faith should feel compelled to praise and thank God for this great gift.

Since the world has come forth from the hand of God it is by its very nature sacred and holy. Think about the prayers during the preparation of the gifts. They are, "Blessed are you Lord, God of all creation." These prayers are based on Jewish meal prayers, which at one time were a form of blessing before meals. Notice that the prayers do not ask God to bless his creation as if it needed to be made holy. Rather the prayers bless God. To bless God in the Bible means to praise and to thank him. In other words, these prayers reflect the belief that we are privileged to share God's creation. It is holy simply because it has been made by God.

Perhaps we have tended to make too fine a distinction between the sacred and the secular. Such an antithesis is alien to God's revelation. Sacred and profane, religious and secular, devotional and worldly, are dichotomies which are not found in the Bible. Nothing created is ever evil in itself, only its misuse.

From the great gifts of creation we should learn of the wisdom and goodness of God, and respond to him through praise and thanksgiving.

Tuesday of the Twenty-eighth Week (II)

In a small Missouri town a dirt road crosses a railroad track. The track is rusty and in disrepair because the route was abandoned over twenty years ago. A stop sign still stands at the crossing and no native of the town would think of driving over the tracks without first stopping. No one has bothered to remove the stop sign even though it no longer serves a purpose. Stopping has become a meaningless custom.

Something like this situation happens in religion. Jesus condemned the Pharisees for insisting on the observance of regulations in religion which had lost their purpose. The washing of hands before eating was not a sanitary precaution but a religious gesture to express inner cleansing before partaking of God's gifts. The Pharisees were more concerned about external observances than they were about purity of heart. They were still stopping at railroad tracks which no longer were in use.

St. Paul reminded the Galatians that they were free of such observances. The former, external regulations no longer mattered. What counted was faith in Christ, a complete and sincere dedication to him and his word. This faith expresses itself through love, the greatest of all the commandments and one which never loses its purpose.

The lesson for us is that we must examine our motivation in all we do. Love, not superstition or selfishness, must underlie our prayers. Love, not hope for a return, must be the moving force for kindness to others. Love was behind everything that Jesus said and did, and love of God and our neighbors must be the foundation of our entire lives.

Wednesday of the Twenty-eighth Week (I)

The only group of people Jesus was really harsh to were the Pharisees. The reason was that they should have known better. As experts in religion they should have realized that external observance of a lot of man-made laws is not the way to please God. In their practices they were self-righteous and complacent.

St. Paul makes the same point in our first reading today. His words are so strong that they indicate how upset he is with any form of self-righteous judgment of others. His somewhat rambling lesson is summed up by saying, "Do you presume on God's kindness and forebearance? Do you not know that God's kindness is an invitation to you to repent?"

God has surely been kind to us. He has given us the great gift of faith. God surely shows us forebearance. No matter what our sins may be, he is always eager to forgive us. If we have an image of God as an all loving and forgiving Father, we are quite correct.

And yet we must not be self-righteous, perhaps thinking that our daily celebration of the Eucharist necessarily makes us better than others. Nor must we become complacent, as if we do all that could possibly be expected of us. To put it another way, we must not presume to take advantage of God because he is so kind and merciful. Rather the feeling that we wish to grow even more holy and more dedicated to God is moving in the right direction. The desire to respond more fully to such a loving God is what is pleasing to him.

Even though we do wish to be very dedicated children of God, it is good for us to hear the warnings of St. Paul today. They are a favor from God to encourage us in our attempts to grow in holiness.

Wednesday of the Twenty-eighth Week (II)

It is important that we not impose on the Scriptures our way of understanding certain matters. An uninformed person might think that St. Paul was referring to body and soul when he spoke of flesh and spirit. The truth is that any notion of a soul as distinct from the body was foreign to the outlook of a Semite like St. Paul. By the word "flesh" St. Paul meant human nature as weakened by sin. His point was that anyone who follows all the inclinations of his humanity as wounded by sin will be led to such things as lewd conduct, hostilities, bickering, jealousy and the like.

In contrast to the flesh he uses the word "spirit." Ultimately this word includes the Holy Spirit, the third person of the Trinity, but in the context it refers more immediately to the grace which comes to us from the Holy Spirit. The first effect of this grace is the forgiveness of sins. The words of absolution spoken by the priest in the sacrament of penance reflect this truth: "God the Father of mercies, through the death and resurrection of his Son, has reconciled the world to himself and sent the Holy Spirit among us for the forgiveness of sins." We enjoy this forgiveness first through baptism, and this forgiveness is renewed for us in the sacrament of penance.

Forgiveness, however, is not a negative thing, a mere destruction of sin. It is also a strengthening grace to live in accord with God's will. That is what St. Paul has in mind when he says that the fruit of the spirit is love, joy, patient endurance, and the like. We are not expected to be good people by our own unaided efforts. God is present with his grace, his strength. Much is expected of us because of this grace. But we can also expect much from God. It is right for us to call upon him in prayer, to beg him to make his grace effective within us so that we can lead lives in accord, not with the flesh, but the spirit.

Thursday of the Twenty-eighth Week (I)

Throughout the epistle to the Romans, parts of which we have been reading at Mass, St. Paul uses two words frequently, law and faith. It is important that we understand these two words as he intended them. First, "law" refers to the law of the covenant of Moses. St. Paul insisted that it was not by observance of this law that people are made holy. His point was that, contrary to the thinking of some early Christians, one did not have to become a Jew in order to be a follower of Jesus Christ.

By "faith" St. Paul means much more than an intellectual acceptance of the truth which God has revealed in Christ. For him faith involves not only the mind but the heart, not only an act of the intellect but a response of the whole person. A man, for example, may believe that his wife is a wonderful person who loves him. That is a kind of faith. But if his faith in her goes no further, they will not have much of a life together. If he gradually comes to ignore her, to spend less and less time with her, to allow himself to become more absorbed in another woman, his faith is meaningless. He may still believe in her love, but his faith is hollow. He has not been faithful.

Being faithful, full of faith, is what St. Paul is concerned with. A person of true faith is so full of his belief in God that it becomes a driving force in his life. It colors all of his thinking and determines all of his actions. His faith becomes a response to God. To put it another way, the kind of faith of which St. Paul writes cannot be separated from love.

This kind of faith is a gift from God. It is not something we can merit or achieve by ourselves. A gift is something freely given, and

God gives us our gift of faith simply because he loves us. Why others may not have the gift of faith we do not know. But we are sure that God has looked upon us with favor. This gift is not a cause for boasting, but should be the reason why we come together here at Mass to praise and thank God for his gift.

Thursday of the Twenty-eighth Week (II)

Loving and devoted couples who really want children look forward to the birth of a child with great eagerness. They pray that the child will be born safely and that he will be healthy and sound. Actually they have no idea of what the child will be like, whether it will be a boy or a girl, or what his future in life will be.

God is not that way with us. The letter to the Ephesians explains that God chose us in Christ before the world began, that he had a plan for us from all eternity. By his almighty power God formed and shaped us according to his plan. He did not have to wait to see how we would turn out. In particular he determined that we would be like his eternal son, the first son of his family. He made us his children, confident to call him Father.

And yet God did not use his almighty power to force us to be what he wanted. He gave to the whole human race the gift of freedom. That freedom allows a return of love which is not forced, but it also allows for sin. As part of the entire human family we share in original sin which is like a birth defect. God does not, however, accept this defect as irreparable. He has confidently turned us over to a divine physician, his eldest son, to repair the damage. Jesus is indeed an unusual physician. He does not operate on us, leaving upon us the scars of his surgery. Rather, he can and does undergo the operation in our place. His death is the means to our recovery. He does not give us a blood transfusion from a donor. Rather it is through his own blood that our sins are forgiven.

Today's passage from the letter to the Ephesians is actually a hymn of praise. In this Mass we should make the sentiments of that hymn our own as we give praise to God the Father who chose us in Christ before the world began and who thought Christ has bestowed upon us every spiritual blessing.

Friday of the Twenty-eighth Week (I)

In the first Eucharistic prayer we refer to Abraham as "our father in faith." This expression means that our faith in the one true God ultimately traces back to Abraham. It also means that Abraham is a model to us of what faith really means.

God had made extraordinary promises to Abraham. He told him that he would be the father of a multitude of nations, that the covenant with him would never be broken. Though Abraham and his wife, Sara, grew old with no legitimate heir through whom God's promises would be realized, Abraham kept his confidence in God. Then when Sara was beyond the natural age of child bearing, she had a son, Isaac. Life was looking bright for Abraham.

But you know the story of how God asked Abraham to sacrifice the life of his son. Abraham was in tremendous mental turmoil. It was terrible enough to be asked to sacrifice his son. What disturbed him the more was that the death of his son would seem to make impossible God's promises about descendants. When Abraham led Isaac to the place of sacrifice on the mountain top, he could not see the bright sunshine of hope but only the dark clouds of confusion which faith alone could penetrate. As the old man stood with the knife clutched in his trembling hand, he was in mental anguish over how this sacrifice would make sense. But because his faith was firm and unwavering, God sent his angel to stay the hand of sacrifice. Isaac's life was spared, and a ram was substituted in his place.

Abraham shows us that faith involves the commitment of our entire selves to God. It is a trust, a reliance, a confident assurance, a firm conviction that God is good, that he is a true Father to us in every circumstance of our lives. It is the faith we express in the first eucharistic prayer in these words of the priest: "You know how firmly we believe in you and dedicate ourselves to you." That is true faith: the complete dedication of ourselves to God.

Friday of the Twenty-eighth Week (II)

G.K. Chesterton, the Catholic author in England who died in

1936, wrote "How odd of God, to choose the Jews." From a human standpoint it would have made more sense to choose the Romans with their genius for government and administration or the Greeks with their high culture and philosophical wisdom. But God for his own good reasons did indeed choose a group of undistinguished nomads and form them into his people. To them he revealed himself as a personal God and called them to worship him alone and to be a sign of his goodness before the nations. He eventually filled them with hope for a messiah, a hope which our faith teaches us was fulfilled in Jesus Christ.

The first reading today reminds us that in Christ we too were chosen, and that when we believed in the good news, the message of the gospel, we were sealed with the Holy Spirit. The word "sealed" is derived from a practice of the time for authenticating important letters or documents. Next to the signature a drop of hot wax was poured. Before the wax cooled, the king or other official who was the author of the document, placed his ring with his "seal" into the wax. This seal showed that the document was authentic and identified the sender without doubt. A signature could be forged but not the seal.

In choosing us God the Father has imprinted his seal upon us. This seal is the Holy Spirit who marks us out as belonging to God, as being his children. This Holy Spirit is also the pledge or promise of our inheritance. Since we are children of God, we will inherit the riches of his love and the family home of heaven. All of these blessings are ours not because of any merit of our own but simply because God has chosen us and given us the gift of his Holy Spirit. It really wasn't odd of God to choose the Jews, nor is it odd of him to choose us. His fatherly love has reached out to embrace us according to his eternal plan.

Saturday of the Twenty-eighth Week (I)

Some years ago with the publication of the book, *Roots*, and its successful presentation on television, many people became interested in their own personal roots. Some even paid large sums of money for experts to trace their ancestry. It is quite proper to be interested in our ancestry, and we as Catholics ought to be aware of our spiritual ancestry. What is recorded in the New Testament takes on its full meaning only when seen in the light of the Old Testament. The reason is that our spiritual roots are in the original chosen people. Their history is our history because their God is our God.

Abraham is prominent in the thinking of St. Paul, as we have heard in the readings yesterday and today. Abraham is the father of the chosen people, and he is our father in faith. Pope Pius XI pointed out that we are all spiritually Semites. The coming of Christ is a fulfillment of the covenant made with Abraham, and the entire Old Testament is a salvific act of God which reaches its climax in the person of Jesus Christ. In other words, the coming of Jesus did not occur in an historical or spiritual vacuum. Rather it was the culmination of all the wonderful works of God during the Old Testament era.

The coming of Jesus in relation to the Old Testament is roughly somewhat like the relation of modern space technology to earlier developments. The technology which landed men on the moon developed only through all that had gone before, even back to the invention of the wheel in prehistoric times. Any scientist, working on the moon project, who did not realize his dependency on previous inventions and findings was grossly ungrateful, even snobbish.

Today in this eucharist we lift our minds and hearts to God in thanks and praise for all the wonderful events of his providence which prepared for and led up to the coming of our Savior, Jesus Christ.

Saturday of the Twenty-eighth Week (II)

These days it is almost imperative that we drive small, gas-saving cars. Sometimes, as in mountain travel, the lack of power can be something of a problem. You can imagine a car with a tiny four cylinder engine struggling to make it up a steep grade. The former eight cylinder cars with huge engines had reserve power for such occasions.

When we think about our human condition, we should be aware of how weak we are, even weaker than one of those economical cars struggling up a long mountain climb. In one sense we can say that life is a mountain to climb to get to our eternal home. We do not have the power to make the journey, but there is someone who does, and that someone is God.

How great is God's power? Does he have power in reserve? St. Paul says that the power which God uses within us is like the power which raised Jesus from the dead. Death is a reality more universal and more overwhelming than the pull of gravity which forces a car to slow down in its ascent of a mountain. Nothing can resist death's pull into the dark unknown—not money, or prestige or influence. Medical science can prolong life but it cannot prevent death. Death recognizes no distinction among people. It overcomes the rich and the poor, the elderly and the young, male and female.

Although death is inevitable, it is difficult for us to accept our mortality. We know in a theoretical way that one day we will die, but we almost feel that it will not happen to us. But accept death we must. And we can do so without regret or sorrow because our faith in God's power to raise us from the dead should fill us with hope.

Today's first reading contains a prayer that we may know the great hope to which God has called us and the wealth of his glorious heritage. This hope depends on our trust in the immeasurable scope of God's power which is like the strength he showed in raising Christ from the dead. That same power he will bring to bear on us in order to raise us with Christ to everlasting life.

Monday of the Twenty-ninth Week (I)

Something every adult seeks is a sense of security. Commercials on radio and television for savings companies appeal to this desire within us. Save we must, but Jesus warns us that security cannot be found in money or material things. Not only is money itself an insecure item, as the great stock market crash in 1929 proved, it cannot purchase the kind of security for which we all ultimately yearn. The reason is that nothing can buy spiritual, eternal security.

Sometimes we may be led to believe that somehow we can purchase heaven by what we do in this life as if eternal life were a commodity which can be bought. Heaven is not like a home which a family purchases. It is not even like a retirement pension which a person deserves after long, dedicated years of service to a firm. Heaven is a gift, pure and simple, from a munificient God.

St. Paul insists that faith is the starting point and the foundation of our relationship with God, and faith is not something we can acquire by our own efforts. It is helpful to wonder why we have faith and others do not. Some people have diligently read the Bible, they have studied theologians, they have discussed religion often with others, but they do not come to faith. Others seem to live a life in which the furthest thing from their mind seems to be religion and God. We do not know why they have not received faith. Why have we? God, for his own good inscrutible reasons, has given us a gift. Faith like life itself, is something which no one can deserve. It is given freely.

We are here today because of our faith. It is right and just that in this eucharist we give praise and thanks to God for our gift of faith.

Monday of the Twenty-ninth Week (II)

A firm foundation is necessary for any building. The more solid the foundation, the higher may the building rise toward the sky. The foundation of our lives is a conviction that we are completely dependent on God for everything.

The rich farmer in the gospel lacked this foundation. There is no indication that he acquired his riches dishonestly or that he mistreated those who worked his farm for him. His mistake was the thought that his abundant wealth was the foundation of his happiness. He believed that his wealth gave him security and that he did not need God. In practice he was an atheist.

Although we are mindful of God as the rich man in the parable was not, there is a temptation for us to be more like the rich man than we may suspect. What I mean is that it is easy for us to have the idea that our relationship with God is based on a spiritual economic system. The rich man thought that all his wealth could buy happiness and we may be led to believe that our good deeds merit God's favor and the ultimate gift of heaven. We have a great wealth from God and what is to come is even greater, but God's favor is not a reward for our good deeds. St. Paul is quite clear about that. He insisted that salvation is God's gift, not our own doing. God's favor is freely given by his own choice and is not a reward for anything we may have accomplished.

Heaven cannot be purchased. It is God's gift to us. The foundation upon which our lives rise toward heaven is a firm conviction that everything comes from God. Without him we can do nothing.

Tuesday of the Twenty-ninth Week (I)

In 1906 an earthquake and subsequent fires leveled the proud and beautiful city of San Francisco. Undaunted, the people of that city set to work at rebuilding. From stubble and ruin rose a more beautiful, modern city. And very proud of their city are the natives of San Francisco.

The human race came forth from the creating hand of God beautiful and sinless. In granting the gift of freedom, God opened the possibility of sin. Sin became a reality, shook the race to its foundations and almost devastated it. But God was undaunted. Included in his overall plan of creation was a way of rebuilding the human race into an even more beautiful work of his art and wisdom. He came to our rescue by his power as God, but he wanted us to be saved by one like us. Through a man sin entered the world, and through a man God's grace would abound in a measure beyond imagining. That man was Jesus Christ. But he was more than a man. He was God's own Son, divine himself.

As Jesus Christ, our redeemer, is greater than any human person, so is the restoration he brought to mankind greater than the devastation of sin and even greater than the first state of sinlessness. To be redeemed by Jesus Christ himself should be a source of great joy for all of us. God thought enough of us that he sent his own son to repair sin. It is something we could never have guessed.

And very proud of his redeemed children is God our Father. In us he sees the handiwork of his almighty power and love. We need not be proud of ourselves. We leave pride to God for he has accomplished all the good that is within us.

Tuesday of the Twenty-ninth Week (II)

Some children go through a stage in life when they become dissatisfied with their family and their home. Usually it is not a very serious or disruptive phase. They simply envy a friend his home and think they would like to be part of his family. The fact is that they experience the family of the friend on a very superficial level when they are at their best. It is the old idea that the grass looks greener on the other side of the fence.

And yet there is a profound sadness when anyone senses that he is on the outside looking in, when he feels excluded from some relationship which he sees as beautiful. God entered into an especially beautiful relationship with the chosen people. He was their God and they were his beloved people. With the coming of Jesus Christ that relationship was broadened. As we say in the second Eucharistic prayer, "For our sake he opened his arms on the cross." He did so to embrace us and all mankind with his Father's love.

Our first reading explains that "this means that we are strangers and aliens no longer." We are not on the outside looking in. We are "fellow citizens of the saints and members of the household of God." By God's favor and the sacrifice of his Son on the cross we have been drawn into God's family, made full members of that family with the right of inheritance. That inheritance is the family home of perfect and everlasting life in heaven.

In our case the grass on the other side of the fence of death is indeed greener. Even now, however, we ought to rejoice in the truth that we have been embraced by God who is truly our Father. We need envy no one—not anyone here on earth or anyone who has gone before us to heaven. We are part of God's family. He shares his love with us now and promises us the joys of his eternal home.

Wednesday of the Twenty-ninth Week (I)

We as Americans are blessed to be a free people. Freedom is so precious that the founders of this country were willing to sacrifice anything in order to achieve it. This nation's struggle for freedom is so fundamental to human dignity that every person passes through stages, often painful and confusing, in his growth into a free person. Adolescents, in whom the instinct to be free is awakening, become confused and mistake rebellion for freedom. Impatient with parental authority they suffer frustration and annoyance. Some adults never come to understand freedom, assuming that it means the right to do anything. That is a childish idea.

Freedom is not the right to do anything we please. Rather, it is the context in which we have the ability to do what God pleases. Confusion about freedom leads to slavery, as St. Paul today warns us. Indulging one's weak aspects, giving in to temptation, refusing to accept a discipline based on moral principles, a person becomes addicted to sin. Sin becomes something of a compulsion, whether it be a matter of never resisting gossip or becoming trapped by an unfaithful marital relationship. God's will recedes from consciousness and becomes a blur.

Sin produces a tension, wherein God draws us to himself and we try to pull in the opposite direction. Jesus by his redemption has given us the grace to be free from slavery to sin. Strengthened by him, especially by means of the eucharist, we can rise above human weakness to be dedicated to God's will. Such dedication begets a peace, a serenity and calm in our lives, the joyous feeling of true freedom.

Wednesday of the Twenty-ninth Week (II)

I find it hard to imagine what life would be like without faith in God. I have heard of people who maintain that they are quite content with the idea that all there is to life is what appears on the surface. Life to them means being born, growing up, searching for some drop of happiness within an ocean of sorrow, and death is

498 / Thursday of the Twenty-ninth Week of the Year

nothing more than falling asleep, never to awaken. They insist that
there is no God and they protest that there is no need for one.

Some atheists explain that their ethic is to do no harm to
anyone. They judge that their lives are based on humanitarian
principles which are higher than those of Christians whose lives are
based on fear of damnation. A superficial reading of today's gospel
would indeed confirm them in their view that fear is the motive for
Christian living. The punishment of the unworthy servant would
occupy their attention, and they would miss the point of the parable
which comes at the end. Jesus states, "When much has been given
a man, much will be required of him." Christian living is a response
to God's goodness, not his wrath.

More devotion and dedication to a family is expected from its
members than from outsiders. Those in the family share a common
life, a common affection, and a common home. The old saying is
that blood is thicker than water. Friends may indeed be very loving,
but it is quite right to expect even greater love among members of
the family, and children especially should respond in great love to
their parents from whom they have received the gift of life.

God is our Father. We are his children. He has given us
everything—our lives, our faith, our hope and our love. It is quite
right that he expect us to respond in love to him and to reach out in
love to our brothers and sisters. What we have received from God is
the motive for Christian living. Since we have received everything
from him, our response must be total without reservation.

Thursday of the Twenty-ninth Week (I)

Sometimes you hear people say that they just cannot believe
that God will send anyone to hell for all eternity. The sentiment is
not a bad one, expressing as it does a great faith in God's goodness. On the other hand you may hear someone talking about
doing some good deed or saying certain prayers in order to earn or
merit a higher place in heaven. The idea reflects the sentiment that
God will reward efforts at goodness.

In a simple but extremely important sentence in today's first reading St. Paul gives a view different from both these ideas. He states that "the wages of sin is death, but the gift of God is eternal life in Christ Jesus our Lord." We need to pay close attention to the words he uses.

The death of which he speaks is eternal separation from God, what we would call hell. He says that this death is the wages of sin. A wage is something which one earns by his own efforts. Some politicians have been so earnest about the justice involved in paying workers that they have established what is known as the minimum hourly wage. With the use of the word "wage" St. Paul is indicating that hell is not something which God imposes on a sinner but something which the sinner himself has earned and deserves. Hell is a matter of justice.

On the other hand St. Paul is very careful not to suggest that the wages of goodness is eternal life. Rather he proclaims that eternal life is the gift of God. In contrast to wages, a gift is something which is freely given, something which is not earned. No justice is involved in a gift, only love. The truth is that there is absolutely nothing we can do by our unaided efforts to earn heaven. It is beyond all human powers. It is God's gift.

As people of faith and godness we are called, in this eucharist, to give thanks and praise to God for all his gifts, and in particular for the gift of heaven, eternal life in Christ Jesus our Lord.

Thursday of the Twenty-ninth Week (II)

Trying to understand God is like trying to put the ocean in a thimble. God is simply too vast, too deep, too big, too everything for us to comprehend. And yet we must open our minds, as well as our hearts, to his revelation, for it is in knowing him better that we come to love him more. St. Paul's prayer for us today is that Christ may dwell in our hearts through faith so that we may be able to grasp the breadth and length and height and depth of his love for us.

With faith, then, let us together look upon this man, Jesus, who is God in the flesh. He declares, "I have come to light a fire on the earth." Fire is usually a symbol of judgment. But the sense is different here. This fire means that all consuming love which separated the disciples of Jesus from all others. Jesus wishes to kindle that fire in our hearts, and he wishes to do so by his expression of love for us. He goes on to say, "I have a baptism to receive." This is not the baptism by John in the Jordan, nor is it the baptism we receive. Rather it refers to his passion and death.

We have become so used to the idea that Jesus suffered and died on the cross that we may not approach this mystery with sufficient wonder and awe. What kind of a God is this whose mission it is to accept suffering and death? Would any human do what Jesus did? Imagine that you are a millionaire. You have everything life can offer: money, prestige, power, and pleasure. Would you be willing to give up all your money, surrender your prestige, abandon your power, and turn your back on pleasure? If you are willing to do all that, you only begin in a remote fashion, to approach what the eternal Son of God did in becoming human and in willingly making himself vulnerable to all human suffering.

Would that we could grasp the breadth and length and height and depth of Christ's love, for indeed his only motive for all that he did for us was love. If we could grasp that love, then no sacrifice would be too great to return his love. Nothing would prevent us from daring to be different in our lives. Through faith in what Christ did we can become true disciples.

Friday of the Twenty-ninth Week (I)

It is always consoling to me to remember that the great saints, like St. Paul, were human like us after all. They had to struggle, they became discouraged and confused and ultimately had to depend completely on God.

The first reading today clearly shows a man who was struggling to be a better person. St. Paul was discouraged by apparent lack of progress. Above all he became confused. How could it be, he wondered, when all he wanted to do was good and yet all that seemed to come out of him was evil. I suspect that the same happens to all of us. Perhaps we see clearly enough that we have to be more loving toward a particular person or that we must give up our rash judgment of other people and their motives. It may even be that we hate within ourselves a "holier-than-thou" attitude without being able to do much to overcome it. Why is it that we seem to make such little progress?

St. Paul cries out, "Who can free me from this body under the power of death?" His answer is only implicit at the conclusion of our reading wherein he says, "All praise to God, through Jesus Christ our Lord." From later parts of the epistle it becomes clear that he turns in praise to God because he knows that only God can help by the power of his Holy Spirit. The real problem is that we tend to depend too much on ourselves, rather than God, to have the attitude that we are the ones who must accomplish our progress rather than placing ourselves completely in God's loving care.

Ordinary people like ourselves become saints not by their own efforts but by being open to God's grace. It is God who will make all the difference in our lives if we are only willing to allow him to enter in and do his work within us.

Friday of the Twenty-ninth Week (II)

Some people seem to be disruptive by nature. Their conversations usually end in arguments. If everyone wants to do one thing, they insist on doing the opposite. When they don't get their way, all they do is complain. If something goes wrong, they take great delight in saying, "I told you so."

St. Paul makes a plea for a different attitude. He tells us, "Make every effort to preserve the unity which has the Spirit as its origin and peace as its binding force." The Holy Spirit is personified love and as such is a unifying force. From all eternity the Holy Spirit unites the Father and the Son in an unbreakable embrace of love. In the fullness of time the Holy Spirit united divinity and humanity in the person of the Son of God made flesh in the womb of Mary. And in the womb of the Church, the sacrament of baptism, he has united us with each other through our oneness with Christ. The Holy Spirit is at work in us. He has formed us into the mystical body of Christ of which he is the soul. That is what St. Paul meant when he wrote, "There is but one body and one Spirit."

Our unity as the body of Christ is a reality which can be deepened. It is especially through the Eucharist that the Holy Spirit is at work within us. We pray in the third Eucharistic prayer that we who are nourished by the body and blood of Christ may be filled with his Holy Spirit and become one body, one spirit in Christ. Growth in unity should be one of our primary purposes in celebrating Mass together. Catholics are diverse, including every economic level, every age, every race and every culture. The Spirit wishes to unite us so that we are one in mind and one in heart. As Christ excludes no one, so by the working of the Spirit we must strive to include everyone in our affection.

Our Catholic, our universal call is not easily achieved. We must pray that we may be open to the grace of the Holy Eucharist so that we may indeed live the unity which has the Spirit as its origin and peace as its binding force.

Saturday of the Twenty-ninth Week (I)

The cold of winter is a time of desolation. The trees, like the fig tree in the gospel, do not bear fruit. The days are often cloudy and dark, the nights long and dreary. Imagine a person, perhaps lost in the woods, during the worst part of winter. Without a fire and sufficient clothing he is exposed to the cold. His activity slows down with his preoccupation for warmth. Shivering and desperate to ward off the cold, he wraps his arms around himself. He can think of only one thing, getting warm.

That is the picture of what St. Paul means by a person who lives according to the flesh. "Flesh" does not mean the human body, as in our thinking. Rather it means the human person turned in upon himself in selfishness and away from God and others. Sin stems from selfishness, a spiritual narcissism, an abject egoism. Sin is the expression of a person who has wrapped his arms around himself.

In contrast is the person who lives according to the spirit, the Spirit of Christ, the Holy Spirit. Often the Spirit is symbolized by fire, which gives both light and heat. The work of the spirit is to give us the light of his wisdom and the warmth of his love. With the power of the Spirit within us we no longer need to wrap our arms around ourselves in selfishness. Rather we can open our arms to embrace God and his people in our love. That is wisdom. It is the right way to live, and it is the kind of "reform" of which Jesus speaks in the gospel.

Think of Jesus himself in his act of sacrifice. Even in the moment of great suffering he opened his arms on the cross in a gesture of love for his Father and for all mankind. God the Father responded to his love by raising him from the dead. In the words of St. Paul, "If the Spirit of him who raised Jesus from the dead dwells in you, then he who raised Christ from the dead will bring our mortal bodies to life also through his Spirit dwelling in you."

Saturday of the Twenty-ninth Week (II)

In nature there are living creatures which consist of but a single cell, such as the amoeba. This single cell must perform all of the functions necessary for life: sensation, ingestion, assimilation, reproduction and so on. By contrast the human body is made up of many parts, each one with its own specific function. All the parts of the body, internal and external, work together for the good of the whole person. The eyes cannot do the work of the hands. Cooperating together these organs allow us to do simple but marvelous things. A complex coordination of eyes and hands make it possible to thread a needle. We may take such a thing for granted until we realize that a blind person cannot do it.

The Church is not like an amoeba. If it were, only those who are ordained would constitute the Church. Rather the Church is like a body, made up of many people with various talents and roles. St. Paul explains for us that through Christ the whole body grows and with the proper functioning of all the members this body builds itself up in love. Some members are more prominent, such as the Pope, the visible head of the Church, making Christ the head present among us. But the Pope would be the first to say that the Church cannot function or even survive without the other members. We are those members and we must never underestimate the contribution we are called to make.

Some people in the Church are noticeable, as are the external organs of a body. But the internal organs of the body, unseen and sometimes unthought of, perform hidden functions which are absolutely necessary. Just let your stomach become upset and your whole body suffers for it. On the other hand, when the internal organs are working well, you feel good and can do what must be done. Many Catholics are like the internal organs, hidden and taken for granted. None of us, however, must fail to make our contribution to the well-being of the whole Church through the goodness of our lives and the devotion of our prayers. We must remember that with the proper functioning of all the members the whole Church builds itself up in love.

Monday of the Thirtieth Week (I)

Frequently in a family there are pet names for the children, and even between husband and wife. They are more than nick names, which often play on personal eccentricities, for they manifest a warmth and affection. And little children rarely call their parents by the formal names of mother and father. More often it is something like mommy and daddy.

When Jesus taught us to call upon God as our Father, he did not use the formal word, "Father." In the Aramaic language which he spoke he used the informal name which a little child would use in speaking to his male parent. That word is "Abba." It even sounds like our English word, "Papa," and that is exactly what it means.

Although the New Testament was written originally in Greek, the authors preserved this Aramaic word. Today we hear St. Paul in his letter to the Romans telling us that we have received the spirit of adoption through which we cry out, "Abba." That expression used by Jesus himself was considered so precious that the early Christian community did not want to lose it. Nor should we. This simple word expresses both the profundity and the simplicity of our relationship to God.

Jesus demanded respect for the woman in the gospel and sympathy for her need because she was a daughter of Abraham. He would reveal, especially through the "Our Father," that we are more than children of Abraham. We are children of God. And God, "Abba," looks upon us with the same affection which good parents show toward their little son or daughter.

Today as in every Mass, we are invited to pray to God as Father. How joyful, confident and serene we should feel to know that the almighty creator of the universe is truly our heavenly Father, our "Abba."

Monday of the Thirtieth Week (II)

Although sin brought evil into this world, we must be careful not to accuse the woman in the gospel of any personal sin. We know neither the cause nor the nature of the affliction which forced her into a stooped position. The gospel tells us only that she was quite incapable of standing erect in that posture of dignity which sets humans apart from animals. Jesus cured the woman on the sabbath, that day on which God rested from his work of creation. Even though the chief of the synagogue objected, the day was a fitting one. God had created all things good, and Jesus showed that he had come to heal the wounds which had been inflicted on creation.

Jesus through the forgiveness of our sins has lifted us up and given us the ability to stand erect in personal worth and dignity. Now he rightly expects that we will live in accord with the dignity he has given us. That is what St. Paul had in mind when he wrote, "Follow the way of love, even as Christ loved you." A life of sin is a contradiction of the way of love. Every sin is not only an offense against God but a blow against our own dignity. Sin demeans us and pushes us downward toward a stooped position. In that posture we become self-centered, quite incapable of looking up to God or even outward to our neighbors.

St. Paul presents another image to help us appreciate our redemption in Christ. He says, "There was a time when you were darkness, but now you are light in the Lord." A person who is darkness itself cannot see either God or others. But a person who is light recognizes God as creator and savior and appreciates the worth of his fellow human beings.

The woman in the gospel suffered a terrible affliction, but we must be wary of a still greater affliction, the only true evil, which is sin in any form, small or great. We must pray in this Mass and every day of our lives that we may be free from sin, able to stand erect before God, conscious of the dignity he has given us.

Tuesday of the Thirtieth Week (I)

Growth is a reality which is all around us, but it is usually a slow process. Parents who see a child every day scarcely notice his growth, but grandparents who are once in a year visitors immediately remark to their grandchild, "My, how you have grown!"

The Church began as a very small number of faithful followers of Jesus Christ, indeed much like a tiny seed planted in the earth. Now the Church is worldwide and counts millions as its members. And this growth will continue until Christ comes again to present his kingdom all glorious and beautiful to God the Father. But the growth of the Church has often been characterized by pain, much like the "growing pains" we experienced as children. The Church has seen her children martyred and she has seen herself divided by heresies and schisms. Nor will the struggle end until Christ comes again.

What is true of the Church as a whole is true of each one of us individually. In God's mysterious plan suffering is part of our growth. Today we are called to put our "growing pains" into perspective. Ours should be the attitude of St. Paul who says, "I consider the sufferings of the present to be as nothing compared to the glory to be revealed in us." That glory is our hope. It is not something we can see now any more than a child can see himself as an adult. St. Paul adds, "Hoping for what we cannot see means awaiting with patient endurance." The word "endurance" is well chosen since it suggests a lasting strength in the face of a series of unbroken trials. Such endurance is a necessary part of the Christian life.

Throughout our time of endurance now we have the firm hope that one day God our Father will receive us warmly into his arms and declare, "My, how you have grown!"

Tuesday of the Thirtieth Week (II)

Heroes are an important part of life. Every kid who plays baseball admires some major leaguer whom he would like to imitate. The quarterback on a high school football team tries to model himself on a favorite professional quarterback. And if truth were to be told, even adults have their idols whom they would like to resemble in one way or another.

As Christians we all have one model, one hero whom we should try to imitate. Whether we are male or female, young or old, married or single, the one model for all of us is Jesus Christ. In today's first reading St. Paul directs husbands to model themselves on Jesus Christ: "Husbands, love your wives as Christ loved the Church." And yet he could have held up Christ as the model for wives in their relationship to their husbands. The fact is that Christ is the model for all of us.

Jesus became human like us in all things but sin, so that we could see in him what it means to live as a child of God. That is our basic calling, to be children of God, no matter what other aspects there may be to our lives. St. Vincent de Paul developed the practice of asking himself this question in any situation: "What would Christ do now?" What the Son of God would do is the example to be followed by all the children of God.

Give St. Vincent's practice a try. Resolve that you will always try to ask yourself, "What would Christ do?" It is a much better practice than counting to ten before losing your temper. Following the example of Christ is the safe, sound way to live a true Christian life.

Wednesday of the Thirtieth Week (I)

If you have ever had to give a public speech, you were probably pretty nervous. You were worried about whether what you wanted to say would come out right or not. Sometimes you can feel the same nervousness even in talking to one person, as perhaps during an interview for a job.

Should we be nervous before God when we speak to him in prayer? If we had to rely on our own resources, we should indeed be terrified. But the truth is that, although we do not know how to pray as we ought, the Spirit helps us in our weakness. He helps us in many ways, the most important of which is by leading us here to Mass.

In the Mass we are invited to call upon God confidently as "Our Father." The prayers of the Mass, especially "the Lord's prayer," show us that the most important aspect of our prayer to God is our relationship with him. He looks upon us as his children. More specifically he sees within us the person of his beloved Son, Jesus. Together with Jesus we form God's own family.

That we are God's family is no mere sentiment. It is a great truth of our faith. St. Paul declares today that God "has predestined us to share the image of his Son, that the Son might be the firstborn of many brothers." God's plan that we share the image of his Son took shape in the sacrament of baptism. We grow in sharing the image of the Son principally through our sharing in the Eucharist, the body and blood of the Son, who gradually transforms us into himself.

There is no need for us to wonder how we should pray, nor should we be full of anxiety. How should a little child speak to a loving parent? That is how we, in union with his beloved Son, Jesus, should pray to God, who is "Abba," our Father.

Wednesday of the Thirtieth Week (II)

If St. Paul could have his way, the disintegration of marriage and the family would be reversed immediately. In yesterday's reading he pleaded that husbands and wives live in mutual love and respect. Today he encourages children to obey their parents. He urges parents not to anger their children but to bring them up with training and instruction befitting the Lord.

Among those who have grown sour on life, his clear but simple advice is greeted with cynicism. It is all too easy to dismiss his directives as naive, far removed from the pressures and tension of modern living. But St. Paul is correct. True happiness comes from unselfish love, a love manifested by Jesus himself in his life and in his death. Why be willing to give up on such a beautiful ideal, why abandon the only possibility for real fulfillment in life?

When a person gives up trying to achieve an ideal, he dooms himself to failure. When an entire society abandons ideals, the result is catastrophe. The complaint, "It just won't work," is a surrender when surrender is not necessary. Life calls for growth, sometimes slow and unnoticeable, but the will to grow must last. In the gospel yesterday Jesus said that his kingdom is like a small seed which becomes a large shrub. What is true of his kingdom is true of all of us. In today's gospel, Jesus warns us to try to come in through the narrow door, which means that we should not seek the easy way adopted by those who have given up on ideals.

In the Mass we have the means to grow; the Eucharist is our nourishment. We also have the means to keep trying to follow the hard way; the Eucharist is our strength. With the gift of the Eucharist we can grow toward fulfilling the ideal of Christian living which alone can give us happiness.

Thursday of the Thirtieth Week (I)

One of the most frightening of human experiences is to be all alone and in trouble. Imagine your car breaking down very late at night on a stretch of road which has been known to be the scene of many muggings and robberies. Being all alone like that is terrifying. Your only thought is to get home safely.

As we struggle through life against forces which would wish to deprive us not of our money but of eternal life itself, we are never alone. God is for us and God is with us. If we are faithful to him, he will guide us through the greatest of dangers to our heavenly home.

Think of Jesus in the gospel. Certain Pharisees warned him that

Herod was trying to kill him. Such was only a single incident among many in which Jesus was threatened. In fact, in going up to Jerusalem he fully expected to be put to death. And yet he was undaunted. The source of his strength was his realization that his Father was ever with him, guiding him through the Spirit of love so that he could fulfill his destiny.

The same love of the Father which Jesus experienced is ours as well. As Jesus was on a journey to Jerusalem to fulfill his Father's will so we are on a journey through life to our destiny, our home in heaven. In our desire to get home safely, we should not be afraid. The Father is with us. He even gives us a nourishment to strengthen us for this journey. That nourishment is the body and blood of his Son, the person who has made the passage through life before us, the one who knows how it is. Fortified with this spiritual food we should be confident that we will take our place at the feast in the kingdom of God, our true home.

Thursday of the Thirtieth Week (II)

Some history books seem to be little more than a chronicle of battles and wars as if nothing other than conflict has marked the story of the human race. It would seem at first hearing that St. Paul reflects this sad aspect of humanity when he warns us "to put on the armor of God." Be ready for battle, he is telling us, but of course he is not speaking of those bloody conflicts motivated by political, economic, and territorial considerations. He is speaking of the conflict with sin, the ultimate cause of evils which men perpetrate.

The Second Vatican Council observed that "a monumental struggle against the powers of darkness pervades the whole history of man" (*Church in the Modern World*, 37). Even Jesus himself met with this conflict from sinful men, as we saw in today's gospel: Herod was planning to kill Jesus. We cannot expect to be immune. The Council also warned that "when the order of values is jumbled, and bad is mixed with the good, individuals and groups pay heed solely to their own interests, and not to those of others. Thus it happens that the world ceases to be a place of true brotherhood." The gravest sins are usually those which violate justice and charity.

More is needed of us than the determinate effort to treat everyone justly and charitably. Conscientious Catholics are called to help right wrongs. The securing of justice for workers, dignity for the downtrodden, and assistance to the poor is a Christian concern. Jesus met conflict head-on by insisting on the dignity and rights of individuals. We must continue the concern which Jesus showed for the indigent and the underprivileged.

Friday of the Thirtieth Week (I)

Almost every Catholic has a relative or close friend who no longer practices his faith. It is a painful experience to see someone we love no longer enjoying the benefits of spiritual values which we hold dear. But we do not lose our love for them.

Such was the feeling of St. Paul about his kinsmen, his brothers, the Jews, who did not choose to follow Christ as he did. He experienced not only a deep affection for them but also a continued sense of unity because of who they were as the chosen people. Paul realized, perhaps more than we appreciate, the fact that Jesus came not to destroy the old covenant but to bring it to perfection. Jesus himself was born a Jew from a Jewish mother of the house of David. His coming into the world was a fulfillment of the eternal covenant God had made with Abraham, the father of the chosen people. Despite their failures and infidelities, Paul's people had preserved faith in the one true God and had prepared the way for the Messiah.

Our reaction to the touching words of St. Paul should be positive. First, we should appreciate our heritage, that our religion is Jewish in its roots, for there is but one God: the God of Israel is the God of Christians. Secondly we ought to have a respect and affection for those of the Jewish religion with whom we live. Any form of bigotry is contrary to the gospels, but anti-Semitism is particularly abhorrent. How can we fail to love a people God in the past made his own? How can we reject a people whose ancestors are the ancestors of Jesus Christ?

As good Catholics we should realize that with our Jewish brothers and sisters we share a common faith and a common God.

Friday of the Thirtieth Week (II)

Today we began reading from the letter of St. Paul to the Philippians. These Philippians were Paul's favorite converts because of the warmth with which they received him and because of their generosity to the poor. Paul was convinced that God had begun a good work in them and that he would bring it to completion. They seemed very close to being an ideal Christian community. Even this letter from Paul was occasioned by their goodness.

The Philippians learned that Paul had been inprisoned in Rome. They were worried about him and sent one of their number, a man with the unusual name of Epaphroditus, to Rome to try to help Paul. While in Rome Epaphroditus became ill and almost died. When he recovered Paul decided to send him back home and he asked Epaphroditus to deliver his letter to the Philippians.

The Philippians were not perfect; there were some rather serious dissensions among them. And yet they had caught the essential spirit of the faith. Affection toward others and a concern for their well-being had become part of their outlook. They knew that their love for God must overflow into love for their neighbors. In direct and shocking contrast is the attitude of the Pharisees who objected to Jesus' healing of the man with dropsy on the sabbath. They were more concerned with legalism than with the spirit of religion. The example of Jesus shows us that coming to the help of others in need is what he expects from us.

God has begun a good work in us. He wants to bring it to completion by forming us into a people who reflect his kingdom here on earth. His kingdom is one of justice, love, and peace.

Saturday of the Thirtieth Week (I)

None of us is really born a Catholic. We had to be reborn

through baptism, and if we were baptized as infants, later we had to accept our faith. In a real sense we can all be called "converts." The only question concerns the time of our conversion.

Originally in God's plan people were born into their faith as members of the chosen people. Faith and religion were an inheritance. The reason that we are "converts" to the faith is that, as St. Paul tells us, "blindness has come upon part of Israel." As a whole the people failed to accept Jesus Christ. Gentiles now have the opportunity to fill up their number.

But God has not abandoned his people. In fact God does not abandon anyone of sincere faith, no matter what his religion may be. Although we should rightly wish that everyone could enjoy the benefits of our religion, we should realize that God wills the salvation of all men. And we must never limit what God can do. God can save people in anyway he chooses.

The spirit of ecumenism which means appreciating the sincere faith of those who are not Catholic does not mean lessening the value of our own faith. Rather it means recognizing the overwhelming goodness and mercy of God. It means not being snobbish or complacent as if Catholics had a corner on God's love.

As we praise and thank God for the love he has shown us as Catholics, we whould also praise and thank him for the love which he shows to the entire family of the human race.

Saturday of the Thirtieth Week (II)

People have varied approaches to the awesome reality of death. Some see it as a step into oblivion. Others are completely uncertain about what follows the moment of death. As people of faith we should accept death with great hope. And yet for nearly everyone the time is one of a certain amount of fear. More often than not even the sickest of people cling to life and refuse to give themselves up to death.

For St. Paul death was a confident leap into the waiting arms of his Savior. He said, "I long to be freed from this life and to be with Christ." He saw death as the greatest gain possible. And yet he knew that there was still work to be done for his people. He was willing to postpone his ultimate union with Christ in order to continue serving Christ's people. In a way I see St. Paul like a doctor who is about to sit down to a magnificent Christmas dinner with his family only to be called away on an emergency. The doctor's sense of duty motivates him to leave the celebration for the good of a patient.

It is difficult for us to get a balanced view of life and death. As Christians we should not fear death. We should look forward to it as the fulfillment of life. But such is not an easy attitude to have, especially in the face of imminent death. On the other hand, we ought to accept God's will for whatever our alloted span on this earth may be. We may not be as certain of our mission or purpose in life as was St. Paul, and yet we know that we are part of God's plan. He has a purpose for each one of us.

We may not think of our place as very exalted. We may feel that it is quite right for us to take the lowest place at the table of life, as Jesus urges in the gospel. Nonetheless, if we have gone through life trying to find and to do God's will, we should be confident that in death Jesus will say, "My friend, come up higher."

Monday of the Thirty-first Week (I)

God's ways are strange but they are full of mercy. God calls all mankind to his kingdom; he will never take back that call. Unfortunately human freedom allows for a rejection of God's invitation. Throughout history human beings have turned away from God by disobedience. But God remains undaunted. In his mercy God continues to extend the invitation.

The advice which Jesus gives in the gospel follows the pattern of his Father's action. Jesus says that whenever one gives a lunch or dinner he should not invite those who will invite him in return. God invites us human beings to his everlasting banquet, and we are represented in the gospel by the beggars and the crippled, the lame and the blind, that is, by those who are not in a position to return God's favor. We have nothing to offer God except our thanks, and yet "our prayer of thanksgiving adds nothing to God's greatness, but makes us grow in his grace" (cf. Preface 40).

Here in the Eucharistic banquet we have a sign and example of God's gratuitous call. The bread and wine which we bring to the altar are really not ours. They belong already to God, for they are the fruit of the earth which God has created and the work of human hands which God empowers. God takes these materials and through the Holy Spirit transforms them into the most marvelous gift imaginable, the body and blood of his Son, our spiritual banquet. This choice food and drink are themselves a sign of the everlasting banquet of heaven to which we are invited. "Happy are those who are called to his everlasting supper" (Rev 19:9).

Monday of the Thirty-first Week (II)

Part of the American dream is to get ahead. Some people like to observe that in this country you can become anything you want. In climbing the ladder of advancement it is often necessary for one to ingratiate himself with the right people. "Who you know" is frequently more important than what you can do. As a result the wife of an ambitious husband finds herself lavishly entertaining guests who are influential in her husband's field of endeavor.

Jesus presented the opposite picture. He insisted that he had come not to be served but to serve. He associated with the poor and the lowly. His spirit was not "what can people do for me," but "what can I do for people." He wanted his followers to have his outlook. And it was this broad outlook he envisioned, and not merely dinner invitations, when he said, "Invite beggars and the crippled, the lame and the blind. You should be pleased that they cannot repay you, for you will be repaid in the resurrection of the just."

St. Paul had the mind of Christ when he wrote: "Let all parties think of others as superior to themselves, each of you looking to others' interests rather than his own." To abandon our own interests for the sake of others is a program for life. To adopt this program requires faith. The first act of faith is the conviction that there is more to life than what the American dream proposes. It is an assurance that Jesus is the model for the right way to live, and that he shows us that true fulfillment and happiness come from acting unselfishly. We need think only of how Jesus in every circumstance put himself at the disposal of people's needs. The second act of faith is the conviction that the Christian dream is a reality, the hope of resurrection to the fullness of life with Christ. It is the assurance that if we follow the example of Jesus, he himself will be our reward on the day of resurrection.

At Mass we receive the body of Christ given up for us and drink his blood poured out for us. The true meaning of life is the willingness to give ourselves to others as generously as Jesus gives himself to us.

Tuesday of the Thirty-first Week (I)

This is the season of football. This rather rough game with its oddly shaped ball and complicated rules has something to teach as a specialized team sport. Each player has his own talent and responsibility, and the team needs each player to do his part. Most of the glory usually goes to the quarterback or a running back, but without a good offensive line a quarterback will never have time to throw passes and a back will never get the blocking he needs to make good gains. Nothing will ruin a team quicker than the failure of each player to accept and to do his part.

St. Paul compares the Church to a physical body. If he were alive today, I would not at all be surprised to hear him compare the Church to a football team. In the Church not many of us have noticeable roles. After all, only one man can be Pope and only a select number can be bishops. A few more can be priests, but, as we are fully aware, women are excluded from the priesthood. Leaving aside the controversy about women priests, we all need to recognize that Jesus himself has arranged his Church much like a team. All the members are important and all must work together for the good of the whole Church. Not a single person is insignificant in God's plan. Rather each one of us must recognize the talent God has given us as well as our position in the Church and then do our best.

Those people in the gospel who were invited to the dinner gave weak, even ridiculous excuses for not accepting. Resentment against anyone in the Church or jealousy over someone else's position is a weak, even ridiculous excuse for not fulfilling our own role in the Church. As a Church we are God's team, and his will and directions are what count.

Tuesday of the Thirty-first Week (II)

In Shakespeare's tragedies a hero occupies center stage. The play opens with the hero rising to fame, wealth, or power. Within him, however, there is a flaw of character at work. Just when he appears to have reached the top, fortune begins to turn against him. His flaw is his undoing, and he tumbles from the height of success to the depth of tragedy. The hero's death is his end.

Just the opposite was true of Jesus Christ. Jesus is the eternal Son of God, equal to him in everything. His human story began with his descent into the human scene. As. St. Paul wrote, "he emptied himself and took the form of a slave, being born in the likeness of men." A supreme virtue, rather than a flaw, was at work within Jesus. That virtue was loving obedience to his heavenly Father. This virtue led him to death on the cross and at first he appeared to be a tragic figure. But precisely because of Jesus' loving obedience, God the Father highly exalted him in his resurrection from the dead. Jesus is indeed just the opposite of a tragic hero. Death for him was not the end, but led to eternal glory with his Father.

God the Father has the same plan for us. Actually his plan is an invitation, such as that from the man in the gospel who was giving a large dinner. It is up to us to accept his invitation. To do so, we first need faith. This faith should lead us to see that in the life of Jesus Christ we find the plan for our lives. Death is not the tragic end. Rather it can lead to resurrection and exaltation. We have a flaw within us, and that flaw is sin. With God's help, however, we can respond to his invitation with loving obedience like that of Jesus.

Jesus himself taught us to pray, "Thy will be done." We must mean that prayer. It should be our expression of loving obedience to God both in life and in death. Let not life end in tragedy. Rather, let it be with Christ a great success.

Wednesday of the Thirty-first Week (I)

At first glance it would seem that the words of Jesus in the gospel are a contradiction of the statement of St. Paul, "He who loves his neighbor has fulfilled the law." Jesus talks about the necessity of turning one's back on his parents, spouse and children, brothers and sisters. Jesus is using a typically Semitic way of making a point by means of exaggeration, but he does have a point to make. What he wants to emphasize is that nothing and no one can be allowed to stand in the way of our Christian duty which binds us to love one another.

I presume that we can rather readily think of obstacles to Christian duty which are within ourselves rather than outside ourselves. Such human weaknesses as selfishness and a wrong sense of values are definite obstacles. Putting our own comfort and pleasure ahead of the needs of those with whom we live violates the commandment of love, as does a form of possessiveness which makes us cling to our money when a donation is called for.

The hard, cold fact is that people outside us can become obstacles too. This is a delicate matter which requires sound judgment in order to get our priorities straight. Nonetheless those closest to us can at times be so overbearing that they keep us from our Christian duty. A person can resent the amount of time the spouse spends in helping a neighbor. Parents can put pressure on adult children to go into a financially rewarding profession when the children prefer to work at a job which pays less but helps people more.

There is no necessity of trying to multiply examples. The lesson is that love does not mean backing down from principles. Rather, praying for the guidance of the Holy Spirit we must devote ourselves to a life of generous and unselfish love, no matter what or who the obstacles may be.

Wednesday of the Thirty-first Week (II)

Today's gospel sounds pretty shocking. It is disturbing to hear Jesus say that his followers must turn their backs on father, mother, wife and children, brothers and sisters. The words of Jesus reflect a typically Hebrew way of speaking by exaggeration in order to make a point very forcefully. The point which he wanted to make was that no one may be allowed to turn us away from him, even if that person is someone very close to us. Jesus must come first in our lives.

I think we can understand this teaching of Jesus when we remember his equally forceful teaching that we must love one another. But love does not mean giving in to another person when our faith is involved. A long list of martyrs throughout the history of the Church bears witness to the fact that even life itself must be sacrificed in order to remain faithful.

St. Paul had the same teaching in mind when he wrote to his beloved people of Philippi: "Prove yourselves innocent and straightforward, children of God beyond reproach in the midst of a twisted and depraved generation." Without daring to judge the personal guilt of anyone, we should acknowledge that we too live in the midst of a twisted and depraved generation. All around us we see wealth and prestige canonized, we witness the disintegration of marriage and the family, we are plagued with disregard for the sanctity of human life.

We must not let the strong forces of corruption affect us. We must remember that God is our God, not money, or power or personal gratification. We must recognize that our devotion to God calls us to be unselfish and generous in our relationships with each other. We are called to live as children of God beyond reproach in the midst of a twisted and depraved generation.

Thursday of the Thirty-first Week (I)

Jesus in today's gospel is not talking about sheep or coins. He is talking about people, people who are infinitely more precious to

God than a lost sheep to a shepherd or a lost coin to a housewife. We are those people. Jesus went out in search of us lost in sin, and brought us back home to our Father.

We belong to God by a double title. First, God created us. He gave us being without any merit of our own. Life is his great gift to us. Secondly, God through his Son has redeemed us. Even though we were devoid of any worth or merit as sinners, God looked upon us with love and chose to reconcile us to himself. In doing so he freely gave us the means to everlasting life. Created and redeemed, we belong entirely to God.

A person who owns a piece of property may do with it as he chooses. He may build upon it or he may sell it or he may even simply allow it to sit. The property belongs to him. That is not the way in which we belong to God. A piece of property is inanimate. It has no intelligence and no free will. We have both, and God wants a free response of love from us. We belong to God in the sense that as intelligent, loving beings we are responsible to him. He has a right to our love and loyalty in somewhat the same way in which good parents have a right to the devotion of their children.

Surely we have nothing to claim as our own. Everything comes to us from God. That is why St. Paul tells us today that, "While we live we are responsible to the Lord, and when we die we die as his servants. Both in life and in death we are the Lord's."

Thursday of the Thirty-first Week (II)

During his public ministry Jesus managed to make himself notorious in the eyes of the Pharisees for having an attraction for those people whom they considered to be sinners. Although Jesus reached out to everyone, he insisted that he had come to call sinners and not the self-righteous. By the term "sinner," Jesus understood those who were conscious of their weakness and did not have the pride of the Pharisees.

When the Pharisees murmured about the kind of company Jesus was keeping, he took the occasion to teach an important lesson. The lesson is that God attaches a great value to each human person, in whatever category he may have placed himself. God is not willing to give up on even a single person. No one is dispensable in his sight, even if others would consider him worth no more than a single sheep or even a single coin. St. Paul in his conversion caught the same spirit as that of Jesus. From persecuting the Church he became a zealous apostle and gave of himself to preach the gospel so that as many as possible could be brought under God's loving mercy.

As we hear the preaching of Jesus about the preciousness of a sinner, we should not think of ourselves as passive spectators, looking around to see whom Jesus is talking about. He is talking about us. Each one of us has been a lost sheep. But we were too valuable to be abandoned. Jesus the Good Shepherd came in search of us, put us on his shoulders and led us to the fold which is the Church. If ever we wander from the fold by sin, we need never despair. He will come again to find us.

Without having the false pride of the Pharisees, we should see how precious we are to God. Others, like the Pharisees, may view us as unimportant and perhaps treat us with contempt. To God we are more valuable than all the gold and silver in the entire world.

Friday of the Thirty-first Week (I)

You have possibly read a book or seen a movie about a thief who has planned a robbery so completely and cleverly that you find yourself almost hoping that he will not get caught. You know that what he is doing is wrong, but you are in admiration of how he is going about it. That is somewhat the situation in the gospel today. Jesus does not approve of any deviousness or dishonesty on the part of the manager, nor does he recommend that we follow his example. Jesus is concerned only with the initiative and enterprise manifested by the manager in his effort to save his own skin. He was willing to do almost anything to avoid ending up a beggar or a worker. It was the easy life he wanted at any cost.

What we want is everlasting life, but at what price? Do we have as much initiative and enterprise about spiritual values as the manager did about temporal values?

St. Paul is an excellent example for us. Jesus Christ is obviously the center of his life and the driving force behind everything he does. He sees that he is a minister of the gospel only by the grace of Christ Jesus. The only glory he knows he can take is in Christ Jesus, not in himself. He has dedicated himself to nothing but the preaching of Christ Jesus. There is no doubt about his initiative, his enterprise, his dedication.

May it never be true of us that the worldly take more initiative about temporary values than we do about spiritual, everlasting values.

Friday of the Thirty-first Week (II)

In the last century Dostoevsky, the Russian author, wrote great novels about man's search for freedom. He had reached his full maturity when in 1880 he wrote *The Brothers Karamazov*. It is a very long, complicated book, but its theme can pretty well be summed up in a single statement by one of the characters in the novel, Ivan Karamazov: "If there is no God, all is permitted."

Dostoevsky's conviction was that without God there is no true freedom, only chaos. Devotion to God begets true freedom, but without God something must serve as a substitute for a supreme being. St. Paul commented on people for whom God is non-existent, if not in theory at least in practice. He wrote, "Their only god is their belly, and their glory is in their shame." When people make their own desires supreme, when they in effect make themselves their own god, there is no freedom for themselves, only license. They judge that they may do whatever they please, but in doing so they become slaves of their own appetites.

Actually many people who do not practice religion or who question the existence of God act in accord with an instinct within themselves which insists that there must be a God. We are called to live with an explicit and expressed belief in God. We are committed to follow his will and we believe that in following his will we can accomplish the true purpose of human existence. We live for the future, not in the sense that we deny the reality of this present world, but in the understanding that our true and final citizenship is in heaven.

The kingdom of a heaven is the fulfillment of peace and justice and mutual concern. That kingdom must begin with us now. Belief in the goodness and justice of God is our motivation to act with love and concern for others. We put God and not ourselves first in all that we do.

Saturday of the Thirty-first Week (I)

There is something special about one's own name. You can feel close to someone only if he knows your name, and when someone of dignity or authority calls you by your first name you feel honored. In concluding his great letter to the Romans St. Paul mentioned some of the Christians by name. You can imagine how honored they felt that the renowned Paul himself would think so much of them as to give them special mention by name. There is also a spirit of great affection running through this final passage.

Jesus in the gospel gives advice about the use of money, advice which we all need to hear. And yet we all have something much more precious than money, and that something is the love and affection we can show each other. One of the marvels of love is that you can do something with it which you cannot do with money. You can give love away and never suffer any loss of love within yourself. In fact the more you give of love and affection to others, the more will your own love grow.

A parish community should be marked by love more than by any other quality. The average parish is so large that it is impossible to know the names of all the people who attend Mass on Sundays. Of course we should try to reach out to people whom we do not know so that we can get to know them and their names. Here at weekday Mass we really have no excuse. We should easily get to know everyone's name, and in Christian love we ought to treat each other with a special respect and affection. Then our sign of peace to each other during the Mass will take on more meaning and become a reflection of the kind of love for people which we have seen in the great St. Paul.

Saturday of the Thirty-first Week (II)

The Philippians were a kind and generous people. They knew how to make good use of this world's goods. They made considerable contributions for the poor in Jerusalem. Twice they gave donations to St. Paul while he was on a missionary journey, and when they found out that he was under arrest in Rome they sent one of their own to see if he could help. With him he took a gift for Paul.

St. Paul boasted of the fact he had always supported himself and had never insisted on pay for preaching the gospel. And yet he graciously accepted the gifts offered by the Philippians because he saw these gifts as an expression of their affection and love.

Some people find it very difficult to accept money or even a favor from others no matter what their needs may be. It is a matter of pride with them. They cherish what they imagine to be their independence and fear becoming indebted to anyone. On the other hand, when they have the opportunity and ability they are very willing to help others without any thought of being repaid.

We all recognize the need to be charitable to others. What we may not see as clearly is our duty to allow others to exercise their charity. Jesus manifested great concern for the needs of others, and yet he was willing to receive their administration as well. He was happy to be entertained in the home of Martha and Mary and accepted invitations to dinner. And he allowed Joseph of Aramathea the privilege of seeing to his burial.

Not one of us is completely independent, nor should we want to be. We can even be happy that we have needs which others can fulfill or problems which others can solve. Part of God's plan is that we allow others the opportunity to be loving and generous.

Monday of the Thirty-second Week (I)

The Book of Wisdom, which we began reading today, was written about a hundred years before Christ in Alexandria, Egypt where there was a rather large Jewish population. Its purpose was to give encouragement to a people who had experienced suffering and opposition, as well as to offset certain philosophies which were at odds with the Jewish religious approach to reality.

As the Book opens the author is concerned that the people remember a basic truth that God must come first in their lives. Any approach to life which ignores God or puts him in the background is not wise or sound. Jesus gives the same warning in the gospel when he speaks of scandals. The word "scandal" literally means a stumbling block or obstacle. In the gospel it refers to any teaching or action which could occasion people "to fall down" in their approach to God, an obstacle in their way.

The warning is not without meaning for us today. We live in a society in which values opposed to those of the gospel are constantly promoted, especially through the advertising media. Much advertising would have us believe that happiness comes from what money can buy, that personal attractiveness is the result of cosmetics and tooth pastes, and that life is concerned with self-gratification. The moral and good purpose of advertising is to allow people a choice among products based on their merit, but most advertising today seeks to create a desire for superfluous things and to make a necessity of luxuries.

It is a wise person who chooses to live simply and humbly and who in all things makes sure that God and his values come first in his life.

Monday of the Thirty-second Week (II)

Today we began reading from the letter to Titus. It is referred to as a pastoral letter because of its instruction to Titus on the manner of fulfilling the pastoral ministry. He was put in charge of the Church on the island of Crete. And yet it also includes many teachings which are useful for every person in the Church.

The point of today's reading is that bishops and presbyters, whom we now call priests, must see to it that the authenticity of the teachings of Jesus are preserved. Jesus warned that scandals would inevitably come upon the Church, scandals of false doctrine and erroneous practice. Part of the pastoral office is to encourage people to follow sound doctrine and to refute those who contradict it.

In hearing these observations of the letter to Titus every Catholic ought to reflect on his own obligation to follow sound doctrine and to recognize that the source of sound doctrine is the scriptures and the tradition of the Church. Our faith is rooted in the Bible as it has been understood and lived for thousands of years. Our religion did not begin yesterday around the corner and up the street. Nor is it a reality which has been lived only within our own lifetime. The Second Vatican Council did not produce innovations. Rather under the guidance of the Holy Spirit the Council called us back to our roots, to the full tradition of the Church. In a particular way the Council wished to revitalize our knowledge and understanding of the sacred scriptures.

Since the year 1570 until the time of the Council, only a very limited portion of the Bible was read during Mass on Sundays and weekdays throughout the year. The Council directed that "The treasures of the bible are to be opened more lavishly so that richer fare may be provided for the faithful at the table of God's Word" here at Mass (*Const. on the Liturgy*, 51). Now we are hearing readings which had not been heard at Mass for centuries. These readings are for us the source of authentic doctrine and sound practice.

Tuesday of the Thirty-second Week (I)

The passage today from the Book of Wisdom is very frequently used at Masses of Christian Burial. Its purpose then is to give consolation and hope to the bereaved by recalling our faith that death is not the end but the beginning of life with God. Our hope is full of immortality.

All of us have lost loved ones in death, and this passage is a consolation for us at this moment. But today let us try to hear this passage, not as applying to those who have already died, but to us who still must face our own death some day in the future. Death is certain, but the time, place and circumstances of our own death are unknown to us. We cannot be sure how we will approach the moment of our death since it is a unique experience, still in the future for us. No one is allowed the ability to die more than once. If we could die more than once, we would be able to correct any mistakes, but such is not the case. Death is a once in a lifetime event.

The present is the time to prepare for death. This Mass is an occasion for us to renew our faith that God's love for us is so great that death is not an utter destruction. Rather in making the passage through death, as has Jesus before us, we will come to abide with God in love forever. Death is awesome, even fearful, especially without faith. But through faith which begets the hope of immortality, we should approach our own death with complete trust in the goodness of God.

Tuesday of the Thirty-second Week (II)

The early Christian communities, such as the one over which Titus had charge, were rather small groups. It is likely that the people knew each other in a rather intimate fashion. And yet the community was made up of all ages; it was not merely a select group of either the young or the old. Titus received specific instructions about applying the principles of Christian living to older men and women, to husbands and wives who were rearing a family, and to young people. In other words, the community, though small, had much the same makeup as a parish today.

One unfortunate aspect of a modern parish is that parishioners are not sufficiently acquainted with each other. There are so many people that we generally stick with those whom we already know, and usually young people are interested only in other young people, and older people only in those who are more or less of their own age. Sometimes financial status determines our relationships.

The grace of God has appeared among us, offering salvation to all people of every age and station. The Church is never a select group or an exclusive club. All of us are equally children of God through our union with Jesus Christ. It is God's will that we reach out in love and concern to all of our brothers and sisters without exception. Our oneness in Christ is more important than any other source of mutual interest. That is why we should be eager to offer the sign of peace during Mass even to people around us whom we do not know personally.

The union which we all experience through our communion with Christ in the Eucharist should move us to want to know each other better, especially those of us who come to daily Mass regularly. But on Sundays too we should make an effort to greet and become acquainted with others both before and after Mass. We all form but one family of God. We really ought to strive to know and love all of our brothers and sisters.

Wednesday of the Thirty-second Week (I)

Today's first reading was addressed to those in authority who abused their power. I suspect that most of us have a sense of awe about people who are in authority, whether they abuse it or not. Often awe overflows into fear, even toward a person who does not have what could be called great authority. Think about how you feel when you are in your car and you see a policeman pull in behind you. You probably sense a little discomfort in your stomach as you check your speedometer and ask yourself whether you have been violating any traffic law. You keep thinking, "I hope that flashing red light does not go on."

God does not abuse his authority, nor does he wish to inspire fear within us. No one has greater authority than he; in fact all legitimate authority comes from God, as the first reading points out. God in exercising his rightful power over us always acts out of the motive of love. He not only wants what is best for us; he also truly knows what is best for us.

God uses his power and authority to help, not to hinder. In Jesus we see God's power today reaching out to cure the ten lepers. That kindness does not surprise us. What is shocking is that only one of the lepers returned to Jesus. I would think that all of them would want to place their entire lives in the hands of Jesus and tell him that they would do whatever he asks.

We have all experienced the goodness of God toward us. Our response should indeed be one of gratitude, but more profoundly our realization of his love for us should move us to obey his will, to accept his authority over us, and to place our lives completely in his hands.

Wednesday of the Thirty-second Week (II)

The lesson of today's gospel is so obvious that it scarcely needs comment. It is incredible that the nine men who had been cured failed to return and give thanks. We hope that we will always be like the one who was grateful.

The Mass should be a constant reminder of our need to thank God. The word, eucharist, is a Greek word which means thanksgiving. The Mass is always primarily a worship of thanks and praise to God for all of the wonderful things he has accomplished for us and for all of his people throughout the history of salvation. Most expressive of this purpose of the Mass is the fourth Eucharistic prayer.

It is right that we give God thanks and praise through the Mass. But more is required. Our very lives should be a eucharist, a never ending act of thanks and praise, a response to God's goodness through the goodness of our lives. Very often we are reminded that this response is expressed through love of God and our neighbors, and that is the highest form of response.

Today's first reading presents us with still another specific form of response to God's goodness. We were told to be loyally subject to the government and its officials, to obey laws, to be ready to take on any honest employment. In other words, we cannot be good Catholics only at Mass. It is not correct to think that being conscientious citizens who are law abiding has nothing to do with our religion. Nor is it correct to act as if being honest or dishonest in business dealings is something apart from what we do and say at Mass.

Our entire lives, and not just our prayers, must be a response of goodness to God's goodness toward us. The way in which we live is to be an extension of the praise and thanks we give to God in the Mass.

Thursday of the Thirty-second Week (I)

Today's first reading is a beautiful hymn in honor of God's wisdom. The author ascribes twenty-one attributes to God's wisdom, and the number is no accident. Seven in the Bible is the perfect number. Twenty-one is three times seven, which means triple perfect, or perfect beyond our imagining.

And as a matter of fact God's wisdom is beyond our imagining. His values are not our human values. As a result God's ways often seem strange to us. They are indeed mysterious and incomprehensible to us mere mortals. Jesus in the gospel, in speaking of the final day, says that his coming will be like the lightning which flashes from one end of the sky to the other. That is an image which is suggestive of God's majesty. But then Jesus adds a strange statement, reflective of God's unique wisdom. He declares that before he comes in glory he must suffer much and be rejected by his own age. He was referring, of course, to his passion and death.

One of the greatest mysteries of God is that he sent his beloved son to suffer and die. Even more astounding is the fact that it was through his suffering and death that Jesus was brought to the glory of the resurrection. Only God could think of a plan like that.

And it is a plan for us as well. Faith leads us to accept God's wisdom in our lives, to believe that our own suffering and death in this life will lead us with Jesus to the fullness of life in the resurrection. Some may think us too foolish to follow a crucified Lord, but following him is the greatest wisdom.

Thursday of the Thirty-second Week (II)

The background of today's first reading is quite interesting. Philemon was a wealthy man who owned slaves, a not uncommon occurrence in St. Paul's day. This man became a convert of St. Paul, as did most of his slaves. A young slave, by the name of Onesimus, escaped and fled to St. Paul for refuge. Philemon had no idea of where he was, and it would have been very easy for Paul to hide him. But such was not his intention. In a somewhat surprising move, Paul returned the slave to his owner, Philemon.

Paul's idea was that he would not force Philemon to give up his slave. He wanted him to release the slave freely out of a motive of Christian love. Paul sent with Onesimus a letter for his master, Philemon. That letter is the source of our reading today. The whole spirit of the letter is summed up in one sentence: "Although I feel that I have every right to command you to do what ought to be done, I prefer to appeal in the name of love."

By appealing to love rather than force, Paul was acting toward Philemon in the same way in which God acts toward us. God does not compel us to serve him. He wants love, and love which is not freely given is not love at all. Paraphrasing the words of St. Paul, God could say to us, "Although I have every right to force you to do what I want, I prefer to appeal in the name of love."

Sin is possible because of our freedom. It is a risk God is willing to make. We need to recognize that freedom is a gift which makes our response of love pleasing to God.

Friday of the Thirty-second Week (I)

It takes a greater act of faith to be an atheist than it does to believe in God. It seems incomprehensible that anyone can consider the marvel of the universe, or even the magnificence of a single human being, and actually think that it all happened by accident without a Supreme Being. That is one point made today by the author of the Book of Wisdom. On the other hand he seems to have more sympathy for those who took the works of the creator as the divinity because of their beauty. It really makes more sense to worship the sun, or the moon or the stars as being a god than not to believe in any kind of god.

And yet if people could mistake the work of the creator for the creator himself, how much more marvelous is the Lord of creation. A modern example of the situation is that these days people are in awe at what computers can do, but some people seem to fail to realize that a human mind had to invent the computer and a human mind had to program it. Awe and wonder are owed to the people behind computers, not to the computers themselves. Jesus in the gospel talks about signs of his second coming. All around us right now are signs of God's beauty and power in his creation.

One purpose of our participating in the Mass is to worship the God of creation. In the third eucharistic prayer the priest proclaims, "Father, you are holy indeed, and all creation rightly gives you praise." We are the voice of all creation. All of us through baptism are a priestly people who offer praise and thanks to God in the name of all created things. Each day, as we continue to experience the marvels of God's wonderful works, we have a motive to offer this worship with joy and enthusiasm for the beauty of creation should lead us to see how far more excellent than these things is the Lord who made them all.

Friday of the Thirty-second Week (II)

St. Vincent de Paul, the great apostle of charity, used to say, "I have but a single sermon and I twist it a thousand ways." What he meant is that the Christian message is essentially a simple one which has almost unlimited applications. That simple message is: "God loves you; love him in return."

Despite its simplicity, this message is profound. In fact, because of both its simplicity and its profundity, it is easy for us to fail to appreciate its full meaning. How wonderful it would be if we could catch and hold the spirit of new found love in our relationship with God. Think about how a young man feels when he realizes that the girl of his dreams really does love him. He is in a kind of ecstasy. He glides through the day in a trance, oblivious of his surroundings, his heart intent only on his love. For him all is right with the world. He sees everything and everyone in a new light. He is happy to be alive, grateful to have the sun rise on a new day. Other people appear more beautiful and loveable to him than ever before.

Of course not everyone can cause this reaction in him, only the girl whose return of love he ardently desires. He finds it almost incredible that this absolutely wonderful person actually loves him. He will do whatever she wants him to do.

No one is greater than God. No love is more desirable than his. If only we could appreciate fully that God loves us, our whole outlook on life would be transformed. We would be grateful for every day as another opportunity to return his love. We would see each other in a different light, and we could easily respond to the urging of St. John's letter, "Let us love one another." We would want to do whatever God wants of us, and so we would readily accept St. John's teaching that "this love involves our walking according to the commandments."

Saturday of the Thirty-second Week (I)

Today's readings present a typical biblical theme. God casts down the mighty and lifts up the lowly. The pagan king, Antiochus, was sitting on top of the world. He has oppressed the Jews and, greedy for even more wealth, had begun to encounter opposition and started to lose battles. Heart broken over his defeats, he died in shame and despair. The mighty king, because of his sins, had been cast down.

We are ordinary people. We are not the powerful rulers of nations nor are we the beneficiaries of mighty economic empires. In fact we can even be considered those who are oppressed by the enemy of inflation which really affects, not the wealthy, but only the poor and those of moderate income. Perhaps we suffer discrimination because of our faith or our ethnic background. We are the lowly of this world. We should see today that God lifts up the lowly. He will do so, not by lifting us out of economic problem or freeing us from the attacks of prejudice. He will do so by raising us from the dead to a life of glory.

In the gospel Jesus takes the occasion of the question posed to him to teach the great truth of resurrection. He proclaims that we are sons of the resurrection, sons of God.

In the Mass Jesus takes two simple lowly things, bread and wine, and lifts them up by transforming them into his body and blood. His body and blood become our spiritual nourishment and will in turn transform us into the glorified Christ. The Eucharist will lift up these lowly bodies of ours from the grave and we will become like the angels, no longer liable to death, to sorrow or to humiliation.

Through our faith we fit into God's plan whereby he casts down the mighty and lifts up the lowly.

Saturday of the Thirty-second Week (II)

The first reading today is taken from a letter written to a man named Gaius who had welcomed some missionaries and given them hospitality, even though they were strangers. The letter encourages Gaius to give them the means necessary to continue their missionary journeys. The missionaries were in need since they did not ask any support from the pagans to whom they preached the gospel.

Missionary activity was a new idea. The Jews did not proselytize. They believed that one received his religion by birth, not by conversion. The Church, however, moved by the Spirit of Pentecost, went forth to proclaim the good news to all peoples. The first missionaries, of whom St. Paul was the chief, left a legacy which is still with the Church. The Second Vatican Council confirmed this legacy by teaching that "The Pilgrim Church is missionary by her very nature." The faith which we have received is to be shared, not hidden.

The Church began a very long time ago on the other side of the world. Its first center was Jerusalem. From there missionaries spread the faith throughout the area and northward to Antioch in Syria where the disciples of Jesus were first called Christians. Later Rome became the center, as it still is, and missionaries eventually spread the faith to the entire world. We ourselves are the beneficiaries of missionary activity.

As part of the Church we are expected to be missionaries in at least three ways: by contributing to the missions, by being witnesses of our faith to others, and by prayer for the spread of the gospel.

We must remember that the faith we have received is not to be hidden but shared with others.

Monday of the Thirty-third Week (I)

Today we begin reading from the First Book of Maccabees. Basically it tells the story of an attempt to suppress the Jewish religion in Palestine in the second century before Christ. Today's reading records the beginning of the persecution "when terrible affliction was upon Israel." Resistance to the persecution was vigorous and heroic, and the result was that, at least for a time, the people gained religious and political freedom.

Persecution and oppression were not new to the Jews. They had experienced it in Egypt and later in Babylon during their exile there. Nor is such treatment unknown to the Church both in the past and even now in certain countries. Motives for such persecutions are varied and sometimes unexplainable. We can say that a certain blindness comes over those in power, but unlike the blind man in the gospel they seem to have no wish to see clearly the meaning and purpose of religion.

The truth is that we ourselves run the danger of being blind to the fact that we are being persecuted and opposed in our religion. We will not be imprisoned for practicing our faith, nor will we face martyrdom. The opposition is more subtle, and therefore more dangerous. The truth is that we live in a society in which many values are just the opposite of the teachings of Jesus. And they influence us and have as much force as a sword or gun to turn us away from our faith.

By participating in daily Mass we are on the right track. The word of God we hear helps to give us proper values and the eucharist we receive gives us the strength to put that word into practice.

Monday of the Thirty-third Week (II)

The Book of Revelation, from which we began reading today, is probably the least understood book of the Bible. It abounds in symbols and figures of speech, most of which were derived from the Old Testament. Some people want to insist that the book was written with our own era in mind and that one should interpret it in the light of current events. Such is not the case.

The book was written around the end of the first Christian century when the Church was undergoing terrible persecution by the pagan Roman empire. It seemed to the people that the world was overcoming them. The message of the Book of Revelation to these people was one of exhortation to remain steadfast in the face of persecution. It was also an encouragement to them to believe that Christ had already won the decisive victory over sin and death, a victory in which all people of faith will share.

This book has an application for us because circumstances have not changed substantially for us. The early Christians sensed an apparent contradiction between the truth of their faith and their daily experience. We live in a world which contradicts the values of our faith. Not persecution, but the pressures of a money and pleasure centered world flaunt their temptations before our eyes to turn us aside from our faith.

As Jesus gave sight to the blind man, so he wishes to enlighten us as to the true values of life. He wants us to know that we need not give in to sin. He wants us to know that it is possible to live according to his demanding teachings, and that these teachings are worthwhile for they alone can enlighten us on the journey that leads to everlasting life.

Tuesday of the Thirty-third Week (I)

The first reading today tells the story of a real hero, a model of religious courage for all the people. Eleazar was an old man, just the kind of person the persecutors did not fear and actually looked down upon in contempt. But the old man showed a deep, inner strength. Physical force and threats could not make him break the law, and so his persecutors tried to persuade him to make a pretense of eating the forbidden meat. His body may have been weak but his will was strong, and he rejected even that suggestion as unworthy of a person committed to God's law. His strength came not from himself, but from God.

Zacchaeus in the gospel was also a person looked upon with contempt, not only because he was a hated tax collector, but because he was small of stature. He too was the kind of person bullies try to take advantage of.

There is no doubt that the old man, Eleazar, found favor with God as did Zacchaeus with Jesus. Zacchaeus, because of his encounter with Jesus, found dignity as well as the strength to change what was wrong in his life.

As people of faith we should let nothing intimidate us, not people who may ridicule us or values in our society which may pressure us to abandon the teachings of Jesus. We have a strength as great as that found by Eleazar and Zacchaeus. It is the body and the blood of Jesus Christ in our daily communion.

Tuesday of the Thirty-third Week (II)

The Book of Revelation was the last book of the Bible to be composed, possibly around the year 95. In some communities the first fervor of conversion had already worn off. This was true of the community in Sardis, a city which had a reputation for luxurious and licentious living. Some of the Christians had given in to these allurements. Laodicea was a wealthy, commercial city and there too fervor had waned. The first reading today was an exhortation for both groups to repent and return to true devotion and Christian living.

Zacchaeus in the gospel is a good example of Christian conversion. He gave half his belongings to the poor and was willing to pay fourfold to anyone whom he had defrauded. Jesus was so pleased that he went to his home and had dinner with him. We do not know, however, whether Zacchaeus persevered in his good intentions.

As people of faith we are in need of constant conversion. Most of us tend to vary in our degree of devotion and generosity. Moods and feelings afflict us which we cannot fully understand. We must strive to make overall progress in our lives, despite our occasional lapses. The chief means is right here at Mass. Notice that Jesus went to the home of Zacchaeus as a guest to dine with him. At Mass we are the guests of Jesus.

In the first reading Jesus is quoted as saying that he will have supper with those who are faithful. This is probably a veiled reference to the eucharist, for the Book of Revelation often presents Christian truths in such a way as not to allow the pagans to understand them.

Our celebration of daily Mass together is both an expression of our devotion and a way of growing in Christian living. It should be our intention to draw from the eucharist the strength we need to be, not lukewarm, but fervent in our Christian lives.

Wednesday of the Thirty-third Week (I)

What an extraordinary scene we have in today's first reading. The king orders seven brothers and their mother to be tortured to force them to abandon the law of God. Not only do all seven brothers go to their death rather than disobey God, but the mother encourages them all, especially the seventh, to accept death willingly. And she is the last to die.

What the mother did seems almost unnatural. Parents would ordinarily do anything to prevent the death of their children. The point is that the mother had an unusual set of values, based on a profound faith. Of course she would have liked her sons to have had a normal life, blessed with a family and the comforts and pleasures this life has to offer. Beyond doubt she would have been pleased to have become a grandmother many times over. And what a joy it would have been for her to be assisted in her old age by the love and devotion of the families of her seven sons. But she wanted more, much more, for her children. She had an eye on their future, but she was looking far into the future, into the day of eternity. She wanted, not a passing happiness for her sons, but the everlasting happiness of eternal union with God. And she knew that any sacrifice was worth fidelity to God.

This unnamed woman is like the man in the gospel who used

well the money which had been given him. She stands as a beautiful model to us of what real sacrifice for God means. And the gospel reminds us that God will be more than generous in return.

Wednesday of the Thirty-third Week (II)

Nobody knows what heaven will be like. Today's first reading is a symbolic picture of heaven, but it really does not help us to form a picture. The reason is that no human words, not even the inspired words of sacred scripture, are adequate to represent what heaven really is in all of its magnificence.

One purpose of today's reading is to emphasize the holiness of God in whose presence we will live in heaven. Sometimes the word "holiness" calls up images of some reality which is distant, remote, and slightly unappealing. It is good for us to think of holiness in terms of two words, perfection and amplitude.

God's holiness is his perfection. If we have come to understand something of goodness as we see it in other people, then we can begin to see that God's goodness is without limit. If we have witnessed beauty in creation, then we have a notion of God's beauty which is without flaw or blemish. If we have experienced love, then we can have some feeling about God's love which will never fail.

God's holiness is also amplitude. "Amplitude" is an unusual word, one we do not use very frequently. But we need an unusual word to approach the meaning of God's holiness. Amplitude indicates a fullness and a richness. There is nothing small, petty, or stingy about God. He is the fullness of goodness, beauty and love. And he will share this fullness with us in heaven.

These few human words do no justice to the holiness of God. Their message is only that heaven will far surpass any expectation we can possibly have and that the wonder of God is worth praying for, working for, and waiting for.

Thursday of the Thirty-third Week (I)

Today's first reading continues the story of the persecution of the Jews. Mattathias and his sons refused to compromise, and the zeal of Mattathias became so great that he killed a fellow Jew who weakened. Much earlier in their history during the time of Moses Phinehas killed a fellow Israelite who entered into an illicit sexual religious rite with a Moabite woman (cf. Nb 25:1-13). These are extraordinary actions, well intentioned, but not in accord with the compassion we have learned from the teachings of the gospel. The reaction of Jesus himself was to weep over the unfaithful city of Jerusalem.

We are not called to imitate the actions of Mattathias and Phinehas, but we should admire the zeal in their hearts. Theirs was a lonely situation as they saw large numbers abandoning their faith. It was not easy for them to remain faithful.

Perhaps the most practical application for us is to recognize that our chief enemy is not outside us, but within, that our first concern is not to turn against those who have turned against God but to consider our own weaknesses. Our own frailty alone can be the cause of infidelity, and with ourselves we must be honest and uncompromising. First we must be honest in seeing and admitting our own shortcomings. Then we must bring to bear against them every power at our command. Too much is at stake to do otherwise.

One purpose of our daily communion is to give us strength. In our personal battle against evil we need not pursue a lonely path. Jesus is with us as our spiritual food to accompany us and to give us the power we need.

Thursday of the Thirty-third Week (II)

By the time the Book of Revelation came to be written, many Christians had become discouraged under the weight of persecution. Jesus had died and seemed far away. Some wondered whether his death at the hands of evil men was not really a defeat after all and a fate in which they would inevitably share.

Today's reading presents a vision which is symbolic of Christ's victory. He is identified as the Lamb, a term rich in meaning for a people still deeply imbued with the story of the Old Testament. The image of a lamb recalled for them the story of the Exodus to freedom from slavery in Egypt. The blood of a lamb was sprinkled on the doorposts of the homes of the Israelites in Egypt and the angel of the Lord, seeing the blood of the lamb, passed over their families and destroyed only the firstborn of the Egyptians. The Israelites were thereby freed from the power of the Egyptians and made their great journey toward the promised land.

Jesus is the new paschal lamb. By his death sin is destroyed and by his blood we are saved. We have been set free from sin so that we may pursue our journey to the promised land of everlasting life. The scroll, which the Lamb alone may open and read, possibly represents the Old Testament. Jesus, the Lamb of God, alone gives us a full understanding of the events described therein, especially the great central event of the Exodus. The full meaning of exodus to freedom is realized only in Jesus Christ.

Another part of the vision shows the Lamb who had been slain as *standing* in heaven. This posture of standing is a sign of his resurrection. He is pictured not as lying in the repose of death but as standing in the fullness of life. His death was not a defeat but a victory over sin and death which led to his resurrection. The message to the early Christians and to us is: Take heart, be not discouraged. You too will share in the resurrection and enjoy the fullness of life.

Friday of the Thirty-third Week (I)

One hundred and sixty-seven years before the birth of Christ, the pagan king, Antiochus IV, desecrated the temple of Jerusalem and erected there a statue of the pagan god Zeus Olympus. After that the persecutions of which we have been reading for the past week broke out. Three years later Judas Maccabee liberated Jerusalem and, as we heard in the first reading today, rededicated the temple to the glory of God.

More than a century and a half later Jesus himself had to call the people back to an appreciation of the meaning of the temple, that it was a house of prayer in God's honor. It was the great, central place of worship for God's people, and the only place where sacrifice could be offered.

In this, the Christian era, we are not limited to any one place for our worship in which the sacrifice of Jesus Christ is renewed. Wherever Mass is celebrated, there God is worshipped in spirit and in truth. We should have as much respect for and appreciation of our own parish church as we would for St. Peter's Basilica in Rome.

But there is more. By his coming to us in baptism the Holy Spirit has consecrated each one of us as a temple of worship. God is present within us just as surely, although in a different manner, as he is in our churches. Our entire being should be a place of prayer. The great evil of sin is that it is a desecration of God's temple, an erecting within ourselves of a pagan god in place of the true God. Quite rightly we want sin to be no part of our lives. Rather we should want God to find within us a sacred place in which he takes delight as in our hearts he finds a tabernacle where he is honored and loved.

Friday of the Thirty-third Week (II)

The Book of Revelation is filled with symbols and figures of speech. It was written in a veiled style to hide its meaning from the pagans who were persecuting the Church. One result is that some of its meaning remains obscure for us today.

No one is absolutely sure of the meaning of the scroll in today's passage. Since the description of eating the scroll refers back to a much earlier episode with the prophet Ezekiel, the scroll may refer to the Old Testament scriptures, but it can just as easily include the writings of the New Testament. One sound interpretation is to see the bitter-sweet taste of the scroll as a symbol of the Christian life. The scroll is sweet because it proclaims the great triumph of Jesus Christ through his death and resurrection, a triumph in which the whole Church shares. The scroll is bitter because the triumph of Christ was achieved through his sufferings, and the people of the Church must share in his sufferings too.

The obscurity of the Book of Revelation can itself serve as a reminder to us that the ways of God are mysterious, that they are different from our own, that they represent values which are in direct contrast with those of the world. No human person would have thought that the best way to achieve the salvation of the world is through suffering and death. No human parents would want to subject their only son to anything similar to the passion of Jesus. And it is quite understandable that all of us, left to our own inclinations, would shun suffering and seek pleasure and comfort.

The great Christian message is that God's plan is that for Jesus pain led to joy, suffering led to happiness, and death led to life. The same is true for us. We are called to live as Jesus did. In the Mass we offer ourselves with him to the Father in union with his offering of himself on the cross. The offering of the Mass means that we wish to unite ourselves with Jesus, and that we accept our sufferings and ultimately our death as the way to everlasting life.

Saturday of the Thirty-third Week (I)

I suppose that at times it is easy for us to envy the "big" people of this world, those who seem to have everything they want, including money and power. If somehow we feel oppressed by the "big" people, envy quickly turns to resentment, even hatred, and we want justice to be done to them.

King Antiochus was one of the big people of his day. The Jews may have envied him, but they certainly did resent him because of his oppression and persecution, and they wanted God to work his justice against him. Today's first reading shows how the mighty are brought low. Learning that his armies had been defeated, Antiochus realized that he was about to die alone and in disgrace.

The truth is that we should never envy those who seem to be the mighty of this world, nor should we ever wish evil upon them. Justice belongs to God alone and we must patiently allow him to work out his justice in his own way. More positively we ought to realize that God favors the simple and humble people of this world who have learned to depend completely on him. No matter what our problems may be during life, the turning point for us will come in the moment which Antiochus feared and which we should welcome, the moment of death. Death means for us a leap into the arms of God who is the God of the living. As children of God we are children of the resurrection. Death is not an end but a beginning, not a conclusion but only the passage to that state in which we are alive in God.

Our daily eucharist is a pledge and promise of our resurrection to everlasting life. The living, resurrected body of the Lord is our food which will support us on our journey through death to eternal life with God.

Saturday of the Thirty-third Week (II)

Today's first reading is one of the most obscure passages from the Book of Revelation, but its significance can be unlocked. The key is to recognize the two witnesses as Moses and Elijah. (The description given fits them perfectly.) Moses and Elijah represent the entire Old Testament, the Law and the Prophets. Recall that when Jesus was transfigured on the mountain, Moses and Elijah appeared along with him, one on either side.

The transfiguration was a vision of the glory which would come to Jesus through his resurrection from the dead. The presence of Moses and Elijah symbolized the truth that everything that had happened in salvation history before the coming of Jesus found its meaning and fulfillment in him, and specifically in his resurrection from the dead. Today's passage from the Book of Revelation has much the same purpose as the story in the gospels of the transfiguration: Jesus by his death has triumphed over sin and death and has won a victory which is manifested in his resurrection from the dead. In this truth we find the meaning of both the Old and New Testaments.

This message is one of encouragement to beleaguered Christians. It has significance for us. Even if it seems that the whole world is turning against us, or it only seems that our own little world is crumbling, there is no cause for fear. We are in a battle, so to speak, which continues for a while after the war has actually been won. We already share in the victory of Jesus Christ.

Today in the gospel Jesus took the occasion of a silly question posed by the Sadducees to proclaim the truth of our own resurrection. He proclaimed that God is not the God of the dead, the defeated, but of the living, those who share in the great victory of Jesus, our Savior and our Lord.

Monday of the Thirty-fourth Week (I)

Today we begin reading from the Book of Daniel, a work composed during the persecution of Antiochus IV concerning which we heard in the readings last week. The stories in the book are based on much earlier traditions, dating back some four hundred years previously to the time of the exile in Babylon. Daniel is not the author but the hero of the stories, and their purpose was to give courage to the people during the terrible persecution.

In a sense Daniel and his companions represent the entire people. At least, the persecuted people were expected to identify with them. Daniel was just an ordinary person, not possessed of any political influence and with no military forces at his disposal. He was somewhat like the poor widow in the gospel. Because he was simple and humble, he was favored by God and from God came all of his power. He had learned to have great confidence in God.

In this opening episode he knew that he and his companions could remain strong even without the king's food and wine. Of course he realized that vegetables alone could not make him and his companions look healthier and better fed than those who ate from the royal table. It was God who would take care of them, and so God did.

Even without a violent persecution, we have much to learn from Daniel. God is the source of all good things, both our ordinary food and the divine food of the eucharist. God is really concerned about us and takes care of us, both physically and spiritually. All he asks is that we be humble enough to acknowledge that of ourselves we are nothing, that we depend on him completely for our lives and everything that we have.

Monday of the Thirty-fourth Week (II)

The Book of Revelation is concerned about life's fundamental issues of victory and defeat, success and failure. The victory and defeat it treats are not the kind which are the outcome of political or economic wars but of the struggle between good and evil. The success and failure it treats are not the kind which revolve around financial or social matters but the kind which are the substance of the very purpose of human existence.

In these fundamental issues the Book of Revelation reflects the paradox of the gospels. By any worldly standards the woman in the gospel would not be considered a success. She was nothing more than a destitute widow of no consequence; not even her name has been recorded in the gospel. She stands in stark and pitiful contrast to renowned religious leaders, the Pharisees, and powerful political figures, such as Herod and Pilate. And yet she made a success of her life because by God's grace she achieved victory over pride and selfishness. Her goodness manifested in her generosity won praise from Jesus himself.

The one hundred and forty-four thousand people in today's reading are not a mathematical count. The number is symbolic of all those who have shared in the victory of the Lamb of God, a triumph which overcame sin and death. We share in the Lamb's victory celebration every time we participate in Mass. Such is the meaning of the words before communion: "Happy are those who are called to his supper" (cf. Rv 19:9).

Through the Mass we receive the grace to overcome pride and selfishness. Through the Mass we have the means to make a success of our lives. Through the Mass we can become people who because of our goodness and generosity will win the praise of Jesus himself.

Tuesday of the Thirty-fourth Week (I)

All things which are of human construction are temporary at best. We can think of a large city like Los Angeles. To see its great expanse, especially from the air, is to be filled with awe. And yet in a moment an earthquake can level this city. Even without an earthquake this city, and all human construction, is subject to the decay and ultimate desolation which time alone must bring.

Through Daniel God wanted Nebuchadnezzar to know that his kingdom, so precious to him, would undergo destruction and desolation. Other kingdoms would take its place, but they too would last only for a time. The picture is a rather depressing one, especially when we realize that what was true of Nebuchadnezzar's era will be true of ours as well. What Jesus foretold about the destruction of the temple in Jerusalem will be true of the modern temples constructed by human genius. And yet there is hope.

Daniel prophesized that God himself would set up a kingdom that shall never be destroyed or delivered up to another people. Daniel himself did not clearly understand that the ultimate meaning of what he was predicting was realized in the kingdom established by Jesus Christ. This is the spiritual kingdom of the Church which will find its fulfillment in heaven. We are the people of that kingdom under Christ the King. In Christ we have a security which can never be shaken and we have a home awaiting us more magnificent than all the great cities of the world put together.

Tuesday of the Thirty-fourth Week (II)

Oppressed people of all time have yearned for a righting of wrongs and for the achieving of justice. Such was the prayer of the Israelites during their slavery in Egypt and their captivity in Babylon. Their songs of yearning for justice resonated in the hearts of American slaves, and still express the longings of peoples under communistic bondage and those persecuted for their faith in our own day. The Christians of the first century were far from free from similar trials, and it was for them that the Book of Revelation was written.

Today's reading is a vision of the coming of Christ at the end of time. He wears a crown of gold to symbolize that he has conquered sin and he bears a sickle to show that he will judge against evil. He is aided by an angel who also wields a sharp sickle and gathers the grapes to be thrown into the wine press of God's wrath. From the time of the later prophets of the Old Testament, God's judgment against sin was likened to the action of a man crushing grapes underfoot. The image is not unfamiliar to us for often we have sung the verse, "Mine eyes have seen the glory of the coming of the Lord; he is trampling out the vintage where the grapes of wrath are stored."

Injustice and evil abound in our world today. It is God's plan that all conscientious people of faith should work to overcome evil and to secure justice for the oppressed, but we should not delude ourselves into thinking that mere human effort will bring about peace and justice. Nor should we let others convince us that awaiting the final coming of Christ for the sake of peace and justice is nothing more than "pie in the sky." God is patient in unfolding his plan, but he will indeed send his Son again to bring to perfection "a kingdom of truth and life, a kingdom of holiness and grace, a kingdom of justice, love and peace."

Wednesday of the Thirty-fourth Week (I)

Today's episode from the Book of Daniel has given an expression to our language: "the handwriting is on the wall." The expression means that there are signs which a person ought to understand. For example, a small business may be doing so poorly that bankruptcy is inevitable. One day the owner reluctantly admits that "the handwriting is on the wall."

King Belshazzar literally saw the handwriting on the wall. He had profaned the vessels of the temple, in addition to other atrocities, and he had become spiritually bankrupt. The division and loss of his kingdom were inevitable.

In the gospel Jesus also speaks of signs, of handwriting, which are of a different kind. He wanted his followers to know that just as the People of God had been persecuted in the past so they would be too. This persecution was to be a sign that God was calling them to patient endurance and to a faith that such suffering would lead to everlasting life. The message found within persecution was that they were not to become discouraged or to give up.

Our persecution is of a different kind. It may be the tensions people feel as they try to keep a marriage and home together. It may be the pressures all around us to give in to the values of an affluent, materialistic society. It may be personal discouragement. Rather than see these realities in a negative way, we ought to view them as a form of handwriting from God in which he tells us that he is with us, that he cares for us, and that he will see us through the greatest difficulties in our lives.

Wednesday of the Thirty-fourth Week (II)

The great English poet, John Milton, completed his famous epic, *Paradise Lost*, in 1665. The purpose of his monumental work was to "justify the ways of God to men." The question was, "How can an all good God allow sin and evil?" Implicit in this question is a fear that perhaps sin and evil are more powerful than God. Long before Milton lived and wrote, the Bible faced the same problem. An awareness of God and his plan gradually became sharper and was manifested in the coming of Jesus Christ as savior.

The Book of Revelation, the last book of the Bible to be composed, in a sense summarizes all that had gone before in the inspired Hebrew and Christian writings. It proclaims that on the last day God will show forth his goodness and power by the total destruction of sin and evil from the universe. Our reading today from the Book of Revelation contains a brief but beautiful hymn sung by all the saints in praise of God's power and righteousness. On the day of Christ's second coming the saints cry out to God, "Your mighty deeds are clearly seen."

The Church makes use of this hymn in its official prayer book, the *Liturgy of the Hours*. In fact, this hymn is part of evening prayer on every Friday, that particular day of the week on which we recall the events of Good Friday. The use of this hymn on Fridays teaches us an important truth. Victory over sin and evil does not lie in the future. It has already been achieved in the death of Jesus on Good

Friday. Through the ages of the Christian era this victory is unfolding in its effect and will reach completion in the second coming of Christ. Meanwhile we pray in every Mass that God may deliver us from all anxiety as we wait in joyful hope for the coming of our Savior, Jesus Christ.

Thursday of the Thirty-fourth Week (I)

It is very difficult to do a difficult and demanding thing for the first time. That is why the very first astronauts were such heroes. No one had done what they had done or gone where they had gone. It took great courage as well as absolute confidence in themselves and in their space ship. Their journey made things much easier for those who followed them.

In our journey through life we have had many people of God who have preceded us. Their story has been told to us in the Bible in order to give us confidence and to make things easier for us. One of these persons is Daniel. In the face of the greatest threat possible, he remained undaunted. Despite the king's prohibition against prayer, a prohibition which promised certain death for its violation, he remained faithful to God. And God responded by rescuing him from the lions' den.

Today in this Mass we are called to reaffirm our loyalty to God, our promise that we will follow him and his will no matter what. This promise is made from a true faith in God, but our faith is not completely blind. It is based on the truth that what God has done in the past, he will continue to do. As he saved Daniel from certain death in the lions' den, so he will save us from what is the only ultimate evil, everlasting death.

Whenever we are tempted to be discouraged or even to give up, we need to hear again the words of Jesus in the gospel, "Stand up straight and raise your heads, for your ransom is near at hand."

Thursday of the Thirty-fourth Week (II)

Today's first reading presents contrasting pictures. In the first scene we witness a mighty struggle against evil, symbolized by Babylon, a struggle in which we are still engaged. In the second scene we see a vision of the joyful victory celebration in heaven, a victory in which we hope to share. By placing the two scenes next to each other for us to observe, the author wishes us to realize that the battle has really already been won, the war is actually over, and God the Father through his Son has achieved total victory for those who remain faithful to him.

The Book of Revelation proclaimed a message of encouragement to the early Christians in the midst of persecution, and it proclaims that same hope to us in the midst of our own struggles. Of particular significance to us is the declaration, "Happy are they who have been invited to the wedding feast of the Lamb." The wedding feast symbolizes the union of Christ with all the holy people whom he has won for his Father by means of his death. It is the ultimate union which is ours only after our own physical death.

The Church has incorporated this declaration into the communion rite of the Mass. The priest holds up the Body of Christ and says, "This is the Lamb of God who takes away the sins of the world. Happy are those who are called to his supper." The supper referred to is not the Last Supper but the wedding supper of the Lamb in heaven. These words are to remind us that the Eucharist is a pledge or promise of future glory. The Body and Blood of the Lord, our spiritual nourishment, strengthens us on a journey toward eternal life. Actually the Mass is a foretaste of heaven, a prelude to everlasting happiness. Those who are called to celebrate the eucharist are also called to share in the eternal supper of the Lamb in heaven.

The Eucharist is very rich in meaning. Today we should focus the eyes of faith on the fact that the Eucharist is our source of hope and encouragement.

Friday of the Thirty-fourth Week (I)

To say that today's first reading is confusing is indeed an understatement. We must remember that the Book of Daniel was written for a people who were undergoing persecution, and it was composed in symbolic language, a kind of code which the people of that time but not their persecutors could understand. All of the symbolism is no longer clear to us, but scholars have been able to figure out some of the code.

The four beasts represent the kingdoms of Babylon, Media, Persia and Greece. The ten horns represent ten kings, and the little horn stands for King Antiochus who was persecuting the people when this book was written. The great sea is a symbol of the forces of evil against God. The Ancient One is God, and the one who is like a son of man represents the faithful Jews to whom God would give his kingdom. In the New Testament Jesus is this Son of Man because he fulfills in his person the destiny of the entire Jewish people.

Despite the obscurities of this passage, its message is clear. Evil will be overcome by good. God is all powerful and he will not let his people be destroyed by evil. We should have an even greater confidence than the people for whom this passage was written because we have witnessed, as they did not, the sending of God's own Son as our Savior.

Friday of the Thirty-fourth Week (II)

The Book of Revelation was written during a time of persecution when many Christians had to suffer martyrdom. Seeing family members and friends being put to death was a terrible trial for the people. They worried about their own fate but they were also tempted to give up, thinking that perseverance was not worth having to endure painful torture and an ignominious death.

St. John, wishing to reassure the faithful, paid particular attention to those who had undergone martyrdom. He proclaimed that martyrs would receive a special award. They would reign with Christ who had himself endured painful torture and an ignominious death. Since they were like him in his crucifixion, they would be like him in glory.

The word "martyr" is a Greek word which literally means "witness." Martyrs give witness to their faith by means of their death. Although we still have people even in our own day who give their lives in witness to the faith, the Church over the centuries has come to understand "witness" in a broader sense. All those who have died to sin in their lives and have lived in accord with God's will are witnesses to their faith. In other words, the great promises found in today's scripture reading apply to all who remain faithful.

St. John saw a vision of new heavens and a new earth. This is a representation of God's kingdom. The picture is made more graphic in his description of the new Jerusalem, "the holy city, coming down out of heaven from God, beautiful as a bride to meet her husband." We are that new Jerusalem, a people whom God will embrace with living tenderness. Our relationship with God will be something like a marriage, indeed a perfect union in which the spouses truly live happily forever after.

Saturday of the Thirty-fourth Week (I)

The message of today's first reading is that the powers opposing God will be destroyed and the eternal kingdom of God will be given to God's faithful people. This great prophecy of the triumph of good over evil was fulfilled in the death and resurrection of Jesus Christ. "Dying he destroyed our death, and rising he restored our life." But what Jesus accomplished is still being unfolded and will not be completed until the end of time when he comes again in glory to hand over his kingdom to his Father.

Today marks the end of the liturgical year, the season of Advent beginning tomorrow. This is a time for us to consider the ultimates of human existence, death and the end of the world. For many people such thoughts are terrifying. They refuse to think of death and they fear the end of the world. Such must not be our reaction. The message from the readings of this entire past week has been one of great hope and confidence, and the same is true today.

Without Jesus death would indeed be frightening and the end of the world a bleak anticipation. But our faith tells us that Jesus will be there to help us through the awesome, dark doors of death to lead us to his Father's kingdom. Our faith tells us that the end of the world will be the final triumph over evil and on that day we will share fully through our own resurrection in the resurrection of Jesus Christ.

Thanks be to God for our faith and for the gifts he has already given us and still promises us in the life to come!

Saturday of the Thirty-fourth Week (II)

This is the final day of the liturgical year (tomorrow we begin Advent), and the reading from the Book of Revelation presents the final scene of human history, the new Jerusalem, our heavenly home. And yet this final scene calls us back to two beginnings: the beginning of the human race and the beginning of our individual lives as Christians.

In the Book of Genesis the first man and woman, representing all of us, were forbidden to eat of the tree of life. By breaking this commandment Adam and Eve pushed God out of their lives and in effect tried to make gods of themselves. The result was catastrophe, and death entered our world. Paradoxically in the heavenly Jerusalem not one, but twelve trees of life grow luxuriously. Adam and Eve drew a curse upon the race, but in the heavenly Jerusalem "nothing deserving a curse shall be found." All the faithful are invited to eat of the fruit of these trees, which bear fruit in turns every month, a symbol of never ending life with God.

Also in heaven flows the river of life giving water. This image should remind us of the water of baptism, the beginning of our lives as Christians. The water of baptism is the sacramental sign that God gives us his life like a seed which is to grow within us. The water of baptism is usually little more than a trickle but the water in heaven is a river which flows down the middle of the streets. The abundance of water in this image is a symbol of the fullness of life in heaven.

We are a people who quite rightly should look forward to heaven. Today's reading wishes to make us realize that heaven means the removal of all that is evil in life and a multiplication of all that is good. Above all the joy of union with God and all his angels and saints is a joy which will be without end. Heaven will never grow old or stale; it will never be tedious or boring. Heaven is the perfection of happiness and the fullness of life for which we were made and for which we yearn on this earth as we await the glorious coming of our Savior, Jesus Christ.

"By your gift I will utter praise

in the vast assembly" (Ps 22:26).